Soaked, Slathered, and Seasoned

A Complete Guide to Flavoring Food for the Grill

Elizabeth Karmel

WILEY

Photo Copyright © Jamie Tiampo

Published by John Wiley & Sons, Inc., Hoboken, New Jersey

Published simultaneously in Canada

For general information on our other products and services or for technical support, please contact our Customer Care Department within the United States at (800) 762–2974, outside the United States at (317) 572–3993 or fax (317) 572–4002.

Wiley also publishes its books in a variety of electronic formats. Some content that appears in print may not be available in electronic books. For more information about Wiley products, visit our web site at www.wiley.com.

Library of Congress Cataloging-in-Publication Data:

Karmel, Elizabeth.
Soaked, slathered, and seasoned : A complete guide to flavoring food for the grill / Elizabeth Karmel.
    p. cm.
At head of title: Taming the flame
Includes index.
ISBN 978-0-470-18648-0 (cloth : alk. paper)
1. Barbecue cookery. I. Title. II. Title: Taming the flame.
TX840.B3K368 2009
641.7'6--dc22

                              2008024104

Printed in the United States of America

10 9 8 7 6 5 4 3 2 1

Contents

Introduction

If *Taming the Flame* was my love letter to grilling and barbecue, this book is the reaffirmation of my love for outdoor cooking. The reason I fell in love with outdoor cooking is that it is the best way to prepare food, bar none. And, you aren't limited by what you can cook or the flavors you use—"if you can eat it, you can grill it!" is my motto and I cook and eat by that motto.

Every country has a tradition of live-fire cooking so you can capture a world of flavor in your own backyard—all you need is a recipe, the ingredients, and a grill. This book is written under the premise that if you know the difference between direct and indirect heat and when to use it, and employ the Grilling Trilogy to cook your food (see Grilling Basics), you can add any number of marinades, brines, sauces, glazes, mops, salsas, chutneys, relishes, jams, and jellies; sweet sauces, barbecue rubs, spice blends, seasoned salts and peppers; flavored vinaigrettes, compound butters, pestos and tapenades, and dipping sauces to add a flourish and change the flavor of your food.

I love art and have an "if I win a million dollars" fantasy that I will give it all up and move to the south of France to paint. But the truth is I am not a very good painter. Regardless of how clearly I see the picture in my head, I can't get it down on paper.

Luckily, I see and taste food flavors and can put those down on paper. I have transferred all of my desires for creative expression to the art of grilling and barbecue. I love the challenge and the puzzle of putting ingredients and flavors together and creating something new. When I was in Tokyo, I was inspired by a plate of glistening fresh sashimi that was adorned with a deep magenta salt. I couldn't wait to get home and try and make it myself. The simple but arrestingly beautiful result is the Hibiscus Flower Salt on page 217. The same thing happened the first time that I made North Carolina–style barbecue myself—this was long before I even thought that I would grill and barbecue for a living! I had a beautiful Boston butt that I had smoked for eight hours and I needed to dress it with the vinegar dip (a.k.a. sauce). I added a little of this and a little of that from my taste memory of the barbecue joints that I had frequented growing up in North Carolina—and much to my surprise, it worked. It tasted authentic and it is still the way that I make my Barbecue Sauce 101 (page 86).

I am insatiably curious. I love to travel near and far, meet the natives—listening and picking up tips from everyone—you never know who is going to show you something amazing! We all look at things differently and someone else's perspective may start you thinking in a new direction. For example, during the Recipe Testing Boot Camp (page vi) for this book, it was interesting for me to see how the students combined the flavors when they had the chance to compose a dish. So many of the students paired sweet sauces, rubs, and butters with meat because they had yet to be told that they couldn't do that. At first, I was secretly horrified and then one of the students used Smokin' Four-Chile Rub (page 209) and Lemon Butter (page 275) on a flat-iron steak and it was a delicious revelation. That experience reminded me how important it is to break out of the classic culinary paradigms and experiment with unlikely combinations. That story is my way of encouraging you to use this book like a huge pantry of flavor accessories. Think of your meat, fish, poultry, veggies, and fruit as your basic black dress and all the recipes in this book as the accessories to make them look, feel, and taste

different! If you had a year to play around with, you could take a chicken and use the flavorings in this book to create a different recipe every night without repeating the combinations. And the time is now. When I walk the aisles of new food product exhibits, I am amazed by the proliferation of rubs, seasoned salts, sauces, pestos, tapenades, vinaigrettes, flavored vinegars, and so on. They range from exclusive truffle products to branded beer barbecue sauces and represent flavor profiles that span the globe. As a country, our interest in international cuisine and worlds of flavor has exploded. We crave a classic American burger one meal and an Indian curry the next. With all the ingredients and products readily available there is no excuse for a bored palate! And with very little effort (and this book) you can satisfy your cravings yourself. It really is as simple as that. We tend to eat the same foods over and over again—I am no exception! But, if you make a commitment to try something new at least once a week, then it is easier to get in the habit of making new recipes. Writing this book helped me break out of the security of my favorite recipes. Much to my surprise, I discovered a whole new group of favorites and I hope you will, too! Write to me at elizabeth@girlsatthegrill.com and let me know your favorite new dishes and ways to soak, slather, and season your food!

CHOW!

Elizabeth

About This Book

Being creative with flavor is the only way to beat the mealtime rut. There are basically five groups of proteins that home cooks prepare regularly: poultry, including chicken, duck, quail, game hen, turkey; pork; beef; lamb; and seafood, including fish and shellfish. So it is not really what you are cooking, but how you are cooking it and what flavors you are using to complement your choice of protein.

An argument can be made that any flavoring agent can be called a sauce, and there are books on sauces that include marinades, brines, compound butters, and flavored vinaigrettes. For the purposes of this book, I have defined the following sections:

Soaked: This section delves deeply into flavored liquid in which you submerge food before cooking, including marinades and brines.

Slathered: This section covers flavorings that you generously brush or spoon onto almost-cooked food or fully cooked food. This includes sauces both savory and sweet, glazes, mops, salsas, relishes, and jellies.

Seasoned: When "a little dab will do ya." This is light flavoring—the "sprinkle" and "drizzle" section of the book. Rubs, spice blends, and seasoned salt; flavored vinaigrettes; pestos and tapenades and dipping sauces all fit in this category. I've included compound butters in this section, because a little goes a long way.

Using this book, you could grill chicken every night for a year and never repeat a flavor combination. If you are in the mood for barbecue, you can use a dry rub like Mike Mills's Magic Dust and finish it off with the Sweet and Spicy Barbecue Glaze or dunk it in the Alabama White Barbecue Sauce. For classic roasted chicken, the Chef's Seasoning Blend will expertly season the chicken and the Roasted Garlic–Dijon Butter will bring back memories of a French bistro. On a warm summer's night, pound a couple of paillards, grill them, and serve them on top of a Greek salad with the smoky Roasted Red Pepper Vinaigrette or the briny Black Olive Vinaigrette. If you prefer to travel East with your menu, grill boneless skinless chicken breasts and simmer the grilled meat in the Tikka Masala Sauce. I could go on and on, but you get the idea here!

In each chapter there is at least one feature recipe. I chose the recipes based on feedback from my cookcook, *Taming the Flame*. Many of the featured recipes are favorites from my first book. The other recipes are new favorites of both mine and my students, amd I hope they will become favorites of yours.

Recipe Testing Boot Camp

When I set about writing this book, I decided that instead of having the recipes tested by only me or me and a recipe tester, which is typical, I wanted to have a collective opinion.

So I concocted the idea of a recipe-testing boot camp with passionate cooks as my testers. Good idea, but where was I going to find passionate cooks and a kitchen big enough for testing almost 400 recipes? It didn't take me long to think of the Institute of Culinary Education (ICE), where

I am a chef-instructor. The professional students were my perfect idea of passionate cooks. They loved to cook and they could read a recipe, measure, and ask questions if something was unclear. The education level of the students ranged from beginner to recently graduated. They were at skill levels ranging from "interested in cooking" to "very good" cooks. And because the boot camp was a volunteer opportunity, they were motivated to do the job.

With the idea in place, it was time to set a date and organize the boot camp—I know that neither myself, Rick Smilow, or Andy Gold had any idea how much work it was going to be, but it was worth it for me and worth it for the students. I organized two five-hour sessions of recipe testing each day and capped the number of testers per session at 14. We went through the recipes, chapter by chapter and each tester was required to fill out an evaluation sheet on each recipe. Not only were measurements checked, but flavors were described and critiqued and the students had to imagine how to use the recipe that they made in a composed dish. And then I tasted each and every recipe with the tester who made it. This sounds relatively easy but believe me, it was an exercise in culinary imagination the days we tested brines and tasted all of those salty solutions on their own.

It really felt like camp with a strong core group of testers coming back every day. They learned, I learned, and we bonded over our love of food and flavors and cooking. And, it was a unique experience—as far as I know, no cookbook has been tested like this before. And it didn't go unnoticed: Rachel Wharton from the New York *Daily*

News came and spent an afternoon with us and wrote up the experience for the paper. It was nice for me and for the students to have that article as a souvenir of the camp.

It was exciting for me to see my recipes realized from paper to reality and know that they were clear and easy to execute. Out of the 400 recipes that we tested, we only had to retest two recipes. One was operator error and the other was a matter of taste! And, the best outcome was that everyone went home with a few new recipes to add to their everyday repertoire. When students would come in the next day and say that they had already made one of the recipes again at home, I knew that it was not only a winner, but it touched their culinary comfort zone, which is what I hope happens to everyone who cooks out of this book.

I think that the Recipe Testing Boot Camp made this a better book and the experience of working with 42 professional culinary students from all different backgrounds was valuable to me as a cookbook writer, recipe developer, and teacher. I am deeply appreciative to Rick Smilow, Andy Gold, and the staff of ICE for all the behind-the-scenes work that they did to make it happen— it was a huge undertaking, just imagine the grocery list! And, I am especially thankful for all of the students that volunteered their time to test these recipes.

With thanks and gratitude to my mother, Lynn, and my father, Big Lou, who have always been my head cheerleaders—supporting me and celebrating my notions no matter what they were.

Grilling 101

Grilling Basics • Grilling Recipes 101

GRILLING BASICS

Before you soak, slather, or season anything, here are some basic grilling guidelines, tips, and ideas to ensure that your grilling work is efficient and successful and your food is fabulous!

RAPID-FIRE CHECKLIST

○ Preheat a gas grill or wait until the briquettes are covered in a white-gray ash.
○ Know which cooking method to use:
  Direct
  Indirect
  Combo
○ Always brush food with a light coating of olive oil and season with kosher or sea salt and freshly ground pepper.
○ Use two pairs of 12-inch locking chef tongs, one for raw and one for cooked food.
○ Always cover the grill for even and quick grilling.
○ Brush food with sweet barbecue sauces during the last 15 to 20 minutes of the cooking time.
○ Use an instant-read thermometer to test meat for doneness.

Charcoal vs. Gas

The first decision you need to make is what kind of grill to use. Both types of grills produce great food, so choosing is basically a lifestyle choice—although some of us who are grill obsessed avoid making a choice and use both!

To help you decide which type of grill is most suited to your lifestyle, review the following characteristics of each to figure out which one fits your needs. If the grill fits, cook on it!

Charcoal Grill

- Requires building, starting, and maintaining the fire
- Requires disposing of ashes and cleaning of the grill
- Portable, easy to move
- Costs less initially but charcoal has to be purchased for each cookout

If you like the hands-on experience of building a fire and you can wait 30 minutes for the coals to be ready, charcoal is for you.

Gas Grill

- Preheats and is ready to cook in 15 minutes
- Low-maintenance fire
- Easy to light and easy to control cooking temperature
- Easy to operate and clean
- Costs more initially but inexpensive to maintain

If you like being able to push a button and be ready to grill in 15 minutes, gas is for you.

Outdoor Cooking: The Three Methods

Direct Grilling means that you put the food directly over the heat source—similar to broiling in your oven.

Indirect Grilling means that the heat is on either side of the food and the burner(s) under the food are turned off.

Combo Grilling means that you sear the food over direct heat before moving it to indirect heat to finish the cooking process.

It is very simple—remember this rule of thumb:

- If the food takes less than 20 minutes to cook, use the **DIRECT METHOD**
- If the food takes more than 20 minutes to cook, use the **INDIRECT METHOD**

Note to Seasoned Grillers

Once you've mastered cooking by direct and indirect heat, you are ready for the **COMBO METHOD**. This is exactly what it sounds like, a *combo*-nation of the Direct and Indirect Methods. It is as simple as searing the food over direct heat and finishing the cooking over indirect heat. This technique works well for everything from chops and steaks to whole tenderloins and even slices of hard squash and potatoes. It is a time-honored and well-respected tradition and the outdoor-grill version of the way most restaurant chefs cook almost everything—searing on the stove and finishing the dish in the oven.

Searing

Searing food seals in and carmelizes the juices and gives food those beautiful telltale grilling marks. The best way to sear is to place oiled, salted food directly on preheated cooking grates for 2 minutes on each side. Closing the lid during this process will keep the grates hot and allow for a better sear on the other side of the food. Searing quickly brings out the deep *caramelization* that makes grilled food taste so much better.

Prepping the Grill— Charcoal

The first step is to light the fire: This is the most basic step in outdoor cooking, yet many people are still confused about the proper way to start the fire.

Following is a step-by-step guide to the process:

Charcoal Grill

1. Remove the lid and open all air vents.

2. Mound the briquettes into a pyramid-shaped pile or pile the charcoal into a high-capacity chimney starter— *preferred method.*

3. Place either nontoxic fire starters or crumbled newspaper under the pile of briquettes and light.

4. When the briquettes are covered with a white-gray ash (usually 20 to 30 minutes), arrange them according to the cooking method you are going to use.

5. For smoke flavor, consider adding hardwood chips or chunks (soaked in water for at least 30 minutes and drained) or moistened fresh herb sprigs such as rosemary, thyme, or lavender. Place the wet wood or herbs directly on the gray-ashed briquettes just before you begin cooking.

Direct Cooking on a Charcoal Grill

When you prepare the grill, light 50 to 60 charcoal briquettes in either a chimney starter or in a pyramid-shaped mound on the bottom grate that is known as the "charcoal grate." Once they are covered with a white-gray ash, spread them in a single layer. Make sure the air vents are open on both the top and the bottom of the grill, and put the lid on for 5 minutes to preheat the grill and sterilize the cooking grates. Cook as the recipe directs.

Indirect Cooking on a Charcoal Grill

When you prepare the grill, light 50 to 60 charcoal briquettes in either a chimney starter or in a pyramid-shaped mound on the charcoal grate. Once the briquettes are covered in a white-gray ash, you are ready to prepare the grill for the Indirect Method. Pour or rake half the briquettes onto each side of the charcoal grate on the lower section of the grill and place a disposable aluminum drip pan in between the two piles of coals. The drip pan will catch fats and juices as the food cooks. Add soaked wood chips if desired and replace the cooking grate. Place the food in the center of the cooking grate, directly over the drip pan, and proceed with the recipe.

The secret to indirect cooking with charcoal is to add briquettes to the fire as needed to maintain the cooking temperature (add about ten briquettes per side every hour or so—or when the temperature inside the grill falls below 250°F). Charcoal briquettes can be added to the fire by dropping additional unlit briquettes through the opening by the handles on each side of the cooking grate. However, I find that it is more efficient to light briquettes in a chimney starter set in a heavy-duty disposable aluminum pan (or an extra charcoal grill) 20 minutes before you need to add them. This way, the new briquettes are already at their prime temperature and covered with a white-gray ash when you add them.

Chimney Starters

Chimney starters take the hassle out of cooking with charcoal. If you grill over charcoal, it will be the best 20 bucks (or less) you've invested in your cookout experience. A chimney starter is the grown-up version of the 32-ounce tin-can fire starters that I used to make in Girl Scouts. It is a two-level aluminum cylinder with a handle for starting the charcoal. It is called a "chimney" starter because it uses the chimney-flue system of maximizing airflow for optimum burning conditions. A chimney starter, paraffin starter cubes or a crumbled piece of newspaper, and a kitchen match is all you will need to get the fire burning. A good chimney starter will turn an onerous process into an easy one.

LOOK FOR A CHIMNEY STARTER WITH

- A heat-resistant handle
- High enough capacity to hold enough charcoal for one cookout, about 50 briquettes
- Heavy-duty metal construction

Prepping the Grill—Gas

The first step is to light the fire: This is the most basic step in outdoor cooking, yet many people are still confused about the proper way to start the fire.

Following is a step-by-step guide to the process:

Gas Grill

1. Open the lid. Check that all burner control knobs are turned off and that your LP tank is not empty.

2. Turn the LP Gas tank on.

3. Light the grill according to the manufacturer's instructions, using either the igniter or a match, if necessary. Generally, when lighting a gas grill, only one burner should be turned on for ignition. Once the fire has started, other burners can be turned on.

4. Close the lid and preheat all burners on high until the thermometer reaches the maximum heat—more than 500° to 550°F. This will take 10 to 20 minutes. Before cooking, adjust burner controls and lower the heat as recipe directs.

5. For smoke flavor, use the smoker box if your grill has one, or place water-soaked wood chips in a small disposable aluminum pan in the upper left-hand corner of the grill directly on the heat source (heat tents, flavorizer bars, or ceramic rock). This must be done during the preheating stage, when all burners are turned to high.

Direct Cooking on a Gas Grill

Turn all the burners on high as you normally would to preheat the grill. Reduce the heat by turning all the burners to medium—this should result in a temperature of about 450°F. Place the food directly on clean cooking grates and grill as the recipe directs—it's that easy.

Indirect Cooking on a Gas Grill

Setting a gas grill for indirect cooking is just as simple as turning it on. Once the grill has been preheated with all burners on high, simply turn off the burner that is directly underneath the food that is being cooked and reduce the heat of the other burners to medium or medium-low. If your grill has two burners, chances are that the burners are on the perimeter of the grill and the center of the cooking grate is already set up for indirect cooking. A three-burner grill is the easiest to set; after preheating, you turn the center burner off and reduce the heat on the other two. Since there are so many different models of gas grills, it is always best to refer to the manufacturer's instructions. Most new gas grills are designed to be used for both direct and indirect cooking. If you are in the market for a new grill, make sure it can be set for indirect cooking.

Tips for Direct Method of Grilling (Charcoal and Gas)

When using the Direct Method, the fire should be between 450°F and 500°F, which is the traditional broiling temperature. For a gas grill, that means that all burners should be turned on to medium or medium-high, depending on your grill. Most food only needs to be turned once, halfway through the cooking time.

Before placing food on the grill, the cooking grate should be clean and free of debris (this will prevent food from sticking)—use a brass-bristle brush to clean the grill. Always use long heat-resistant mitts and long-handled locking chef tongs to move the food. Using chef tongs instead of traditional "grilling" tongs gives you the most dexterity, and using both tongs and mitts will prevent you from burning yourself.

Once you place the food on the grill, cover the grill with the lid. This helps to keep heat in, which speeds cooking time, and it cuts down on flare-ups. It also keeps the heat consistent and shields the food from dust, wind, and rain.

Direct Grilling Guidelines at a Glance by Food Category

BEEF, LAMB, AND OTHER RED MEAT

Steaks, chops, and burgers are most frequently cooked by the Direct Method. You should *not* try to cook very thick steaks using the Direct Method—the outside of the steak will be burned long before the center is done.

Because of the danger of food-borne illness, the U.S. Department of Agriculture now recommends that all burgers be cooked completely through—i.e., until they are well-done and no longer pink. While individuals are obviously free to follow this recommendation as they see fit, I suggest following USDA guidelines and/or grinding your own meat at home. It is easier than you think. You can use a KitchenAid meat grinder attachment for the standing mixer.

PORK AND VEAL

As with beef and lamb, the Direct Method can be used to cook thinner pork and veal chops and small cuts such as pork tenderloins. Veal can be safely cooked rare, but most people prefer it cooked to medium.

The pork of today is not your mother's pork chop. Hog farmers are bringing a much leaner, and cleaner, animal to market. The National Pork Producers Council recommends cooking pork to medium (160°F). The Combo Method is a better choice for thicker chops, and it is the way that I usually cook smaller pieces of meat.

POULTRY

You *must* cook chicken and turkey all the way through. This is especially true as salmonella becomes more pervasive in the poultry industry. Almost all poultry can be successfully cooked using the Indirect Method. The only cuts of poultry that are easier to cook using the Direct Method are boneless, skinless chicken breasts; small pounded chicken or turkey breasts, i.e., paillards, chicken tenderloins, satays, and small chicken or turkey pieces on kabobs. Duck breasts can also be cooked using the Direct Method and do not need to be cooked until well-done, according to the Duckling Council. However, I prefer my duck cooked to a much higher temperature because I find it more flavorful and tender.

SEAFOOD

Seafood tends to be more delicate than meat or poultry and should be treated carefully. That said, "steaks" of the sea such as firm fillets of tuna, shark, or swordfish and shellfish such as shrimp, oysters, clams, and mussels are best cooked over high direct heat. Other fish fillets, while small, are usually best cooked using indirect heat, as they can burn easily and are difficult to turn. The best tip for cooking fish is to lightly coat the exterior with olive oil and turn only once halfway through the cooking time. Fish should not break apart unless it is turned too soon.

VEGETABLES AND FRUIT

Americans are in love with grilled vegetables of all kinds. Potatoes and corn are still popular, but now so is fennel, asparagus—even Brussels sprouts! Before grilling, vegetables should be lightly coated with olive oil to help prevent sticking and to prevent sliced vegetables from drying out. Vegetables such as asparagus, bell peppers, sliced squash, zucchini, sliced sweet potatoes, eggplant, green onions, onion slices, and large mushrooms such as portobello are best grilled by the Direct Method.

Tips for Indirect Method of Barbecue, Grill-Roasting, Grill-Baking

Indirect cooking is typically used for large cuts of meat or large whole vegetables that require more than 20 minutes to cook through. When cooking via the Indirect Method—especially when preparing traditional American barbecue, think low and slow—low heat, slow cooking. The heat should be significantly lower than it is when using the Direct Method—somewhere between 325° and 350°F—or even lower in some cases. This low heat will enable the food to cook gently and be flavored by the natural fat that renders out while it cooks. This natural fat bastes the meat as it cooks, resulting in tender meat and a deeply caramelized crust. When cooking large cuts of meat, fish, or poultry by the Indirect Method, you don't need to turn the food at all.

Indirect heat is the method used for barbecuing, grill-roasting, and grill-baking. These three types of outdoor cooking are essentially the same technique. The only difference is the type of food you are cooking and the temperature.

- Barbecuing temperature is 300° to 325°F.
- Grill-roasting temperature can be as low as 350°F and as high as 400°F.
- Grill-baking temperature is generally 350°F but for foods like cornbread, it is as high as 400°F.

Before placing food on the grill, the cooking grate should be clean and free of debris (this will prevent food from sticking)—use a brass-bristle brush to clean the grill. Always use long heat-resistant mitts and long-handled locking chef tongs to move the food. Using chef tongs instead of traditional "grilling" tongs gives you the most dexterity, and using both tongs and mitts will prevent you from burning yourself.

Once you place the food on the grill, cover the grill with the lid. This helps to keep heat in, which speeds cooking time, and it cuts down on flare-ups. It also keeps the heat consistent and shields the food from dust, wind, and rain.

Indirect Grilling Guidelines at a Glance by Food Category

BEEF, LAMB, AND OTHER RED MEAT

Prime rib, whole bone-in leg of lamb, beef brisket, and other large cuts are perfect for the Indirect Method. Bear in mind that, unless you first sear the exterior of the meat, the food will *not* have dark searing marks when finished. When cooking beef brisket or other tough cuts of meat, plan on 3 to 7 hours of slow cooking to break down the fibers and produce a tender dish.

PORK AND VEAL

Due to the low fat content in pork and veal—pork is now as lean as chicken—the Indirect Method is (in most cases) the best way to grill. Even in the case of most chops, I call for the Combo Method, which will reduce the amount of time the food spends over a direct flame. In addition to large roasts, ribs—like all barbecue—should only be cooked using the Indirect Method, allowing at least 90 minutes to break down the fibers and make the ribs tender.

POULTRY

Here is the biggest grilling secret, which addresses the biggest misconception that backyard cooks have. Chicken pieces, as well as whole poultry (chicken, turkey, duck), half chickens, and turkey breasts, should always be cooked indirectly—unless they are boneless and skinless. It is essential that all poultry, no matter the preparation, reaches internal temperatures of at least 180°F in the thigh and 165°F in the breast.

SEAFOOD

The Indirect Method is the right choice for whole fish, most large fish fillets, and large shellfish such as lobsters and crabs.

VEGETABLES AND FRUIT

Firm whole vegetables like potatoes, carrots, and other root vegetables; large squash; heads of garlic; artichokes; and corn in the husk are best cooked by the Indirect Method, as are whole fruits like apples and pears and vegetable side dishes such as gratins, casseroles (like baked beans), and other long-cooking foods.

Flare-ups—Covering the Grill

The quickest way to extinguish flare-ups is to put the lid on the grill. The lid will reduce the amount of oxygen that feeds the fire—thus limiting or snuffing out any flare-ups.

Don't be tempted to use a water bottle to extinguish flare-up flames. When the water hits the hot cooking grates and the flames, it can splatter, causing burns to you and/or cracks in the porcelain enamel finish on your grill.

Grilling Trilogy

I developed the Grilling Trilogy of olive oil, salt, and pepper as a simple flavoring for just about anything you can grill. Use the best-quality raw ingredients, and use the Grilling Trilogy principles, and everything that you grill will be delicious. Remember, in most cases—in life and in cooking—less is more, and the Grilling Trilogy is the epitome of that.

The Whys and Hows Behind the Grilling Trilogy

Don't worry about the oil and don't eliminate it. It is truly essential and you don't need to use very much. Coat all the outside surfaces of the food with a thin layer of olive oil. I prefer olive oil for everything, but you can use any kind of oil except butter, because it burns easily. If you don't oil the food, it will dry out and become tasteless. And remember, grilling is intrinsically low fat and healthy because you aren't frying or sautéing in loads of oil or butter.

Likewise, salt is very important. It is a natural mineral and, when used in moderation, I think it is the most important ingredient (besides the food itself) for great taste. There are a few things to keep in mind when cooking with salt. Season food with salt just before it goes on the grill; otherwise it will draw the juices to the surface of the meat. We want the juices to stay inside the meat so it is tender and juicy when we serve it. And a dry surface always results in better sear marks and a more caramelized exterior. Start with a little salt and add to taste. There is a fine line between just right and too much—and it's much easier to add than take away.

Pepper is the classic seasoning accompaniment and balances out the salt. In the case of pepper, there is also a fine line between just right and too much. Use pepper sparingly or according to taste. If you prefer not to use pepper, that is okay, but do not eliminate salt, which enhances the natural flavors of your food.

Salt and Timing

Salt and timing are the keys to grilling success. A fellow chef once told me that the only difference between a restaurant chef and the rest of us is . . . timing and using enough salt. Salt really does make a difference, and I recommend seasoning uncooked food with kosher salt because it has a cleaner taste and an irregular surface that sticks to the food better than table salt. Kosher salt can be found in any grocery store. I recommend seasoning cooked food with fleur de del or coarse sea salt to add both the final salty note and a nice crunchy texture.

Cleaning the Cooking Grates

If you clean the grates before and after each cookout while the grates are hot, you will always have a clean grill, which will help prevent food from sticking and flare-ups. A little daily care will make the grill virtually maintenance free.

After you've preheated the grill, you want to make sure the cooking grates are clean. It is very simple but, like flossing your teeth, requires discipline to do it regularly and thoroughly. You will need a special grill brush for this job. I recommend a long-handled brass-bristle brush. Do not buy a brush with stainless steel bristles or plastic bristles. The steel is too hard and can damage porcelain-enamel finishes on the cooking grates. Plastic isn't stiff enough, and even heat-resistant plastic will melt over time at high temperatures. The brushes will need to be replaced one to two times a year, depending on how much you use your grill. Always brush on hot cooking grates, after preheating and after cooking. Be sure to brush hard, bearing down in the same direction as the grates.

If you find yourself without a grill brush, don't blow off the cleaning step. It is essential to great grilled food, and in a pinch you can make a good substitute brush out of crumpled heavy-duty aluminum foil.

Oil the Food, Not the Grates

And speaking of grates . . . some people recommend oiling the grates. I am emphatic about oiling the food, not the cooking grates. By the time most people put the food on the grill, any oil on the grates has "cooked" and become tacky, making the food stick even more.

Tricks of the Trade

Tongs Tip

Use two pairs of tongs. Mark one pair with red tape (red = stop) and reserve it for handling raw food. Mark the other pair with green tape (green = go) and reserve it for handling cooked food. Or use my red and green Stop 'n Go tongs. Only use the "red" tongs for raw food and the "green" tongs for cooked food. This will keep your outdoor cooking food safe by helping to prevent cross-contamination.

Double-Skewer It, a.k.a. the Ladder Method

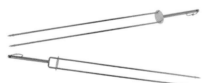

Skewering makes cooking shrimp, vegetables, chunks of meat, and other small items very simple. It eliminates the need to place each small piece of food on the grill and turn it just minutes later. That isn't such an issue with larger pieces of food or even jumbo or large shrimp, but it is with medium-sized shrimp, cherry tomatoes, okra, etc. How many times have you threaded food down the middle of a skewer, only to have it twirl around and around on the skewer? My solution is to double-skewer it. I like to use inexpensive bamboo skewers that I've soaked in water for about 30 minutes. This step is necessary or your skewers will burn. If I were getting ready to make a shrimp kabob, I would do the following: For each kabob, lay out two skewers and thread the shrimp in both ends instead of in the middle. The skewers end up looking like shrimp *ladders* (thus my nickname for the method) and hold the shrimp so they cook evenly on both sides. Now all you have to do is place the shrimp on the cooking grate and turn once halfway through the cooking time. (Note: You can only skewer shrimp that has been peeled.)

Is It Done Yet? Or Testing for Doneness

Besides lighting the grill, figuring out when the food is "done," much less perfectly prepared, makes many of us otherwise confident hosts quiver in our proverbial boots. Not to worry; arm yourself with two tools and one technique:

- A timer
- An instant-read thermometer
- A-OK method (see page 15)

Both tools are inexpensive and worth every penny! Set the timer for the number of minutes that you think the food will need before turning, etc. Base this estimate on the recipe or your past experience. Then use your instant-read thermometer to check the internal temperature to see if your timing is correct. Remember, grilling is much more of an art than a science, and cooking times will vary slightly based on many factors, including wind, thickness of food, starting temperature of food (refrigerator cold vs. room temperature), grill preheating time, and temperature of the fire. Once you get the hang of it, you'll realize that the mystery is part of the game of grilling and what makes it so much fun!

In *Taming the Flame*, I created cooking charts based on USDA-recommended end temperatures at the end of all the chapter 101 sections. They are a good guide for internal temperature/testing for doneness. Remember, the USDA recommends that all ground meat, including hamburger, veal, pork, poultry, and lamb, be cooked until no longer pink. If you still have questions, consult the USDA Meat and Poultry Hotline at 1-800-535-4555 or the USDA Web site at www.usda.gov.

Resting

If you cook meat or poultry, you are familiar with the instructions to let meat "rest." Besides seasoning with the Grilling Trilogy (page 10) and grilling it properly, I find that letting the cooked food rest is the single most important factor in turning out juicy, perfectly cooked meat. When any protein is exposed to high heat, the juices are forced toward the outside of the piece of food. When you remove it from the heat and let it rest, the protein "relaxes" and the juices are redistributed evenly through the food. I prefer to let my meat rest or sit uncovered, but some people cover their food to keep the heat in. I don't do it because the covering starts to steam the food, making my golden brown crusts or skin soggy.

Grilling Dos and Don'ts

We are always looking for tips for preparing foolproof meals. Below are the top ten grilling do's and don'ts. Think of them as the *CliffNotes* for outdoor cooking!

1. Do know the cooking methods: direct and indirect.

2. Don't peek under the lid; every time you lift the lid, heat escapes and the cooking time increases.

3. Don't add volatile fuel to the fire; this means no lighter fluid. Use either crumbled newspaper or fire starter cubes.

4. Do remember to keep the air vents open, or else the fire will go out.

5. Do make sure charcoal briquettes are gray-ashed before cooking.

6. Don't flip food more than once unless a recipe specifically requires it.

7. Don't pierce meat with a fork; this lets all the precious juices and flavor escape.

8. Do control flare-ups with a closed lid, not a spray bottle filled with water.

9. Do use an instant-read thermometer, the only fail-safe way to test for doneness. The thermometer reads the internal temperature of meat and poultry in a matter of seconds.

10. Do know the Grilling Trilogy (page 10).

GRILLING RECIPES 101

In this chapter, I give you the most basic way to flavor (with olive oil, salt, and pepper) and grill foods from steak to fish to veggies. Or, you can soak 'em, slather 'em, or season them with one of the hundreds of marinades, sauces, and seasoning recipes in this book, in the ways that I suggest or using your own combination.

Burgers 101

Serves 6

Who doesn't love a freshly grilled burger?

Grilling Method: Direct/Medium Heat

> 2 pounds ground chuck or other meat
> Kosher salt
> Freshly ground pepper
> Olive oil

1. Build a charcoal fire or preheat a gas grill.

2. Being careful not to overwork the meat, season it with salt and pepper in a large bowl, and mix just until combined. Gently shape the meat into 6 burgers of equal size and thickness (about 3/4 inch thick). Make an imprint in the center of each patty with your thumb. Spread the top and bottom of each patty with a thin layer of olive oil.

3. Place the burgers on the cooking grate over direct medium heat, cover, and grill for 4 minutes. Turn and continue grilling until the meat is cooked through and no longer pink, 4 to 6 more minutes. Remove and let the burgers rest for 3 to 5 minutes before serving.

Tip: If you like rare burgers, try the ice cube burger trick—placing an ice cube in the center of the burger, which melts slowly as the burger cooks and keeps the meat rare and juicy on the inside while the outside develops a crisp coating. Assemble the patties just before you grill them or the ice cube will melt. Enclose an ice cube within each patty, pressing the meat around it, and grill as usual. The USDA recommends that all ground meat should be cooked until no longer pink, but if you grind your own meat or trust your butcher, cooking burgers until rare should be okay.

Soaked, Slathered, and Seasoned

THE A-OK METHOD

This touch test, in which you compare the texture of meat to the feel of your hand in different positions, may be a little tricky at first but will get easier the more you do it. Try focusing on the doneness of meat you prefer and learn how that feels first. This will save you from needing a thermometer or from guessing doneness.

1. With the left hand, make an OK sign, with gentle pressure.

2. Feel the meaty part of the palm just under the thumb with your other forefinger; that texture is the equivalent of raw meat.

3. Move your left middle finger to the thumb and feel how the palm has gotten a little tighter; that is the texture of rare meat.

4. Move your left ring finger to the thumb and feel how the palm is tighter still; that is the equivalent of meat cooked to medium doneness.

5. Move your left pinky finger to the thumb and touch the palm under the thumb again; it should be really tight—that is what well-done meat feels like.

Steak 101

Serves 4

Most people think steak should be cooked over direct high heat, but that often results in overcooked, burned steaks. In this foolproof steak recipe, I grill the steaks over indirect heat. This virtually prevents flare-ups and burned steaks. Just make sure you preheat the grill with all burners on high so the cooking grates are hot enough to sear the meat as soon as you put it on the grill. Once you get the hang of it, try searing over direct heat and then finishing the steak over indirect heat. This combo method is my favorite way to grill steaks and the most common way that restaurant chefs prepare them.

Grilling Method: Indirect/Medium Heat

> 4 New York strip steaks or other favorite steak, each about 3/4 pound and about 1 1/2 inches thick
>
> Olive oil
>
> Kosher salt
>
> Freshly ground pepper
>
> 2 tablespoons softened unsalted butter, optional
>
> Chopped fresh parsley, optional

1. Allow the meat to come to room temperature 20 to 30 minutes before grilling.

2. Build a charcoal fire or preheat a gas grill.

3. Just before grilling, brush both sides of the steaks with oil and season with salt and pepper.

4. Place the steaks on the cooking grate over indirect medium heat, cover, and cook for about 5 minutes or until well marked. Turn the steaks over and continue cooking for 7 to 10 more minutes for medium-rare. Use the A-OK test (see page 15) or an instant-read thermometer to determine if the steaks are done to your liking. They will also continue to cook a little as they rest.

5. Remove the steaks from the grill to a platter or to dinner plates and allow them to rest at least 5 minutes but no longer than 10 minutes before serving. Top the steaks with 1/2 tablespoon of butter and a sprinkle of parsley, if desired.

Note: Use indirect heat for any food that takes longer than 15 to 20 minutes to cook—this includes all bone-in pieces of meat.

Hot Dogs and Sausage 101

Serves 4

The key to making sausages, including hot dogs, that are darkly caramelized on the outside and done on the inside is controlling the heat. The best sausages are cooked over a much lower heat than you would think. Keeping the heat consistent at medium-low will also prevent the skin from splitting, which spills the precious juices (aka flavor) and can cause flare-ups.

Fully Cooked

Grilling Method: Direct/Medium-Low Heat

> 4 fully cooked hot dogs or sausages
>
> 4 hot dog buns or rolls

1. Build a charcoal fire or preheat a gas grill.

2. Place the sausages on the cooking grate over direct medium-low heat, cover, and grill, turning occasionally, for 5 to 7 minutes or until browned, plump, and warmed through.

3. Remove the sausages from the grill, let them rest for about 3 minutes, and then serve on buns with traditional condiments, if desired.

Uncooked

Grilling Method: Indirect/Medium Heat

> 4 uncooked sausages, such as Polish, Italian, chicken, or bratwurst
>
> 4 hot dog buns or rolls

1. Build a charcoal fire or preheat a gas grill.

2. Place the sausages on the cooking grate over indirect medium heat, cover, and grill, turning occasionally, for 20 to 25 minutes or until browned, plump, completely cooked through, and sizzling. If there is any question whether or not they are completely cooked through, leave them

on the grill for another 5 to 10 minutes. If you are using indirect heat, as instructed, they won't burn or overcook.

3. Remove the sausages from the grill, let them rest for about 3 minutes, and then serve on buns with traditional condiments, if desired.

Bone-In Chicken Pieces 101

Serves 4

I recommend grilling chicken pieces over indirect heat so that they are cooked on the inside and golden brown on the outside at the same time. Cooking over direct heat can result in a raw interior and a burned exterior—especially if you put the barbecue sauce on too soon.

Grilling Method: Indirect/Medium Heat

> 4 bone-in chicken breasts or thighs, or other chicken pieces
>
> Olive oil
>
> Kosher salt
>
> Freshly ground pepper

1. Build a charcoal fire or preheat a gas grill.

2. Remove and discard any excess fat from the chicken. Pat it dry with paper towels. Brush lightly with oil and season with salt and pepper. Place the chicken, bone side down, in the center of the cooking grate over indirect medium heat.

3. Cover and grill until the breast meat near the bone registers 170°F and the thigh meat registers 180°F, 35 to 45 minutes, depending on size. You do not need to turn the chicken pieces. If you don't have a thermometer, cook it until the meat is no longer pink and the juices run clear.

4. If preparing barbecued chicken, season with your favorite barbecue rub and brush the sauce on the chicken during the last 15 minutes of cooking time to prevent burning. Remove and let the chicken rest for 10 minutes before serving.

Boneless Skinless Chicken Breasts 101

Serves 4

The size of chicken breasts varies widely. Small chicken breasts will take 6 to 8 minutes total. The larger and thicker the breasts, the longer they will take to cook—up to 20 minutes total cooking time.

Grilling Method: Direct/Medium Heat

> 4 boneless skinless chicken breast halves
> Olive oil
> Kosher salt
> Freshly ground pepper

1. Build a charcoal fire or preheat a gas grill.

2. Pat the chicken dry with paper towels. Brush with oil and season with salt and pepper. Place the chicken in the center of the cooking grate over direct medium heat. Cover and grill for about 15 minutes or until the meat is no longer pink and the juices run clear. Turn the chicken only once during cooking time.

3. If using barbecue sauce, brush on the chicken during the last 5 minutes of cooking time to prevent burning. Remove and let the chicken rest for 5 minutes before serving.

Whole Turkey on the Grill 101

Serves 12 to 15

Once you grill your first turkey, you'll never want to prepare it any other way. The convection action of the grill cooks the turkey faster than a conventional oven and browns the skin picture-perfect! The turkey takes on a slightly smoky grilled flavor, and it is a cinch to smoke with wood chips if you prefer a more intensely flavored turkey. The grill will give the turkey that distinctive pride-of-barbecuer's pink smoke ring next to the skin—so don't think the turkey is undercooked if you see a smoke ring, just congratulate yourself for a job expertly done! This method works well with a whole breast of turkey, too.

Cooking Method: Indirect/Medium Heat

> 1 whole turkey, 14 to 16 pounds, thawed if necessary
> Olive oil
> Kosher salt
> Freshly ground pepper

1. Build a charcoal fire or preheat a gas grill.

2. Remove the neck and giblets; reserve them for other uses or throw them away. Remove and discard any excess fat. Rinse the bird, if desired, and pat it dry with paper towels. Twist the wing tips under the back—this is called "wings akimbo."

3. Brush the turkey with oil and lightly sprinkle with salt and pepper.

4. Place the turkey breast side up on the cooking grate on a charcoal grill or on a roasting rack in a disposable foil roasting pan on a gas grill. The grill should be set for indirect medium heat. There's no need to baste it; the thin coating of oil will promote browning and keep the juices inside the bird.

5. Cover and cook 11 to 13 minutes per pound or until an instant-read thermometer inserted in the thickest part of the thigh (not touching the bone) registers 180°F and the juices run clear. Transfer the turkey to a platter and let it rest for 20 minutes before carving.

Tip: Charcoal grillers will have to add about 12 briquettes to each side every hour. Gas grillers don't need to do any tending; but about 30 minutes before the bird is done, remove the foil roasting pan and place the bird directly on the center of the cooking grate. This allows the bottom of the bird to brown. Use the drippings in the foil pan to make gravy. Make sure to bring the drippings to a boil before mixing them in with the rest of the gravy ingredients.

Seafood Steaks 101

Serves 4

This is the basic recipe for seafood steaks, using the Grilling Trilogy (see page 10). Once you've mastered this technique, start adding your own seasonings. Serve with fresh salsa, pesto, or lemon wedges, if desired.

Grilling Method: Direct/Medium Heat

> 4 fish steaks, such as yellowfin tuna, halibut, swordfish, salmon, or sea bass, about 1 inch thick
>
> Olive oil
>
> Kosher salt
>
> Freshly ground pepper

1. Build a charcoal fire or preheat a gas grill.

2. Brush the steaks on both sides with oil. Season with salt and pepper.

3. Place on the center of the cooking grate over direct medium heat. Cover and grill, turning once halfway through the cooking time, until the fish is opaque but still moist in the center, about 10 minutes. Serve immediately.

Whole Fish 101

Serves 4 to 6

If you've never worked with whole fish, start here with the simplest method, then move on to some of the flavor enhancers.

Grilling Method: Indirect/Medium Heat

> 4 whole fish, such as trout, snapper, or whitefish, about 1 pound each, cleaned
>
> Kosher salt
>
> Freshly ground pepper
>
> Olive oil
>
> 1 cup fresh herbs, such as thyme, tarragon, or marjoram, optional

1. Build a charcoal fire or preheat a gas grill.

2. Rinse the fish and pat it dry. Season the inside and outside with salt and pepper.

Lightly oil the inside cavity and both sides of the fish. Place fresh herbs inside the cavity, if desired. Wrap the fish in aluminum foil, if desired.

3. Set the fish in the center of the cooking grate over indirect medium heat. Cover and cook until opaque but still moist in the thickest part, 15 to 20 minutes, without turning. If you are only grilling one fish, it will take only 10 to 15 minutes.

4. Remove the fish from the grill and slide it onto a platter. Peel off the top layer of skin, if desired. Let rest for 3 to 5 minutes. To serve, slide a wide metal spatula inside the cavity of the fish between the flesh and bones, and lift off each portion.

Skin-On Fish Fillet 101

Serves 4 to 6

Have your fishmonger skin your fillet, place the fish back on the skin, and wrap the fish. When you are ready to grill, lay the fish skin on the cooking grates and place the fillet on top of the skin. The skin will act as a barrier between the fish and the cooking grates and prevent sticking. When the fish is done, slide your spatula between the flesh of the fish and the skin to remove your fish.

Grilling Method: Indirect/Medium Heat

> 1 skin-on fish fillet, such as salmon, trout, or snapper, about 2 pounds and about 1 inch thick
>
> Olive oil
>
> Kosher salt
>
> Freshly ground pepper

1. Build a charcoal fire or preheat a gas grill.

2. Rinse the fish and pat it dry. Brush all over with oil. Season with salt and pepper.

3. Lay the fish, skin side down, on the cooking grate over indirect medium heat. Cover and cook until the fish is opaque but still moist, 15 to 25 minutes. Do not turn the fish during the cooking time.

4. Supporting the fish with a wide metal spatula, transfer it to a platter by sliding the spatula between the skin and the flesh. Leave the skin on the grill to crisp up for serving, or remove and discard it. Serve immediately.

Grilled Lamb Chops 101

Serves 2 to 4

The thicker the chop, the longer it will take to cook. The cooking time will vary slightly based on how hot the grill is, but use this basic rule: Calculate 4 to 5 minutes for every 1/2 inch of thickness for medium-rare. For example, a 1-inch chop will take 8 to 10 minutes total cooking time. Brush each chop with olive oil, season with salt and pepper, and turn only once halfway through the relatively short cooking time. Even 2-inch chops should take less than 20 minutes over direct heat to be cooked to medium-rare perfection.

Grilling Method: Direct/Medium Heat

> 1 rack of lamb (8 bones), frenched (bones trimmed), about 1 1/2 pounds, or 4 lamb loin chops, about 1/3 pound each

Olive oil

Kosher salt

Freshly ground pepper, optional

1. Build a charcoal fire or preheat a gas grill.

2. Pat the lamb dry with paper towels. Place the rack on a secure wooden cutting board.* With a sharp chef's knife, cut through the lamb every 2 bones, using the bones as a guideline. You will have 4 chops with 2 bones each, about 1 1/2 inches thick.

3. Brush all over with oil and season with salt and pepper, if desired. Place the chops on the cooking grate over direct medium heat, cover, and grill for 6 to 7 minutes per side for medium-rare (145°F). Test the internal temperature by inserting an instant-read thermometer in the center of the thickest part of the meat, being careful not to hit the bone. Cook them longer if you prefer your meat more fully cooked.

4. Remove the lamb from the grill and place it on a platter. Let the chops rest for 5 minutes before serving. Season with additional salt and pepper, if desired, and serve.

*Make sure that the cutting board is stable and won't move before cutting on it. Wet a paper towel, wring it out, and lay it flat on the counter. Place the cutting board on top and push away from you. It should not move easily. Now you are ready to wield that knife.

Rack of Lamb 101

Serves 2 to 4

I think that a whole rack of lamb is one of the most elegant main courses around. It used to be that this dish was reserved for restaurants or the occasional home meal because it was so hard to find a rack of lamb. Now, the wide distribution of tender Australian and New Zealand lamb makes it much easier to serve at home, and for a fraction of the restaurant price. One rack, preferably frenched, will serve two adults handsomely.

Grilling Method: Direct/Medium Heat

1 rack of lamb (8 bones), frenched (bones trimmed), about 1 1/2 pounds

Olive oil

Kosher salt

Freshly ground pepper

1. Build a charcoal fire or preheat a gas grill.

2. Pat the lamb dry with paper towels. Brush all over with oil and season with salt and pepper.

3. Place the rack in the center of the cooking grate, bone side down, over direct medium heat. Cover and grill for 45 to 55 minutes or until the lamb is browned on the outside and medium-rare (140°F) on the inside. Test the internal temperature by inserting an instant-read thermometer in the center of the thickest part of the meat, being careful not to hit the bone.

4. Remove the rack from the grill onto a platter and let the lamb rest for 10 minutes before slicing and serving. You can cut the rack in half and serve a 4-bone mini-roast or cut it into 4 pieces, carving every 2 bones.

Tip: The grill-roasting time will change based on the weight of the rack of lamb. A small Australian rack of lamb weighs about 1 1/2 pounds and will be cooked to a perfect medium-rare in 45 to 55 minutes. A larger American rack of lamb can weigh up to 3 pounds and will take about 1 1/2 hours.

Butterflied Leg of Lamb 101, Unstuffed

Serves 6 to 8

There are two ways to prepare leg of lamb: whole and butterflied. For years, I chose the former, preferring the rich flavor of a slowly grill-roasted piece of meat. But then my grill friend John Mose convinced me of the wonders of a boneless (butterflied) leg of lamb, which you can request from your butcher or meat department. The boned meat takes a lot less time to cook since it is so thin; and it is so versatile —perfect for wet or dry rubs, marinades, and stuffing. I also like it grilled quickly with the Grilling Trilogy (see page 10) of olive oil, salt, and pepper, so the natural flavor of the lamb and the smoky goodness of the grill really shine through. This way of grilling works best with a boneless butterflied leg of lamb that is roughly the same thickness throughout.

Grilling Method: Direct/Medium Heat

> 1 leg of lamb, 3 to 4 pounds, butterflied
> Olive oil
> Kosher salt
> Freshly ground pepper

1. Build a charcoal fire or preheat a gas grill.

2. Pat the lamb dry with paper towels. Brush all over with oil. Season with salt and pepper.

3. Place the lamb on the cooking grate over direct medium heat, laying it out as flat as possible. Cover and grill for 8 to 10 minutes per side for medium-rare. The time will vary based on the thickness of the lamb. Use long-handled tongs to turn the lamb over.

4. Remove the lamb from the grill and place it on a platter. Let it rest for 5 minutes before carving and serving.

Whole Bone-In Leg of Lamb 101

Serves 6 to 8

Like any roast, a whole bone-in leg of lamb is one of the easiest pieces of meat to grill. Because it grill-roasts over indirect heat for a long period of time, the meat will naturally caramelize and brown on the outside without any need for turning. The only thing this recipe needs is adequate time, great raw ingredients, and the Grilling Trilogy (see page 10).

Grilling Method: Indirect/Medium Heat

Special Equipment: V-rack roast holder, optional

THOMAS J. FRENCH
> 1 bone-in leg of lamb, 5 to 7 pounds
> Olive oil
> Kosher salt
> Freshly ground pepper

1. Build a charcoal fire or preheat a gas grill.

2. Pat the lamb dry with paper towels. Brush all over with oil. Season with salt and pepper.

3. Place the lamb, fat side up, on the cooking grate or in a V-rack set in a disposable aluminum pan over indirect medium heat. Cover and grill-roast for 1 1/2 to 2 hours or until the lamb registers 140°F in the thickest part of the leg. Test the internal temperature by inserting an instant-read thermometer in the center of the thickest part of the meat, being careful not to hit the bone.

4. Remove the lamb to a platter, and let it rest for 15 to 20 minutes before carving and serving.

Variation
Make random slits in the meat every couple of inches and insert half of a peeled garlic clove in each slit before brushing with oil and seasoning with salt and pepper.

Pork Tenderloin 101

Serves 4

This is a good choice for a special meal when you don't have a lot of time.

Grilling Method: Combo/Medium Heat

> 2 pork tenderloins, about 1 pound each
> Olive oil
> Kosher salt
> Freshly cracked pepper or your favorite barbecue rub

1. Build a charcoal fire or preheat a gas grill.

2. Brush the tenderloins with oil and season with salt and pepper or rub.

3. Place the tenderloins on the cooking grate over direct medium heat to sear. Cover and grill for 2 to 3 minutes per side. Once seared, move to the center of the cooking grate and cook over indirect heat for 12 to 15 minutes, turning once halfway through the cooking time to ensure even cooking. If using an instant-read thermometer, the meat should register 160°F.

4. Transfer the tenderloins to a platter. Let the meat rest for 5 minutes. Slice the tenderloins into 1/2 -inch slices and serve hot.

Pork Chop 101

Serves 4

These are cut somewhat thick, but watch them so they don't overcook.

Grilling Method: Direct/Medium Heat

> 4 bone-in single-cut pork chops, each about 3/4 pound and 1 inch thick
> Olive oil
> Kosher salt
> Freshly ground pepper

1. Build a charcoal fire or preheat a gas grill.

2. Pat the pork chops dry with paper towels. Brush lightly on all sides with oil and season with salt and pepper.

3. Place the chops on the cooking grate, cover, and grill over direct medium heat for 6 to 8 minutes. Turn and continue grilling for another 8 minutes, or until well marked and the meat registers 160°F in the center of the chop on an instant-read thermometer.*

4. Transfer the chops to a platter and let them rest for 5 minutes before serving hot.

*It is difficult to use a meat thermometer on a single-cut pork chop, so try using my A-OK technique (page 15) to check doneness. Take the chop off when it feels medium or you feel a good bit of firm resistance when you touch the center of the chop with your finger.

Boneless Pork Chop 101

Serves 4

Boneless pork chops will take a little less time to cook than chops with the bone.

Grilling Method: Direct/Medium Heat

> 4 boneless pork chops, each about 1/2 pound and about 1 inch thick
> Olive oil
> Kosher salt
> Freshly ground pepper

1. Build a charcoal fire or preheat a gas grill.

2. Pat the pork chops dry with paper towels. Brush lightly on all sides with oil and season with salt and pepper.

3. Place the chops on the cooking grate, cover, and grill over direct medium heat for 5 to 6 minutes. Turn and continue grilling for another 6 to 7 minutes, until they are cooked to medium, checking using the A-OK method (see page 15).

4. Transfer the chops to a platter and let them rest for 5 minutes before serving hot.

Pork Loin Roast 101

Serves 6 to 8

Make sure you plan for enough time to let the roast cook.

Grilling Method: Indirect/Medium Heat

> 1 pork loin roast, about 3 pounds
> Olive oil
> Kosher salt
> Freshly ground pepper

1. Build a charcoal fire or preheat a gas grill.

2. Pat the pork dry with paper towels. Brush lightly on all sides with oil and season with salt and pepper.

3. Place the roast in the center of the cooking grate, cover, and grill-roast over indirect medium heat for 45 to 60 minutes, or until an instant-read thermometer registers 160°F. (There is no need to turn the roast during the grilling time.)

4. Transfer the roast to a platter and let the meat rest for 10 minutes before carving into thin slices. Serve hot.

Pulled Pork 101

Makes 10 servings

Barbecue in North Carolina is defined as pulled pork with a distinctive tangy vinegar sauce—no sweet tomato sauce allowed! The pork is either "pulled" into pieces or chopped with a meat clever and dressed with the sauce. It is served on a cheap, white flour hamburger bun topped with a simple slaw of chopped green cabbage dressed with the same vinegar sauce.

Grilling Method: Indirect/Medium-Low Heat

Pork butt, Boston butt, or untrimmed end-cut pork shoulder roast, 7 to 9 pounds

Olive oil

Kosher salt

Freshly ground pepper

Hickory wood chips, soaked in water for 30 minutes

Barbecue Sauce 101 (a.k.a. Lexington-Style Vinegar Sauce, page 86)

1. Build a charcoal fire or preheat a gas grill for indirect cooking.

2. Do not trim any excess fat off the meat; this fat will naturally baste the meat and keep it moist during the long cooking time. Brush pork with a thin coating of olive oil. Season with salt and pepper. Set aside on a clean tray until ready to cook.

3. Before placing the meat on the grill, add the soaked wood chips. Place the chips directly on gray-ashed briquettes or in the smoking box of your gas grill. If using a charcoal grill, you will need to add charcoal every hour to maintain the heat.

4. Place the pork in the center of the cooking grate, fat-side up, over indirect low heat. Cover and cook slowly for 4 to 5 hours at 325°F to 350°F, or until an instant-read thermometer inserted into the middle of the pork registers 190°F to 200°F. The meat should be very tender and falling apart. If there is a bone in the meat, it should come out smooth and clean with no meat clinging to it. (This is the real test for doneness on the barbecue circuit.) Remember, there is no need to turn the meat during the entire cooking time.

5. Let the meat rest for 20 minutes or until cool enough to handle. Using rubber kitchen gloves (because it is so messy), pull the meat from the skin, bones, and fat. Set aside any crispy bits (fat) that have been completely rendered and look almost burned. Working quickly, shred the chunks of meat with 2 forks by crossing the forks and "pulling" the meat into small pieces from the butt. Alternatively, you can chop the meat with a cleaver. Chop the reserved crispy bits and mix into the pulled pork. While the meat is still warm, mix with enough sauce to moisten and season the meat (about 3/4 cup). The recipe can be made in advance up to this point and reheated with about 1/4 cup additional sauce in a double boiler.

6. Serve hot, with more sauce on the side, if desired.

Shrimp and Scallops 101
Serves 4

Both shrimp and scallops cook in a very short time, so be sure to have everything you need at your fingertips before putting them on the grill.

I prefer mixing the two shellfish, but you can use all shrimp or all scallops; just double the amount of each. If you decide to use peeled shrimp, keep a close watch; they cook more quickly than those with the shells. Use sea scallops, as tiny bay scallops can only be grilled skewered or in foil packages. If you want to use these shellfish in a seafood salad or a cold seafood cocktail preparation, chill them in the refrigerator before using.

Grilling Method: Direct/Medium-High Heat

1 pound unshelled jumbo shrimp

1 pound large sea scallops, preferably Alaskan

Olive oil

Kosher salt

Freshly ground pepper, optional

1. Build a charcoal fire or preheat a gas grill. If frozen, thaw shrimp in cold running water just before cooking.

2. Rinse and dry the shrimp and scallops. Toss them in a little oil to coat all surfaces. Season with salt and pepper, if desired.

3. Using long-handled tongs, place the shrimp and scallops across the cooking grate to prevent them from falling through. Cover and grill over direct medium-high heat for 1 1/2 to 5 minutes on each side, depending on size. The shrimp are done

when they curve and become pink. The scallops are done when they are firm and opaque. Take care not to overcook, or they will be rubbery.

4. Remove the shellfish from the grill and put it on a platter. Let rest for a few minutes, then serve immediately, or let cool briefly before using them in another preparation.

Mollusks in the Shell 101

Serves 4

Shellfish is the general category for aquatic animals that have a shell. They are technically either mollusks (mussels, clams, oysters, snails, squid) or crustaceans (crabs, shrimp, prawns, lobster). It is best to buy in-shell mollusks live (ask the fishmonger if you're not sure). Some varieties, including oysters, are available out of the shell, but to grill or smoke them, you will need to have at least the bottom shells to hold the oysters during the cooking process. For best results, all shellfish should be cooked within 24 hours of purchase.

Grilling Method: Direct/Medium-High Heat

24 fresh oysters, clams, or mussels, in the shell

Cocktail sauce, relish, dipping sauces, or melted butter, as desired

1. Build a charcoal fire or preheat a gas grill.

2. Scrub the mollusks with a stiff brush under cool running water and discard any cracked shells. Place the mollusks on the cooking grate over direct medium-high heat, cupped side down. Cover and grill until the shells pop open (4 to 6 minutes); there is no need to turn mollusks.

3. Remove each shell from the grill when it opens, protecting your hands with tongs or hot pads. Discard any mollusks that have not opened.

4. Season to taste, and drizzle with sauce or butter, if desired.

Lobster 101

Serves 4

If you love lobster but are squeamish about handling them, you can have your fishmonger steam the live lobsters for a few minutes or until they turn red, before you take them home. Store them in the refrigerator and finish cooking them on the grill, or place the live lobster in a freezer for 20 minutes before grilling them. Place the lobsters on the cooking grate right out of the freezer while they are still "asleep."

Grilling Method: Direct/Medium Heat

Special Equipment: Lobster crackers, lobster picks

4 whole lobsters, about 1 1/2 pounds each
Olive oil
Melted butter, optional

1. Build a charcoal fire or preheat a gas grill.

2. Cut off the rubber bands that are holding the lobster claws together. Brush oil on both sides of the lobster.

3. Place the lobsters, bottom-side down, on the cooking grate over direct medium heat. Cover and grill 6 to 8 minutes or until the shells are red. Turn over and finish grilling 2 to 4 more minutes.

4. Remove the lobsters, and using kitchen scissors or shears, cut the soft inside membrane of the bottom of the tail and crack the shells of the claws. Serve the lobsters with metal lobster crackers and picks and warm butter, if desired, or pick the meat from the shells and reserve for lobster rolls, salads, etc.

Veggies 101

I hope that this 101 recipe will give you the confidence to buy whatever produce looks appealing and that it will inspire your curiosity in the grocery store or, better yet, at the curb stand, greenmarket, or nearby farm. Knowing whether to use direct or

indirect heat and using the Grilling Trilogy (see page 10) of olive oil, salt, and pepper should free you up to cook anything without following a specific recipe. This improvising at the grill is my favorite way to cook in the summer.

Grilling Method: Direct/Medium Heat

> Zucchini, eggplant, squash, asparagus, Belgian endive, etc., cut into 1/2-inch-thick slices or rounds or into quarters
>
> Olive oil
>
> Kosher salt
>
> Freshly ground pepper

1. Build a charcoal fire or preheat a gas grill.

2. Coat each vegetable slice with oil by placing clean, dry slices in a resealable plastic bag, pouring in the oil, and massaging to coat each vegetable piece with oil. Sprinkle with salt and pepper and massage again. Leave the veggies in the bag until ready to cook.

3. Place the vegetable slices on the cooking grate crosswise so they won't fall through the grates. Cover and grill over direct medium heat for 6 to 15 minutes, depending on the thickness and tenderness of each vegetable. Turn once or twice during the grilling time to expose all sides to the heat. The vegetables should begin to brown in spots (indicating that their natural sugars are caramelizing) but should not be allowed to char.

4. Move each vegetable to a platter as it is finished. Serve hot or at room temperature.

Hard-Skinned or Root Vegetables 101

Cooking times may vary depending on the thickness and water content of the veggie. If working with different types, place them on the grill in a way that will make them easy to remove in the order that they finish cooking.

Grilling Method: Indirect/Medium Heat

> Butternut, acorn, or delicata squash, or root vegetables such as whole potatoes, any variety
>
> Olive oil
>
> Kosher salt
>
> Freshly ground pepper

1. Build a charcoal fire or preheat a gas grill.

2. Cut squash in half and remove the seeds. Leave potatoes whole or cut them in half. You may need to cut a sliver off the bottom of a round squash so it will stand up straight. Coat the vegetables all over with oil, and season with salt and pepper.

3. Place the vegetables in the center of the cooking grate over indirect medium heat or on the warming rack, cover, and grill for 40 to 60 minutes, depending on the size of each vegetable. There is no need to turn large squash during grilling. Turn sliced potatoes once halfway through the cooking time to mark each side.

4. Remove each vegetable from the grill to a platter as it is finished and serve hot.

Sliced or Small Soft Fruit 101

These will cook almost immediately, so don't walk away from the grill.

Grilling Method: Direct/Medium-Low Heat

Bananas, strawberries, pineapples, melons, apples, plums, oranges, etc.

Walnut or grapeseed oil or melted clarified butter

Sugar, optional

1. Build a charcoal fire or preheat a gas grill.

2. Cut each fruit in half, wedges, or rings 1/2 inch thick. Leave on any skin that can be eaten or easily peeled before eating, such as for oranges, bananas, apples, and plums. It will be necessary to remove the skin from pineapple, mangos, etc. Brush the fruits lightly with oil. Sprinkle with sugar, if desired.

3. Place the fruit, cut side down, over direct medium-low heat, cover, and grill for 1 to 3 minutes or until they have grill marks. Turn the fruits over and continue cooking until warmed through. You can usually tell that the fruit is done when the skins starts to pull away.

4. Remove each fruit from the grill to a platter as it is finished. Serve warm, or let cool and refrigerate if desired.

Whole or Halved Hard Fruit 101

Baked apples, pears and other fruits can be grill-baked as a savory side dish or a sweet dessert.

Grilling Method: Indirect/Medium Heat

Apples, pears, pineapple halves, or other very firm (hard) fruits

Walnut or grapeseed oil or melted clarified butter

Sugar, honey, or maple syrup, optional

Spices, such as ground cinnamon, ground ginger, etc., optional

1. Build a charcoal fire or preheat a gas grill.

2. Cut each fruit in half, wedges, or rings 1/2 inch thick. Leave on any skin that can be eaten or easily peeled before eating. Wrap the bottom side of each piece or half with aluminum foil, but leave the top of the fruit exposed. Brush the cut surfaces with oil, and season with sugar and spices, if desired.

3. Place each piece in the center of the cooking grate over indirect medium heat, cover, and grill-bake until soft and fragrant, anywhere from 30 to 60 minutes, depending on how hard the fruit is.

4. Remove each fruit from the grill to a platter as it is finished. Serve hot, warm, or cold as a dessert or side dish.

Soaked

This section delves deeply into flavored liquids in which you submerge food before cooking, including:

Marinades • **Brines**

Marinades

Seasoned mixtures of an acid (vinegar, citrus) and a base (oil, yogurt) that impart flavor through soaking. Meat, poultry, fish, and vegetables marinate for at least 30 minutes, but generally not for more than 2 hours.

Marinades 101

RAPID-FIRE CHECKLIST

○ You need base, acid, and seasoning ingredients.

○ Be careful not to add too many sweet ingredients in a marinade, because the sugars burn quickly.

○ The oil locks in the flavor, promotes caramelization, and keeps the food moist and juicy.

○ The acid helps to "soften" the food and adds brightness and flavor.

○ When marinating, you need a relatively short soak (generally 30 minutes to 2 hours) for most foods.

○ Rule of thumb: The smaller and more delicate the food, the shorter the soak.

○ Much more than an hour or two in an enzyme-rich marinade can overtenderize and result in a mushy texture. A long soak in an acid-rich marinade can toughen food.

○ Always marinate in a glass, plastic, or stainless steel container, never aluminum, which will react with the acid.

○ If you plan to serve the marinade as a sauce at the table, you must bring it to a roaring boil and let it continue to boil for 3 minutes before it is considered safe.

○ Do not rinse off marinade. Drain the food and pat excess off with a paper towel—but do not rub, as you want to leave a coating of the marinade, and especially the oil, on the food.

Americans love to marinate what they grill. It's the first thing that weekend grillers think of when they want to add flavor to food.

And they're not alone: The Indian tandoori chef won't let fire touch his food until it's marinated in a rich aromatic yogurt marinade. Mojo is the signature marinade of Cuban cuisine, and all the delicious grilled and roasted Cuban meats start with a soak in this sour-orange and garlic mixture. And my own grandmother, like most Southern cooks, always threw her chicken in a buttermilk bath before baking or frying it. The whole world of cooking has a long history of marinating food.

It is commonly believed that people began the practice of adding flavor to foods by marinating or soaking them in seasoned and salted liquid between the mid-1600s and the mid-1700s. There are several ideas about the origin of the word *marinade*; it is commonly thought to come from both the French and the Italian, from the French word *mariner*, which means "to pickle," or the Italian word *marinare*, which means "to marinate." It is also said that the origin alludes to the use of brine, a.k.a. *aqua marina* (seawater or saltwater), in the pickling process, which goes reinforces the French origin of pickling.

Regardless of how and where they started, marinades are a great way to add flavor to meat, fish, poultry, vegetables, and fruit. At their simplest, marinades have one acidic ingredient (for penetrating foods) and a base ingredient (to lock in flavors and keep food moist), usually vegetable oil, extra-virgin olive oil, nut or seed oil, or sometimes full-fat yogurts. You can also use flavored oils like hot chile oil, lemongrass oil, basil oil, truffle oil, etc. to add both flavor and the oil component. Good acid choices include cider vinegar; lemon, lime, or orange juice; wine; beer; and buttermilk. (Juices from raw pineapple, papaya, melon, figs, ginger, and kiwi contain powerful tenderizing enzymes that can turn meat into mush—a short soak is perfect but the longer the time, the mushier the meat gets.) Yogurt is one of my favorite marinating ingredients, and it is actually both an acid and a base (unless you choose the fat-free variety). Thick, full-fat Greek yogurt (one commonly found brand is FAGE Total) is my favorite yogurt to use because the excess whey (liquid) is already drained out.

Once the oil and acid are in place, flavoring elements are added to create marinade flavor profiles. Favorite and common ingredients include fresh grated or minced ginger, fresh or dried herbs, spices, garlic, onion, hot sauce, ketchup, soy sauce, fish sauce, Tabasco sauce, chutney, jellies, jams, marmalades, Worcestershire sauce, and Thai chile-garlic sauce (*sriracha*).

Note: Some people like leaving the oil out of the equation; I don't recommend it. If you don't have the oil to temper the acid, the acid and enzymes can "cook" or toughen the food and prevent the seasonings and moisture from being absorbed and locked in. The food may be tough, mushy, and dried out once it is cooked. The oil locks in the flavor, prevents a quick "cook" by the acidic ingredients, promotes caramelization, and keeps the food moist and juicy.

Not-Too-Sweet Tip: Be careful not to add too many sweet ingredients to your marinade since sugars burn quickly. This is also why it's not advisable to put barbecue sauce on the food at the beginning of the cooking time. By the time the meat is cooked, the outside will be burned.

The best part of marinating is that you can vary the flavors of your food just by adding herbs, spices, and flavorings indicative of a particular cuisine. It is an especially appealing option these days when so many international cuisines are available to us. Most of the food I ate growing up was Southern, Continental, or French—and the French was courtesy of Julia Child beaming onto the tiny black-and-white television set in my mother's kitchen. My mother's mother never made a French dish in her life, but already things were changing when her daughter cooked for my sisters and me using family recipes, and with recipes provided by the TV station. Growing up in North Carolina, it was highly unusual to have extra-virgin olive oil (or any olive oil, for that matter!) and Dijon mustard in our pantry. Today, those two items are standard grocery store items and not exotic at all—even in the smallest town in North Carolina!

Today, we all have access to restaurants specializing in international cuisine regardless of where we live. And it is natural that we want to replicate (or at least mimic) food at home that we eat in restaurants. Who wouldn't like to make grilled chicken taste like that fragrant oregano chicken that we've all had in Greek Town or recreate the smoky, moist tandoori meats from our neighborhood Indian restaurant? I often eat something great in a restaurant and then come home and riff on the dish to create my own version. Most of the time it is just as pleasing and sometimes even better than what I remember from the restaurant. You no longer need to learn the traditional techniques and details of a world of cuisines—you can stock your pantry and create exotic meals on the grill with just a few palate-pleasing seasonings.

That is where marinades come in handy. Marinades are the easiest way to impart grilled food with these distinctive flavors. For that reason, I have included marinades that will capture all your favorite restaurant flavors. My Double Happiness Chinese Marinade (page 61) captures all the prominent flavors from that cuisine. Truth be told, there are so many styles of Chinese food that my Chinese friends would probably laugh at the idea that one marinade could bring you all the flavors of China. That said, if you are used to eating American versions of Chinese food and like those flavors, you'll love this marinade. The same is true for all of my international marinades. For all but the most extreme purists, these marinades will deliver just what you are looking for—a hint of Italian, French, Mexican, Vietnamese, or Indian, etc., flavor in your own backyard cuisine.

A note on the process of marinating: Most of the time, a marinade does not penetrate food much beyond the surface. Unless you use a vacuum marinator such as the Vacu Vin Instant Marinater, you only flavor the first 1/4 inch of the food. (The instant marinater eliminates the oxygen within food and creates a vacuum seal, which locks in flavor. The marinade takes up the space where the air used to be.)

Generally, every bite includes this flavored layer, and it is enough to nicely flavor the dish. In addition, the acids or enzymes in marinades change the texture of (the food during the process of marinating (the term *tenderize* is often used

but is technically incorrect unless it is an enzyme-rich marinade that will breakdown tough meat fibers). When marinating, I recommend a relatively short soak for most foods—30 minutes to 2 hours. Much more than an hour or two in the marinade can oversoften food and result in a mushy texture, especially if the marinades contain enzymes from ingredients like pineapple or papaya, or a tough texture if the marinade has a lot of acid-rich citrus juice and/or vinegar. My rule of thumb is the smaller and more delicate the food, the shorter the soak.

I know that some of my BBQ Buddies disagree with me and marinate food in acid-rich baths for days at a time. If you look at the meat during the marinating process, you can literally see the acid or enzymes "cooking" the meat and changing the molecular structure. One visual sign of over-marinated meat is a gray or dark blueish color instead of a healthy red color (see photo below). In my experience, when you grill or barbecue meat that has already been "cooked" by the acid, the result is meat with mushy texture and flavor. If you think about how quickly citrus juice and vinegar "cooks" raw seafood when you make a ceviche, this will make sense to you.

If you have a marinade recipe that calls for letting it soak for days, and you love the results, keep making it. But try it my way and see what you think of a quick, flavor-filled soak that leaves the meat firm and full flavored. The only exception to my short-soak approach is an olive oil and dry herb marinade (devoid of any liquid acid) that can be used for up to 3 days to great effect.

Tenderizing Tip

Marinades penetrate meat with flavor. One note of caution when using acid-rich or enzyme-rich marinades: Soaking meat for too long can result in a mushy, tough, or overprocessed texture. Be careful not to put too much of these ingredients in your marinade. For example, both ginger and pineapple contain natural enzymes that quickly break down proteins. One or two acidic ingredients will add dimension to your marinade, but more than that will rapidly ruin your meat and make it tough.

Marinating Tools

Since marinades are acidic, always marinate in a glass, plastic, or stainless steel container, never aluminum, which will react with the acid. This is what recipe instructions are referring to when they call for a "nonreactive bowl or container."

I like to use large resealable plastic bags for marinating, brining, and oiling foods before grilling—I even packaged two sizes of heavy-duty, leakproof bags for my line of Grill Friends products. Look for the Turkey Brining Bag around the holidays and the Everyday Brining and Marinade Bag year-round. The bags are airtight and you can move the food through the plastic so all parts are exposed to the liquid easily and without any mess.

How to Safely Turn a Marinade into a Sauce

Although it's common knowledge to many cooks, it's worth repeating: Don't repurpose used marinade as a serving sauce. Raw meat, fish, and especially poultry have natural bacteria when raw. These bacteria are cooked off during the grilling process. However, the bacteria may have transferred from the protein to the marinade during soaking. For this reason, if you want to serve the marinade as a sauce at the table, you must bring it to a roaring boil and let it continue to boil for 3 minutes before it is considered safe. That said, most of my marinades are designed to impart raw food with bold, bright flavors—not to be cooked and used as a table sauce. Unless the recipe specifically calls for cooking the marinade down and serving the marinade, I'd toss it, confident that it has already served its primary purpose.

Shelf Life

Most of my marinade recipes say that you can make them and store them in the refrigerator for 2 days or so. This is correct; they won't go bad, but know that all marinades are best made just before you want to use them. The fresher a marinade is, the brighter and more intense the flavor will be.

Marinade 101: Viva! It's Homemade Italian Dressing!

Makes 1 1/4 cups

I chose a homemade Italian "dressing" for Marinade 101 because everyone I know has taken a bottle of store-bought dressing and doused it over chicken, fish, shrimp, and vegetables before grilling. And it is the "secret" marinade of just about every competition barbecuer I know. My home-made version is a simple and so-much-better version. I give you the choice to use olive or canola oil. My personal preference is extra-virgin olive oil, but feel free to use canola if you prefer a more neutral flavor. I've listed individual spices, but you may substitute your favorite Italian spice blend. You can also make the marinade lighter and more contemporary by substituting basil for the oregano.

Good for Soaking: Zucchini, cut vegetables, chicken pieces, pork tenderloin, salad greens

1/2 cup white wine vinegar
1/4 cup white wine, preferably Chardonnay
1 teaspoon mayonnaise, preferably Hellmann's*
2 cloves garlic, chopped
2 teaspoons dried oregano or 1 tablespoon chopped fresh
2 teaspoons chopped fresh curly parsley
1 teaspoon granulated onion
1 teaspoon granulated garlic
1/2 teaspoon red chile flakes
1/2 teaspoon fine-grain sea salt
1/2 cup olive or canola oil

In a medium bowl, mix the vinegar and wine together and whisk in the mayonnaise until the color is milky white and there are no lumps. Mix in the fresh garlic, oregano, parsley, granulated onion and garlic, red chile flakes, and salt. Slowly whisk in the oil until it is completely incorporated. Taste and adjust the seasoning. The marinade will keep, tightly covered, in the refrigerator for up to 5 days.

*The mayonnaise may seem like a strange addition to this list of ingredients, but it's there to help the dressing blend together. If you like a creamy Italian dressing, increase the mayonnaise until it has the creaminess that you like.

Red Wine Marinade for Beef and Lamb

Makes 3 1/2 cups

This classic marinade is great for all cuts of red meat, and, it is a great use for a half-finished bottle of wine. That remaining wine may not be good enough to drink, but it'll be just perfect for this marinade.

Good for Soaking: Any kind of red meat, veal, mushrooms, onions

2 cups favorite red wine
1 cup water
1/4 cup packed dark brown sugar
1/2 cup extra-virgin olive oil

2 tablespoons coarse kosher salt, preferably Morton, or sea salt

1 tablespoon chopped fresh or dried rosemary leaves

6 cloves garlic, smashed

Combine all the ingredients in a large nonreactive bowl and whisk until the sugar and salt are dissolved. (Alternatively, warm the water, dissolve the sugar and salt in it, and then add the rest of the ingredients.) Refrigerate for at least 30 minutes before using. The marinade will keep for up to 2 days.

White Wine Marinade for Fish, Poultry, and Pork

Makes 3 1/2 cups

Think of this as the classic marinade for "white" meat.

Good for Soaking: Meaty fish fillets, salmon, Arctic char, chicken, pork cutlets, pork loin

2 cups favorite white wine

1 cup water

1/4 cup packed light brown sugar

1/2 cup extra-virgin olive oil

3 teaspoons coarse kosher salt, preferably Morton, or sea salt

Zest of 1 large lemon

1 tablespoon each of 3 herbs such as chopped fresh or dried tarragon, basil, sage, and/or rosemary leaves

1 tablespoon dehydrated garlic

Combine all the ingredients in a large nonreactive bowl and whisk until the sugar and salt are dissolved. (Alternatively, dissolve the sugar and salt in warm water and then add the rest of the ingredients. Make sure the marinade is cool before using.) The marinade will keep, tightly covered, in the refrigerator for up to 1 week.

Classic French Marinade

Makes 3 1/3 cups

This marinade is inspired by my favorite French chicken recipe, which Julia Child published in her first cookbook—I can't make it without hearing her wonderful, warbling voice. I've taken the most prominent flavors and turned them into a paste-like marinade that will turn you into a bona fide bistro cook. The key is to leave as much of the marinade on the food as possible; don't rub it off before cooking.

Good for Soaking: Flat-iron steak, pork, butterflied chicken, chicken pieces

One 7.5-ounce jar Dijon mustard

2 cups white wine

1/2 cup (1 stick) melted unsalted butter

1 teaspoon fine-grain sea salt

1/2 teaspoon coarsely ground black pepper

4 to 5 scallions, cleaned and chopped

In a medium nonreactive saucepan over low heat, whisk together the mustard and wine until smooth. Add the melted butter, salt, pepper, and scallions and mix until the salt is dissolved. Cook, whisking occasionally, for 2 to 3 minutes to emulsify the mixture. The marinade will keep, tightly covered, in the refrigerator for up to 2 days.

Pete the Greek's Marinade

Makes about 1 cup

Everyone has a Greek neighbor or neighborhood restaurant that is famous for marinated and grilled meats. This lemon, garlic, and oregano marinade is my version of what my friend Pete (and every Greek restaurant I've ever been to) uses. He says that you can use this on anything that is good grilled except fruit! I especially like to use it for lamb chops.

Good for Soaking: Lamb, swordfish, octopus, chicken, whole fish, vegetables

- 1/2 cup extra-virgin olive oil
- 1/4 cup fresh squeezed lemon juice (about 2 lemons)
- Zest of 1 large lemon
- 2 tablespoons fresh oregano, chopped, or 2 teaspoons dried
- 1 teaspoon dried thyme
- 4 cloves garlic, grated
- 1/4 teaspoon sea salt

Combine all the ingredients in a medium nonreactive bowl and whisk until the salt is dissolved. The marinade will keep, tightly covered, in the refrigerator for up to 2 days.

Korean Barbecue Marinade

Makes about 1 3/4 cups

Korean barbecue restaurants are all the rage. Here's a way to enjoy those flavors at home and a great way to get the whole party in on the cooking! The classic dish is marinated strips of beef (sirloin) called bulgogi. The term means "fire meat" in Korean, which makes sense, as the marinated meat is grilled by diners over live fire. The classic marinade is soy sauce, sugar, garlic, and sesame oil. I've added other traditional (and some not-so-traditional) Korean ingredients to make this a marinade that is good for all grilled meats and is dynamite with small Japanese eggplant.

Good for Soaking: Thin pieces of beef, chicken, pork, snow peas, broccoli, Japanese eggplant

- 1 cup low-sodium soy sauce
- 1/4 cup Sugar in the Raw (turbinado)
- 2 tablespoons pure maple syrup
- 2 tablespoons sherry vinegar
- 3 tablespoons toasted sesame oil
- 2 tablespoons peanut or canola oil
- 3 large cloves garlic, grated
- 4 scallions, including green tops, finely chopped, about 1/4 cup
- 1/2 piece fresh ginger root, grated on a Microplane, about 2 tablespoons
- 1 tablespoon sesame seeds

In a medium nonreactive bowl, whisk together the soy sauce, sugar, maple syrup, sherry vinegar, oils, garlic, scallions, ginger, and sesame seeds. Mix until the sugar is dissolved. The marinade will keep, tightly covered, in the refrigerator for up to 3 days. Before marinating, reserve 1/2 cup to use as a dipping sauce, if desired.

Note: Make sure whatever food you grill is thin and/or small, since the sugar in the marinade will burn if left on the grill for a long time.

Rosé Marinade with Herbes de Provence

Makes 2 1/2 cups

This marinade was inspired by long nights spent drinking rosé wine in the south of France. I am thrilled that rosés are coming into their own in the United States—these days, fewer and fewer people look at me with a wrinkled nose when I recommend drinking or cooking with rosé. I love marinating leg of lamb or fresh ham in this light and savory marinade, but it is equally delicious paired with scallops, shrimp, or delicate white fish, such as flounder or sole.

Good for Soaking: Lamb, fresh ham, beef tenderloin, fish, shellfish, eggplant, tomatoes

> 2 cups favorite rosé wine, preferably from the south of France
>
> 2/3 cup extra-virgin olive oil
>
> 1/8 cup lavender honey
>
> 2 tablespoons coarse kosher salt, preferably Morton, or sea salt
>
> 2 tablespoons herbes de Provence with lavender buds
>
> 1 tablespoon grated garlic

In a large nonreactive bowl, combine all the ingredients and whisk until the salt and honey are dissolved. The marinade will keep, tightly covered, in the refrigerator for up to 2 days.

Garlicky Lemon Marinade

Makes 1 3/4 cups

The simple flavors of garlic and lemon can be found throughout the Mediterranean. In Greece, they may add oregano and dill to the garlic-lemon base. In France, you'll often find the addition of white wine and herbes de Provence. And in Italy, it is best quality olive oil.

I like to use this marinade for shellfish, meat, poultry, and veggies, but I most often use it for shrimp or chicken skewers. Leave as much marinade on the food as possible—you will love the salty, lemony garlic crust that forms during grilling.

Good for Soaking: Fish, shellfish, chicken, lamb

> 6 tablespoons fresh lemon juice (2 large lemons)
>
> 1/2 cup best-quality extra-virgin olive oil
>
> Zest of 1 large lemon
>
> 16 cloves garlic, peeled
>
> 1 1/2 teaspoons kosher salt
>
> Pinch red chile flakes

1. In a small nonreactive bowl, whisk the lemon juice and oil together until blended. Add the lemon zest and set aside.

2. Mash the garlic cloves and salt together in a mortar and pestle or with the back of a fork in a shallow bowl to form a thick paste. Add the paste and the red chile flakes to the lemon-oil mixture and mix well. The marinade will keep, tightly covered, in the refrigerator for up to 2 days.

Garlicky Lemon and Herb Marinade Variation

Reduce the number of garlic cloves to 8. Make the marinade as directed, and add 1 teaspoon dried crumbled rosemary or other favorite herbs to the marinade and mix well.

Papaya-Lime Marinade

Makes about 2 1/2 cups

On a recent trip to Mexico, I spent a week at a very simple yoga retreat. It was undeniably beautiful—I looked out at the Mayan Riviera and ate fresh fish every day! But even paradise can get monotonous. The "mess hall" specialized in basic food, but after several days of eating plain broiled fish, I suggested that they marinate my fish in a mixture of locally available ingredients—papaya, lime juice, garlic, and cilantro. And so this colorful and delicious marinade was born. Before pureeing, reserve some of the ingredients and make a roughly chopped salsa to serve on top of your fish.

Good for Soaking: Fish, shellfish, chicken, pork loin

   1 large ripe but not mushy papaya, peeled and roughly chopped
   1/2 cup fresh lime juice (about 6 limes)
   5 cloves garlic, chopped
   1/2 cup loosely packed fresh cilantro
   1 teaspoon kosher salt
   1/2 cup peanut oil
   1/4 teaspoon minced habanero pepper or ground cayenne pepper

Using a blender, puree the papaya with the lime juice. Add the garlic, cilantro, and salt and puree to combine. Add the oil and the habanero pepper. Pulse to combine. The marinade will keep, tightly covered, in the refrigerator for up to 2 days.

Note: The enzyme in the papaya is a "super-tenderizer" and very powerful. Make sure you do not leave this on food for very long; up to 30 minutes for fish and shellfish and up to 1 hour for poultry and pork.

Fire-Roasted Poblano, Peach, and Onion Marinade

Makes about 2 cups

I created this marinade one summer when I had an over-abundance of peppers and peaches. The essence of this recipe is in the sweet heat from the roasted poblano peppers mixed with the tangy sweetness from ripe peaches and the savory layer of flavor from the caramelized onions. It is so good that I sometimes make it and eat it as a salsa.

Make a double batch and use half of it as a marinade and the other half as a grilling sauce. Try grill-roasting boneless pork chops in the marinade in a pan on the grill. You can use a disposable aluminum pan or the greener choice of a cast-iron skillet. I like using a skillet because it goes from the kitchen to the grill to the table for a great rustic presentation.

Good for Soaking: Chicken, whole fish, shellfish, pork, beef

3 to 4 poblano peppers, roasted, peeled, and seeded (see Roasted Peppers, right)

2 large sweet onions, slow roasted (see Forgotten Onion, below)

1 to 2 ripe peaches, unpeeled and pitted

1/2 cup peach or apricot nectar, preferably Goya

2 tablespoons balsamic vinegar

1/2 cup loosely packed fresh basil

1 teaspoon kosher salt

1/2 cup extra-virgin olive oil

1/4 teaspoon Tabasco Green Pepper Sauce

Using a blender, puree the peppers, onions, and peaches with the juice and vinegar. Add the basil and salt, and puree to combine. Add the oil and the Tabasco. Pulse to combine. The marinade will keep, tightly covered, in the refrigerator for up to 2 days.

Forgotten Onion

Grilling Method: Indirect/Medium Heat

2 whole unpeeled medium onions, preferably Vidalia

Extra-virgin olive oil

Kosher salt or fleur de sel

1. Coat the onion with olive oil and salt. Place it in the center of the cooking grate over indirect heat.

2. Grill, covered, for 60 to 90 minutes or until the skins are blackened and the onion is deeply caramelized. Remove from the grill, remove the skins, and use as directed, or serve whole with a sprinkle of olive oil and salt.

Roasted Peppers

Grilling Method: Direct/Medium-High Heat

Bell or poblano peppers

1. Place the peppers directly on the cooking grate over medium-high heat. Turn occasionally until the skins blacken and blister all over.

2. Remove the peppers from the grill with tongs and place in a paper bag or a sealed plastic or glass container until cool enough to touch, about 30 minutes. Using your fingers, remove the skins and seeds. Use as directed.

Tequila-Honey-Lime Marinade

Makes 1 3/4 cups

One night, I was cooking at home while enjoying a cocktail, and I accidentally poured tequila into a mixture of lime juice and honey that I was whisking into a salad dressing (I thought it was the walnut oil). I was about to throw it out, but I tasted it first. It was really yummy and I decided to use it on my jicama slaw. I then made a bigger batch and tried it with a couple of catfish fillets. Needless to say, it was a winner dinner and has worked with everything I've tried it on. It's the best excuse to open a bottle of tequila that I've had in a long time!

Good for Soaking: Chicken thighs, whole chicken, chicken pieces, prawns, whole fish, pork tenderloin

> 1/2 cup blue agave tequila
>
> 1/2 cup untoasted walnut oil
>
> 1/2 cup honey
>
> 1/4 cup fresh lime juice (about 4 large limes)
>
> Zest of 1 lime
>
> 1 teaspoon kosher salt
>
> Optional add-ins: 2 cloves garlic, grated; 1/2 teaspoon ground cumin; 1 small jalapeño pepper, minced; 2 shallots, minced

In a small nonreactive bowl, whisk the tequila and oil together until blended. Add the honey, lime juice, zest, salt, and any optional add-ins, if using. Mix well. The marinade will keep, tightly covered, in the refrigerator for up to 2 days.

Note: Since that first day, I've used this as a base for adding other aromatics and especially classic Mexican ingredients. Add one or all of my optional add-ins for a fuller-flavored marinade. This marinade can also double as a salad dressing.

Turkish Delight Yogurt and Pomegranate Marinade

Makes about 1 cup

India is famous for its yogurt marinades, but Turkish cooks use them almost as often. Here I've combined pomegranate, which is native to the region, with rich spices and a hint of fresh mint for a marinade that is reminiscent of Turkey and delightful on meat, poultry, or vegetables—especially kabobs, which are also common in Turkey. In Turkish *shish* means "skewer."

Good for Soaking: Lamb chops, leg of lamb, chicken, eggplant

> 1 cup predrained whole-milk yogurt, such as FAGE Total
>
> 1 large shallot, chopped
>
> 1 teaspoon ground coriander
>
> 1/2 teaspoon ground cardamom
>
> 1/4 teaspoon ground cinnamon
>
> 1/4 cup chopped fresh mint
>
> 1 tablespoon unsweetened pomegranate juice
>
> 1/4 cup pomegranate seeds
>
> 1 teaspoon kosher salt
>
> 1/2 teaspoon ground white pepper

In a small nonreactive bowl, mix together the yogurt, shallot, spices, and mint. Add the juice, seeds, salt, and pepper and mix until well blended. The marinade will keep, tightly covered, in the refrigerator for up to 2 days.

Green Tabasco Marinade

Makes about 2 cups

My friend and fellow Southern food lover Bill Smith is famous for his Green Tabasco Chicken. On a recent trip to his renowned restaurant, Crook's Corner, in Chapel Hill, N.C., I had the pleasure of tasting it myself, and it inspired this simpler green Tabasco marinade. If you like this recipe, you'll love his book, *Seasoned in the South*.

Good for Soaking: chicken, wings, skirt steak, white fish, potatoes, chayote, corn, squash

> One 5-ounce bottle Tabasco Green Pepper Sauce or other green hot pepper sauce
>
> 1 cup dry white wine
>
> 1/2 cup bacon drippings or melted butter
>
> 5 cloves garlic, smashed
>
> Zest and juice of 1 lemon
>
> 1 teaspoon kosher salt
>
> 1/2 teaspoon freshly ground black pepper
>
> 1 small jalapeño pepper, seeded and minced

In a small nonreactive bowl, whisk together the Tabasco sauce and wine. Set over low heat, and gradually whisk in the bacon drippings. Add the garlic, lemon juice and zest, salt, pepper, and jalapeño. Mix until well blended. The marinade will keep, tightly covered, in the refrigerator for up to 2 days.

Southern Buttermilk Marinade

Makes 2 1/4 cups

Contrary to what many people think, buttermilk does not contain any butter. Made in the traditional way, it is the liquid that is rendered during the process of making butter. Though it is fat free, it is full of wonderful tenderizing agents and for that reason is a mainstay in Southern cooking. In fact, if you have ever eaten a piece of Southern-fried chicken (and I don't mean from a fast-food chain), chances are that the cook marinated the chicken in buttermilk before coating and frying it. Though the marinade is made for chicken, it is also great for pork or hearty fish fillets.

Good for Soaking: Chicken, pork cutlets, turkey cutlets, fish fillets

> 2 cups buttermilk
>
> 1/4 cup olive or peanut oil
>
> 1/2 to 1 teaspoon ground cayenne pepper
>
> 1/2 teaspoon kosher salt
>
> 1/2 teaspoon freshly ground black pepper

In a medium nonreactive bowl, whisk together the buttermilk and oil. Add the cayenne pepper, salt, and black pepper. Mix until well blended. The marinade will keep, tightly covered, in the refrigerator for up to 2 days.

Asia-Lite Marinade

Makes about 3/4 cup

There are many Asian marinades—and most are heavy on the soy sauce. That's great when you want to impart a dark, salty rich flavor but not when you want a marinade with a lighter touch. This marinade is as light in color as it is in flavor, due to the fact that the soy sauce is an accent instead of the main flavor. This has become one of my favorite marinades, and the lettuce-wrapped "tacos" (see facing page) are a real crowd-pleaser for adults and kids alike—my sister Mary Pat makes them for her three young boys several times a month!

Good for Soaking: Chicken; flank steak; sea bass, catfish, sea bass; Asian slaw

- 1/4 cup peanut or canola oil
- 1/4 cup toasted sesame oil
- 1/8 cup unseasoned rice vinegar
- 1 tablespoon Thai chili-garlic sauce (*sriracha*)*

- 2 tablespoons low-sodium soy sauce
- Pinch sea salt
- Zest of 1 orange
- 3 to 5 cloves garlic, grated
- 1 small knob (1 inch) fresh ginger, grated

In a medium bowl, combine the oil, sesame oil, rice vinegar, chili-garlic sauce, soy sauce, salt, zest, garlic, and ginger. Mix until well blended. The marinade will keep, tightly covered, in the refrigerator for up to 2 days.

*_Sriracha_ is that delicious pungent hot sauce in the clear bottle or jar with a kelly-green plastic top and a picture of a rooster. It is made from sun-ripened chile peppers, vinegar, garlic, sugar, and salt and has a thick, almost ketchup-y consistency. It is easily found in Asian grocery stores or online. If you don't have it, omit it or add a few dashes of Tabasco sauce—it won't be the same, but you'll get the heat. However, I strongly urge you to add it to your pantry—it lasts forever and is a great ingredient to have on hand.

Oy Vey! French Onion Soup Marinade

Makes 3 1/2 cups

It wouldn't be an all-American grilling cookbook without at least one recipe that calls for Lipton onion soup mix. The mix has become such a popular recipe ingredient that the company has actually changed the name of the product to "recipe, soup, and dip mix." In fact, this—and chili sauce—is the secret to many a Jewish grandmother's brisket! And it makes a great marinade and a great grilling sauce as well. Instead of discarding the marinade, grill-roast the marinade and the brisket

Asian Tacos: Grilled Chicken Wrapped with Mint and Lettuce

Serves 4

Grilling Method: Medium Direct heat

- 1 recipe Asia-Lite Marinade
- 1/4 cup peanut or canola oil
- 1/4 cup toasted sesame oil
- 1/8 cup unseasoned rice vinegar
- 1 tablespoon Thai chili-garlic sauce (*sriracha*)
- 2 tablespoons low-sodium soy sauce
- Pinch sea salt
- Zest of 1 orange
- 3 to 5 cloves garlic, grated
- 1 small knob (1 inch) fresh ginger, grated
- 2 boneless skinless chicken breasts

TACO FIXINGS

- Bunch fresh mint
- 1 head Boston lettuce, leaves separated
- Large bean sprouts, optional
- 1 lime, cut into wedges

1. Preheat a gas grill or build a charcoal fire.

2. Reserve one-third of the marinade. Add the chicken to the remaining marinade, making sure all surfaces are coated. Cover and marinate in the refrigerator for 30 minutes to 1 hour, turning occasionally to coat all sides.

3. When ready to grill, remove the meat from the marinade and discard the marinade. Place the chicken directly on the cooking grates. Grill for about 10 minutes, turning the chicken once halfway through the cooking time or until the chicken is completely cooked through.

4. When the chicken is done, remove from the grill and drizzle with a little of the remaining marinade. Let sit for 5 minutes.

5. Meanwhile, arrange the mint, lettuce leaves, bean sprouts, and lime wedges buffet-style on one or several platters. Thinly slice the chicken on the diagonal and add the chicken slices to the platter. Place the reserved marinade in a bowl and serve on the side as a dressing.

(or chicken thighs) together in a pan on the grill over indirect medium heat until the meat is done and the sauce is bubbling. You'll become the new "Bubbie" of the family!

Good for Soaking: Brisket, country ribs, short ribs; chicken

- 1 package Lipton Recipe Secrets onion soup mix
- 1 cup red wine
- One 12-ounce bottle Heinz Chili Sauce
- 1/4 cup extra-virgin olive oil
- 1 teaspoon granulated garlic
- 1 teaspoon sweet smoked paprika
- 1/2 teaspoon ground white pepper
- 1 yellow onion, chopped, about 1 cup
- 1 carrot, grated, about 3/4 cup

In a medium nonreactive bowl, whisk together the soup mix and wine. Add the chili sauce, oil, garlic, paprika, pepper, onion, and carrot. Mix until well blended. The marinade will keep, tightly covered, in the refrigerator for up to 2 days.

Yogi Yogurt Marinade

Makes 1 1/2 cups

This marinade is transcending! The toasted cumin seed infuses the rich yogurt and olive oil marinade with explosive flavor and helps to create a crispy, crunchy skin and silken chicken meat. The success of the marinade hinges on two things: buying full-fat yogurt and draining it or buying Greek or Greek-style yogurt such as FAGE Total that is already drained, and toasting the cumin seeds. Toasting spices will increase the flavor and aroma exponentially.

Good for Soaking: Butterflied chicken, game hen, quail; lamb

- 1 cup predrained whole-milk yogurt, such as FAGE Total
- 1/2 cup extra-virgin olive oil
- 3 cloves garlic, minced
- 1 teaspoon whole cumin seeds, toasted
- 1 teaspoon coarse kosher salt, preferably Morton, or sea salt
- Freshly ground pepper
- Pinch red chile flakes or ground cayenne pepper
- 1 teaspoon ground turmeric, optional*

Put the yogurt in a bowl and stir in the remaining ingredients. Use immediately.

*Adding ground turmeric to the marinade will give the food that distinctive golden hue common in Indian food.

In a small nonreactive bowl, whisk together the oil and curry powder. Add the granulated onion, salt, and cayenne pepper. Add the beer and mix until well blended. The marinade will keep, tightly covered, in the refrigerator for up to 2 days.

*Madras curry is the readily available curry powder that I call for in this recipe. It usually contains a blend of curry leaves, turmeric, coriander, cumin, cinnamon, cloves, chile pepper, bay leaves, fenugreek, allspice, and black pepper.

Madras Curry Marinade

Makes 1 1/2 cup

Madras shorts and Madras curry powder conjure up images of a party right out of an Austin Powers's sequel! Interestingly, both the shorts and the spice mixture have origins in the same Indian city. They are both brightly colored and a mixture of many things, whether patterns or spices. Curry powder does not refer to one spice, but rather to a mixture of many spices, and most Indian cooks make their own signature blends, just as we barbecuers blend our own spice rubs.

Good for Soaking: Quail, squab, chicken; lamb; salmon, shrimp; mushrooms, sliced vegetables

> 1/2 cup extra-virgin olive oil
> 2 tablespoons Madras curry powder*
> 1 teaspoon granulated onion
> 1 teaspoon kosher salt
> Pinch cayenne pepper
> 1 cup Indian or other beer, such as Kingfisher or Foster's

Orange Teriyaki Marinade

Makes about 1/2 cup

Due to the popularity of the Soy Vay! brand of teriyaki marinade, you can't be faulted for thinking it is a traditional Jewish food—but it comes from Japan. Traditional teriyaki sauce is a sweetened soy sauce, and the name comes from the word *teri*, which refers to the shine or luster the cooked food gets from the sugar content in the sauce, and the word *yaki*, which refers to the cooking method of grilling (or broiling). Teriyaki restaurants use small, thin pieces of meat that cook quickly—before the sugar in the marinade burns. In Japan, this teriyaki sauce is used as both the marinade and the grilling sauce. If you want to cook your meat and veggies like the Japanese, double the recipe and use half for marinating and half for brushing while cooking.

Good for Soaking: Beef skewers, flank steak; chicken; eggplant, green beans

1/2 cup low-sodium soy sauce

1/4 cup sake, mirin (sweetened rice wine), or dry sherry

1 tablespoon sugar

3 tablespoons orange marmalade*

2 large scallions, minced

2 cloves garlic, minced

1 tablespoon minced fresh ginger

You can prepare this marinade two ways:

You can whisk together the soy sauce, sake, sugar, and marmalade in a small saucepan and simmer until the mixture is reduced and thick. Then add the scallions, garlic, and ginger.

Or you can mix all the ingredients together in a small bowl and use it uncooked. The cooked version is more authentic and deeper in flavor than the uncooked version.

*As you can imagine, orange marmalade is not traditional, but I love the sweet and bitter orange mixed with the soy sauce. The dry sherry is another substitute that I make when I don't have mirin or sake on hand.

"I Think My Pig Is Sexy" Marinade

Makes about 5 1/2 cups

Think of this marinade as a "bubble bath" for pork! A few years ago, my sister Mary Pat and brother-in-law, Karl, joined me on the banks of the Mississippi for Memphis in May—the Mardi Gras of the barbecue circuit. Arriving just in time for the "Miss Piggy" contest, we stared in delight as a chorus-girl lineup of Miss Piggys (as in fat,

hairy men in bikinis, Mardi Gras beads, and pig noses) began singing "I think my pig is sexy..." Needless to say, this became our signature barbecue song, and to this day, we sing it as we barbecue our "sexy pig"—winter, spring, summer, or fall!

Good for Soaking: Pork! ribs, butt, shoulder; chicken; salmon, trout

2 cups apple cider vinegar

One 12-ounce bottle beer, such as PBR (Pabst Blue Ribbon)

1/2 cup peanut or olive oil

1/2 cup ketchup

1/2 cup molasses

5 cloves garlic, smashed

1 tablespoon kosher salt

1 tablespoon fine-ground white pepper

1 tablespoon red chile flakes

2 teaspoons freshly ground black pepper

2 tablespoons sugar

1/4 cup packed dark brown sugar

In a large nonreactive bowl, whisk together the vinegar, beer, oil, ketchup, and molasses. Add the garlic, salt, peppers, and sugars. Mix until well blended. The marinade will keep, tightly covered in the refrigerator, almost indefinitely. Shake well before using.

Note: The longer the sauce sits, the spicier it gets, since the heat from the red chile flakes is brought out by the vinegar. Start with 1/2 tablespoon red chile flakes and then add more to taste.

4 cloves garlic, grated
1 teaspoon kosher salt
1/4 teaspoon freshly ground pepper
1 large red onion, cut into 1-inch rings*

In a small nonreactive bowl, whisk together the beer and olive oil. Add the parsley, garlic, salt, pepper, and onions. Mix until well blended. The marinade will keep, tightly covered, in the refrigerator for up to 2 days.

*If you like, after you use the marinade, you can remove the onion rings before discarding the marinade and grill them.

Irish Marinade: Guinness Is Good for You

Makes 3 cups

Don't believe everything you read is what I told my always-up-for-a-challenge friend Bob Blumer. He was in Ireland and the "Guinness is good for you" slogan was everywhere . . . he began to believe it, and ever a *Glutton for Punishment*, he decided to test its veracity. For an entire week, he neither ate nor drank anything except that Irish tonic, Guinness. The good news is that he made it through the whole week sober and his doctor pronounced him healthy as a horse. This is the perfect marinade for flank steak, deepening the flavor and promoting a nice dark crust—absolutely gorgeous!

Good for Soaking: Flank steak, other cuts of beef; red onions; duck breast

One 14.9-ounce can Guinness
1/2 cup extra-virgin olive oil
2 tablespoons fresh parsley

Tango Tangerini Marinade

Makes 1 1/2 cups

The Hungry Cat restaurant in Hollywood is a temple of fresh juice cocktails. Bowls full of exotic citrus fruits line the bar and are pressed to order. During my last visit, the very handsome, must-be-looking-for-work actor obliged my curiosity by "testing" recipes on me all night long. My favorite was a muddled tangerine "martini" that he mixed and shook before pouring into a tall glass. I took a long sip and instantly thought it would be a perfect marinade for fish—I was hungry, after all!

Good for Soaking: Shrimp, white fish; pork; beef; fruit

2 to 4 tangerines, juiced (about 1 cup)

Zest of 1 tangerine

Zest of 1 lime

1/4 cup vodka

3 tablespoons mirin or sweetened rice wine vinegar

1/2 cup almond oil or your favorite nut oil

2 tablespoons pickled ginger, roughly chopped

1 teaspoon kosher salt

In a small nonreactive bowl, whisk together the juice, zests, vodka, and mirin. Gradually add the oil until well blended. Add the ginger and salt and mix until combined. The marinade will keep, tightly covered, in the refrigerator for up to 2 days.

Caribbean Jerk Marinade

Makes about 2 1/2 cups

The two most important ingredients in an authentic jerk spice mixture are allspice and Scotch bonnet peppers. The Scotch bonnet pepper is a cousin of the habanero and insanely hot. If you do not like extra-spicy food, make the marinade but eliminate the Scotch bonnet. There is plenty of kick in the dry spices alone! I've "juiced up" the traditional Jamaican marinade with dark rum, which is not authentic but is a natural with the jerk seasoning—this marinade is a party in your mouth!

Good for Soaking: Pork; chicken; grouper, catfish

DRY JERK SEASONING

3 teaspoons ground allspice

2 teaspoons ground thyme

1/4 teaspoon freshly ground pepper

1/4 teaspoon ground star anise

1 tablespoon dried parsley

1 teaspoon red chile flakes

1 tablespoon dried granulated onion

2 teaspoons granulated garlic

2 teaspoons cayenne pepper

1 teaspoon grated nutmeg

1/2 teaspoon ground cinnamon

1 tablespoon brown sugar

1 1/2 teaspoons kosher salt

MARINADE

5 limes, juiced

1/2 cup dark rum, preferably Jamaican

1/2 cup olive or peanut oil

1 Scotch bonnet chile, stemmed and seeded, optional

1 large Spanish onion, roughly chopped

1. Make the jerk seasoning: Mix together all the spices in a small bowl. Set aside.

2. Make the marinade: Put the juice, rum, oil, chile, and onion in a blender and puree until smooth. Add half the dry jerk seasoning, process to combine, and taste. If it is not spicy enough, add more of the dry seasoning and blend again. The marinade should be thick and very dark. The marinade will keep, tightly covered, in the refrigerator for up to 2 days.

3 tablespoons cherry kirsch or maraschino cherry juice

2 tablespoons grenadine

1 tablespoon sugar

1 teaspoon fine-grain sea salt

1/4 cup almond or extra-virgin olive oil

In a small nonreactive bowl, whisk together all the ingredients. Mix until well blended. The marinade will keep, tightly covered, in the refrigerator for up to 2 days.

Bahama Mama Marinade

Makes about 3 1/4 cups

In the late 1990s, I spent a lot of time in the Bahamas, where I fell in love with the tropical cocktails, fresh fish, and white beaches. Of all the drinks, my favorite was the Bahama Mama—a combination of citrus juice, pineapple juice, a touch of coconut rum, and maraschino cherry juice. They say this drink is the most fun you can have with your clothes on. Since my food is already naked, I say it is the most fun way to "dress" your food before it hits the grill—paper umbrellas are optional!

Good for Soaking: Fruit, summer vegetables; shellfish, tuna; chicken; pork

Juice and zest of 1 large lemon

1 cup fresh orange juice

Zest of 1 orange

1 cup pineapple juice

1/2 cup dark rum

1/4 cup coconut rum

Sparkling Campari Marinade

Makes about 4 cups

The fruity bitterness of Campari—an Italian aperitif that is part of the family of bitters—pairs perfectly with the hearty flavors of beef, lamb, and game. The addition of sparkling wine or champagne makes the effervescent marinade light and fragrant—perfect for a midsummer night's cookout.

Good for Soaking: Game, chops, lamb, flank, skirt steak, and tenderloin

1/2 cup Campari

1/2 cup extra-virgin olive oil

1 medium onion, thinly sliced

Zest of 1 lemon

2 cloves garlic, flattened with the side of a cleaver

3 sprigs fresh parsley, chopped

2 cups dry champagne or sparkling wine

2 teaspoons whole juniper berries, cracked

1 teaspoon whole black peppercorns, cracked

Put the Campari, oil, onion, zest, garlic, and parsley in a blender and puree. Add the sparkling wine, juniper berries, and peppercorns to the mixture and whisk just to mix. The marinade will keep, tightly covered, in the refrigerator for up to 2 days (though you will lose the fizz after 1 day.)

Cajun Turkey Marinade

Makes about 5 cups

This marinade is just what the turkey ordered. The high salt content makes this marinade work like a brine and a marinade all in one, flavoring, tenderizing, and keeping the turkey juicy! I've provided a recipe for Cajun seasoning, but if you'd rather substitute Tony Chachere's Original Seasoning or Zatarain's, they are good options. But be advised that they are mostly seasoned salt blends, so you may need to increase the amount of spice and decrease the salt in this marinade. (Use 1/2 cup of the prepared seasonings and eliminate the seasonings and the salt from the recipe below.)

Good for Soaking: Turkey (legs, breast), chicken; shrimp, crab, red potatoes, corn

CAJUN DRY SEASONING

2 tablespoons freshly ground pepper

2 tablespoons onion powder

2 tablespoons garlic powder

2 tablespoons sweet Hungarian paprika

2 tablespoons dried parsley

1 tablespoon dried basil

1 tablespoon dried thyme leaves

1 tablespoon cayenne pepper

2 teaspoons chili powder

1 cup kosher salt

MARINADE

1 cup apple cider vinegar

2 lemons, cut into quarters

1/2 cup liquid crab boil*

1/2 cup honey

One 12-ounce bottle beer

1/2 cup extra-virgin olive oil

1/2 cup melted unsalted butter

1/4 cup Cajun seasoning

1/4 cup kosher salt

1 teaspoon Tabasco sauce

1. Make the Cajun seasoning: In a medium bowl, mix together all the ingredients. Reserve 1/4 cup and place the rest in a clean glass jar with a tight-fitting lid for future use.

2. In a small nonreactive bowl, put the vinegar, lemons, crab boil, honey, beer, olive oil, melted butter, the 1/4 cup Cajun seasoning, salt, and Tabasco, and whisk together until well blended. The marinade will keep, tightly covered, in the refrigerator for up to 2 days.

*In Louisiana, liquid crab boil (a.k.a. liquid spice) is used for seasoning everything from crabs and shrimp to potatoes, corn, gravies, etc. Most of the spice companies have a version, but I like Zatarain's or Rex brand. If you can't find it near you, you can order it at www.cajungrocer.com. And if there is no time to order, you can make a substitute by adding 2 tablespoons Old Bay Seasoning to 1/2 cup olive oil—it's not the same, but it is still very good.

Note: Make the marinade and put the turkey and all the liquid in a nonreactive container or a Turkey Brining Bag.

Mojo Marinade

Makes 2 cups

Mojo means many things. In African-American folklore, mojo is commonly thought of as a magic charm (or just plain charm). In Cuba, mojo is the signature marinade. That's a country that is high on my list to visit and one where I imagine everyone has a lot of "mojo" with the steamy climate and hot salsa dancing! Think of this marinade as a love potion for your fish, pork, or poultry, and for whomever you are serving it to! And if you are looking for appropriate music, everyone from Muddy Waters and Joni Mitchell to Jim Morrison has sung about "mojo" rising.

Good for Soaking: Pork (tenderloin, shoulder); chicken pieces

> 7 cloves garlic, grated or coarsely chopped
> 2 teaspoons fine-grain sea salt
> 1 teaspoon ground cumin
> 1/2 teaspoon dried oregano
> 1/2 teaspoon freshly ground pepper
> 1/2 cup fresh lime juice (about 6 limes)
> 1/2 cup fresh lemon juice (about 4 lemons)
> 1 cup fresh orange juice

In a mortar or small bowl, mash the garlic and salt together until it forms a paste. Place the garlic paste and the rest of the ingredients in a blender and blend to a smooth puree. Use immediately.

Bloody Mary Marinade

Makes about 7 cups

Talk about a killer brunch! Make a pitcher for yourself and a pitcher for the grill. This spicy horseradish-rich marinade works with all savory foods, vegetables, fish, meat, and poultry alike! And if you are ambitious, simmer the used marinade until it is reduced by half for a rockin' sauce!

Good for Soaking: Steak; chicken; shrimp; pork chops

> Juice and zest of 2 large lemons
> One 6-ounce jar prepared horseradish (not cream-style)
> One 14.5-ounce can chopped stewed tomatoes
> 1/2 small jalapeño, seeded and roughly chopped
> 1 Spanish onion, roughly chopped
> Tops from a bunch of celery or parsley, chopped (about 1/3 cup)
> 3 cups Spicy Hot V8
> 1/4 cup Worcestershire sauce
> 1/4 cup maple syrup
> 1 teaspoon coarsely ground pepper
> 1 teaspoon granulated garlic
> 1 teaspoon kosher salt

Place the lemon juice and zest, horseradish, tomatoes, jalapeño, onion, and celery tops in a blender and puree until smooth. Add the juice, Worcestershire sauce, maple syrup, pepper, garlic, and salt and taste. If desired, add more pepper, garlic, and salt and blend again. The marinade should be thick and very dark. The marinade will keep, tightly covered, in the refrigerator for up to 2 days.

Coffee-Crusted New York Strips

This steak preparation is for those of us who like dark chocolate, espresso, red wine and red meat. Theses dark, fruity and slightly bitter flavors combine to make a perfectly harmonious marinade and rub that deepens the flavor of the meat without being over-powering. It reminds me of what dry-aging does to a good steak. Be sure to dry off the marinade, oil and salt the steaks just before grilling.

Serves 4

Grilling Method: Combo/High Heat

> 2 tablespoons unsweetened cocoa powder
> 3 tablespoons ground espresso coffee
> 2 tablespoons freshly ground pepper
> 2 teaspoons sugar
> 4 New York strip steaks, about 14 ounces and 1 1/2 inches thick
> 1 recipe Java Joe Steak Marinade (below)
> Olive oil
> Kosher salt

1. In a small bowl, mix the cocoa, coffee, pepper, and sugar. Set aside.

2. Build a charcoal fire or preheat a gas grill. Marinate the steaks in the Java Joe Steak Marinade for 30 minutes. Remove from the marinade and wrap the steaks in paper towels to remove all surface moisture.

3. Brush the steaks lightly with olive oil. Sprinkle all over with the rub, pressing the mixture evenly and lightly on both sides of the steak. (**Note:** Too much rub will over-season the meat.) Just before grilling, season with salt.

4. Place the meat on the cooking grate directly over the heat. Sear on both sides, about 2 minutes per side. Move to indirect heat and continue grilling for 6 to 8 more minutes for medium-rare.

5. Remove the meat from the grill and place on a platter. Let the steaks rest for 5 minutes before serving.

Java Joe Steak Marinade

Makes about 2 1/2 cups

This marinade is inspired by my favorite steak rub of espresso and black pepper (see above). Although I love the rub, it is a little strong for some. I created this rich marinade to impart the same flavors but in a milder form. Try this once and it will become your signature preparation for steak. It is equally good on any cut of steak, from the more expensive and marbled big prime rib-eye to the leaner "value" cuts like flat-iron or flank steak. The more tender the cut, the less time you want to let it soak before cooking. And remember to salt your steaks just before grilling.

Good for Soaking: Any cut of beef or steak

1 cup brewed espresso or very strong black coffee

1 cup full-flavored red wine, such as Cabernet Sauvignon, Shiraz, or Zinfandel

2 tablespoons Dijon mustard

2 tablespoons dark brown sugar

1 tablespoon Worcestershire sauce

4 cloves garlic, grated

1/2 cup extra-virgin olive oil

2 teaspoons coarsely ground pepper

1 teaspoon cinnamon chips or a cinnamon stick broken into pieces

In a medium nonreactive bowl, whisk together the coffee, wine, mustard, sugar, Worcestershire sauce, garlic, oil, pepper, and cinnamon until well blended. The marinade will keep, tightly covered, in the refrigerator for up to 2 days.

Moroccan Spice Market Marinade

Makes about 3 cups

Morocco is famous for the noisy, chaotic, and brightly colored spice markets whose vendors mount pyramid-shaped mounds of vibrantly colored ground spices that look like art installations. I love this marinade because it is a pinch of this and a pinch of that—a pinch of most of the spices that Morocco is known for. I mix the spices and add them to yogurt, olive oil, and slices of lemon for a thick pasty marinade that enhances all meat, red or white. If you have preserved lemons on hand, substitute them for the fresh lemons for an even more authentic Moroccan experience!

Good for Soaking: Chicken kabobs; lamb (leg, kabobs); shrimp, hearty fish

MOROCCAN RUB (MAKES 1/4 CUP)

2 tablespoons hot smoked Spanish paprika

2 tablespoons dark brown sugar

1 tablespoon sesame seeds

1 tablespoon ground cinnamon

2 teaspoons ground cumin

2 teaspoons ground ginger

2 teaspoons ground coriander

1 teaspoon ground turmeric

2 teaspoons kosher salt

1 teaspoon freshly ground pepper

1/2 teaspoon anise seeds

MARINADE

2 cups predrained whole-milk yogurt, such as FAGE Total

1/2 cup extra-virgin olive oil

1/4 cup Moroccan Rub

2 lemons, cut into thin slices

1. Make the rub: Mix all the ingredients together in a small bowl. Set aside 1/4 cup for the marinade and reserve the rest for another marinade or for use as a rub. It will keep in a jar with a tight-fitting lid for up to 3 months.

2. Make the marinade: In a medium nonreactive bowl, whisk together the yogurt, olive oil, and reserved spice rub until smooth. Add the lemon slices and mix until blended. The marinade will keep, tightly covered, in the refrigerator for up to 2 days.

Smoked Spanish Paprika Marinade

Makes about 2 cups

Sometimes there is nothing better than the "less is more" adage. And this is one of my favorite examples of it. This simple marinade relies on the best possible sweet smoked Spanish paprika that you can buy. The absence of any acid in this unusual marinade allows you to prep the food up until a day before you cook it. It is equally good on tuna steaks, chicken pieces, and slices of vegetables.

Good for Soaking: Fresh sardines, tuna steaks, bluefish; chicken; peppers, potatoes

- 1/8 cup sweet smoked Spanish paprika
- 2 teaspoons kosher salt
- 3/4 cup extra-virgin olive oil

In a small bowl, mix the paprika and salt together. While whisking, slowly add the oil and mix until it is smooth and there are no lumps. The marinade will keep, tightly covered, in the refrigerator for up to 2 days.

Under the Tuscan Sun Marinade

Makes 2 1/4 cups

Every time I make this marinade, it takes me back to a lazy summer day in Tuscany when I sat under a huge olive tree with a group of friends, drinking wine and eating a whole fish that we had marinated in this bright citrus, garlic, and basil mixture. For a simple but flavorful final dish, reserve some of the marinade before putting the food in it to drizzle on the food as it comes off the grill.

Good for Soaking: Chicken; salmon, swordfish, calamari, shrimp

- Zest and juice of 2 oranges
- 3 lemons, juiced
- 1 large lime, juiced
- 5 cloves garlic, grated or minced
- 1 teaspoon fine-grain sea salt
- 1/2 teaspoon red chile flakes
- 1/2 cup extra-virgin olive oil
- 3 sprigs coarsely chopped fresh curly parsley, leaves only (1 tablespoon)
- 5 sprigs coarsely chopped fresh basil, leaves only (4 tablespoons)

In a medium nonreactive bowl, combine the orange, lemon, and lime juices, orange zest, garlic, salt, and hot chile flakes and mix until well combined. Whisk in the olive oil and add the herbs. If necessary, stir again before using. Reserve one-quarter of the marinade to drizzle on food as it comes off the grill. The marinade will keep, tightly covered, in the refrigerator for up to 2 days.

Persian Marinade

Makes about 2 1/2 cups

This marinade is my best guess of the secret recipe from my favorite Persian restaurant. Everything that they grill—from chicken to lamb, beef, shrimp, salmon—

is moist, juicy, and perfectly seasoned. When I've asked what the secret is, everyone tells me something different. Over the years, I've worked on putting the marinade together like a puzzle, and finally I discovered the missing piece: It is the wine that makes the difference!

Good for Soaking: Lamb; chicken; salmon; beef fillets; zucchini, eggplant

    1 cup white wine*
    1 cup predrained whole-milk yogurt,
    such as FAGE Total
    1/4 cup extra-virgin olive oil
    3 cloves garlic, minced
    1 bay leaf, crumbled
    1 teaspoon dried oregano
    1 teaspoon ground turmeric
    1 teaspoon kosher salt
    Zest of 1 lemon
    2 lemons, juiced
    3 tablespoons chopped fresh parsley
    2 tablespoons chopped fresh mint

In a medium nonreactive bowl, whisk together the wine and the yogurt until smooth. Add the oil, garlic, bay leaf, oregano, turmeric, and salt. Whisk to combine. Add the zest and lemon juice, parsley, and mint and mix together. The marinade will keep, tightly covered, in the refrigerator for up to 2 days.

*If you like the pine-resin flavor of Greek retsina, it is a good choice for this marinade.

TGIF Fajita Marinade
Makes 1 cup

Sizzlin' platters of hot grilled meat—can't you smell it now? Use this marinade on strips of red and green peppers and sweet onions as well as on pieces of chicken, beef, and/or shrimp that will be grilled hot and quick over a live fire.

Good for Soaking: Lamb; beef; chicken; pork cutlets; burgers; peppers, onions

    1/4 cup fresh lime juice,
    (about 4 large limes)
    Zest of 1 lime
    1/2 cup peanut or canola oil
    6 cloves garlic, grated
    2 teaspoons ground cumin
    1 teaspoon kosher salt
    1/2 teaspoon red chile flakes

In a small nonreactive bowl, whisk together the lime juice, zest, oil, garlic, cumin, salt, and pepper flakes. The marinade will keep, tightly covered, in the refrigerator for up to 2 days.

Modern Madeira Marinade
Makes 1 cup

Although this marinade is good on almost anything it touches, it is tailor-made for infusing mushrooms with flavor before grilling. If you are in the mood for a quick steak-house dinner, make a batch and soak your steak and mushrooms at the same time. Grill them together for a fancy dinner made quick and easy—I especially like skirt or hanger steak made this way.

Good for Soaking: Mushrooms, asparagus; steak; chicken; lamb chops

> 2 teaspoons kosher salt
> 8 large cloves garlic, smashed
> 1/3 cup Madeira
> 2/3 cup extra-virgin olive oil
> 2 tablespoons chopped fresh curly parsley
> 1/2 teaspoon freshly ground pepper

In a mortar or a small bowl, mash the salt and garlic cloves together until they form a paste. If using a mortar, transfer the paste to a bowl. Add the wine and whisk to combine. Slowly add the oil in a slow stream and whisk until thoroughly blended. Add the parsley and pepper. The marinade will keep, tightly covered, in the refrigerator for up to 2 days.

Ginger-Soy Marinade

Makes about 1 cup

This marinade takes just a few seconds to whisk together and imparts an alluring Asian flavor to almost any fish.

Good for Soaking: Fish steaks, shellfish; beef; chicken; pork; mushrooms

> 1/4 cup extra-virgin olive oil
> 1/4 cup toasted sesame oil
> 1/8 cup unseasoned rice vinegar
> 2 tablespoons low-sodium soy sauce
> 1 tablespoon Thai chili-garlic sauce (*sriracha*)

> 1/4 teaspoon kosher salt
> Zest of 1 lemon
> 3 to 5 cloves garlic, grated
> 1 small knob (1 inch) fresh ginger, grated

In a small nonreactive bowl, combine the olive oil, sesame oil, rice vinegar, soy sauce, chili-garlic sauce, salt, zest, garlic, and ginger. Mix to combine. The marinade will keep, tightly covered, in the refrigerator for up to 2 days.

Memories of Asia Marinade

Makes about 2 cups

This big, bold Asian marinade has it all! It works best with heartier foods and is terrific with pineapple—turning it into a side dish instead of a dessert. The combination of the lime and orange juice adds a nice sweetness to the meaty flavors of the soy sauce and the toasted sesame oil. I love the texture of the scallions and sesame seeds, which stick to the food and stay on during grilling.

Good for Soaking: Steak; chicken; pork; shrimp; salmon, vegetables

> 1/2 cup fresh lime juice (about 6 limes)
> Zest and juice of 1 orange
> 2 tablespoons unseasoned rice vinegar
> 1/4 cup low-sodium soy sauce
> 1/4 cup toasted sesame oil
> 2 tablespoons extra-virgin olive oil
> 1 tablespoon dark brown sugar

One large knob (5 inches) fresh ginger, grated

2 teaspoons sesame seeds

1 bunch scallions, trimmed and finely chopped

In a medium nonreactive bowl, combine the lime juice, orange juice and zest, vinegar, soy sauce, oils, brown sugar, ginger, sesame seeds, and scallions. Mix to combine. The marinade will keep, tightly covered, in the refrigerator for up to 2 days.

Double Happiness Chinese Marinade

Makes 1 cup

I recently visited China with my friend and grill products distributor Robert Laub. We were in Dongguan City for a trade fair and decided to venture outside of the hotel and go to a "real" Chinese restaurant. We were lucky enough to have one of our Chinese colleagues, David, with us or else we wouldn't have been able to order. Before settling into a private room complete with our own team of cooks and servers, we went outside to the parking lot to choose our catch of the day from an aquarium. Of all the fish we chose, our favorite fish was a giant purple prawn that was marinated in this sweet mixture and flash-fried until it was crispy —no batter at all. The prawns were so good that Robert and I asked for a second helping—doubling our happiness with finding a new Chinese treat!

Good for Soaking: Shrimp; prawns; pork ribs; chicken; scallions, bok choy, carrots

1/4 cup low-sodium soy sauce

1/4 cup dry sherry

2 tablespoons honey

2 tablespoons low-sugar hoisin sauce

2 teaspoons dark brown sugar

2 teaspoons Thai chili-garlic sauce (*sriracha*)

2 teaspoons Chinese five-spice powder

1/2 teaspoon freshly ground pepper

3 cloves garlic, crushed

1 small knob (1 inch) fresh ginger, roughly chopped

3 scallions, sliced on the diagonal

In a medium nonreactive bowl, whisk together the soy sauce, sherry, honey, hoisin sauce, brown sugar, sriracha, five-spice powder, black pepper, garlic, ginger, and scallions until well mixed. The marinade will keep, tightly covered, in the refrigerator for up to 2 days.

BRINES

Classic brines are saturated solutions of salt and sugar. Flavor brines are saturated solutions of salt, sugar, and other seasonings. They both improve the texture, moisture content, and flavor of lean meat, poultry, and hearty fish. Brines were originally only saturated salt solutions used for preserving food. Food soaks in brine for 30 minutes minimum and up to 24 hours.

Brines 101

brining is the ticket! And now, their pork chops taste like a pork chop should—or at least just as good as the ones they order from their favorite restaurant.

Ten years ago, brines were a well-kept restaurant secret. Whenever my students ask me why the pork chops they grill at home don't taste as good as the ones from their favorite restaurant, I tell them to brine their pork chops (this works wonders with chicken, too) before grilling them. In every case, they come back and tell me that

Brining grew popular with restaurant chefs because they were looking for a way to add flavor and juiciness to increasingly lean and tasteless factory-processed meat and poultry. Even a simple salt and sugar brine adds moisture and seasons the meat inside and out, and thereby increases the flavor. Up the ante by using a flavor brine rich with herbs, spices, fruit juice, beer, wine, and/or whiskey and you've got better texture, juicy meat, and flavor. Recently, brining has been embraced by a growing number of home cooks. While there is no doubt that brining adds moisture and flavor to less-than-perfect-ingredients, it works magic on the best-quality meats, poultry, and fish as well.

Originally, a brine (a strong saltwater solution) was used for preserving meat. Today, cooks use a salt-and-sugar-water solution to enhance the flavor of lean meat like pork loin, chops, and country-style ribs, as well as chicken, turkey, and hearty fish and shellfish like catfish, monkfish, salmon, jumbo shrimp, and clams. A flavor brine adds spices, fruits, juices, and other ingredients to the basic brine formula. I think of a brine as a simple marinade.

Brining simply calls for submerging the food into the salt-and-sugar-water solution and letting it soak. Times vary and, like marinating, the rule-of-thumb is the smaller and more delicate the food, the less time you want to brine, and the larger and heartier the food, the longer you can brine. Think 30 minutes for small cuts of poultry, pork, or shellfish, and up to 24 hours for a turkey.

In the brining process, the meat absorbs a portion of the seasoned salt-and-sugar water, making the meat juicier and more flavorful. A brine technically only has to be a strong salt solution, but the sugar balances the salt and promotes browning (caramelizing) of the food. This browning of the natural sugars in the food intensifies and concentrates the flavors, making the food taste great. Think about the difference between a steamed piece of food and a grilled piece of food and—if you are like me and prefer bold flavors—you'll understand why browning is so important.

A simple moderate brine formula is 1/2 cup of kosher salt and 1/2 cup of sugar for every gallon of water. If you like a stronger brine, increase the salt and sugar to 1 cup each for every gallon of water. (**Note:** I call for kosher salt in my brines, but you can substitute table salt; just use half as much and purchase the noniodized version.) The way a brine works is that the water that is inherent in all foods is replaced or balanced out by the brining liquid. If you remember your lessons in osmosis from school, you'll remember that the liquid will try to balance itself out by traveling through the semi-permeable membranes. What that means here is that since there is more salt in the brine than in the meat, the tissue absorbs the salt water, balancing the salt proportion between the meat's "water" and the brining water. Once in the meat, the salt denatures the protein molecules, causing them to unwind and form a matrix that traps the water, the salt, and all the flavoring seasonings that you added to the saltwater solution. Because this water has salt, sugar, and other flavorings in it, the food is seasoned inside and out. Because the salt present causes the food to retain water, the food is juicier and does not dry out during the grilling process.

After you become familiar with the basics of brining, the next step is to use flavor brines in your pre-grilling preparation. Think of these brines as a combination of a brine and a marinade without the acid or the oil. I love flavor brines and use them often.

Choosing Salt

Any salt can be used to make a brine, although I prefer using kosher salt. I steer away from using iodized salt for anything. I believe that the added potassium iodide in the salt gives food an off-flavor, a tin-like, metallic flavor. I also do not like the perfect round shape of the crystals, which have a tendency to bounce off the food. I prefer the irregularly shaped flakes of kosher salt for simple seasoning and making brines. If you've read my other entries on salt, you know that I prefer the hard, crunchy flakes of Morton kosher salt for seasoning and salt-crusting food because it doesn't melt or dissolve quickly. When I am making brines, I prefer Diamond Crystal kosher salt because it does dissolve quickly! This may be a moot point since distribution for both brands is somewhat regional, but if you have a full pantry of salt, here's your chance to put that Diamond Crystal to good use.

The small grains of salt in a cup of table salt weigh much more than those in a cup of either Morton or Diamond Crystal kosher salt. So, 1 cup of table salt will render the brine twice as salty as the lighter, airier Diamond Crystal and three-quarters stronger than the larger, flakier Morton kosher salt. This is a little confusing to most home cooks. If you don't have either brand of kosher salt, use half as much table salt as these recipes call for. And regardless of the type of kosher salt that you have, follow the recipe or your own taste buds.

Best Candidates for Brining

Anyone who has brined a Thanksgiving turkey knows firsthand what a wonderful effect a brine can have on lean meat. The juicy seasoned meat debunks the tradition of dry turkey meat that has to be smothered in gravy in order to eat it. The following list is in no particular order, but reflects what I personally brine most often. As you can imagine, I never grill, smoke, or oven-roast a turkey without brining it.

- Turkey
- Chicken parts or whole chicken
- Game hen
- Pork, especially chops, loin and tenderloin, ribs, and fresh hams (it takes the "porkiness" out of pork)
- Hearty fish, such as catfish and salmon
- Shellfish in the shell, such as jumbo shrimp, mussels, and clams

Note: Brines are not for delicate fish like sole or tilapia but need meatier, tougher fish like catfish, snapper, or salmon to appreciate their charms. Shellfish like shrimp, clams, oysters, and mussels are also good candidates, but you need to brine them in their shells and only for a short time.

Brining Beef

It is rare to find a recipe or recommendation for brining beef unless you are looking to make a homemade corned beef or pastrami. Homemade corned beef is near and dear to my heart, as I had an aunt who would make her own, brining it for a month before slowly roasting it in the oven (see page 73). If you have the patience and the room in your fridge, it is worth planning in advance and making your own, grill-roasting the beef for a brined and smoky flavor. But watch out—you'll want to pair this succulent meat with fresh homemade rye bread!

Shelf Life

A basic brine can be made up to a week in advance as long as there are no herbs or fresh ingredients in the mixture. If you want to add fresh citrus fruit and other perishable ingredients, it is best to make it the day you use it.

Basic Brine 101

Makes 2 gallons

This brine is my basic brine recipe and the base solution for all my flavor brines. I use equal parts salt and sugar, 1/2 cup of each per gallon of liquid. I use this brine for most of my everyday foods. For large pieces of meat or a whole turkey, use the Basic Strong Brine 101 (see page 68).

Good for Soaking: Lean pork (tenderloin or chops); whole chicken, chicken pieces, (boneless skinless chicken breasts); hearty fish

> 8 quarts cold water, divided
>
> 1 cup kosher salt
>
> 1 cup sugar or sweetener, such as honey, maple syrup, or brown sugar

1. Boil 2 quarts of water; add the salt and sugar, stirring until completely dissolved.

2. Add the rest of the water and let cool before submerging meat, poultry, or fish in a nonreactive container or the Grill Friends Everyday or Turkey Brining Bag.

3. Cover if necessary and refrigerate brined food for the entire brining process. If the food weighs less than 1 pound, brine for 30 minutes; 1 to 3 pounds, 45 minutes; 3 to 5 pounds, 1 hour; 5 to 8 pounds, up to 6 hours; and more than 8 pounds, 12 hours or overnight. The food is brined when you notice a plumper, fuller look to the food. This is easiest to see in smaller foods. It is more difficult to see a change in whole chickens, turkeys, and roasts.

Notes:
* This recipe can be multiplied to accommodate larger pieces of meat.
* This brine combined with 2 gallons of water can accommodate up to 2 whole chickens, 8 chops or bone-in chicken pieces, or 4 racks of ribs. If you have more food, use a stronger solution.

BRINE TIME

The rule of thumb is the smaller and more delicate the food, the less time you need to soak it in the brine. Larger and denser pieces of meat and poultry need more time. You will read recipes that call for brining for days. In my experience, that results in overseasoned and mushy-textured food with a purplish white cast. I generally cap my brines at 24 hours for a whole turkey, fresh ham, or other large piece of meat. The only exceptions are when you brine or "cure" tougher cuts of meat before smoking or cooking to create specialized deli meats like bacon and traditional corned beef or pastrami. This process can take up to a month to brine the meat (see Brining Beef, facing page).

Tip: You can add ice cubes to the boiled salt-sugar solution to cool the brine down faster.

Basic Strong Brine 101

Makes 2 gallons

For those who want a stronger salt-sugar solution, use this as your solution. This recipe calls for a ratio of equal parts salt and sugar, but twice as much of it as in the Basic Brine 101 (see page 67).

Good for Soaking: Whole turkey, whole chicken, pork shoulder, fresh ham, larger pieces of meat

- 8 quarts cold water, divided
- 2 cups kosher salt
- 2 cups sugar or sweetener, such as honey, maple syrup, or brown sugar

1. Boil 4 quarts of water; add the salt and sugar, stirring until completely dissolved.

2. Add the rest of the water and let cool before submerging meat, poultry, or fish in a nonreactive container or the Grill Friends Everyday or Turkey Brining Bag.

3. Cover if necessary and refrigerate brined food for the entire brining process. If the food weighs less than 1 pound, brine for 30 minutes; 1 to 3 pounds, 45 minutes; 3 to 5 pounds, 1 hour; 5 to 8 pounds, up to 6 hours; and more than 8 pounds, 12 hours or overnight. The food is brined when you notice a plumper, fuller look to the food. This is easiest to see in smaller foods. It is more difficult to see a change in whole chickens, turkeys, and roasts.

Notes:
*This recipe can be multiplied to accommodate larger pieces of meat.
* This brine combined with 1 gallon of water can accommodate up to 1 whole turkey, 1 bone-in Boston butt, 1 fresh ham, 3 whole chickens, or 8 racks of ribs. It is not suited for smaller, more delicate foods like fish, pork tenderloin, boneless pork chops, or boneless skinless chicken breasts.

Orange Spice Brine

Makes about 1 1/2 gallons

Nothing will improve your Thanksgiving more than a brine. Brining is the single most important thing you can do to ensure that the turkey stays extra-juicy during the roasting process. This orange brine complements the Montreal Maple Syrup Glaze (page 131) and scents the turkey with fall's favorite seasonings. Depending on how much time you have, you can brine the turkey for as few as 8 hours or as long

as 24 hours. The longer you brine, the more seasoned your turkey will be.

Good for Soaking: Turkey breast or whole turkey; pork; chicken pieces

1 gallon plus 6 cups water, divided
1 cup sugar
2 cups kosher salt
2 oranges, quartered
1 tablespoon whole cloves
3 bay leaves
2 teaspoons whole black peppercorns

1. In a large saucepan over high heat, bring 6 cups of the water, the sugar, and salt to a boil, stirring to dissolve the sugar and salt. Add the oranges, cloves, bay leaves, and peppercorns while still hot. Stir and let cool to room temperature.

2. In a Turkey Brining Bag, 3-gallon plastic bucket, or other food-safe container large enough to hold the food, add the remaining 1 gallon water and the rest of the brine. Stir well.

3. Submerge the food in the brine. If necessary, add more water to cover and top with a weight (such as a resealable plastic bag filled with water) to make sure it is completely covered with the liquid. Refrigerate covered, for 8 to 24 hours.

Dr. T's Cranberry Turkey Brine

Makes about 1 1/2 gallons

My dear friend and collaborator, John Lineweaver, aka Dr. T, is part of my Thanksgiving tradition. Every year he hosts a growing crowd at his home in Atlanta, and every year we discuss the pros and cons of fresh versus frozen, to grill or not to grill—for those traditionalists who need to smell the turkey roasting. The one thing we never have to discuss—and the one thing that John will never change—is this cranberry brine that the two of us made up on the fly many years ago. The tart, rosy red cranberry juice, sweet brown sugar, and Southern Comfort is the very essence of Thanksgiving, and produces one kickin' turkey—on the grill of course!

Good for Soaking: Whole turkey; chicken; veal chops; venison

1 gallon plus 6 cups water
1 cup packed dark brown sugar
2 cups kosher salt
2 oranges, quartered
2 cups cranberry juice
1 tablespoon whole cloves
3 bay leaves
2 teaspoons whole black peppercorns
1/2 cup Southern Comfort

1. In a large saucepan over high heat, bring 6 cups of the water, sugar, and salt to a boil, stirring to dissolve the sugar and salt. Add the oranges, cranberry juice, cloves, bay leaves, and peppercorns while still hot. Stir and let cool to room temperature. Add the Southern Comfort.

2. In a Turkey Brining Bag, 3-gallon plastic bucket, or other food-safe container large enough to hold the food, add the remaining 1 gallon water and the rest of the brine. Stir well.

3. Submerge the food in the brine. If necessary, add more water to cover and top with a weight (such as a resealable plastic bag filled with water) to make sure it is completely covered with the liquid. Refrigerate, covered, for 8 to 24 hours.

Basic Beer Brine

Makes about 1 gallon

The key to this simple flavor brine is the beer. As the salt and sugar season the food, the beer adds a yeasty depth to hearty fish and poultry—especially catfish and boneless skinless chicken breasts. It is so easy to make and is my back-pocket standard when I want to throw a quick brine together.

Good for Soaking: Chicken pieces, boneless, skinless chicken breasts, game hens; quail; catfish, prawns

> 4 cups water
> 1 cup kosher salt
> 1/2 cup packed dark brown sugar
> 1 tablespoon whole black peppercorns
> 4 bay leaves, crumbled
> 3 cans cold beer
> 8 cups ice cubes

1. In a large saucepan over high heat, bring the water, salt, sugar, peppercorns, and bay leaves to a boil, stirring to dissolve the sugar and salt. Transfer hot liquid to a large container. Add two medium bowls of ice cubes, about 8 cups, to cool the brine and add more volume to the brine. Stir and let cool to room temperature.

2. Add the cold beer to the brine. Whisk well to remove the carbonation. When the brine is cool to the touch, submerge food in the brine. Refrigerate for 2 to 4 hours, covered.

Beer-Brined Smoked Catfish Spread

Serves 4 to 10 as an appetizer

Special Equipment: Cameron Stovetop Smoker; wood chips, soaked in water for outdoor grill only. If using a Cameron Stovetop Smoker, you do not need to soak the chips

- 1 recipe Basic Beer Brine (facing page)
- 4 large catfish fillets, about 3/4 pound each
- Olive oil
- One 8-ounce block cream cheese, at room temperature
- 1/2 to 3/4 cup sour cream
- 2 large shallots, minced
- 2 tablespoons capers in liquid
- 2 to 4 teaspoons caper juice
- 1/4 teaspoon granulated garlic
- 5 shakes Tabasco sauce
- Freshly ground pepper

1. When the brine is cool to the touch, submerge the fish in the brine. Refrigerate for 2 to 4 hours, covered. Remove the fish from brine, and let air-dry for 5 minutes before smoking.

2. When ready to smoke, brush the fish lightly with olive oil and place it in the center of the cooking grate, skin side down. Preferably, smoke in a Cameron Stovetop Smoker for 20 to 30 minutes. The fish will be a dark caramel color. Alternatively, smoke-cook on an outdoor grill for 1 hour or until the fish is cooked through and is caramel colored. At this point, the fish can be served by itself, but it is even better made into the spread.

3. While the fish is still warm, break the fillets into pieces, removing any bones or burned bits. Add the cream cheese and mix well. Add 1/2 cup of the sour cream and mix well. Add the shallots, capers, caper juice, garlic, and Tabasco. Taste for seasoning, adding more sour cream at this point if the spread is a little dry or tastes a little salty. Adjust the level of Tabasco and caper juice, and add freshly ground pepper to taste.

4. Refrigerate for at least 3 hours or preferably overnight. Taste once more before serving and adjust the seasonings as desired. Serve on the cold side of room temperature on Melba toast or your favorite crackers. Top with a dollop of sour cream if desired.

Note: Do not add any salt to this dish, because the brine and the smoke "salt" the fish before it is mixed into the spread.

Old Bay Beer Brine

Makes about 1 gallon

When I was growing up, I would go to shrimp boils at the beach where they cooked shrimp, oysters, corn, sausage, and potatoes in great vats of boiling beer and seawater seasoned with Old Bay. I created this brine to infuse familiar flavors of the boiling liquid in one shot. This brine is especially helpful if your shrimp dries out as you grill it. Brine it shell-on for 30 minutes in this spiced beer brine. Though unconventional, I love brining precooked red potatoes and smoked sausage with the jumbo shrimp and grilling it all for a smoked take on the traditional shore dinner—feel free to add a few cobs of fresh corn as well.

Good for Soaking: Shrimp, crab; chicken; potatoes, corn; uncooked smoked sausage

> 4 cups water
>
> 1 cup kosher salt
>
> 1/2 cup packed dark brown sugar
>
> 2 tablespoons Old Bay Seasoning
>
> 1 teaspoon each whole black and green peppercorns
>
> 8 cups ice cubes (or cold water)
>
> 1 lemon, cut into slices
>
> 3 cans cold beer

1. In a large saucepan over high heat, bring the water, salt, sugar, Old Bay, and peppercorns to a boil, stirring to dissolve the sugar and salt.

2. Add ice or cold water to the hot brine to cool and add more volume to the brine. Add the lemon slices and cold beer. Stir to combine. Add more cold water if more liquid is necessary to cover the food. When the brine is cool to the touch, submerge food in the brine. Refrigerate for 2 to 4 hours, covered.

Sweet Tea Brine

Makes about 1 gallon

Take the traditional Southern sweet tea and add salt to it, and it makes a brine that will rock any kind of poultry. Use green tea and substitute apricot nectar for the lemonade and you've got an exotic tea brine that works perfectly with pork.

Good for Soaking: Chicken pieces, whole chicken; pork

> 4 cups water
>
> 1 cup kosher salt
>
> 1/2 cup sugar
>
> 1 cinnamon stick
>
> One 12-ounce can lemonade concentrate
>
> 4 cups strong freshly brewed tea, cooled
>
> 1 lemon, cut into slices
>
> 6 cups ice cubes

1. In a large saucepan over high heat, bring the water, salt, sugar, and cinnamon stick to a boil, stirring to dissolve the sugar and salt. Stir and let cool to warm.

2. Add the frozen lemonade and brewed tea. Stir and add the lemon slices. Add ice to cool and add more volume to the brine.

Stir well. Add more cold water if more liquid is necessary to cover the food. When the brine is cool to the touch, submerge the food in the brine. Refrigerate for 3 to 6 hours, covered.

Corned or Pastrami Brine

Makes about 1 gallon

If you love the flavor of homemade pastrami but you don't have 3 to 4 weeks to wait for a brisket to cure, use this brine to impart the classic deli flavor. The brine makes a mean salmon or turkey pastrami, and you only need to brine either for a few hours. But at least once in your cooking lifetime, plan ahead and try your hand at the real thing! Curing a brisket in the fridge requires 3 to 4 weeks of brining before cooking. Interesting note: Corned beef and pastrami use the same brine; it is the cooking method that differentiates the two. Corned beef is oven-braised and pastrami is smoked.

Sodium nitrate is a preservative added to many meat products to help keep meats a pleasing red color; if you want to make what people are used to seeing, add it to make it visually appealing.

Good for Soaking: Brisket; fillet of salmon; turkey breast

- 4 cups water
- 2 cups kosher salt
- 1 cup packed dark brown sugar
- 2 tablespoons each whole black and green peppercorns
- 1 tablespoon whole allspice
- 1 cinnamon stick, snapped in half
- 2 teaspoons whole cloves
- 2 teaspoons whole mustard seeds
- 2 teaspoons whole coriander seeds
- 1 teaspoon whole cardamom pods
- 1/2 head garlic, cloves separated and crushed but not peeled
- 1 ounce sodium nitrate, to keep the meat red if making corned beef or pastrami (optional)
- 8 cups ice cubes

1. In a large saucepan over high heat, bring the water, the salt, sugar, peppercorns, allspice, cinnamon, cloves, mustard seeds, coriander, and cardamom to a boil, stirring to dissolve the sugar and salt. Add the garlic cloves, sodium nitrate (if using), and ice. Stir and let cool.

2. Add more cold water (up to 8 cups) if more liquid is necessary to cover the food. When the brine is cool to the touch, submerge the food in the brine. Refrigerate for 8 to 24 hours, covered. Brine a brisket for 3 to 4 weeks.

Pickle Brine

Makes about 2 quarts

Southern pickled shrimp is the inspiration for this brine. Pickled shrimp is a specialty from the Carolina low country—where you can find it stored in jars in cupboards, in old-fashioned country stores, and sometimes in farmer's markets. Here, I am reversing the process. Instead of par-cooking the shrimp (or vegetables) before brining them, I suggest you brine shrimp or any garden vegetable first and then grill it quickly over a hot fire—a minute or two should do.

If you don't want to eat immediately, prepare another batch of the brine and cover the shrimp or veggies in sealed and refrigerated mason jars for up to 1 week. Because this brine is tailor-made for shrimp, the quantity is sized smaller to fit the small size of the shrimp. If you want to use this brine for a larger piece of fish, double the recipe.

Good for Soaking: Shrimp, bluefish; chicken; cucumbers, pearl onions

  8 cups water, divided
  1/2 cup kosher salt
  1/2 cup sugar
  1/4 cup pickling spice
  3/4 cup white vinegar
  3 teaspoons celery seeds
  5 dashes Tabasco sauce
  1/2 cup chopped celery hearts with leaves
  4 white onions, sliced into rings, about 3 1/2 cups
  1 bunch fresh dill, roughly chopped, or 2 tablespoons dried dill

1. In a large saucepan over high heat, bring 4 cups water, salt, sugar, pickling spices, vinegar, and celery seeds to a boil, stirring to dissolve the sugar and salt. Stir and let cool to warm.

2. Add the Tabasco, celery, onions, and dill and stir. Let sit for 10 minutes, and then add about 4 cups cold water or ice cubes. Stir and let cool.

3. Add more cold water if more liquid is necessary to cover the food. When the brine is cool to the touch, submerge the food in the brine. Refrigerate for 2 to 4 hours, covered.

Southern Buttermilk Brine

Makes about 2 quarts

Adding buttermilk to a flavor brine combines the top two Southern tricks for juicy, tasty chicken. The buttermilk tenderizes the chicken and the brine seasons it and makes it juicy. Although my original inspiration was for fried chicken, it is terrific for pork tenderloin, chops, and all manner of poultry—grilled or fried!

Good for Soaking: Chicken; pork; catfish

  2 cups water
  1 cup kosher salt
  1/2 cup packed light brown sugar
  2 tablespoons dried or fresh rosemary, leaves only
  1 teaspoon whole black peppercorns
  1 cup ice cubes
  4 cups cold buttermilk
  1 teaspoon Tabasco sauce or cayenne pepper

1. In a large saucepan over high heat, bring the water, salt, sugar, rosemary, and peppercorns to a boil, stirring to dissolve the sugar and salt. Stir and let cool to room temperature.

2. Add the ice cubes, buttermilk, and Tabasco. Whisk well. When the brine is cool to the touch, submerge the food in the brine. Refrigerate for 2 to 4 hours, covered.

Pernod Brine for Salmon

Makes about 2 quarts

A few years back, I was lucky enough to take a week-long class with grilling expert Chris Schlesinger at the Culinary Institute of America-Greystone campus in Northern California. On the last day, he let us riff on our own. I wanted to try my hand at smoking a side of salmon at the lowest possible temperature and decided to brine it for 24 hours with Pernod. The result was so exciting that it sealed my future as a grill jockey—although I didn't know it yet! I owe Chris a great big thanks for fanning my thrill of the grill, and you will too when you taste this brine!

Good for Soaking: Salmon, Arctic char

> 4 cups water
> 1 cup kosher salt
> 1/2 cup honey
> 1 tablespoon whole green peppercorns
> 4 whole star anise
> 1 teaspoon whole coriander seeds
> 3 cups cold water or ice cubes
> 1 cup Pernod

1. In a large saucepan over high heat, bring 4 cups water, salt, honey, peppercorns, star anise, and coriander to a boil, stirring to dissolve the sugar and salt. Add 3 cups cold water or ice cubes. Whisk well and add the Pernod. Stir and let cool to room temperature.

2. When the brine is cool to the touch, submerge the food in the brine. Refrigerate for 2 to 4 hours, covered.

Apple Cider Brine for Pork

Makes 2 quarts

The classic pairing of apples and pork is unbeatable. Brine a pork loin or chops in this apple cider brine and drizzle the grilled meat with Red-Eye Gravy Glaze (page 130) for a dressed-up American classic.

Good for Soaking: Pork chops, pork loin, fresh ham; chicken; turkey

> 2 cups cold water
> 1 cup kosher salt
> 1 cup packed light brown sugar

2 teaspoons dried thyme, or 2 sprigs fresh thyme

1 teaspoon whole black peppercorns

1 teaspoon whole cloves

4 cups unfiltered apple cider

2 cups ice cubes

1. In a large saucepan over medium-high heat, bring the water, salt, sugar, thyme, peppercorns, and cloves to a boil. Cook for 2 to 3 minutes, stirring occasionally, or until the sugar and salt dissolve. Remove from the heat, add the apple cider and ice cubes, and stir well.

2. Put the meat in a nonreactive pan or extra-large resealable bag and cover with the cooled brine. Cover or tightly close the bag and refrigerate for 6 to 12 hours. If you are using a resealable bag, rotate the pork a few times to make sure all of the meat gets brined. Before roasting, remove the pork and pat dry with paper towels.

Salty Dog Brine

Makes about 2 quarts

Grapefruit, a touch of vodka (or gin), and salt make a refreshing brine that any whole snapper, chicken, or pork would jump at the chance to swim in. Serve the grilled food with a jicama and pink grapefruit salad and a tall, cool drink—a salty dog, perhaps?!

Good for Soaking: Snapper, scallops, tuna; chicken; pork tenderloin, chops

4 cups water

1 cup kosher salt

1/2 cup packed light brown sugar

1 tablespoon whole pink peppercorns

1 tablespoon whole juniper berries

2 cups ice cubes

2 cups ruby red grapefruit juice

1/2 cup gin or vodka

1. In a large saucepan over high heat, bring the water, salt, sugar, peppercorns, and juniper berries to a boil, stirring to dissolve the sugar and salt. Add the ice cubes. Stir and let cool to room temperature.

2. Whisk well and add the grapefruit juice and vodka. When the brine is cool to the touch, submerge the food in the brine. Refrigerate for 2 to 4 hours, covered.

Espresso Brine

Makes about 2 quarts

This brine makes me think of the red-eye gravy that my grandmother used to make out of the bits of ham that stuck to her blackened pan. She made it by deglazing the browned bits with a steaming cup of thick, black coffee. As the coffee hit the hot cast iron, the steam of coffee and ham smelled so good! This rich, peppery coffee brine is my more contemporary take on the flavors of her red-eye gravy. Try it with pork chops, and serve them with creamy, rich cheese grits.

Good for Soaking: Pork chops, tenderloin, pork cutlets; chicken pieces; ham steak

- 4 cups hot water
- 1 cup kosher salt
- 1/2 cup Sugar in the Raw (turbinado)
- 1 teaspoon whole white peppercorns
- 1 teaspoon whole black cardamom pods (available in Indian food stores)
- 3 shots strong espresso, or 2 tablespoons instant espresso powder
- 4 cups ice cubes

1. In a large saucepan over high heat, bring the water, salt, sugar, peppercorns, and cardamom pods to a boil, stirring to dissolve the sugar and salt. Stir and let cool to room temperature.

2. Add the espresso. Add the ice cubes to cool the brine and add more volume to the brine. Add more cold water if more liquid is necessary to cover the food. When the brine is cool to the touch, submerge the food in the brine. Refrigerate for 2 to 4 hours, covered.

Rum-Honey Brine

Makes 2 quarts

Brining gives meat a silky texture—and this brine is the ultimate in silky, honeyed flavor and texture. Use spiced golden rum for the best flavor and serve your fish,

poultry, or pork with grilled plantains, pineapple, and beans and rice for a lip-smacking taste of the Caribbean.

Good for Soaking: Shrimp, catfish, snapper; pork loin; poultry

- 4 cups water
- 1 cup kosher salt
- 2 cups wildwood honey
- 1 cup spiced golden rum, preferably Captain Morgan
- One 8-ounce can crushed pineapple
- 1 bunch scallions, roughly chopped
- 3 cups ice cubes

1. In a large saucepan over high heat, bring the water and salt to a boil, stirring to dissolve the salt. Remove from the heat and add the honey, rum, pineapple, and scallions. Add the ice cubes and stir to combine. Let cool to room temperature.

2. When the brine is cool to the touch, submerge the food in the brine. Refrigerate for 2 to 4 hours, covered.

Molasses and Guinness Brine

Makes about 2 quarts

If the Southern pantry collided with the Irish pantry, you'd naturally have molasses and Guinness sitting side by side. The dark, slightly bitter ingredients in Guinness and molasses seem like fraternal twins, so alike in flavor yet so far removed by geography, which makes them the perfect pairing for this beef, chicken, and pork marinade.

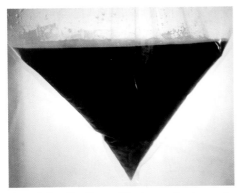

Good for Soaking: Venison; flank steak; pork roast; chicken thighs

    3 cups water
    1 cup kosher salt
    1/2 cup molasses
    2 tablespoons sliced crystallized ginger
    2 tablespoons Dijon mustard
    1/2 cup Worcestershire sauce
    2 cans cold Guinness
    2 cups ice cubes

1. In a large saucepan over high heat, bring the water and salt to a boil, stirring to dissolve the salt. Stir and remove from the heat. Add the molasses, ginger, mustard, Worcestershire, and Guinness. Add the ice cubes; stir and let cool to room temperature.

2. When the brine is cool to the touch, submerge the food in the brine. Refrigerate for 2 to 4 hours, covered.

Slathered

This section covers flavorings that you generously brush or spoon onto almost-cooked food or fully cooked food, including:

Sauces • Glazes • Mops
Salsas, Relishes, and Jellies • Sweet Sauces

SAUCES

Highly flavored liquids that are brushed on the food at the end of the cooking time to add another layer of flavor, visual appeal, and moisture. Regional American barbecue sauces are slathered on food during the final cooking time and classic sauces are spooned on food after cooking.

Sauces 101

RAPID-FIRE CHECKLIST

○ Don't overseason the sauce. All the food that you put it on will already be seasoned.

○ Most barbecue sauces are made to taste good once they are cooked on the food. This is the major difference between the regional American sauces in this chapter and the dipping sauces (see pages 300–334).

○ Brush food with barbecue sauce during the final 5 to 15 minutes of cooking time, depending on the length of the total cooking time. For quick-cooking foods, brush on during the final 5 minutes of cooking; for medium foods like beer-can chicken, during the final 10 minutes, and for the larger foods, during the final 15 minutes.

○ You are the boss! Adjust the seasonings to your taste. For example, if you like things hotter, add more heat. If you want more garlic, add more garlic, and vice versa.

○ Most sauces can be made in advance, and some sauces are actually better the next day.

○ Plan your menus in advance so that you can do one to two things a day. That way, on the day you plan to serve the food, it's not a big job.

Sauces are the foundation of all cuisines and the most traditional way to add flavor to food. After all, a chicken is a chicken, but add a sauce and you have myriad possibilities. In fact, my "saucy" friends say that chicken is just an excuse to eat barbecue sauce! I know that I love the Tikka Masala Sauce (page 105) so much that I could pour it over rice and enjoy it just as much as I do when I eat it with chicken. If you like this traditional Anglo-Indian sauce, just wait until you try it over grilled chicken, shrimp, or scallops. The smokiness from the grill complements the sauce perfectly.

Sauces can be savory or sweet and are a perfect way to dress up plain grilled food. Think about that chicken again; you can grill chicken pieces or a whole chicken every night using the Grilling Trilogy (see page 10), but now you can also go to Italy and slather your grilled chicken with Speedy Amatrici-Style Sauce (page 119), or go to Greece and eat your chicken with Tzatziki (page 318), or come back home with any number of regional American barbecue sauces. You can eat around the world using the same chicken preparation, simply by adding a different sauce.

Sauces have been used in food preparation since medieval times and were so important to medieval feasts that every wealthy home had a staff "saucier" who was responsible for nothing but making sauces. Often the saucier had assistants to help him prepare that part of the menu. And anyone who has ever eaten at a French restaurant knows that sauces are a defining characteristic of French cuisine.

In the 1800s, Antonin Carême, considered one of the fathers of classic formal cooking techniques, classified French sauces into four groups. Each group was based on one "mother" sauce, with variations that became separate sauces. Another French cooking expert, Auguste Escoffier, updated this list of sauces in the 1900s to include the best and most popular examples of how a mother sauce inspires other important sauces. For example, hollandaise is a mother sauce, and the tarragon-flavored béarnaise is one of the sauce variations made from the basic hollandaise recipe. In this chapter, I have a blender hollandaise that is made every weekend by my friends Bill Barrick and Tony Kemp for the guests at their inn, Irish Hollow, in Galena, Illinois. Their version is foolproof and makes a normally finicky sauce a cinch for anyone who owns a blender. Once you make their hollandaise, you can make any number of variations, including béarnaise, with the addition of a few ingredients.

This being a *barbecue* (and grilling) book, the bulk of the recipes in this chapter are for regional American barbecue sauces. These sauces are almost indestructible and can be doctored up to your own personal liking (see chart, page 85). I have seen barbecue sauce recipes that are as simple as a bottle of ketchup and a box of brown sugar and as complicated as making a labor-intensive demi-glace.

Shelf Life

Most sauces can be made in advance and some sauces are actually better the next day. Store sauces in a clean glass jar with a tight-fitting lid in the refrigerator. If necessary, warm or bring to room temperature before serving.

For many people, barbecue sauce is the heart and soul of barbecue flavor. The most popular types of barbecue sauces are sweet, red, tomato-based sauces, even though there are many other varieties. Vinegar sauces have made North Carolina famous, and yellow mustard–based sauces are popular in some parts of South Carolina and Georgia. There is even a white mayonnaise-based sauce popularized by Alabama-based Big Bob Gibson. But typical sauces start with a base of either ketchup, American chili sauce, tomatoes, or tomato sauce and are heavily flavored with onions, garlic, and other aromatic vegetables like sweet peppers or celery that have been cooked down and pureed into the liquid. The key ingredient is actually Worcestershire sauce, as the tangy tamarind flavor in that sauce is what most of us associate with barbecue sauce. Other common ingredients include hot pepper sauce, cider vinegar, red wine vinegar, whiskey, cola, honey, molasses or brown sugar, coffee, cocoa, soy sauce, dried fruits, juices, herbs, and spices.

Barbecue sauces are made to sauce or glaze the meat at the end of the cooking time. Because of their high sugar content, sauce should only be brushed on during the final 5 to 15 minutes of cooking time. And, even though we are accustomed to dipping our food in barbecue sauce, the rule on the barbecue circuit is that the sauce is made to taste good once it is cooked on the meat, not necessarily on the side as a dipping sauce.

Liquid Smoke: To Use or Not to Use?

Early in my barbecue career, I visited a natural liquid smoke factory. It was fascinating to watch how wood was burned in the absence of oxygen and the natural condensation was collected and funneled into small bottles of liquid smoke for home use and huge 18-wheeler trucks for industrial (read: hot dogs) use. So I do know that some liquid smoke is actually natural smoke that is captured under a plastic tent and sent to be bottled.

That said, I am not a lover of liquid smoke. I think that the concentrated smell and flavor is artificial, no matter whether it's a drop in a sauce or a drop in a stadium "dog." If you are looking for a smoky note to goose up your recipes, I suggest using Spanish smoked paprika. Smoked paprika is made by roasting and smoking pimentón over a special oak wood fire and then dehydrating the smoked red peppers before grinding them into a powder. The smoked paprika comes in sweet, hot, and bittersweet versions. It is advisable to taste before using because some hot versions taste just like the sweet, but other hot versions are almost as fiery as cayenne pepper. If it's smoke and not heat that you are after, use the sweet—you can use lots of it!

Plastic Squeeze Bottles

Clear plastic squeeze bottles look like the ubiquitous red and yellow ballpark squeeze bottles except that you can see what's inside. They are great for storing sauce (get the bottles that have a top to seal the sauces for storage), for decorating food and plates, and for serving so that you don't waste your precious homemade sauces when someone gets too much on their plate. These bottles can be found in some gourmet kitchen stores or at all restaurant supply stores. They are very inexpensive and dishwasher safe.

Measuring Sticky Ingredients

Most of the sauce recipes call for sticky or clinging ingredients like molasses, honey, and even ketchup. To make these ingredients literally "slip" out of the measuring cup, coat the empty cup with a little olive oil or spray it with a nonstick vegetable spray. It won't add any flavor to the sauce, and you'll make sure to get all the good stuff, down to the last drop.

DOCTOR, DOCTOR, BARBECUE SAUCE DOCTOR

Here is a quick look at how to doctor up store-bought barbecue sauce and make it taste homemade. This list is just a start, so feel free to experiment with all your favorite add-ins. Start with a small amount and increase to taste.

Add 1	Add 1 to 2	Add 1	Add 1
Favorite spice or barbecue rub	Sautéed onions	Lemon juice	Wine
Salt	Cooked and crumbled bacon	Lime juice	Beer
Pepper	Sautéed garlic	Orange juice	Whiskey
Pepper juice (see page 91)	Sautéed shallots	Pineapple juice	Southern Comfort
Ginger juice	Sautéed grated apples	Crushed pineapple	Bourbon
Molasses	Chipotles in adobo	Apple cider or other vinegar	Tequila
Cocoa powder		Raspberries	Sweet liqueurs
		Blackberries	Soft drinks, such as Coca-Cola
		Canned cranberry sauce	
		Jams and jellies	

Timing Tip

Don't apply barbecue sauce or sweet glazes until the last 5 to 15 minutes of cooking time. That way your food will be done inside and the sauce will coat them with a nice warm glaze. Putting the sauce on earlier runs the risk of burning the sauce. Use this rule of thumb:

- Large pieces of meat can take the sauce up to the final 15 minutes of cooking time.

- Brush medium foods, like a whole chicken or slab of ribs, during the final 10 minutes of cooking time.

- Brush sweet sauces on small foods, like boneless chicken breasts, during the last 5 minutes of cooking time.

- Brush shrimp and quick-cooking fish during the final 1 to 2 minutes of cooking time.

Barbecue Sauce 101: a.k.a. Lexington-Style Vinegar Sauce

Makes about 3 cups

Though not the most traditional, this sweetened-up version of the Eastern North Carolina Sauce (recipe follows) is my 101 sauce because it enhances the natural flavor of well-smoked barbecue. It is traditionally used to dress pulled pork from Lexington west to the mountains.

Good for Slathering: Pulled pork; pulled chicken; chopped beef

- 2 cups cider vinegar
- 1 tablespoon kosher salt
- 1/2 to 1 tablespoon fine-ground white pepper, to your taste
- 1 to 2 tablespoons red chile flakes (the more flakes, the hotter the sauce)
- 2 tablespoons sugar
- 1/4 cup packed dark brown sugar
- 1/2 teaspoon freshly ground black pepper
- 1/2 cup ketchup

1. In a large bowl, mix all the ingredients together and let sit for at least 10 minutes. The sauce will keep, tightly covered, in the refrigerator almost indefinitely.

2. Use this sauce to moisten pulled barbecue, especially pulled pork. If desired, serve extra on the side.

*The longer the sauce sits, the hotter it gets, since the heat from the red chile flakes is brought out by the vinegar. Start with 1 1/2 teaspoons red chile flakes and then add more to taste.

Eastern Carolina–Style Barbecue Sauce

Makes 4 cups

This eastern Carolina–style sauce is little more than vinegar and red pepper. It is the simplest of the Carolina sauces, and the most piquant, which is why it is sometimes diluted (like I did here) with water. This simple mixture is also referred to as "dip" because the pork gets dipped into the sauce to moisten and season it after it has been pulled or chopped.

Good for Slathering: Pulled pork; pulled chicken; chopped beef

- 2 cups cider vinegar
- 1 cup distilled white vinegar
- 1 cup water
- 1 tablespoon kosher salt
- 1 tablespoon sugar
- 1 teaspoon fine-ground white pepper
- 1 teaspoon freshly ground black pepper
- 1 1/2 teaspoons red chile flakes (the more flakes, the hotter the sauce)

1. In a large bowl, mix all the ingredients together and let sit for at least 10 minutes. The sauce will keep, tightly covered, in the refrigerator almost indefinitely.

2. Use this sauce to moisten pulled barbecue, especially pulled pork. If desired, serve extra on the side.

South Carolina Mustard Sauce

Makes 2 1/4 cups

As a girl from North Carolina, it took me a very long time to try the "Carolina Gold" sauce, because it wasn't what I was used to. But a few years ago, I bit the butt, so to speak, and went to one of the most famous and most controversial (it still supports the "Confederacy") barbecue joints—the original Piggie Park in South Carolina's capital, Columbia. After I got over the shock of the self-published propaganda that Mr. Bessinger papers his restaurant with, I settled into my "Big Pig" sandwich with the golden mustard sauce. I was pleasantly surprised; it is sweet and tangy with enough vinegar to complement the smoky meat.

Besides the sauce, there are two other significant differences in the way the pork is served. South Carolinians make their sandwiches minus the coleslaw on top, and the bun is buttered and toasted before being piled high with the mustard-dressed pulled pork.

Good for Slathering: Lamb chops; pork, pork ribs; fish; dilute with beer to make a mop for brisket and other large meats

- 3/4 cup cider vinegar
- 1 cup yellow mustard
- 1/2 cup molasses
- 1/4 cup honey
- 2 tablespoons peanut oil
- 2 1/2 teaspoons Worcestershire sauce
- 1/2 teaspoon fine-grind white pepper
- 1/2 teaspoon freshly ground black pepper
- 3 dashes cayenne pepper
- 2 teaspoons fine-grain sea salt, optional

1. In a stainless steel or nonreactive saucepan, combine the vinegar, mustard, molasses, honey, peanut oil, and Worcestershire sauce. Whisk to combine and bring to just under a boil, stirring well. Add the white, black, and cayenne peppers and the salt and whisk again.

2. Reduce to a simmer and let cook for an additional 5 minutes, stirring occasionally. Let cool before using. The sauce will keep, tightly covered, in the refrigerator for up to 2 weeks.

3. Brush it on food 5 to 15 minutes before the cooking time is finished. If desired, serve extra on the side.

Note: The most popular Carolina mustard sauces do not include salt; a very sweet single-note sauce is preferred. I think that the pork tastes a little bland without the salt, so I add it, giving the sauce a little more complexity.

Mama Faye's Winning Barbecue Sauce

Makes 2 1/2 cups

This sauce is known to most people as Apple City Barbecue Sauce. It won Mike Mills three Grand Championships at Memphis in May and more accolades and trophies than you can count. During a recent trip to Murphysboro, Illinois, Mike took me to see a few "antiques" in his attic. As soon as I got out of the elevator, I saw more trophies than I had ever seen, literally hundreds of them. And these are the trophies that he doesn't display; he has hundreds more decorating his seven restaurants in southern Illinois, St. Louis, and Las Vegas! And best of all: The trophies were won in three years' time!

Mike got the recipe for the sauce from his mother, Mama Faye, who made it from scratch for his restaurant and his competitions until the day she went to the big barbecue contest in the sky. I thought it was time she got her rightful praise.

Good for Slathering: Ribs, pork; chicken; steak; shrimp

    1 cup ketchup, preferably Hunt's
    2/3 cup seasoned rice vinegar
    1/2 cup apple juice or apple cider
    1/4 cup apple cider vinegar
    1/2 cup packed dark brown sugar
    1/4 cup soy sauce
    2 teaspoons yellow mustard
    3/4 teaspoon garlic powder
    1/4 teaspoon fine-ground white pepper
    1/4 teaspoon cayenne pepper
    4 slices bacon, cooked until crisp and
    ground in a spice grinder
    1/3 cup peeled and grated apple
    1/3 cup grated onion
    2 teaspoons grated green bell pepper

1. In a large saucepan, combine the ketchup, rice vinegar, apple juice, cider vinegar, brown sugar, soy sauce, mustard, garlic powder, white pepper, cayenne, and bacon bits. Bring to a full boil over medium-high heat.

2. Stir in the apple, onion, and bell pepper. Reduce the heat and simmer, uncovered, for 10 to 15 minutes or until it thickens slightly. Stir it often. If you want a thicker sauce, reduce for a longer time.

3. Let cool, then pour into clean glass bottles. The sauce will keep in the refrigerator for up to 2 weeks.

4. Brush it on food 5 to 15 minutes before the cooking time is finished. If desired, serve extra on the side.

Alabama White Barbecue Sauce

Makes about 2 cups

Chris Lilly is the celebrated pitmaster of Big Bob Gibson's Bar-B-Q in Decatur, Alabama. Chris is widely known as one of the nicest guys on the circuit, and he hasn't let all the fame go to his head. In all the years I've known him, I have never heard him toot his own horn! But I guess he doesn't need to, since Chris and the restaurant have earned countless barbecue-contest awards and accolades in the press for their pork shoulder.

Big Bob Gibson's is equally famous for an unusual white barbecue sauce. It's so different that folks who aren't from Alabama sometimes look askance when I first mention it, but one taste is all you need. In Chris's restaurant, freshly smoked chickens are dunked in this sauce before serving. Pulled chicken doused with this sauce is also very good.

Good for Slathering: Whole chicken, pulled chicken steak; grilled asparagus

- 1 cup mayonnaise
- 1 cup apple cider vinegar
- 1 tablespoon sugar
- 2 teaspoons freshly ground black pepper
- 1/2 teaspoon salt, plus more to taste
- 1/2 teaspoon cayenne pepper
- 1/2 teaspoon prepared horseradish (not cream-style)
- 1 lemon, juiced

1. In a large nonreactive bowl, whisk all the ingredients together. The sauce will keep, tightly covered, in the refrigerator for up to 2 weeks.

2. Brush it on food 5 to 15 minutes before the cooking time is finished or dunk your hot-off-the-grill food in a bowl of the sauce like they do in Alabama. If desired, serve extra on the side.

Rick Bayless's Oklahoma Barbecue Sauce

Makes about 1 1/2 cups

Mexican food expert and culinary champion Rick Bayless is a barbecue legacy. He grew up in his family's barbecue restaurant in Oklahoma. Every year, he treats his staff to a taste of American barbecue with a fabulous pig roast in his backyard garden. I've been fortunate to attend several of these barbecues, and his family's sauce is always served alongside some Mexican condiments. Rick says, "This [sauce] is the simple essence of barbecue sauce . . . starting with ketchup. So it's easy, too. If you have any meat drippings from your barbecue, stir them in for fabulous added flavor." I say, it's good eatin' no matter what you slather it on!

Good for Slathering: Pork; beef; chicken

- 2 cloves garlic, minced or grated
- 1 cup ketchup
- 1 tablespoon apple cider vinegar
- 2 tablespoons Worcestershire sauce
- 1/3 cup packed dark brown sugar
- 1/2 to 1 teaspoon barbecue rub, store-bought or homemade (Rick says you can substitute chili powder)
- 1/4 teaspoon freshly ground pepper
- 3/4 cup water
- 1/8 teaspoon kosher salt

1. In a small saucepan, over medium-low heat, simmer all the ingredients for 15 minutes.

2. Taste and season with more salt if necessary. The sauce will keep, tightly covered, in the refrigerator for up to 2 weeks.

3. Brush it on food 5 to 15 minutes before the cooking time is finished. If desired, serve extra on the side.

Sweet Cherry Cola Barbecue Sauce

Makes 2 cups

I love iconic American foods made out of popular grocery items. Think of the Tater Tot casserole: I'm not sure that I could bring myself to make it, but I love the spirit of it. What I do make all the time is cola-based barbecue sauces. Try to find the Mexican Coke that is made with real sugar instead of high-fructose corn syrup. The flavors are brighter and you get more dimension from the cola than the one-note—all sweet—corn syrup–sweetened drinks. If you can't find it, you can substitute any boutique cola made with sugar. This ramped-up cherry cola sauce is the bomb!

Good for Slathering: Chicken; sirloin, burgers; grilled mushrooms

    4 tablespoons (1/2 stick) unsalted butter
    1 large red onion, chopped
    4 large cloves garlic, grated
    One 12-ounce can Coca-Cola
    One 12-ounce can cherry cola
    1 cup ketchup
    1/2 cup raspberry or cherry vinegar
    1/4 cup no-sugar-added cherry jam

    1/3 cup Worcestershire sauce
    2 teaspoons ground ancho or New Mexican chili powder
    2 teaspoons sweet smoked Spanish paprika
    1 teaspoon kosher salt
    1/8 teaspoon cayenne pepper
    Freshly ground pepper

1. In a heavy saucepan, melt the butter. Sauté the onion and garlic in the butter until translucent, about 10 minutes. Add all the remaining ingredients and simmer for about 15 minutes, until the flavors have blended. Note: Do not add the seasonings directly to the colas, as the mixture will foam up and bubble over.

2. Continue cooking until the sauce begins to thicken, 20 to 25 minutes. Taste and adjust the seasonings with salt and pepper if desired. Remember, anything you sauce will already have plenty of spice rub on it, so don't overseason the sauce.

3. Let the sauce cool for about 10 minutes or until it is warm but no longer "boiling" hot. Puree with an immersion or traditional blender.

Let cool. The sauce will keep, tightly covered, in the refrigerator for up to 2 weeks.

4. Brush it on food 5 to 15 minutes before the cooking time is finished. If desired, serve extra on the side.

Dr. Pepper Barbecue Sauce

Makes 5 cups

My students make this barbecue sauce every month in my Southern-barbecue classes. It is the only red sauce that we make in the class, and we always double the recipe because the class slathers it on everything! This sauce has been printed in many places and thousands of students have the recipe, but I couldn't write a sauce chapter and not include it here. The Dr. Pepper gives this sauce an edge over most basic sweet barbecue sauces.

Good for Slathering: Pork; beef; duck; ribs

- 4 tablespoons (1/2 stick) unsalted butter
- 1 large yellow onion, chopped
- 4 cloves garlic, chopped
- 1 cup ketchup
- 3 tablespoons tomato paste
- One 12-ounce can Dr. Pepper
- 1/2 cup cider vinegar
- 1/3 cup Worcestershire sauce
- 1/2 cup packed dark brown sugar
- 2 teaspoons ancho or New Mexican chili powder
- 1 teaspoon fine-ground white pepper
- 1 teaspoon kosher salt

1. In a heavy saucepan, melt the butter. Sauté the onion and garlic in the butter until translucent, about 10 minutes. Add all the remaining ingredients and simmer for about 15 minutes, until the flavors

---

CHAR-ROASTED PEPPER JUICE FOR BARBECUE SAUCES

My good friend Jeff Belmonti tipped me off to the best idea that I've ever heard for doctoring up store-bought barbecue sauce. Buy an assortment of your favorite fresh chile and bell peppers, both sweet and hot, such as poblanos, red and yellow bell peppers, jalapeños, banana peppers, etc. Grill-roast them over high heat (see page 43) until the skins are charred and the flesh is roasted and soft. Peel, seed, and grind the peppers. Take the mixture and push it through a fine-meshed strainer. Add a little salt to the liquid and mix it into your favorite store-bought barbecue sauce. This "pepper juice" thins out commercial sauce, which is almost always too thick, and gives a fresh, smoky flavor and touch of heat that you can't get by adding any bottled hot sauce or other processed ingredients. Can't you just taste it?

---

have blended. Continue cooking until the sauce begins to thicken, 20 to 30 minutes. Taste and adjust the seasonings with salt and pepper if desired. Remember, the ribs will have plenty of spice rub on them, so don't overseason the sauce.

2. Let the sauce cool for about 10 minutes or until it is warm but no longer "boiling" hot. Puree with an immersion or traditional blender—this will make the sauce thicker. Let cool. The sauce will keep, tightly covered, in the refrigerator for up to 2 weeks.

3. Brush it on food 5 to 15 minutes before the cooking time is finished. If desired, serve extra on the side.

Backyard Barbecue Ribs with Dr. Pepper Barbecue Sauce

Serves 6

Grilling Method: Indirect/Medium-Low Heat

> 4 slabs pork ribs, about 2 pounds each, St. Louis cut, if possible
>
> Hickory or apple wood chips, soaked in water for 30 minutes
>
> 1 recipe Hot and Sticky BBQ Rub (page 205)
>
> 1 recipe Dr. Pepper Barbecue Sauce (page 91) or your favorite barbecue sauce

1. Build a charcoal fire or preheat a gas grill. Remove the silver skin from the back of the ribs, if desired. Set up the grill for indirect heat and, if using wood chips, place the soaked chips directly on the charcoal or in the smoking box of the gas grill. Rub the ribs liberally with the spice rub and let sit, covered, for 15 to 20 minutes.

2. Place ribs (bone side down) in the center of the cooking grate or in a rib holder or rack, making sure they are not over a direct flame. Grill covered (at 300° to 325°F, if your grill has a thermometer) for 2 to 3 hours or until the meat is tender and has pulled back from the ends of the rib bones.

3. Leave the ribs untended for the first 30 minutes—this means no peeking (especially important if using wood chips). If the ribs start to burn on the edges, stack them on top of one another in the very center of the grill and lower your fire slightly. Twenty minutes before serving, unstack if necessary and brush with the barbecue sauce. Remove from the grill and let rest for 10 minutes before cutting into individual portions. Warm the remaining sauce in a saucepan and serve on the side.

Red Zin Barbecue Sauce

Makes about 3 1/2 cups

This sauce is tailor-made for beef. Zinfandel is called the "barbecue wine" because of its affinity for the bold smoky flavor notes, which overpower many other red wines. Reducing a spicy, fruity bottle of Zinfandel by half and using it as a base for a barbecue sauce is one of the best ways to create a sophisticated layer of flavor that is a change of pace from the classic barbecue sauces.

Good for Slathering: Smoked short ribs, brisket, or even a thick grilled steak; wild game, venison; duck; pork

- 1 bottle "Old Vines" or other red Zinfandel
- 1/2 cup plus 2 heaping tablespoons seedless blackberry or raspberry jam
- 1 cup ketchup
- 2 tablespoons tomato paste
- 3 tablespoons balsamic vinegar
- Pinch ground cloves
- 1/2 teaspoon ground cinnamon
- 1 teaspoon sweet Hungarian paprika
- 1/2 teaspoon Tabasco sauce
- Kosher salt and freshly ground pepper

1. In a heavy saucepan, bring the wine to a boil, then reduce the heat and simmer until it is reduced to about half of its original volume, about 25 minutes. Add the jam and stir until combined. Simmer for 5 minutes. Add the ketchup, tomato paste, vinegar, cloves, cinnamon, paprika, and Tabasco sauce to the saucepan.

2. Simmer for 15 minutes, stirring occasionally. Season to taste (I like about 1 teaspoon salt and 1/4 teaspoon pepper) and let cool. The sauce will keep, tightly covered, in the refrigerator for up to 2 weeks.

3. Brush it on food 5 to 15 minutes before the cooking time is finished. If desired, serve extra on the side.

Kicked-Up Orange-Tequila Barbecue Sauce

Makes 2 1/2 cups

The smoky hot chipotles in this sauce give you a big bang! But the complex sauce is not just hot, it is also sweet with fresh orange juice and marmalade tempering and complementing the savory ingredients. The tequila takes the place of vinegar in this recipe for a rich sauce that is balanced sweet heat—not too sweet and not too hot—just right!

Good for Slathering: Wild game; quail, duck, chicken; pork

- 2 tablespoons vegetable oil
- 1/2 cup finely chopped yellow onion
- 2 cloves garlic, minced
- 1 to 2 tablespoons pureed chipotles in adobo sauce, to your taste
- 1 tablespoon dry mustard
- 3/4 teaspoon dried thyme
- 1 1/4 teaspoons ground ginger
- 1 teaspoon ground cumin, preferably from toasted seeds
- 1 teaspoon freshly ground pepper
- 2 bay leaves

1 3/4 cups ketchup
1/2 cup fresh orange juice
1/4 cup orange marmalade
1/2 cup tequila
1/4 cup molasses
1 tablespoon Worcestershire sauce
2 tablespoons soy sauce

1. In a medium heavy saucepan over low heat, warm the oil. Add the onion, garlic, chipotle, mustard, thyme, ginger, cumin, pepper, and bay leaves.

2. Cover and cook, stirring occasionally, for 10 minutes. Add the ketchup, orange juice, marmalade, tequila, molasses, Worcestershire sauce, and soy sauce and bring to a simmer. Cook, uncovered, stirring often as the sauce begins to thicken, for 20 minutes.

3. Remove from the heat. If desired, refrigerate for 24 hours before using to allow the flavors to mellow. Bring to room temperature and discard the bay leaves before using. The sauce will keep, tightly covered, in the refrigerator for up to 2 weeks.

4. Brush it on food 5 to 15 minutes before the cooking time is finished. If desired, serve extra on the side.

Sassy 2B Barbecue Sauce

Makes about 4 cups

I love anything that includes 2 of my favorite Bs . . . in this case, bourbon and brown sugar. And this is one of my favorite barbecue sauces. It is made with crushed tomatoes and just a touch of ketchup for a lighter, sassier sauce that is at home on anything you want to put it on. The secret to this sauce is a touch of cocoa that is whisked in at the end; it deepens the color and the flavor.

Good for Slathering: Brisket; chicken; pork; ribs

One 28-ounce can crushed tomatoes
1 cup packed brown sugar
2 tablespoons molasses
1/2 cup bourbon, preferably Maker's Mark
1/2 cup ketchup
1/4 cup Heinz Chili Sauce
1/4 cup apple cider vinegar
1/8 cup red wine vinegar
1/4 cup Worcestershire sauce
2 teaspoons Grilling Guru Rub (page 205)
Kosher salt and freshly ground pepper
1 tablespoon unsweetened cocoa powder

1. In a large saucepan, combine the tomatoes, sugar, molasses, bourbon, ketchup, chili sauce, vinegars, and Worcestershire sauce, stirring after each additional ingredient to combine. Add the spice rub and simmer until the flavors have blended and the sauce has thickened somewhat, about 30 minutes.

2. Let the sauce cool for about 10 minutes or until it is warm but no longer "boiling" hot. Puree using an immersion or traditional blender. Taste and adjust the seasonings with salt and pepper, if desired. Remember, the food will be seasoned as well, so don't overseason the sauce. Add the cocoa powder and mix well to combine. Let sit for 5 minutes, and then stir again to make sure the cocoa powder is well distributed. Let cool. The sauce will keep, tightly covered, in the refrigerator for up to 2 weeks.

3. Brush it on food 5 to 15 minutes before the cooking time is finished. If desired, serve extra on the side.

sauce will keep, tightly covered, at room temperature indefinitely.

2. Sprinkle a few drops into any dish/ recipe as desired.

*Bird peppers are also known and sold as Chinese Tien Tsin chile peppers.

Note: The longer the mixture sits, the hotter it will get. You can also add more heat to suit your taste.

Rattlesnake Bite Hot Sauce

Makes about 1 cup

I love making homemade hot sauces, and I find that the best liquid to pull out the heat from the peppers is distilled alcohol. These days, tequila is my favorite medium for a simple hot sauce that is all chilies. Use the Gecko brand black tequila for a deep, dark, Texas "Black Gold" version of this hot sauce.

Good for Slathering: Grilled or raw oysters, fish; all barbecued meats; vegetables, salads; scrambled eggs

Special Equipment: bottle with shaker spout or half pint tequila bottle

> 1/4 to 1/2 teaspoon cayenne pepper, to your taste
>
> 3 whole dried red bird peppers* or cayenne peppers
>
> 1 cup blue agave tequila or apple cider vinegar

1. Pour the cayenne into a glass jar or the tequila bottle, add the dried peppers, and top with the tequila. Let sit at room temperature for a few days before using. The

Caribbean Hot Sauce

Makes 2 cups

This hot sauce is a little more than just "hot" sauce. It is great mixed into recipes or on its own for a subtle but definitely tropical splash of flavor. Try your own combinations of whole spices, dried peppers, and alcohols—almost anything goes, but just don't use any sugar-fortified liqueurs.

Good for Slathering: Grilled fish, grilled or raw oysters, ceviche, conch; all barbecued meats; vegetables, salads; fruits; scrambled eggs

> One 1-pint bottle dark rum
>
> 5 to 6 whole fresh or dried red bird peppers or small Scotch bonnet chilies
>
> 6 whole cloves
>
> 4 whole allspice berries
>
> 3 whole black peppercorns

1. Pour 1/4 cup rum out of the bottle into a measuring cup. Place the peppers, cloves, allspice, and peppercorns and spices into the bottle of rum. Top up the bottle with the remaining rum. Tightly cap the bottle.

2. Let the pepper rum "ripen" for at least 2 weeks, preferably 1 month, before serving. The pepper rum will keep at room temperature almost indefinitely.

3. Sprinkle a few drops into any dish/recipe as desired.

Spiced Rum Variation

If you want to make this hot sauce even spicier and add dimension to the heat, substitute Captain Morgan or another spiced rum for the regular rum.

Reuben's Sauce Vera Cruz

Makes 2 cups

On my first day of a yoga retreat in Mexico, I arrived late because of airport delays and was starving! After a speedy check-in, I walked to the beachside restaurant and was greeted by the congenial Reuben. Reuben recommended the grilled grouper with sauce Vera Cruz—so naturally, I ordered it. A big fan of grouper, I relaxed and looked forward to my dinner when Reuben came scurrying to the table. Full of apologies, he said that the kitchen didn't have the ingredients and I needed to choose another preparation. No problem, as long as it was grilled grouper it didn't matter. Then, out of the blue, the grilled grouper smothered with Reuben's sauce Vera Cruz appeared! He excitedly explained that he really wanted me to try it, so he borrowed the ingredients from another "kitchen." When I looked down at the plate, I saw a perfectly grilled grouper fillet smothered in a steaming sauce of chunky tomatoes, strips of white onions and green peppers, and green olives.

Everything but the olives is standard in a Mexican kitchen. So instantly, I knew that a few martinis would be missing their olives that night and the neighboring "kitchen" was really the bar next door! I devoured the fresh-caught fish with its sweet, tart, sour, briny, and slightly spicy sauce as I listened to the waves crashing. Interestingly enough, it reminded me of home and a sauce my mother used to make (minus the olives) to top pork chops—Mexican or Southern, it is delicious.

Good for Slathering: Grilled fish (grouper, red snapper, salmon, shrimp); chicken thighs; pork chops

> 3 tablespoons olive oil
>
> Kosher salt
>
> 1 medium white onion, halved and cut into 1/4-inch slices
>
> 1/2 green bell pepper, cut into strips
>
> 4 fresh tomatoes or one 15-ounce can plum tomatoes, roughly chopped
>
> 2 cloves garlic, grated
>
> 1/4 teaspoon habanero hot sauce or Tabasco Green Pepper sauce, or more according to taste
>
> Freshly ground pepper
>
> 1/2 cup brined green olives, pitted

1. In a medium saucepan, heat the olive oil and a pinch of salt for about 2 minutes. Add the onion and green pepper and sauté over high heat until the vegetables are wilted, soft, and beginning to brown, about 5 minutes. Add the tomatoes and all their liquid. Reduce the heat and stir. Add the garlic and hot sauce. Stir well and simmer for another 5 minutes. Season with salt and pepper and add the olives. Cook for 1 to 2 minutes more or until the olives are warmed through. You do not want the tomatoes to be cooked down into a sauce; they should keep their shape. Remove from the heat. Use immediately.

2. Spoon over cooked food just before serving. If desired, serve extra on the side.

Creating a sauce for Hill Country restaurant in New York City, where I am the executive chef, was a lot harder than it sounds. First off, the Texas barbecue that we celebrate doesn't use sauce—it's a no-sauce zone! But since we were going to be in the Big Apple, we knew that we had to have a sauce—thus the "if you gotta have it" name. The owner, Marc Glosserman, and I must have tasted 300 or more sauces to find a style that we thought would go with our simple salt-and-pepper-rubbed barbecue. At one pre-opening cookout, we had three long tables literally covered with different sauces! We finally decided on a sweet, red, high-vinegar sauce studded with chunks of the famous Fredericksburg, Texas, peaches and infused with a smoky bite from chipotles. It's great, but don't just take my word for it; it won an award of excellence from the National Barbecue Association!

Good for Slathering: Brisket, beef ribs, chopped beef, sausage; chicken; pork ribs, chops

Hill Country "If You Gotta Have It!" Peach Chipotle Sauce

Makes about 4 cups

One 28-ounce can crushed tomatoes
1 cup packed brown sugar
2 tablespoons molasses
3/4 cup chunky peach preserves, divided
1/2 cup ketchup
1/4 cup Heinz Chili Sauce
1/4 to 1/3 cup apple cider vinegar
1/8 cup rice vinegar
1/4 cup Worcestershire sauce
1/2 teaspoon chipotle chile powder
1/2 to 1 teaspoon kosher salt

1. In a large saucepan, combine the tomatoes, sugar, molasses, 1/2 cup of the peach preserves, the ketchup, chili sauce, vinegars, and Worcestershire sauce, stirring after each additional ingredient to combine. Add the chipotle powder and simmer until the flavors have blended and the sauce has thickened somewhat, about 30 minutes. Taste and add more vinegar if needed; you should taste a tang of vinegar and then the sweetness of the sauce.

2. Let the sauce cool for about 10 minutes or until it is warm but no longer "boiling" hot. Puree using an immersion or traditional blender. Add the remaining 1/4 cup peach preserves. Taste and adjust seasonings with the salt. Let sit for 5 minutes, and then stir again. Let cool. The sauce will keep, tightly covered, in the refrigerator for up to 2 weeks.

3. Brush it on food 5 to 15 minutes before the cooking time is finished. If desired, serve extra on the side.

true-friend colors showed. He made his sauce for my dinner for 100, helped shepherd all nine courses out to the diners, and even posed with the girls for pictures. When Richard makes this sauce, he uses ketjap manis, an Indonesian sauce that is thick like molasses but flavored with garlic, star anise, and palm sugar. If you have it on hand, replace the molasses in my recipe with the ketjap manis.

Good for Slathering: Pork ribs, pork; steak, beef ribs; duck, chicken

2 chipotle chilies in adobo sauce
5 whole cardamom pods
2 whole star anise
1 shallot, diced
3 cloves garlic, chopped
1/4 cup tomato paste
1/4 cup honey
1/4 cup molasses
1/2 cup pomegranate juice
1/4 cup pomegranate syrup or Pama Liqueur
1 1/2 cups ketchup
1/8 cup apple cider vinegar
2 teaspoons salt
1/2 teaspoon freshly ground pepper

Pomegranate Barbecue Sauce

Makes about 2 1/4 cups

This wonderful barbecue sauce is my take on my friend Richard Ruben's "Spicy Barbecue Sauce." Many years ago, when I kicked off my new life as a girl at the grill, I was invited to be the guest chef at the James Beard House. I gathered a bunch of my (girl) grill friends and Richard. Undaunted by this girls' grilling affair, his

1. In a 4-quart saucepan, combine all the ingredients and bring to a boil. Lower the heat and simmer for 20 minutes.

2. Discard the cardamom pods and star anise and blend until smooth either using an immersion or traditional blender. The sauce will keep, tightly covered, in the refrigerator for up to 2 weeks.

3. Brush it on food 5 to 15 minutes before the cooking time is finished. If desired, serve extra on the side.

Big Lou's Root Beer BBQ Sauce

Makes about 3 cups

Call it crazy, but there is a whole range of soft drink–based barbecue sauces in the land of barbecue. If you think about it, it's not really so strange, since it is a great way to get flavor and sugar into the sauce in one step. Root beer is not used very often—maybe because it isn't a staple in most people's pantry like Coke and Pepsi. But in my family, we drank root beer more than any other soda, probably because my father, Big Lou, loves it and would make us root beer floats when we were kids. Because I am continuing the tradition, root beer is very often the only "pop" (soda) I have in the house, so I make this sauce more than the others. I find that the sassafras-based soda is tailor-made for barbecued and grilled foods.

Good for Slathering: Pork ribs, pork tenderloin; chicken; beef ribs, brisket, chopped beef

Two 12-ounce cans root beer, preferably Dad's Old Fashioned Root Beer

1 cup Heinz Chili Sauce

1/4 cup ketchup

2 tablespoons molasses

2 tablespoons sherry vinegar

1 1/2 tablespoons soy sauce

1 tablespoon dark brown sugar

1 teaspoon kosher salt

1 teaspoon freshly ground pepper

3 vanilla beans, scraped, or 1 teaspoon real vanilla bean paste

1/2 teaspoon ground allspice

1/2 teaspoon ground coriander

1/2 teaspoon ground ginger

1/2 teaspoon ground anise

1. In a large, heavy-bottomed nonreactive saucepan, combine all the ingredients and gradually bring to a boil over medium heat. Reduce the heat and gently simmer the sauce until it is slightly reduced, 30 to 45 minutes. This is a thin basting sauce with a distinctive flavor, not a traditional thick tomato-based sauce.

2. Taste for seasoning, adjusting with more vinegar, salt, and pepper if desired. Let cool. The sauce will keep, tightly covered, in the refrigerator for up to 2 weeks. Serve at room temperature or gently reheat.

3. Brush it on food 5 to 15 minutes before the cooking time is finished. If desired, serve extra on the side.

Apricot-Mustard Barbecue Sauce

Makes about 2 1/4 cups

When you are in the mood for grilled food with a very different flavor profile from traditional barbecue sauce, this is like a ray of sunshine for anything that you put it on. I created this sauce for my sister Mary Pat, who loves apricots and fruit of any kind. The mustard tempers the sugar and turns it from a sweet to a savory sauce.

Good for Slathering: Pretzels; deviled eggs; pork; chicken pieces

> 2 cups dried Turkish apricots
> 1 cup apricot nectar, preferably Goya
> 1/2 cup Sauvignon Blanc
> Zest of 1 lemon
> 1 cinnamon stick, snapped in half
> 2 tablespoons light brown sugar
> 1 tablespoon rice vinegar
> 1/8 teaspoon sea salt
> 1/2 cup Dijon mustard
> 2 tablespoons yellow mustard
> 2 tablespoons Southern Comfort
> 1/4 teaspoon salt
> Pinch fine-ground white pepper

1. Put the apricots, nectar, wine, zest, cinnamon stick, sugar, vinegar, and sea salt in a large heavy-bottomed saucepan set over medium heat. Cover and bring to a boil; stir and reduce the heat. Let simmer for about 35, minutes until the apricots are soft enough to puree and the liquid is syrupy. If is too thin, remove the lid and let the liquid reduce. If the sauce is too thick, add 1/4 cup water or apricot nectar and continue cooking.

2. Remove from the heat and remove the cinnamon stick. Puree the mixture in a food processor or blender. Add the mustards, Southern Comfort, salt, and pepper. Process and mix well. Taste and adjust the seasonings as desired. Let cool. The sauce will keep, tightly covered, in the refrigerator for up to 2 weeks.

3. Brush it on food 5 to 15 minutes before the cooking time is finished. If desired, serve extra on the side.

Pumpkin Butter Barbecue Sauce

Makes about 2 1/2 cups

This is just the thing for a fall cookout. The rich sauce is filled with all the spices of fall and is as good on squash as it is on pork, chicken, or duck! You can make your own pumpkin butter very easily (see below) or use any local pumpkin butter—Trader Joe's makes a very good one, as do lots of local orchards and farms. It's actually fun to make and is a great hostess or holiday gift. If you use a purchased pumpkin butter, make sure that it is sweetened and well spiced with ginger, cinnamon, cloves, and nutmeg; otherwise you may need to adjust the sauce recipe accordingly.

Good for Slathering: Pork chops; turkey; beef ribs, steak; spaghetti squash

- 1 cup (2 sticks) unsalted butter
- 2 cups pumpkin butter
- 1 cup Laird's Applejack
- 2 tablespoons pure maple syrup
- 1/2 teaspoon ground allspice
- Pinch salt
- Freshly ground pepper

1. Melt the butter in a medium heavy-bottomed saucepan. Add the pumpkin butter and whisk until it is smooth. Add the applejack, mix until well combined, and add the maple syrup, allspice, salt, and pepper. Bring to a gentle boil, and then reduce the heat to a simmer. Cover and let cook for about 10 minutes or until the flavors meld. Taste and adjust the seasonings as desired. If it is too thin, add more pumpkin butter. If it is too thick, add a bit more applejack.

2. Transfer the sauce to a clean glass jar and let cool to room temperature. The sauce will keep, tightly covered, in the refrigerator for up to 2 days. Serve at room temperature or gently reheat.

3. Brush it on food 5 to 15 minutes before the cooking time is finished. If desired, serve extra on the side.

Pumpkin Butter

Makes about 6 cups

- Two 15-ounce cans pumpkin puree
- 1 cup apple juice
- 1 lemon, juiced
- 2 teaspoons ground ginger
- 1/2 generous teaspoon ground cloves
- 1/2 cup packed dark brown sugar
- 1/2 cup pure maple syrup
- 2 teaspoons ground cinnamon
- 1 teaspoon ground nutmeg
- 1/2 teaspoon sea salt
- 1/2 cup toasted pecan pieces, coarsely ground, optional

1. In a large heavy-bottomed saucepan, combine the pumpkin, apple juice, lemon juice, ginger, cloves, brown sugar, maple syrup, cinnamon, nutmeg, and salt; stir well. Bring the mixture to a gentle boil. Reduce the heat, and simmer for 30 minutes or until thickened. Stir frequently. Remove from the heat when thick enough. Taste and adjust the seasonings as desired and add the pecans, if desired.

2. Pour into canning jars, filling to within 1/4 inch of the tops. Remove air bubbles and wipe jar rims. Cover at once with metal lids and screw-on bands. If you are making this for future use, process the jars in a boiling-water bath for 10 minutes.

Note: This recipe can be halved.

Elvis Is in the House Sauce

Makes about 3 cups

When I first moved to Chicago, I worked with an Elvis-obsessed woman. I had met Elvis fans before—I've even been known to belt a few of his best choruses when I've been sipping on the grape—but this woman was a die-hard fan you had to see to believe. It should not have come as a surprise, then, that her contribution to the group Christmas party was grape jelly–glazed meatballs. I am not sure how Elvis became associated with this pass-a-long recipe, but it is reported that he loved grape jelly. Here's a sauce in honor of the King of Rock 'n' Roll and his excellent taste in comfort food! The grape jelly turns this sauce into a rockin' finale for a sweet-and-sour mixed grill that will make Memphis proud.

Good for Slathering: Meatballs, burgers; flank steak; kielbasa; pork chops; chicken wings

    One 12-ounce bottle Heinz Chili Sauce
    One 12-ounce jar Welch's grape jelly
    2 tablespoons yellow mustard
    2 tablespoons Worcestershire sauce
    1 teaspoon sea salt
    1 teaspoon freshly ground pepper
    Pinch granulated garlic
    1 tablespoon apple cider vinegar (optional)

1. In a medium heavy-bottomed saucepan over medium heat, combine the chili sauce and jelly. Stir occasionally until the jelly has melted and you can whisk the two together.

2. When the mixture is smooth and begins to bubble, add the mustard, Worcestershire sauce, salt, pepper, and garlic. Taste and adjust the seasoning if desired. If it is too sweet, add the vinegar. Let cool. The sauce will keep, tightly covered, in the refrigerator for up to 2 weeks.

3. Brush it on food 5 minutes before the cooking time is finished. If desired, serve extra on the side.

Spicy Love Apple Sauce

Makes about 2 cups

Did you know that it was once thought that tomatoes were aphrodisiacs? Well, it makes sense to me—there is nothing more sensual that an over-the-sink-juicy, vine-ripe-tomato sandwich! And do you know anyone who doesn't fall in love with barbecue? It could be all those tomatoes in the sauce! Here, I've combined fresh vine-ripened tomatoes and spicy apple butter as my ode to the love apple and the real apple. If you prefer, you can smoke the tomatoes on the grill before making the sauce.

This sauce is best made in late summer or early fall, when you still have gorgeous tomatoes bursting from the vine and fresh apple butter from local orchards. It's that time of year when summer meets autumn in perfect harmony.

Good for Slathering: Steak; veal, chicken; shrimp, scallops; veggies

5 to 6 large, vine-ripe summer tomatoes

10 to 12 cloves garlic, cut into slivers

2 to 3 tablespoons olive oil

Kosher salt

1 cup well-spiced apple butter

1 tablespoon unseasoned rice vinegar

1 teaspoon chili powder

1 teaspoon sweet smoked Spanish paprika

1/8 teaspoon chipotle chile powder

1. Preheat the oven to 275°F. Cut the core out of each tomato. In the core of each tomato, place about 2 cloves garlic, unless the cloves are very large; then use only 1 per tomato.

2. Place the tomatoes on a sheet pan fitted with a silicone liner or waxed paper. Drizzle the olive oil over the tomatoes and sprinkle with salt. Bake for 2 1/2 hours or more, depending on the size of the tomatoes. When the tomatoes are roasted and soft, remove from the oven.

3. Process the tomatoes one or two at a time through a food mill. Discard the skins and seeds and reserve the roasted tomato "sauce." This step can be done up to 3 days in advance.

4. Place the tomato "sauce" in a heavy-bottomed 4-quart saucepan over medium-low heat. Bring to a gentle simmer, and then add the apple butter. When the mixture is hot, whisk in the vinegar, chili powder, smoked paprika, chipotle powder, and a pinch of salt. Stirring frequently, bring to a gentle boil. Reduce the heat and let simmer for 5 to 10 minutes or until

thickened. Taste for seasoning and adjust if desired. The sauce will keep, tightly covered, in the refrigerator for up to 2 weeks.

5. Brush it on food 5 to 15 minutes before the cooking time is finished. If desired, serve extra on the side.

Three-in-One Mango Curry Sauce

Makes about 3 1/2 cups

This bright and sunny barbecue sauce is "just what the chef ordered" for fish and shellfish. Because this sauce is not cooked, it is important to use the freshest, most flavorful mangos that you can find. The versatile sauce will make you wish you had a mango tree in your yard. It can actually be used as a marinade, a basting sauce, and a dipping sauce.

Good for Slathering: Scallops, shrimp; lamb; chicken; pork tenderloin

4 ripe mangos, peeled and cut into pieces

1 large shallot, roughly chopped

1/2 cup mango juice (Odwalla makes a good one)

2 tablespoons unseasoned rice vinegar or sherry vinegar

2 to 3 tablespoons curry powder, to your taste

1 tablespoon agave nectar

1 tablespoon fresh cilantro, chopped

1/2 teaspoon ground coriander

1/2 teaspoon sea salt

1 cup macadamia or almond oil

1. Put the mango pieces, shallot, and mango juice in a blender and puree. When there are no more chunks of fruit or shallot, add the vinegar, curry powder, agave nectar, cilantro, coriander, and salt.

2. Slowly drizzle in the oil in stages as the blender is mixing on low speed. Do not add more oil until each batch is fully incorporated. Repeat until all the oil is incorporated into the sauce.

3. Taste and adjust the seasonings as desired. The sauce will keep, tightly covered, in the refrigerator for up to 3 days.

4. Brush it on food 5 to 15 minutes before the cooking time is finished. If desired, serve extra on the side.

Tikka Masala Sauce

Makes about 2 1/2 cups

This "Indian" dish was created in England for the British palate; the very popular but not authentic chicken tikka masala has actually been hailed as that country's national dish! It is so tasty that restaurant diners have demanded that the dish be made worldwide. And I am no different! If you read the introduction to this chapter, you already know how much I love this sauce. It is the perfect thing to brighten up a boneless skinless chicken breast and will "dress to impress" grilled shrimp, pork, and countless vegetables. I used to think that I could only have this exotic sauce in an Indian restaurant, but truth be told, it is one of the easiest pan sauces to make.

Good for Slathering: Grilled chicken; shrimp; pork; beef; vegetables

2 tablespoons clarified butter (ghee)

1 tablespoon olive oil

3/4 cup finely chopped white onion

3 cloves garlic, grated

1 small knob (1 inch) fresh ginger, peeled and grated

3 tablespoons tomato paste

2 teaspoons sweet smoked Spanish paprika

1 teaspoon ground cumin

1/2 teaspoon cayenne pepper

1 teaspoon sea salt

1/2 teaspoon ground turmeric

1/4 teaspoon ground cinnamon

1 1/2 cups canned crushed tomatoes

1/2 cup heavy whipping cream or sour cream

1. Heat the clarified butter and olive oil in a medium heavy-bottomed saucepan over medium heat. Sauté the onions until translucent. Add the garlic and ginger. Stir to combine, and continue sautéing until the garlic and ginger begin to turn golden.

2. Add the tomato paste, paprika, cumin, cayenne, salt, turmeric, and cinnamon. Sauté for a couple more minutes to "toast" the spices.

3. Add the crushed tomatoes. Bring to a boil; then reduce the heat and simmer for about 10 minutes. Stir in the cream. Continue to simmer over medium heat until the sauce is reduced and the consistency of thick gravy. The sauce will keep, tightly covered, in the refrigerator for up to 2 days.

4. To use: Toss food hot off the grill in the sauce, and serve.

Irish Hollow Hollandaise and Four Variations

Makes about 4 cups

Bill Barrick and Tony Kemp are dear friends who own a charming inn located in Galena, Illinois. Besides the natural beauty of the place and the gorgeous private cottages, it is the breakfast that has customers reserving years in advance. Bill and Tony are known for their sumptuous classic fare. And homemade hollandaise is a weekly feature. One weekend, I went to Galena to help the boys finish a couple of new cabins and got pressed into breakfast service. As I was making up 20 fruit plates, I watched Bill make a perfect blender hollandaise. It was foolproof and brilliant! Bill's trick to making it creamy is a little hot water—never fear a broken hollandaise again!

Good for Slathering: Asparagus; fish; chicken; veal; duck; poached eggs

13 egg yolks
1 pound (4 sticks) unsalted butter
1/4 cup fresh lemon juice (about 2 lemons)
1/2 teaspoon cayenne pepper
1 teaspoon fine-grain sea salt
1 to 3 tablespoons hot water, as needed

1. Put the egg yolks in a blender and process until creamy.

2. Melt the butter in a saucepan over low heat—do not let the solids separate from the liquid. (If that starts to happen, remove it from the heat immediately.) Add the lemon juice and cayenne to the melted butter. Bring the mixture to a boil.

3. Pour the hot butter mixture slowly over the egg yolks while the blender is running at medium speed. When smooth, add the salt and enough hot water to reach the desired texture. You may make this several hours in advance and hold it in a water bath in a warm oven. It will keep, tightly covered, in the refrigerator for up to 1 week. Reconstitute with a small amount of hot water and warm in a double boiler. Spoon over cooked food just before serving.

Béarnaise Variation

With the hot water, mix in 2 tablespoons chopped fresh tarragon leaves and 1 teaspoon tarragon vinegar.

Orange Béarnaise Variation

With the hot water, mix in 2 tablespoons chopped fresh tarragon leaves, 2 teaspoons fresh orange juice, and the zest of 1 large orange.

Cucumber Hollandaise Variation

With the hot water, mix in 1 cup of peeled and chopped seedless cucumbers and 1 teaspoon of rice wine vinegar.

French Mustard Variation (Mustard Sauce)

With the hot water, mix in 2 tablespoons strong Dijon mustard, 2 teaspoons Colman's dry mustard, 1/2 teaspoon ground white pepper, and substitute 1/3 cup fresh lemon juice for the sherry vinegar.

Mother's Cheese Sauce

Makes 1 cup

Talk about a mother sauce! This is the cheese sauce that my mother, Lynn, made at least once a week when my sisters and I were kids. She initially made this sharp cheddar cheese sauce to get us to eat our veggies—especially broccoli. It is based on a traditional white sauce—meaning once you master it, you can add all kinds of flavoring ingredients. We soon discovered that this simple but rich sauce is great on all kinds of food. A little leftover cheese sauce makes the best cheeseburger as the heat of the burger warms up the sauce and makes it all soft and melty.

Good for Slathering: Steak, cheese-steak sandwiches, burgers; chicken; ham; veggies

3 tablespoons unsalted butter
3 tablespoons all-purpose flour
1 teaspoon dry mustard, preferably Colman's
1/4 teaspoon sea salt
1/8 teaspoon fine-ground white pepper
1 3/4 cups whole milk, plus more as needed
1 cup grated sharp cheddar cheese
Tabasco sauce

1. Melt the butter in a heavy-bottomed sauté pan. When it begins to bubble, sprinkle in the flour and stir with a wooden spoon. Continue stirring and cooking until the flour is golden and no longer raw. At this point, you have made a roux.

2. Blend in the dry mustard, salt, and pepper, stirring until the mixture is smooth and bubbling.

3. Slowly add the milk, mixing it into the roux until it is smooth and there are no lumps. Bring to a boil for 1 to 2 minutes or until it begins to thicken. Continue cooking for 5 to 10 more minutes to thicken. If it is too thick, add a little more milk. When the sauce is thickened to the desired consistency, add the cheese and Tabasco and let the cheese melt while stirring it into the white sauce. Taste for seasonings and adjust if necessary.

4. Spoon over cooked food just before serving.

Note: The key to this sauce is making a roux, or sauce base, made with flour and fat—usually butter. To make the roux, melt the desired amount butter in a sauté pan. Add an equal amount of flour and cook, stirring, until the flour is golden and the butter and flour are incorporated into a paste. You can keep this roux in a clean glass jar in the refrigerator for 1 to 2 months.

Beer-Cheese Sauce Variation

Beer-cheese soup is popular in the Midwest, and though I don't love it as a soup, I love it in this sauce! Use 1 cup of milk and 2/3 cup of beer for the liquid. You need to use a full-flavored beer, as light beer won't deliver enough flavor.

Rich White Sauce Variation

Use half-and-half or heavy cream instead of the milk. You can also do this for the cheese sauce, but be forewarned that it will be very rich.

Blue Cheese Sauce Variation

Use 1/2 cup sharp white cheddar and 1/2 cup French Roquefort or Danish blue cheese.

Four-Cheese Sauce Variation

Experiment with a combination of cheeses for a more sophisticated cheese sauce that can be the basis of a killer homemade mac and cheese. I like combining sharp cheddar, parmesan cheese, Gruyère, and fontina.

Smoked Tomato Sauce

Makes about 2 cups

This sauce in classic French cooking is called a coulis. Though it sounds fancy, *coulis* simply refers to a fruit or vegetable sauce that is strained. Tomatoes are the perfect vegetable for a coulis because they have a soft texture with a high liquid-to-solid ratio and can be easily strained. Smoking the tomatoes gives them a rich depth, for a simple but elegant sauce.

Good for Slathering: Grilled fish, shellfish; steak; grilled vegetables; savory pancakes

Grilling Method: Indirect/Medium-Low Heat

> 6 large, ripe (but still firm) tomatoes
> 2 large shallots, cut in half
> 3 tablespoons extra-virgin olive oil, plus extra for coating tomatoes
> Kosher salt
> 2 tablespoons red wine vinegar
> 1 tablespoon sweet smoked Spanish paprika
> 1/2 teaspoon fleur de sel

1. Build a charcoal fire or preheat a gas grill. Core the tomatoes; coat the tomatoes and shallots lightly with olive oil and season with salt. Place in the center of the cooking grate and let grill for 1 hour or until the tomatoes and shallots are soft and the skins are bursting. You can also grill-smoke the tomatoes and shallots in a shallow disposable aluminum tray to catch any juices that escape during cooking. Alternatively, you can smoke the tomatoes and shallots in a Cameron Stovetop Smoker. Remove from the grill.

2. While the tomatoes and shallots are still warm, place in a blender and puree. When the vegetables are liquefied, add the vinegar, the 3 tablespoons olive oil, paprika, and fleur de sel and blend until smooth. Taste and adjust the seasonings if desired. Remove from the blender and process through a food mill or or fine-mesh strainer to remove the large pieces, seeds, and skins.

3. The strained flavorful liquid is the sauce. It will keep, tightly covered, in the refrigerator for up to 1 week.

4. Spoon over cooked food just before serving. If desired, serve extra on the side.

Meyer Lemon Butter Sauce

Makes 1 cup

This sauce is an updated take on the classic French beurre blanc butter sauce. Think about how delicious Dover sole and asparagus are when they are served with this sauce; quite frankly, cardboard would taste good slathered with this sauce. I don't make it very often, but it is my secret weapon when I want to make a "nice" dinner. I think of it as my string-of-pearls sauce! You can drizzle it on the plate and over any grilled meat or vegetable and your dish will be elevated to black-tie status. The sweet-sour Meyer lemon cuts the richness of the butter for a sauce that presents itself as light and elegant.

Good for Slathering: Grilled fish, sole, crab, lobster, scallops; asparagus

2 large Meyer lemons

1 large shallot, minced

1/4 cup dry white wine

1 tablespoon heavy whipping cream

1 cup (2 sticks) cold unsalted butter, cut into cubes

Dash Tabasco or your favorite hot sauce, optional

Fine-grain sea salt and fine-ground white pepper

Zest of 1 Meyer lemon

2 to 6 teaspoons minced fresh curly parsley or other herbs

1. Cut the rind off the lemons and slice into 1/4-inch-thick slices. Combine the shallot, wine, and lemon slices in a small saucepan. Bring to a boil. When the lemons break down and the liquid is reduced, add the cream and whisk it until it is incorporated. This addition of the cream will help prevent the sauce from breaking. Next start adding the butter, cube by cube. Whisk continually. When the first cube of butter is almost melted, add another, and so on. Repeat until all of the butter is incorporated.

2. Add the dash of Tabasco if desired, a pinch of salt, and a few grinds of pepper.

3. While the mixture is still warm, strain through a fine-mesh strainer. Mix in the lemon zest and herbs. Use immediately, or keep in a pitcher in a warm water bath. If it breaks, you can reincorporate by whisking in a little heavy cream or by using an immersion blender.

4. Spoon over cooked food just before serving. If desired, serve extra on the side.

Note: Once you master this sauce, you can add different flavors to it. I love adding fresh and dried herbs, such as a few teaspoons of minced tarragon or basil.

Green Peppercorn Variation

Substitute 3 tablespoons champagne or white wine vinegar for the lemon slices. Substitute 3 tablespoons brandy for the wine. Stir in 1 tablespoon of Dijon mustard before adding the cream and butter. Substitute 1/2 cup heavy cream for half the butter (you will use 1 stick of butter and 1/2 cup of cream) and add it in after the butter has been completely incorporated. Stir in 1 to 2 tablespoons brine-packed green peppercorns that have been drained and the excess moisture pressed out. This sauce is also good with 1 teaspoon of dried tarragon.

Smoked Paprika Variation

Substitute 3 tablespoons sherry vinegar for the lemon slices and whisk in 1 tablespoon smoked sweet paprika at the end, eliminating the parsley or other herbs.

Pan "Duck" Sauce

Makes about 1 cup

There is nothing Asian about this classic cassis sauce for duck, but I couldn't resist the playful name! This sauce is my take on my friend Bob Blumer's signature pan sauce. Since I am always grilling rather than pan-frying duck, I don't have the flavorful liquids and bits of meat at the bottom of the pan to reduce and turn into a simple sauce. Thus I've created a technique of caramelizing shallots and sugar to take the place of the browned bits of meat. This trick is a great way for grillers and vegetarians alike to make simple pan sauces to accompany their main dishes.

Good for Slathering: Duck, chicken, quail; dilute for a great marinade

- 1 tablespoon unsalted butter
- 1 tablespoon olive oil
- 4 shallots, minced
- 1 tablespoon light brown sugar
- 1 tablespoon sugar
- 1 teaspoon sea salt
- 1/4 cup crème de cassis
- 1/4 cup balsamic vinegar
- 1/2 cup no-sugar-added black currant black cherry, boysenberry, or similar berry jam
- 1 teaspoon coarsely ground pepper

1. Place a medium heavy-bottomed sauté pan over medium heat. Put the butter and oil in the pan and slowly melt the butter as the pan heats up. Stir together and add the shallots. Let the shallots cook for 2 minutes, stirring to make sure that the shallots are coated with the butter-oil mixture. Add the sugars and stir to ensure even coating. Watch the pan closely and let cook until the sugar has darkened (caramelized) and the shallots are soft and brown on the edges, 5 to 7 minutes. Add the salt and stir to combine.

2. Increase the heat to medium-high, and when the sugar begins to bubble, turn the heat off and pour in the cassis, whisking continually.

3. Turn the heat to medium and add the vinegar. Stir continually, loosening up any browned bits of shallot or caramelized sugar. Add the jam and pepper, and stir occasionally for 2 to 3 minutes or until warmed through. Remove from the heat and use immediately.

4. Spoon over cooked food just before serving. If desired, serve extra on the side.

Shortcut Sauce Nantua

Makes about 3 cups with the crayfish

When I lived in New Orleans, my favorite Sunday brunch meal was eggs Nantua. I got this poached egg dish for the sauce alone, which was swollen with big, fat, spillway crayfish. The eggs were almost forgotten as I picked through the sauce and ate the crayfish one by one. I soon realized that I could do this at home and serve it with many foods.

For traditional sauce Nantua, chefs cook down the crayfish heads until they are red, grind them, and make a stock with sautéed garlic, onions, celery, and carrots. I've eliminated the time-consuming nature of the classic sauce and cook the crayfish right in the sauce to get the approximate flavor.

Good for Slathering: Grilled fish, shellfish; chicken; veal paillards; eggs; cheese grits; rice; pasta

> 2 tablespoons unsalted butter
> 2 tablespoons all-purpose flour
> 1 large shallot, chopped
> 1 cup shellfish or chicken stock
> 1/2 cup dry white wine
> 2 tablespoons tomato puree or paste
> 2 tablespoons Cognac
> 1/2 cup heavy whipping cream
> Pinch dried thyme
> 1/2 teaspoon sweet Hungarian paprika
> 1/2 to 1 teaspoon sea salt
> Pinch cayenne pepper
> 1 pound crayfish, thawed if frozen

1. Melt the butter in a heavy-bottomed sauté pan over medium heat. When the butter begins to bubble, sprinkle in the flour and stir with a whisk or blending fork. Add the shallot and continue stirring and cooking until the flour is golden and no longer raw, about 7 minutes. This is a roux.

2. Gradually add the stock and wine, stirring after each little bit is added until it is all incorporated. Add the tomato paste, Cognac, cream, thyme, paprika, salt, cayenne, and crayfish. Stir gently until the mixture begins to thicken, 10 to 15 minutes. Use immediately.

3. Spoon over cooked food just before serving. If desired, serve extra on the side.

Nutty Browned Butter Sauce

Makes about 1/2 cup

Browned butter is easy to make, and you can use whatever nuts you like. My favorites are pecans, hazelnuts, and slivered almonds, but pistachios and macadamia nuts are delicious as well. The sauce can be made in advance and gently reheated just before serving.

Good for Slathering: Firm white fish (swordfish, tilapia, sturgeon); veal chops; chicken

> 1/2 cup (1 stick) unsalted butter
> 1 cup pecan, hazelnut, or almond pieces
> 1/2 teaspoon fleur de sel or sea salt
> 1/8 teaspoon fine-ground white pepper

1. Put the butter in a cold sauté pan. Over medium-low heat, slowly melt the butter. Add the nuts, stirring occasionally as they brown.

2. Season with the salt and white pepper. You will need to watch the pan closely, as the butter can burn very quickly.

3. When the butter reaches the desired color (dark caramel) remove from the heat, cover, and set aside. Either keep warm or gently reheat before using. Best made the day you want to use it.

4. Spoon over cooked food just before serving. If desired, serve extra on the side.

Nantucket Swordfish with Browned Butter and Sautéed Pecans

Serves 4

Grilling Method: Direct/Medium Heat

> 4 center-cut swordfish steaks, about 1 inch thick
> Olive oil
> Sea salt
> Fine-ground white pepper
> 1 recipe Nutty Browned Butter Sauce (left)

1. Build a charcoal fire or preheat a gas grill.

2. Brush the fish steaks on both sides with oil. Season with salt and pepper. Place on the cooking grate and grill for about 5 minutes on each side or until the fish is opaque and releases easily from the grill.

3. Remove from the grill and to a clean platter. Top with the sauce, and serve immediately.

Fresh Herb Oil Infusion

Makes 1/2 cup

It's no secret that good home cooks (and cookbook writers) get some of their best ideas from eating in restaurants. Vibrantly colored and brilliantly fresh herb-infused oils are used by chefs all over the world, and they are easier to make than a smoothie! In restaurants, chefs often add a step, quickly blanching (briefly boiling) herbs and plunging them in an ice bath before pureeing them with oil. This helps preserve the vibrant green color, which is important since we eat with our eyes before we taste with our palates. If you go the extra step, make sure the herbs are dry before pureeing them with the oil.

Good for Slathering: Grilled fish; chicken; vegetables; stir into risotto; use to decorate plates

> 1 to 2 cups fresh herbs, such as parsley, basil, chives, cilantro, chervil, sorrel, tarragon, or arugula (almost any green herb will work)
>
> 1 cup best-quality extra-virgin olive oil or untoasted nut oil like hazelnut, macadamia, or walnut
>
> Pinch fine-grain sea salt

1. Place half of the herbs in a blender with about 1/3 cup of the oil and the salt. Puree and taste. Based on the taste, add the rest of the herbs and the rest of the oil as desired.

2. Allow the puree to sit for 30 minutes. Strain through cheesecloth into a plastic squeeze bottle. Discard the solids. The infusion is best used the day you make it but will keep refrigerated for up to 2 days, but the color of the herbs will darken.

3. Brush, spoon or squirt on cooked food just before serving. If desired, serve extra on the side.

Cherry-Chile Steak Sauce

Makes about 1 1/4 cups

The fruitiness of ancho chilies has always reminded me of dried cherries, and in fact one of my signature desserts is a bittersweet chocolate brownie with dried cherries and ancho chilies. Maybe you could say that this steak sauce was inspired by chocolate, cherries, and chilies—a combination that is hard to beat whether in a sauce or a brownie! It's so good that I suggest doubling the recipe to keep the sauce on hand.

Good for Slathering: Steak; pork loin; venison

> 4 dried ancho chilies, stemmed and seeded
>
> 1/8 cup unsweetened dried cherries
>
> 7 cloves garlic, peeled
>
> 1/4 cup Worcestershire sauce
>
> 1 teaspoon freshly ground pepper
>
> 1/4 teaspoon ground cumin
>
> 2/3 to 1 cup beef broth
>
> 3 tablespoons olive oil
>
> 1 cup cherry juice or cider or cherry-pomegranate juice
>
> 2 tablespoons red wine vinegar

2 teaspoons dark brown sugar

2 teaspoons unsweetened cocoa powder

1 teaspoon salt

1. In a small bowl, cover the chilies and cherries with boiling water and let sit for 30 to 40 minutes, stirring occasionally to ensure that all the chilies are under the water. Drain and discard the water.

2. Combine the garlic, Worcestershire sauce, pepper, and cumin in a food processor or blender. Puree and add the drained chilies and 2/3 cup of the broth. If the puree is too dry, add more broth. Blend to a smooth puree.

3. Heat the oil in a 4-quart heavy-bottomed saucepan. When the oil is hot, add the chile puree and stir constantly until it bubbles and resembles a paste, 4 to 5 minutes. Stir in the cherry juice and vinegar. Cover and let simmer for 20 minutes. Remove the cover, add the sugar, cocoa powder, and salt, and simmer, stirring occasionally, for about another 25 minutes. If the sauce is too thick, add more broth or cherry juice to thin it out. You want it to be the thickness of steak sauce. Taste and adjust the seasoning if desired with salt and/or vinegar. The sauce will keep, tightly covered, in the refrigerator for up to 2 weeks.

4. Spoon over cooked food just before serving. If desired, serve extra on the side.

New York Grill Steak Sauce

Makes 4 cups

The best meal that I had in Tokyo was at the New York Grill at the Park Hyatt Hotel. Situated on the top floor of the Park Hyatt, it is a restaurant so high that on clear days you can see hundreds of miles away to Mount Fuji. It was here that I had my first and only taste of true Kobe beef. I had seen the lavishly marbled raw cuts earlier in the day and, interestingly enough, the cooked meat actually tasted lighter and less rich than its leaner American cousin. All of these fine marbled steaks come from the Wagyu cow. Kobe is the most famous region that raises these cows, but you can find many other variations from many other towns—all Wagyu, not Kobe. It reminded me of the way that wine is categorized in France by regions instead of by grape. My steak was grilled simply with a little salt (see the Grilling Trilogy, page 10) and served with this sauce on the side.

Good for Slathering: Steak, prime rib; burgers

> 1/4 cup olive oil
>
> 1 1/4 cups diced white onions
>
> 2/3 cup diced carrots
>
> 1/3 cup peeled and diced celery
>
> 1 tablespoon chopped garlic
>
> 3 1/2 tablespoons tamarind paste
>
> 1/3 cup anchovies

3 tablespoons molasses

6 whole cloves

1 bay leaf

1/3 cup packed brown sugar

1/3 cup sugar

2 1/3 cups balsamic vinegar, divided

2/3 cup sherry vinegar

One 750-ml bottle red wine

8 cups veal or beef stock

1. In a large sauté pan, heat the olive oil and sauté the onions, carrots, celery, and garlic. Add the tamarind paste, anchovies, molasses, cloves, and bay leaf. Let cook for 5 minutes or until the onions are translucent. Add 1/3 cup of the balsamic vinegar to deglaze the pan. Stir to dislodge any browned bits and set aside.

2. Cook the sugars in a sauté pan until browned (caramelized). Deglaze the pan with the remaining balsamic vinegar and sherry vinegar and reduce by two-thirds. Add the red wine, and reduce by half. Put the stock in a large pot and add the vinegar-wine reduction and the reduced vegetables to the stock.

3. Simmer sauce until it is again reduced by half. When the sauce is still hot, strain it through cheesecloth or a fine-mesh strainer. Let the sauce cool for about 10 minutes or until it is warm but no longer "boiling" hot. The sauce will keep, tightly covered, in the refrigerator for up to 2 weeks.

4. Spoon over cooked food just before serving. If desired, serve extra on the side.

Merlot Wine Steak Sauce

Makes about 3 3/4 cups

I have my good friend Sarah Powers to thank for this recipe. Sarah introduced me to St. Francis Reserve Merlot, the wine that changed my mind about Merlots and got me to give this wine its due respect. I had wrongly looked at Merlot as thin and not so flavorful. The wine is full of plums and berries and rich spice, and it is the perfect liquid complement to grilled red meat and any other big-flavored meals. This recipe for steak sauce reflects all my favorite flavors from the wine. I like drizzling a little on the plate before I place the steak on the plate to rest before serving; it soaks up the sauce as the meat rests.

Good for Slathering: Steak; Berkshire pork chops; venison; duck

4 cups Merlot

1/2 cup balsamic vinegar

1/2 cup Worcestershire sauce

2 tablespoons fig or pomegranate molasses

1 cup packed light brown sugar

1 cup dried plums, cut into quarters

1/2 cup dried unsweetened cherries

1 teaspoon whole cloves

1 teaspoon whole black peppercorns

Pinch salt

1/2 cup (1 stick) unsalted butter, cut into pieces

1. In a heavy saucepan, combine the wine, vinegar, Worcestershire sauce, molasses, and brown sugar and bring to a boil. Reduce the heat and simmer for about 30 minutes or until the liquid is reduced by half, to 2 1/2 to 3 cups. Add the dried plums, dried cherries, cloves, peppercorns, and salt. Reduce the heat and simmer gently for 5 to 10 more minutes. At this stage, watch carefully that the sauce does not thicken too much, or it will resemble toffee instead of a thick sauce. Be careful not to overcook, as the sauce burns easily.

2. Strain the sauce through a fine-mesh strainer or pick out the peppercorns and cloves by hand. (The liquid should be very dark in color and syrupy, and not have a strong winey aroma.) Taste for seasoning and adjust if desired. Pour the strained sauce back into the pan, and gradually incorporate the cold butter, piece by piece, waiting until the first piece is fully incorporated before adding the next. Stir to combine. If you want a smoother sauce, puree until smooth (but I love the chunky texture of leaving the fruit in pieces).

3. Let the sauce cool for about 10 minutes or until it is warm but no longer "boiling" hot. The sauce will keep, tightly covered, in the refrigerator for up to 1 week.

4. Spoon over cooked food just before serving. If desired, serve extra on the side.

Jack Daniel's Steak Sauce

Makes about 2 cups

I couldn't write a sauce chapter without featuring Jack Daniel's, since it is one of my favorite sauces to hit! Kidding aside, we all know that bourbon makes anything taste better, and although Jack Daniel's is not technically considered bourbon (contrary to what most people think, you don't have to be in Bourbon County, Kentucky, to officially be called bourbon), this fine Tennessee sipping whiskey is just the thing to turn a simple sauce into a stately steak sauce.

Good for Slathering: Beef (prime rib or flank or skirt steak); chicken

- 2 tablespoons olive oil
- 1/2 cup chopped white or yellow onion
- 1 tablespoon dark brown sugar
- 1 tablespoon sweet smoked Spanish paprika
- 1 tablespoon sweet Hungarian paprika
- 2 teaspoons dry mustard, preferably Colman's
- 1 teaspoon kosher salt
- 1/2 teaspoon chili powder
- Pinch cayenne pepper
- 2 tablespoons Worcestershire sauce
- 1 cup Coca-Cola or other cola
- 1 cup Spicy Hot V8 juice
- 3/4 cup ketchup
- 1/4 cup Jack Daniel's
- 1/4 cup rice vinegar
- 1 tablespoon low-sodium soy sauce

1. Heat the oil in a large heavy-bottomed saucepan over medium heat. Add the onion and stir to coat with the oil. Add the sugar and stir again. Cook for 2 to 3 minutes or until the onions and sugar begin to darken in color and caramelize, stirring occasionally.

2. Add both of the paprikas, the dry mustard, salt, chili powder, and cayenne. Stir until the spices are well mixed, and let them toast in the pan. When the onions are soft and the spices are fragrant, add the Worcestershire sauce, cola, V8, ketchup, Jack Daniel's, vinegar, and soy sauce.

3. Let simmer over medium-low heat for about 15 minutes or until thickened. If you want a smooth texture, strain through a fine-mesh strainer. You can also use an immersion blender to blend the sauce. Let the sauce cool for about 10 minutes or until it is warm but no longer "boiling" hot. The sauce will keep, tightly covered, in the refrigerator for up to 1 week.

4. Spoon over cooked food just before serving. If desired, serve extra on the side.

Mushroom Ragoût

Makes about 2 cups

It's no secret how much I love mushrooms. (For example, this sauce is enough for four regular people or one mushroom lover like me!) Lucky for me, my good friend and associate Kirsten Newman-Teissier lives right next to the largest mushroom farm in America—most mushrooms are cultivated in controlled farms, not foraged from the woods. A few years ago, we took a fascinating tour of the Kennett Specialties Farm in Kennett Square, Pennsylvania. The best part of the day was picking our own mushrooms to take home by the case. We immediately canceled all our dinner reservations and cooked every conceivable mushroom dish for the next three days. This mushroom ragoût was my favorite. We served it alongside a simple grilled steak. For the best caramelization, use a seasoned cast-iron pan.

Good for Slathering: Steak; pork; chicken; serve as a side dish for anything, such as pasta

2 pounds assorted mushrooms, such as shiitake, hen of the woods, chanterelle, morel, king oyster, baby bellas, reconstituted dried porcini, etc.

2 tablespoons extra-virgin olive oil

2 tablespoons unsalted butter

1/4 teaspoon plus 1 pinch kosher salt

2 cloves garlic, grated

1 small shallot, grated

1/4 teaspoon dried ground thyme, or 1 teaspoon fresh thyme leaves

1/2 cup cream sherry

1/2 cup crème fraîche (see below)

1 to 2 teaspoons truffle oil

Sea salt

Freshly ground pepper

Fresh thyme leaves or chopped fresh parsley, for garnish

1. Trim the ends of the mushrooms and slice them into large pieces. Be creative—you want to be able to see the shape of the mushrooms, and some of them will lend themselves to slices and some will be easy to cut into chunks. Set aside.

2. Heat a large cast-iron skillet or heavy-bottomed sauté pan over medium heat. Add the oil and butter and the pinch of kosher salt. Let the butter melt and then stir to combine. Add the garlic, shallot, the 1/4 teaspoon kosher salt, and the thyme to the pan and stir. Cook without stirring for 2 minutes. Add the mushrooms and sauté over medium-high heat until well caramelized on both sides, 7 to 10 minutes.

3. Pour in the sherry and stir to scrape up any browned bits and deglaze the pan. Cook for another 3 to 4 minutes or until the liquid has reduced a bit and the mushrooms have absorbed the sherry. Remove from the heat and quickly stir in the crème fraîche and the truffle oil. Add sea salt and pepper to taste. Serve immediately, garnished with the thyme.

4. Spoon over cooked food just before serving. If desired, serve extra on the side.

Homemade Crème Fraîche
Makes about 3 cups

Crème fraîche can be used in so many ways, enriching sauces or as a sauce on its own (try dipping strawberries in it). Homemade is not only better tasting than store-bought, but it is also less expensive and a fun at-home science experiment. You'll just need to plan to make it several days before you need it.

> 4 cups heavy whipping cream
> 2 tablespoons buttermilk

Pour the cream into a clean glass jar with a lid. Add the buttermilk, shake gently, and close the lid. Place the jar in the warmest part of your house (e.g., on top of the refrigerator) and let sit for 2 to 3 days, until thickened. When the cream has cultured and thickened, use immediately, or refrigerate for up to 2 weeks. Spoon over cooked or raw food just before serving.

Speedy Amatrici-Style Sauce
Makes about 2 1/2 cups

Once you make this sauce, you will find yourself making it over and over again. The combination of smoked peppered bacon, red chile flakes, and tomatoes make an Italian-style sauce that tastes like you slaved all day when it only took you five minutes—this is a great sauce to keep in your entertaining arsenal!

Good for Slathering: Grilled double-cut veal or pork chops; pasta with grilled pork, chicken, shrimp, or veggies; use as a sauce for grilled pizza

> 8 slices center-cut bacon, chopped, preferably Nueske's pepper-crusted bacon
> 2 tablespoons extra-virgin olive oil, divided
> One 14.5-ounce can chopped tomatoes, any flavor
> 1 clove garlic, minced or grated
> 1/2 teaspoon red chile flakes
> Sea salt and freshly ground pepper

1. Preheat an 8-inch skillet over medium-high heat for 1 to 2 minutes. Add the bacon and a little of the oil. Cook, stirring, to brown the bacon and render the fat.

2. Add the tomatoes and cook, stirring, until warmed through, then add the garlic, red chile flakes, and the rest of the oil. Simmer for another minute, then remove from the heat.

3. Season to taste with salt and pepper and let cool before using. The sauce will keep, tightly covered, in the refrigerator for up to 3 days.

4. Spoon over cooked food just before serving. If desired, serve extra on the side.

Thanksgiving Pan Gravy

Makes about 2 cups

Every November, the thought of making gravy puts fear in the heart of American cooks! Gravy is so important on Thanksgiving Day, even to those who don't touch gravy any other day of the year. Inevitably, as the meal is being prepared, the host or hostess asks a guest to be the "gravy-maker" to whip up a gravy on the spot, forgetting that you need either pan drippings or the broth from turkey giblets that have simmered for hours.

My "gravy-maker" friend Sharon Franke gets chosen every year to make or "fix" the gravy. Because she anticipates this happening and she doesn't want to have to perform "under fire," she keeps a batch of gravy on reserve. Twenty minutes before dinner is served, when the Great Gravy Panic has set in, she calmly goes out to her car and retrieves her expert gravy. Once she reheats it, she's the hero of the day, and the guests can't believe how she made such a great gravy in minutes! This recipe relies on white wine for a flavor boost.

Good for Slathering: Grilled turkey, chicken

> Giblets, neck bone, and back from turkey
> 2 stalks celery with leaves, cut into 2-inch pieces
> 1 small onion, cut into eighths
> 2 to 3 cups chicken stock or water
> 1/4 cup Wondra flour
> 1/2 cup (1 stick) unsalted butter
> 1/2 cup white wine
> Kosher salt and freshly ground pepper

1. Preheat the oven to 400°F. Put the neck bone, giblets, and back in a roasting pan and roast for 30 minutes or until browned.

2. Put the turkey parts in a large saucepan with the celery and onion and 2 cups of chicken stock. If the liquid is too low, add more chicken stock. Let simmer, covered for 1 1/2 hours.

3. Strain through a fine-mesh strainer into a large bowl. Discard the vegetables. If you want a chunky gravy, pick the meat off the bones, chop the meat and giblets very fine, and set aside. If you don't want a chunky gravy, discard the turkey parts.

4. Mix the Wondra with a small amount of the cold chicken stock to make a slurry and set aside (this will prevent the flour from clumping). Melt the butter in a sauté pan over medium heat, add a little of the chicken stock and the flour "slurry," and whisk for 3 to 5 minutes, until the flour is browned. Stir in the wine and the giblet liquid. Add the chicken stock a little at a time. Add a little more of the giblet liquid until the consistency is smooth and thick. Season to taste with salt and pepper.

5. Add the finely chopped turkey giblets and meat if using. The gravy will keep, tightly covered, in the refrigerator for up to 3 days. Reheat before using. Spoon over cooked food just before serving. If desired, serve extra on the side.

GLAZES

Thin sauces with a high sugar content that are brushed on food for flavor and a glossy finish during the final minutes of the cooking time or just as the food is removed from the grill.

Glazes 101

RAPID-FIRE CHECKLIST

○ Glazes give a glossy sheen to cooked food and add subtle flavor.
○ Melted jam is a glaze in its simplest form and works for sweet and savory foods.
○ If you don't have a fine-mesh strainer, place cheesecloth in a colander.
○ Brush glaze on food at the end of the cooking time or as soon as the food comes off the grill.
○ Use a silicone brush for best results and easy cleaning.
○ Most glazes are best made the day they are used.

My earliest memory of making a glaze—or helping to make a glaze—was when my mother made a Julia Child's French apple tart for my sister's birthday. I got the job of straining the bits of apricot out of the apricot jam. The resulting smooth jam was heated just enough to melt, and then it was brushed on the top of the tart, enrobing each apple slice in a glossy glaze of sweet-tart jam that protected the apples as they cooked and made the tart glisten.

But jam isn't just for sweets; it makes a great glaze for savory foods as well. You can use your favorite jam to glaze any fruit or meat, and the good news is that since we are grilling, you can leave in the bits of fruit. Just heat your favorite jam or jelly to a liquid consistency and brush away. To balance the sweet notes for savory foods you can thin it out with your favorite vinegar—I particularly like using rice vinegar.

Glazes work well when you want a hint of flavor but you don't want the strong presence of a sauce. Glazes generally have a high proportion of sugar or some kind of oil or fat that will give a shiny appearance to the top of the food. It is important to brush on a sweet glaze only during the final cooking time so that it doesn't burn—the last 5 to 10 minutes or as soon as the food is removed from the grill.

A glaze can be as simple as a brush of olive oil, coconut milk or heavy cream, or melted jam. The purpose of the glaze is to give a sheen to the food, seal in all the flavors, and then with the more robust glazes, contribute to the overall flavor of the food with a first taste that reflects the brightness, sweetness, or savoriness of the glaze. The classic sweet glaze is melted and

strained jam. Jams and jellies are all good additions to glazes because the sugar and pectin give your food a glossy "lacquered" sheen. Glazes are very versatile; you can put them on the food during the final minutes of cooking time or brush them on the food as soon as it comes off the grill, or just before serving. Next Thanksgiving, try melting the traditional canned cranberry sauce roll and glazing your turkey—not only is it gorgeous but delicious as well.

Most cooked glazes should be used shortly after they are made. The noncooked glazes, like the Savory Glaze 101: Sweet and Spicy BBQ Glaze (page 126), can be made a few days in advance and kept covered in the refrigerator.

I love using sweeter, tarter glazes on fattier cuts of meat like duck, pork shoulder, and pork belly because the tartness cuts through the natural richness and the sweetness adds a complementary flavor dimension. For an unusual taste experience, try a slow-cooked brisket glazed with the Red-Eye Gravy Glaze (page 130). The slightly bittersweet and salty coffee and molasses–rich glaze balances the rich beefy brisket that is barbecued until the fat cap (the layer of fat that is on the top of the brisket) is rendered out (melts off) and the meat is crispy.

Glaze Tip

When I use a glaze, I always brush the food with a generous amount of fresh glaze as soon as I take the food off the grill. The glaze will set as the food rests and it adds a fresh uncooked layer of flavor to the food. For best results, use a silicone brush.

Plastic Squeeze Bottles

Just like for sauces, a plastic squeeze bottle is just the thing for squirting and storing glazes and reductions.

Shelf Life

Most glazes are best made the day they are used. Any glaze that uses jam or jelly and is melted needs to be made just before using and brushed on while still warm and in a liquid state. Glazes that can be made in advance should be stored in a clean class jar with a tight-fitting lid in the refrigerator. If necessary, warm or bring to room temperature before serving.

Savory Glaze 101: Sweet and Spicy BBQ Glaze

Makes about 1/2 cup

Thinner than a traditional barbecue sauce, thicker and sweeter than a mop, this sauce will make your ribs, chicken, or pork chop picture-perfect and finger-lickin' good!

Good for Slathering: Chicken; pork, ribs; shrimp

- 1/4 cup apple cider vinegar
- 2 teaspoons your favorite barbecue dry rub, finely ground
- 1 tablespoon ketchup
- 1 1/4 teaspoons yellow mustard
- 1 tablespoon honey
- 1/4 to 1/3 cup vegetable oil

In a nonreactive bowl, whisk together the vinegar, dry rub, ketchup, mustard, and honey until well mixed. Slowly add the vegetable oil until it is completely incorporated and balances the vinegar. To use the glaze, brush it on meat 20 minutes before the cooking time is finished. If desired, serve extra on the side.

Note: If you choose a rub that doesn't have salt in it, you will need to add salt; otherwise it should be seasoned well enough.

Sweet Glaze 101: Ginger-Honey Glaze

Makes about 3/4 cup

Sweet from the honey but full of spicy ginger, this glaze is just the thing for brushing on grilled fruit when you want to add a touch of sweetness but not mask the delicious natural flavors—I use it all summer long.

Good for Slathering: Grilled pineapple, mango, peaches; grilled vanilla or chocolate pound cake, gingerbread

- 1 cup honey
- 2/3 cup diced crystallized ginger
- 2 teaspoons fresh lemon juice
- Zest of 1/2 lemon
- Pinch salt

1. In a small, heavy-bottomed saucepan over very low heat, warm the honey and mix in the ginger, but do not bring to a simmer or boil.

2. When the honey begins to bubble, take the pan off the heat and add the lemon juice, zest, and salt. Stir until well mixed. You can use warm, or let cool and transfer to a clean glass jar. The glaze will keep, tightly covered, in the refrigerator for up to 2 days

Steak Love Glaze

Makes 3 cups

When I had the opportunity to "guest chef" at one of the country's top steak houses, I discovered one of their best-kept secrets. It was one of those great "aha" moments, as in, why doesn't my steak taste like this when I make it at home? Before each steak goes to the diner, it is generously brushed with a bit of this Steak Love. So, now you want to know what's in the Love? Rendered beef fat is all there is to it. And of course it makes sense, since the flavor is in the fat. Oh yeah, and a sprinkle of fleur de sel. That's the secret, and now you have it! I haven't served a steak without the Love since!

Good for Slathering: Any type of steak, including strip, filet, flank, porterhouse

> 2 pounds beef fat trimmings, coarsely chopped
>
> Spring or bottled water

1. Place the beef trimmings in a medium-sized, heavy-duty saucepan. Cover with water, 1 to 2 cups. Place over medium heat and simmer slowly until all the meat solids have cooked and floated to the top and the water has evaporated. This will take about 2 hours total. You will need to add water periodically as it cooks to keep the fat covered.

2. Pour the rendered beef trimmings through a fine-mesh strainer to get rid of any lingering pieces. You can use warm, or let cool and transfer to clean glass jar. The Steak Love will keep, tightly covered, in the refrigerator for up to 1 week. Warm gently to a liquid state before using.

The 3 B's Glaze Variation (Brown Sugar, Bourbon, and Bacon)

Try the same technique with 2 pounds of thick-cut bacon or pork belly with a high fat-to-meat ratio. When the fat is rendered and strained, add 2 tablespoons of dark brown sugar and 2 tablespoons of bourbon to the mixture.

Hot Pepper Jelly Glaze

Makes 1 1/3 cups

Hot pepper jelly is one of those one-stop flavorings for all ingredients. In its simplest form, you can melt the jelly and use the melted liquid as a glaze or juice it up with a little vinegar and seasonings before brushing it on! Try making your own hot pepper jelly using the recipe on page 163.

Good for Slathering: Pork; lamb; whole roasted chicken; fish such as salmon; grilled vegetables; use as a dip for sausages;

or spread over a block of cream cheese for an appetizer with crackers

> One 12-ounce jar hot pepper jelly
> 2 tablespoons unseasoned rice vinegar
> Pinch red chile flakes, optional
> Pinch salt

1. Put the hot pepper jelly in a small, heavy-bottomed saucepan set over low heat. Melt the jelly, stirring occasionally until it is smooth, making sure it doesn't burn.

2. When the jelly is melted, add the vinegar and stir to combine. Add the red chile flakes, if desired, and the salt and stir again. If the glaze is too thick, add a bit more vinegar. Mix and taste. Adjust the seasoning if desired.

3. You can use warm, or let cool and transfer to clean glass jar. The glaze will keep, tightly covered, in the refrigerator for up to 1 week but will need to be re-heated before using.

Mint Glaze Variation

Use mint jelly instead of the hot pepper jelly and add 1/4 cup of chopped fresh mint.

Elvis Glaze Variation

Use grape jelly instead of the hot pepper jelly.

Mustard-Molasses Glaze

Makes about 1/3 cup

This glaze was inspired by the unusual South Carolina Mustard Sauce (page 87). When there's not enough time to barbecue a pork shoulder, I grill-roast a pork tenderloin with this sweet and tangy yellow mustard (yes, ballpark mustard) glaze.

Good for Slathering: Pork, ham; hot dogs, sausage; flank steak

> 3 tablespoons yellow mustard
> 1 tablespoon molasses
> 1 tablespoon apple cider vinegar
> 1 tablespoon olive oil
> 1 teaspoon Worcestershire sauce
> 1 large pinch kosher salt
> 2 shakes Tabasco sauce

In a small bowl, combine all the ingredients and whisk well. You can use warm, or let cool and transfer to a clean glass jar. The glaze will keep, tightly covered, in the refrigerator for up to 2 days.

Note: If you want a thicker glaze with a more pronounced mustard flavor, double the quantity of mustard.

Cranberry Jelly and Balsamic Glaze

Makes about 2 cups

This is a glaze that you will make on Thanksgiving and then find yourself using all year long. It is versatile and is one of the few glazes that tastes good on both red

Pork Tenderloin with Mustard-Molasses Glaze

Serves 6 to 8

Grilling Method: Combo/Medium Heat

> 2 center-cut pork tenderloins, 2 to 3 pounds total
> Olive oil
> Kosher salt
> 1 recipe Mustard-Molasses Glaze (left)

1. Dry off any excess moisture from the pork with paper towels. Coat lightly with olive oil and season with salt.

2. Place the pork in the center of the cooking grate over indirect heat. Grill for 5 minutes over direct heat, turning occasionally to mark all sides of the tenderloin. Switch to indirect heat and cook for 5 more minutes.

3. Brush generously with the glaze. Cook for 5 more minutes, and then brush more glaze all over the pork, turning if necessary. Continue cooking for 5 more minutes or until the internal temperature is 145°F. The total cooking time should be 20 to 25 minutes.

4. Remove from the grill, place on a clean platter, and let rest for 5 to 10 minutes before carving.

and white meat. Rich balsamic vinegar is reduced and mixed in with the jellied cranberry sauce that comes in a can. You can easily turn this glaze into a barbecue sauce by adding ketchup and a few dashes of Worcestershire sauce.

Good for Slathering: whole turkey, turkey legs, turkey cutlets, chicken; pork; duck; salmon; beef

One 12.7-ounce bottle balsamic vinegar
One 16-ounce can jellied cranberry sauce
Zest of 1 orange
2 tablespoons Southern Comfort, apple cider, or fresh orange juice
2 tablespoons Wild Turkey
Pinch salt
Freshly ground pepper

1. Pour the balsamic vinegar into a medium heavy-bottomed saucepan. Cook over medium heat for about 20 minutes, or until it is reduced by one-half. When the vinegar has reduced, add the cranberry sauce, zest, and Southern Comfort. Let cook, stirring occasionally, over medium-low heat until it bubbles, about 10 minutes.

2. Remove from the heat and add the Wild Turkey, salt, and a few grinds of pepper. Taste and adjust the seasonings if desired.

3. You can use warm, or let cool and transfer to clean glass jar. The glaze will keep, tightly covered, in the refrigerator for up to 2 days.

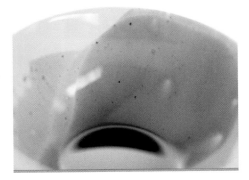

Red-Eye Gravy Glaze

Makes 1/2 cup

Even though I am a proud card-carrying Southerner, I don't smother my food with heavy gravies, preferring the flavors in a lighter application like this glaze. I fondly remember the sizzle and steam coming from my grandmother's blackened pan as she made red-eye gravy in the mornings. After browning the ham, she'd deglaze the pan with the thick black coffee from her morning cup. As a child, its allure was a mystery to me, and I decided it must be an adult-acquired taste! Today, I use it as a glaze on just about everything, including brisket, pork butt, and catfish.

Good for Slathering: Brisket; grilled ham, pork butt; catfish, salmon; grits

1 ham steak or piece of slab bacon, or several pieces of country ham or thick-cut bacon, about 8 ounces
3/4 cup brewed espresso or strong coffee
1/2 cup molasses
1 tablespoon dark brown sugar
Pinch salt

1. Heat a cast-iron skillet over medium heat. Add the ham steak. Cook on both sides until browned and warmed through. Remove the meat from the pan when browned on the edges. (If using bacon, pour out any excess fat.)

2. Raise the heat, and when the pan is really hot, pour in the espresso and scrap up the seasoned food bits from the pan surface. Add the molasses and brown sugar and stir into the coffee. Bring to a simmer, add salt, and taste. The glaze should be thick and black. Use immediately.

1. Put the maple syrup, apple cider, and sugar into a small, heavy-bottomed saucepan set over low heat. Stir to combine and add the cinnamon stick, star anise, and cloves. Cook over low heat until the liquid is reduced by about one-quarter. Stir in the soy sauce and taste. Adjust the seasoning if desired with more apple cider or maple syrup. Let cool to room temperature and remove the spices before storing.

2. You can use warm, or let cool and transfer to clean glass jar. The glaze will keep, tightly covered, in the refrigerator for up to 2 days.

Montreal Maple Syrup Glaze

Makes about 1 1/3 cups

This glaze seems to do it all. It actually reminds me of that sweet-salty sauce that sushi chefs use to glaze certain pieces of fatty sushi, like eel and salmon.

Good for Slathering: Grilled apples, pears, and winter squash; fatty fish like salmon and sturgeon

> 1 cup pure maple syrup
> 1/4 cup apple cider
> 1/4 cup packed dark brown sugar
> 1 cinnamon stick
> 2 whole star anise
> 5 whole cloves
> 2 teaspoons soy sauce

Pennsylvania Dutch Raisin Glaze

Makes about 2 cups

This glaze is a cross between the Pennsylvania Dutch black vinegar sauce and the Southern raisin sauce that is often made for glazing hams. I love the aroma of the sauce, heavy with vinegar, and the taste surprises as the brown sugar and raisins lend it a sweetness that is not unlike an old tawny port—minus the alcohol.

Good for Slathering: Ham; ribs; pork loin; duck; cheese

> 1 cup balsamic vinegar
> 3 cups red wine vinegar
> 2 tablespoons molasses
> 1 2/3 cups packed brown sugar
> 1 cup raisins
> 1/2 to 1 cup apple cider

(continued on page 134)

Butter-Rum Glaze

Makes 1/2 cup

Using a spiced rum eliminates the need to add anything else to the glaze. This flavorful glaze is not sweet, and it enhances anything you put it on.

Good for Slathering: Grilled pineapple and other tropical fruit; ham, pork

> 2 tablespoons unsalted butter, melted
>
> 1/2 cup golden spiced rum, preferably Captain Morgan

1. In a small saucepan, mix the butter and rum. Set over low heat to melt the butter. Stir until well blended.

2. You can use warm, or let cool and transfer to clean glass jar. The glaze will keep, tightly covered, in the refrigerator for up to 1 week but reheat before using.

Rum-Spiked Carpaccio of Pineapple with Toasted Coconut

Serves 4 to 8

Grilling Method: Direct/Medium Low Heat

> 1 Golden pineapple, peeled and cored
>
> 1 recipe Butter-Rum Glaze (left)
>
> 1/8 cup dried unsweetened coconut, toasted
>
> 1 fresh sprig mint for garnish

1. Using a pineapple slicer or a knife, cut the pineapple into very thin rings and set aside. Pour the Butter-Rum Glaze into a shallow plate. Dip the pineapple slices into the glaze. Reserve the remaining glaze for serving.

2. Place the pineapple rings on a very clean cooking grate and grill for 2 to 3 minutes per side, or until marked and warmed through. Be careful not to leave them on much longer, as the pineapple burns easily.

3. Place the grilled pineapple on a plate in an overlapping circle. Brush lightly with remaining butter-rum mixture and sprinkle with the toasted coconut. Serve immediately or at room temperature, garnished with the mint.

1. In a medium heavy-bottomed saucepan, combine the vinegars, molasses, and brown sugar and bring to a boil. Reduce the heat and simmer for 30 to 40 minutes or until the liquid is reduced by one-half, to about 2 1/2 cups. Add the raisins, reduce the heat, and simmer slowly for 5 to 10 more minutes. At this stage, watch carefully so that the sauce does not thicken too much, or it will resemble toffee instead of a thick sauce.

2. Strain the sauce through a fine-mesh strainer to remove the raisins. (The liquid should be black and syrupy and not have a strong vinegar aroma. Be careful not to overcook as the sauce burns easily.)

3. Let the sauce cool for about 10 minutes or until it is warm but no longer "boiling" hot. Mix in 1/2 cup of the apple cider; if the sauce is still too thick, add the remaining apple cider bit by bit until you get to the desired consistency.

4. You can use warm, or let cool and transfer to clean glass jar. The glaze will keep, tightly covered, in the refrigerator for up to 1 week.

Note: Don't discard the raisins; the simmered raisins are particularly good in spiced muffins and carrot cake.

Ice Wine and Orange Blossom Glaze

Makes 3/4 cup

A good ice wine can be like delicious liquid candy. On the one hand, it is a shame to cook with it. But on the other hand, when cooked down to its syrupy essence and then finished with a splash of orange blossom water, it is so ethereal that you'll wonder how you ever lived without it!

Good for Slathering: Salty cured meats; grilled fruit; serve over pound cake, angel food cake, ice cream

> 1 375 ml bottle ice wine
> 2 teaspoons orange blossom water

1. Pour the wine into a large heavy-bottomed saucepan. Simmer over medium heat for about 1 hour or until the wine is reduced by about one-half and has a sweet taste and syrupy consistency.

2. Mix in the orange blossom water. Let cool and transfer to a clean plastic squeeze bottle. The glaze will keep, tightly covered, in the refrigerator for up to 1 week.

Elderflower Lemonade Glaze

Makes 3/4 cup

I discovered elderflower lemonade when I visited Darina Allen, owner-instructor of the Ballymaloe Cookery School in Ireland. Every afternoon, someone set out a huge iced pitcher of the loveliest cool, fruity-but-floral drink. I couldn't get enough of it. Darina told me how they picked the elderflower blossoms and infused them in a simple syrup to make the afternoon lemonade.

Until recently, elderflower was difficult to find in the U.S. That is, until St-Germain elderflower liqueur (www.stgermain.fr) became available in the United States. Buy it, drink it, cook with it—if you are like me, you'll love it so much that you'll want to always have it on hand.

Good for Slathering: Grilled strawberries, watermelon or other fruit—hot off the grill; serve over angel food cake, cocktails, lobster

SIMPLE SYRUP

1 cup water

1/2 cup sugar

LEMONADE GLAZE

1/2 cup fresh lemon juice (about 4 lemons)

4 tablespoons simple syrup

1/2 cup elderflower liqueur, preferably St-Germain, or 1/3 cup elderflower syrup

1 tablespoon Chambord or crème de cassis

1. Make the simple syrup: Mix the water and sugar together in a small, heavy-bottomed saucepan. Heat over low heat until the sugar is completely dissolved and the syrup is clear. Bring to a low simmer for 5 minutes and then remove from the heat.

2. Let the syrup cool and transfer to a clean glass jar. The syrup will keep, tightly covered, in the refrigerator for up to 1 week.

3. Make the glaze: Mix the lemon juice and simple syrup together and taste. You want it to still be tart, but not so sour that it will overpower the elderflower. Mix it with the elderflower liqueur and add the Chambord.

4. You can use warm, or let cool and transfer to a clean glass jar. The glaze will keep, tightly covered, in the refrigerator for up to 2 days.

Note: My favorite way to use this glaze for fruit is to add fruit to the glaze when it is warm and let sit for 5 minutes. Serve fruit in the glaze, or remove it just before serving.

Orange Marmalade and Grand Marnier Glaze

Makes about 1 cup

Marmalade is the perfect starter for a glaze. You can use your favorite marmalade, or if you don't already have a favorite marmalade, try one of the organic fruit combinations made by California jam artisan June Taylor (www.junetaylorjams.com). I especially like the delectable Meyer lemon and her equally good lime version.

Good for Slathering: Game, turkey, chicken; lamb; pork; fall fruit and squash, sweet potatoes; gingerbread

> 1 cup your favorite orange or clementine marmalade
> 3 tablespoons Grand Marnier
> Pinch sea salt

1. Put the marmalade in a small, heavy-bottomed saucepan over low heat. Melt the jelly, stirring occasionally so that it doesn't burn.

2. When the jelly is melted, add the Grand Marnier and stir to combine. Add the salt and stir again. If the glaze is too thick, add a bit more Grand Marnier. Mix and taste, adjusting the seasoning if desired.

3. You can use warm, or let cool and transfer to a clean glass jar. The glaze will keep, tightly covered, in the refrigerator for up to 1 week but will need to be reheated before using.

Lemon Marmalade Variation

Mix lemon marmalade with gin (for game).

Lime Marmalade Variation

Mix lime marmalade with aged blue agave tequila (for whole fish such as snapper or grouper, or shrimp or scallops).

Port and Cherry Reduction Glaze

Makes 1/2 to 3/4 cup

This is one of those easy-to-make—all it takes is a little time and patience—culinary flourishes that every good cook should keep on hand.

Good for Slathering: Veal; game; pork; grilled pears; cheese plate

> 1 750 ml bottle port
> 1 cup dried cherries
> 3 whole cloves
> 2 whole black peppercorns
> 2 teaspoons red wine vinegar
> Pinch sea salt

1. Pour the port into a 4-quart, heavy-bottomed saucepan. Add the cherries, cloves, and peppercorns and simmer over medium heat for 60 to 80 minutes or until the port is reduced by about one-half and has a sweet taste and syrupy consistency. This is slightly thinner than a traditional port reduction; if you want it thicker, continue to cook.

2. Add the vinegar and salt, stir to dissolve, and taste, adjusting the seasoning if desired.

3. Let cool, and strain the cherries and spices out of the reduction. Transfer to a clean plastic squeeze bottle. The reduction will keep, tightly covered, in the refrigerator for up to 1 week.

Chinese Lantern Glaze

Makes about 3 cups

This glaze makes everything shine bright with a sticky, deep red varnish. Sweet with brown sugar and red currant jelly, spicy with sharp fresh ginger and chili sauce, this is a glaze that is equally at home on silky halves of grilled eggplant or Chinese baby back ribs.

Good for Slathering: Grilled vegetables (Chinese eggplant, bok choy, asparagus, broccoli rabe); pork; chicken; beef short ribs

3 cloves garlic, minced
1 1/2 tablespoons grated fresh ginger
1 tablespoon chile paste
6 tablespoons light brown sugar
1/4 cup molasses
3/4 cup hoisin sauce
3/4 cup dark soy sauce
3/4 cup red currant jelly

1. In a large saucepan, combine all the ingredients. Stir gently and simmer for 3 to 4 minutes until melted and well mixed.

2. You can use warm, or let cool and transfer to a clean glass jar. The glaze will keep, tightly covered, for up to 2 days.

Spicy Watermelon Glaze

Makes 2 cups

This is easy, but the trick is using fresh juice. Once you master the juicing step, try using the juice to make Irene's Hot Pepper Jelly (page 163)—it's a jelly and a glaze in one!

Good for Slathering: Baby back pork ribs; butterflied chicken, pork, chicken, shrimp and scallop kabobs, grill-roasted game birds

1 small watermelon, cut from the rind in chunks (about 8 cups fruit)
One 12-ounce jar apple jelly
Juice and zest of 1 small lime
2 teaspoons red chile flakes
1 teaspoon jalapeño hot sauce
Pinch sea salt

1. Place the watermelon in a food mill or juicer and collect the juice. Reserve 1 cup (4 cups of fruit) for this recipe and drink the rest—it's delish! Discard the seeds and solid bits.

2. Put the apple jelly in a small, heavy-bottomed saucepan over low heat. Melt the jelly, stirring occasionally so that it doesn't burn. When the jelly is melted, add the watermelon juice and stir to combine. Add the lime juice and zest and stir again. Add the red chile flakes, jalapeño hot sauce, and salt. Mix and taste, adjusting the seasoning if desired.

3. You can use warm, or let cool and transfer to clean glass jar. The glaze will keep, tightly covered, in the refrigerator for up to 2 days.

MOPS

Thin, savory basting sauces that are mopped (or dabbed) on the food during cooking. Mops are mostly used when making authentic barbecue to keep the meat moist and to add a little flavor during the long cooking time. Mops are called mops because the thin sauce has traditionally been "mopped" onto the meat with a mop—a brush-size version of a floor mop with many bristles.

- Don't oversalt or overseason your mopping liquid—the meat will already be highly seasoned.
- Almost anything can be a mop as long as it is thin and doesn't have too many sweet ingredients.
- Use a silicone mop head or a plastic squeeze bottle for best results.
- Only mop after the first 45 to 60 minutes.
- Try flavored oil mops on more classic grilled foods.

Mops are a competition barbecuer's secret weapon. The thin, savory liquid is "mopped" on the meat to add moisture to the food and the (grill) cooking box during the long, slow barbecuing process.

Although barbecuers rarely make mops exactly the same way twice, everyone on the barbecue circuit has his (or her) favorite mop. When I was competing with my team, Bubba Meets Bacchus, I was appointed Mop Queen. Although all I did was mix beer, barbecue sauce, and rub together, the rest of my teammates loved mine so much that they didn't think anyone else could match it. I remember this distinctly, because after a night of debauchery (very common at Memphis in May!) and a bottle of Bulleit Bourbon provided by my good friend Billy, a 6:00 a.m. call for my "secret" mop didn't feel like a compliment! I did, however, get myself together enough to rejoin the team and make my mop! The best ending to my story would be that we won the contest. We didn't win, but we sure had fun trying! These days, backyard grill jockeys have adopted the very fun and effective technique of mopping their food.

Mops 101

In its simplest form, a mop is a thin basting sauce that is mopped or brushed on ribs (or other barbecue) during cooking. It can be a leftover marinade, although most barbecuers like to mix a special mop for the cooking process. The simplest and most common mops are water, beer, or juice mixed with enough barbecue sauce to season the liquid.

To this base, add whatever spices and seasonings you like, but be careful with the seasonings because most contain a large percentage of salt, and if you add too much salted rub to a salted barbecue sauce or tomato juice, you can wind up overdoing it on the salt content. To use a mop, check on your barbecue periodically as it cooks, about every 20 minutes. Baste your food with the mopping sauce and close the lid. If using wood chips, let the meat cook unchecked for at least 45 minutes before adding the first mop.

Even if you're not familiar with mops, don't discount them. A good mop adds moisture and subtle flavor and promotes caramelization. It is the perfect complement to a dry spice rub. Feel free to try one of my recipes or make your own concoctions. Mops are an approved and encouraged way for barbecuers to play with their food! You can borrow this mopping tradition for grill-roasted meats—just make sure they are larger pieces of meat.

Quick Mop

Turn your favorite barbecue sauce into a mop. Just add water, beer, fruit juice, etc. until the consistency is almost as thin as the liquid itself.

Oil Mops

Flavored oils also make great mops, especially when you don't want to impart a lot of extra flavor to the food but you want to increase the sheen and promote caramelization. I use an oil mop frequently when I grill. Olive oil will do the trick, but a rich basil or lemon oil is great on fish and shellfish, and I love the burst of clean herbs and spices when I mix a tablespoon or teaspoon of a favorite dried herb or spice with the oil before mopping. One of my favorite oil mops is 1/2 cup olive oil mixed with 1 teaspoon curry powder. I mix the two and place the mixture in a squeeze bottle. You don't need much, and besides flavor, the curry oil imparts a nice golden sheen to the food. This is especially great on grilled halibut.

Cook's Tools

Nonreactive Bowls

I generally use stainless steel mixing bowls no matter what I am making. Years ago, I went to a restaurant supply store and bought a bunch of bowls in the sizes that I use most often. These bowls are indestructible and nonreactive. Both qualities are important because the bowls are easy to clean, don't hold odors, are dishwasher safe, and will not react with acidic ingredients. This last quality is very important, as many barbecue mops, sauces, brines, etc. contain a lot of acidic ingredients. If you don't have stainless steel bowls, glass is the next best thing. However, I urge you to buy a few of these prep bowls in the sizes that you use most often; they aren't expensive and they last forever. Some of the housewares companies have recently come out with versions with silicone or rubber bottoms that prevent them from skidding across your kitchen counters—a nifty addition, indeed!

What Is a Mop?

For the uninitiated, a "mop" is both the liquid and the tool. For years, a cloth barbecue mop, which looks like a miniature version of the traditional floor mop was used for applying the "mop" basting sauce. I think it is really much more of a novelty than a functional barbecue tool. The biggest downside to this kind of mop is that the cotton mop head has to absorb as much liquid as it can hold before any liquid will come off the mop onto your food. And you can't clean it thoroughly.

I looked for a better alternative for a long time and when I couldn't find one, I designed the Grill Friends Super Silicone Angled BBQ Mop. It is a silicone mop head with nearly 200 bristles that holds but doesn't absorb liquid. My angled BBQ mop helps keep your hand away from the fire, is made of washable,

heat-resistant silicone, holds a lot of liquid, and can be washed in the dishwasher. You can find the award-winning Grill Friends mop in both bakelite and stainless steel in stores nationwide or on the online at www.BBQProShop.com.

If you don't have the silicone mop, I recommend mopping one of two ways, one traditional, one way all my own. The traditional way is using a bowl and a brush, but be sure to use a brush with silicone bristles—the natural and synthetic bristles have a tendency to fall out and stick to the food. The other technique is to use a plastic squeeze bottle. Funnel the mop into the squeeze bottle, screw the top on, and squeeze away, aiming the stream at the top of the ribs or other barbecue so it will flow down, covering the whole surface equally. Don't aim at the fire, as doing so will cause a serious flare-up. This way is also much faster and generally cleaner than using a brush. Just don't leave the bottle too close to the fire or the plastic will melt.

Shelf Life

Most mops are best used the day they are made. The exceptions are the oil mops and any mop that doesn't have an acidic or uncooked carbonated ingredient. The good news is that most of the mops take just a few minutes to prepare and use ingredients that barbecuers generally have on hand. Mops that can be made in advance should be stored in a clean class jar with a tight-fitting lid in the refrigerator. If necessary, warm or bring to room temperature before serving.

Mop 101: Simple Apple Cider Mop

Makes about 2 1/2 cups

It doesn't get any easier than this! And this mop is probably what 90 percent of the competition barbecuers use—with maybe a little beer mixed in for good measure!

Good for Slathering: Pork; chicken, turkey, duck; beef; lamb

- 1 tablespoon your favorite dry rub
- 1 1/2 cups apple juice
- 1 1/2 cups water
- 1 1/2 teaspoons fine-ground sea salt

1. In a medium nonreactive bowl, mix the dry rub with the apple juice, water, and salt until the salt is dissolved.

2. Funnel into a plastic squeeze bottle or put in a clean glass jar until ready to use. The mop will keep, tightly covered, in the refrigerator for up to 2 days. (If you add beer, use the mop the same day.) Shake before using.

Bloodshot Mop

Makes about 2 1/2 cups

This recipe was created in honor of the bloodshot eyes that the barbecue pit masters have after a night of tending the 'que and the brew! This unusual mop is spicy and not sweet at all. It matches best with simple rib recipes or a whole brisket.

Good for Slathering: Whole brisket, steak; ribs, beef and pork, chicken

- One 12-ounce bottle or can beer, preferably Budweiser
- 1 cup Spicy Hot V8 juice
- 1 tablespoon Worcestershire sauce
- 2 tablespoons prepared horseradish
- 1 teaspoon finely ground pepper
- 1/4 teaspoon sea salt
- 1 teaspoon granulated garlic
- 1 teaspoon Tabasco sauce

1. Pour the beer into a medium nonreactive bowl and whisk to remove the carbonation. Add the remaining ingredients and mix well.

2. Funnel into a plastic squeeze bottle or put in a clean glass jar until ready to use. The mop will keep, tightly covered, in the refrigerator for up to 1 day. Shake before using.

Apple Loves Pork Mop

Makes 2 cups

Apple loves pork and pork loves apples: apple juice, apple wood, apple cider—all things apple. Maybe that is why whole hawgs are always presented with an apple instead of, say, a lemon in their mouths! I've tripled the apple ingredients in this recipe to intensify the apple flavor in the sweet and sour notes. This mop is also good cooked down and pureed to make a sauce; just double the ingredients and simmer for an additional 20 minutes.

Good for Slathering: Pork butt, pork shoulder, pork tenderloin, pork chops, ham steak—or use it to simmer grilled pork sausages

> 2 cups apple cider
> 1 large shallot, minced
> 2 tablespoons hot pepper jelly
> 1 Granny Smith apple, peeled and grated on the large side of a box grater
> 2 tablespoons apple cider vinegar
> 2 tablespoons tomato paste

> 2 tablespoons dark brown sugar
> 2 teaspoons ground ginger
> 1/8 teaspoon ground cloves
> 1/2 teaspoon kosher salt
> 1/4 teaspoon freshly ground black pepper

1. In a small saucepan, combine the apple cider, shallot, and hot pepper jelly. Bring to a boil and simmer for 10 minutes. Add the remaining ingredients, bring to a boil, and remove from the heat.

2. Let cool, then strain through a fine-mesh strainer and transfer to a clean glass jar. The mop will keep, tightly covered, in the refrigerator for up to 2 days. Shake before using.

Lemon-Garlic Mop

Makes 1 1/2 cups

This is a little mop that I created for fresh hams, pork loins, veal chops, roasted chicken, game hen and quail, and all manner of fish and shellfish. It is decidedly un-barbecue in flavor but absolutely delicious on grill-roasted meats! Mop on during cooking, or try dunking a whole chicken cooked beer-can style as soon as you take it off the grill.

Good for Slathering: Fresh hams, pork; veal; fish steaks (tuna, mahi-mahi, salmon), whole fish, shellfish; chicken, game hen, quail

> 10 cloves garlic, grated
> 1 teaspoon kosher salt
> 1 cup fresh lemon juice (about 8 lemons)

Zest of 2 lemons

Zest of 1 orange

1 tablespoon mayonnaise (not salad dressing)

1/2 cup olive oil

In a medium nonreactive bowl, mix the garlic and salt together to make a paste. Add the lemon juice and whisk to combine. Add the zest and mayonnaise and whisk again. Slowly add the oil to the lemon mixture, incorporating it little by little until it emulsifies or blends together. The mop is best used immediately, but it will keep, tightly covered, in the refrigerator for up to 2 days. Shake before using.

Coca-Cola Mop

Makes 2 cups

This is the mop that saves the day in the Bible Belt—and much of the barbecue belt is in the Bible Belt! Coke is a classic, and the Worcestershire and soy sauce balance the sweet quotient, making this a mop that gives a sweet, salty, and savory finish to meat, fish, fowl, and hearty veggies like portobello mushrooms. If you aren't in the Bible Belt, feel free to add a couple of shots of Jack Daniel's to the mop—I'm sure that is what everyone does when no one is looking! The mop can be doubled and used as a marinade in a pinch.

Good for Slathering: Pork (tenderloin, chops, butt, ribs); skirt steak; chicken; catfish; portobello mushrooms, sweet onions

One 12-ounce bottle or can Coca-Cola

1/4 cup low-sodium soy sauce

1 tablespoon Worcestershire sauce

1 tablespoon peanut or olive oil

1 tablespoon toasted sesame oil

1 shallot, grated

3 cloves garlic, grated

1 teaspoon coarsely ground pepper

1. Pour the bottle of Coke into a medium nonreactive bowl. Add the soy sauce and Worcestershire sauce and whisk in the oils. Stir in the shallot, garlic, and pepper and let sit for 10 minutes before using.

2. Funnel into a plastic squeeze bottle or put in a clean glass jar until ready to use. The mop will keep, tightly covered, in the refrigerator for up to 2 days. Shake before using.

This Swine Is Mine Beer Mop

Makes 2 cups

This is the mop that made me the Queen of Mops. It is made in the style of the classic barbecue circuit mop. I've given you measurements, but feel free to adjust them to meet your needs and taste.

Good for Slathering: Ribs; pork butt, pork chops; chicken; flank steak

> One 12-ounce bottle or can of your favorite beer
>
> 1/2 cup of your favorite barbecue sauce
>
> 1 tablespoon apple cider vinegar
>
> 2 to 4 teaspoons of your favorite barbecue rub that isn't too salty

1. Pour the bottle of beer into a medium nonreactive bowl. Add the barbecue sauce and vinegar and whisk to combine. Stir in the barbecue rub and let sit for 10 minutes before using.

2. Funnel into a plastic squeeze bottle or put in a clean glass jar until ready to use. The mop will keep, tightly covered, in the refrigerator for up to 1 day. Shake before using.

Pineapple–Lemon Juice Mop

Makes 5 cups

Both lemon and pineapple juice are used on the barbecue circuit to tenderize and mop ribs, chicken, and pork shoulder.

I love the light, tangy citrus flavors as a change of pace from the tomato-based flavors most often associated with classic American barbecue.

Good for Slathering: Whole chicken, duck; pork chops; ribs, whole fish such as snapper or grouper; green vegetables

> 2 cups canned pineapple juice
>
> 1/2 cup fresh lemon juice (about 4 lemons)
>
> 2 cups water
>
> 1/2 cup vegetable oil

1. Mix all the ingredients together in a medium nonreactive bowl.

2. Funnel into a plastic squeeze bottle or put in a clean glass jar until ready to use. The mop will keep, tightly covered, in the refrigerator for up to 2 days. Shake before using.

Sweet and Spicy Crushed Pineapple and Ginger Mop

Makes about 2 1/4 cups

Pineapple and ginger are both natural tenderizing agents, so you don't want to use this with ribs or other meat that has been marinated in any mixture that contains either fresh ginger or pineapple. Instead, use this mop with a chile-intense rub for a spicy-sweet flavor with tropical hints. But beware—the collective spices are not for the weak at heart!

Good for Slathering: Ham; whole fish; Hawaiian-style ribs; chicken, wings

1 cup ginger beer or ginger ale

1 cup canned pineapple juice

1/2 cup crushed pineapple

1 tablespoon jalapeño (green) hot sauce, preferably Tabasco

1 small knob (1 to 2 inches) fresh ginger, peeled and grated

1 tablespoon honey

1/4 cup Thai chili-garlic sauce *(sriracha)*

Sea salt and fine-ground white pepper

1. Pour the ginger beer into a medium bowl and whisk to remove the carbonation. Add the remaining ingredients and mix well. Let the mop sit for a minimum of 30 minutes or up to overnight, stirring occasionally.

2. Strain the mop using a fine-meshed strainer and funnel it into a squeeze bottle or put it in a clean glass jar until ready to use. The mop will keep, tightly covered, in the refrigerator for 1 day. Shake before using.

"The Bath" Mop

Makes about 1/2 gallon

Gary Pantlik is one of my favorite BBQ buddies, and we are both former members of the Swine and Dine barbecue team. Gary was a founding member, and since I live in Chicago, I was an out-of-town member. No matter the difference in our 'que status—he was happy to let me hang around the pits and pick up all his secrets. It's Gary who came up with the Cook's Ribs (page 148) and coined the term "bath." "The bath" mop recipe is poured into a large loaf pan that sits on the grill during cooking—making this a warm bath. Every so often, the ribs are submerged into the bath, replacing basting with bathing! Here I've mixed all the ingredients together for a bath you can use every night!

Good for Slathering: Pork (ribs, butt, chops); butterflied chicken

4 cups Barbecue Sauce 101 (page 86) or vinegar-based marinade (such as Wicker's)

1 cup spring or bottled water

2 cups (one 16-ounce bottle) Italian dressing, homemade (see page 38) or any brand

1/2 cup John Willingham's W'ham dry rub (page 200) or your favorite rub

1/2 cup clover honey

Put all the ingredients in a large bowl. Stir until the honey is mixed evenly in the liquid and is no longer solid. Pour enough into a large loaf pan so that it is halfway full. Stir again before using. The bath will keep, tightly covered, in the refrigerator for up to 2 days.

The Cook's Ribs

Serves between 4 and 16, depending on appetite and number of racks cooked

Grilling Method: Indirect/Low Heat

Special Equipment: Rib racks(s), smoker box, hickory or oak chips or pellets, large disposable aluminum loaf pan (13 x 5 x 3 1/2)

> 4 to 8 racks back loin or St. Louis ribs
>
> 2/3 cup John Willingham's W'ham dry rub (page 200) or your favorite rub, divided
>
> 2 recipes (1 gallon) "The Bath" Mop (page 147)
>
> One 8-ounce jar clover honey (preferably a squeeze bottle or honey bear)

1. The night before you want to serve them, prepare the ribs: Remove the membrane on the back, if desired, and season generously with some of the dry rub—you will need about ½ cup. Once rubbed, take each rack and cut in half. Place in a large resealable plastic bag and refrigerate overnight.

2. When you are ready to cook, remove the ribs from the refrigerator and allow them to reach room temperature. Build a charcoal fire or preheat a gas grill and set the temperature at 250°F.

3. Place the "mop" in an aluminum loaf pan. Place the pan on the grill to keep warm.

4. Once the grill has reached 250°F, place all the ribs on the grill using a rib rack and let the smokin' begin. The temperature may drop a bit, but that's okay. Make sure to maintain a temperature of 225°F. After 1 hour has passed, the ribs will be ready for their first bath. Using a sturdy pair of locking chef tongs, submerge each slab in the bath pan. Give them all a good dousing and return them to the heat. Repeat this process each hour until the ribs have been on the grill for 3 to 4 hours.

5. Finish the ribs: Take a half-slab and give it one last bath. Place on a large piece of aluminum foil for wrapping (see photos below). Drizzle honey over the slab and finish off with one last dash of dry rub. Repeat the dunking and drizzling process for each half slab. Stack 3 to 4 slabs on top of each other per foil package and wrap tightly (see below). After the ribs have been wrapped, place them back on the grill for 1 1/2 more hours. Let them cook slowly in the foil packages over indirect low heat, at about 225°F. These ribs will take 4 1/2 to 5 1/2 hours to cook. Remove the foil packages from grill as needed and serve.

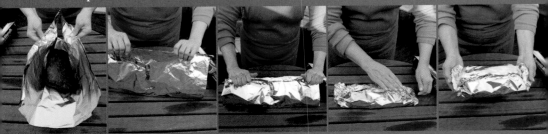

Wrapping is also known as the Texas crunch. It is said on the circuit, "If you aren't wrapping, you are either lying or losing!"

Sesame-Soy Mop

Makes 1 1/4 cups

This mop is a quick and easy way to impart some Asian flavor to anything you grill. This is a chameleon mop that will enhance anything from vegetables to meat to fish—even fruit.

Good for Slathering: Flank steak, skirt steak; sea bass, shrimp, scallops, pineapple, scallions, mushrooms

> 1 cup low-sodium soy sauce
> 1/2 cup fresh orange juice
> 1/2 cup toasted sesame oil
> 2 tablespoons rice vinegar
> 1 tablespoon Worcestershire sauce
> 3 cloves garlic, grated
> 2 teaspoons sesame seeds
> 1/4 teaspoon coarsely ground pepper

1. Pour the soy sauce, orange juice, oil, vinegar, and Worcestershire sauce into a medium nonreactive bowl. Whisk together and add the garlic, sesame seeds, and pepper. Let it sit for 10 minutes before using.

2. Funnel into a plastic squeeze bottle or put in a clean glass jar until ready to use. The mop will keep, tightly covered, in the refrigerator for up to 2 days. Shake before using.

The Gaucho's Mop

Makes about 1 cup

Today Argentina is considered the Paris of South America. In years past, it was a land of South American cowboys called gauchos. My friend Bob Blumer's father, Jack, was a steak master using the tricks taught to him by his great-uncle, who was a gaucho. The trick is to make up the mixture and mop it on the meat constantly during the cooking time. As soon as the water has evaporated, mop it again so that you build up a complex layer of flavor on the crust of the meat. But, beware—do not taste the sauce on its own, for it is made to make the meat taste good—not your finger! The sauce tastes like nothing on its own, but as it cooks into the meat, the salt and cayenne mix with the natural beef flavors for a perfectly seasoned steak.

Good for Slathering: Any kind of steak, especially porterhouse, skirt, sirloin; veal; lamb; chicken pieces

> 1 tablespoon cayenne pepper
> 3 tablespoons fine-grain sea salt
> 1 cup hot spring or bottled water

1. In a small nonreactive bowl, dissolve the cayenne and salt in the hot water. Let sit for 10 minutes before using.

2. Funnel into a plastic squeeze bottle or put in a clean glass jar until ready to use. The mop will keep, tightly covered, in the refrigerator for up to 1 week. Shake before using.

Cabernet and Fresh Rosemary Mop

Makes 1 3/4 cups

I created this mop for my annual Christmas dinner of prime rib studded with garlic and rosemary. My sister and I usually grill a 5- to 7-bone prime rib that takes 2 to 3 hours to grill-roast. After the first hour, when the fat has started to cook, I mop it with this complementary Cabernet mop. The mop is almost good enough to drink (it doesn't need long, deep cooking for flavor), so I started using it on quick-cooking pieces of beef and steaks as well.

Good for Slathering: Any kind of beef, such as prime rib, all steaks including flat-iron, flank, and skirt

1 1/2 cups Cabernet Sauvignon
3 tablespoons extra-virgin olive oil
1 tablespoon red wine vinegar
3 cloves garlic, grated
4 sprigs fresh rosemary, leaves only
1 teaspoon coarse sea salt
1/2 teaspoon coarsely ground pepper

1. Pour the wine, oil, and vinegar into a medium nonreactive bowl. Whisk together and add the garlic, rosemary leaves, salt, and pepper. Let it sit for 10 minutes before using.

2. Funnel into a plastic squeeze bottle or put in a clean glass jar until ready to use. The mop will keep, tightly covered, in the refrigerator for up to 1 day. Shake before using.

Salsas, Relishes, and Jellies

Chunky condiments that may be raw or cooked and served over food as a sauce or with food as an accompaniment. Some of these can be warmed to become a glaze.

Condiments 101

It's time to tell my dirty little secret. I am obsessed with condiments. Everywhere I go, I buy jars of jams, jellies, chutneys, oils, mustards, sauces, relishes, salsas, and more. I can't help myself! When you open my refrigerator, there is hardly any room for fresh food because the jars, stacked on top of each other, take up so much real estate. If that weren't bad enough, I also make my own homemade versions of these lovely jarred ladies—half the jars are mine and half are purchased. Part of the reason is that I love the promise of opening a jar of a new combination of ingredients, and the other part of the reason is that these condiments or quick-to-make raw salsas and relishes are the real secret to mouth-watering, soul satisfying 30-minute meals. I love to grill a pork tenderloin and slather it with Jezebel Sauce (page 164), and some of my most simple and enjoyable meals are grilled fish or meat with a hearty accompaniment of a chunky raw salsa, sweet chutney, relish, jam, or jelly. These rough-and-ready "sauces" or condiments complement the flavor of simple grilled foods. They have eye appeal and their texture enhances everything you serve with them.

If you are a seasoned cook, you know that we eat with our eyes before we taste the food, and we are halfway to deciding whether or not we like the food as soon as we see it. But texture plays an equally important role in whether or not we love a dish. If the texture of what we eat is always the same, we get bored with eating it way before we are finished. Think about a crème brûlée. Even if the custard is delicious by itself, it's breaking through the caramelized sugar top and having both the bittersweet crispy crust and the smooth custard together that makes the dessert such a time-honored favorite. The contrast in texture and flavors keep most of us going until we've licked the bowl (or want to)!

Salsa: This contrast in color, flavor, and texture is the reason that I love topping food with these often uncooked "sauces." Practically anything can be a salsa. *Salsa* is simply the Mexican word for "sauce" (and is used to describe both chunky salsas and smooth cooked sauces), but since Mexican cuisine is known for these raw, roughly chopped relishes, that is what we think of when we think of salsa. A fresh fruit or vegetable salsa that combines sweet, sour, and spicy flavors and is quickly mixed together is a perfect complement to smoky grilled fish.

Chutney: I've borrowed the Indian tradition of chutney to make two heady, sweet, fruit-rich mixtures that are perfect to keep on hand for grilled meat, fish, and poultry, especially duck, and as a complement to great stinky aged cheese or soft, fresh goat cheese. And a short note of disclosure: The chutneys that I have here are my interpretation of chutney and not at all authentic! They are delicious and could have just as easily been called compote, sauce, or jam. I just happen to love the sound and the connotation of the word *chutney*!

Relish: The American farmhouse tradition of relish trays offers other pantry staples that will brighten just about everything you serve with them. The combination of sharp vinegar, sweetness, and crunchy vegetables give relish that distinct Southern and/or farm-stand flavor.

The tangy, vinegary relishes and sweeter chutneys are full of complementary flavors for sharp, smoky barbecued foods. Irene's Hot Pepper Jelly (page 163) and Jezebel Sauce (page 164) can be made long in advance and stored in the fridge until you need that little something extra for your grilled pork. Jellies also make great quick glazes—just heat them up and brush them on the food.

In this chapter, I have included a few of my favorite salsas, chutneys, relishes, and jellies as a point of departure. Feel free to experiment, improvise, and substitute. For example, in the spring I love substituting or adding the pulp of passion fruit in place of the pomegranates in the Pomegranate and Mint Salsa (page 172). In the fall, I often add raw or sautéed apples to the relish depending on what I am serving it with.

I'd love to know your favorite recipes or recipe variations for relishes, salsas, etc. E-mail me at elizabeth@girlsatthegrill.com.

Shelf Life

Most condiments can be made in advance, and some of them are even better after "curing" in the refrigerator. But all fresh salsas and uncooked relishes are best made and tossed together just before serving. Sweet condiments that can be made in advance should be stored in a clean class jar with a tight-fitting lid in the refrigerator. If necessary, warm or bring to room temperature before serving.

Raw Salsa/Relish 101: Rough and Raw Tomato-Basil Relish

Makes 3 to 4 cups, depending on the size of the tomatoes

I make this relish all the time. Not only is the color a perfect feast for the eyes, but it's easy to prepare. It is best in the summer months, but the small hothouse grape or cherry tomatoes available year-round add a burst of sweet-tart tomato flavor even in the dead of winter. In the summer, try making it with yellow, red, and baby green zebra tomatoes for an heirloom tomato salsa that you will relish by itself like a salad, on top of fresh mozzarella or its creamier cousin, burrata. It is equally nice served on top of grilled chicken or fish.

Good for Slathering: Grilled fish, shrimp; chicken; beef; serve as a side dish

- 2 pints ripe cherry or grape tomatoes, cut in quarters, or 2 pounds vine-ripened or heirloom tomatoes, diced
- 2 tablespoons extra-virgin olive oil
- 1 1/2 teaspoons balsamic vinegar
- 1 teaspoon kosher salt
- 2 cloves garlic, minced
- 3 sprigs fresh basil, leaves only, chopped just before using (about 1/3 cup)

1. In a large nonreactive bowl, mix the tomatoes, olive oil, vinegar, salt, and garlic. If serving within 1 to 2 hours, let stand at room temperature so the tomatoes release their juices and the flavors meld. Or refrigerate, covered, for up to 24 hours.

2. When ready to serve, if refrigerated, allow at least 30 minutes to bring to room temperature. Mix all the ingredients together again, then drain excess juice from the tomatoes. Just before serving, mix in the basil.

Fresh Corn Variation

In the summer, when corn is at its peak, remove the kernels from 2 ears of fresh white corn and mix the raw kernels in with the relish. Delish!

Note: You can save the drained liquid to toss with fresh greens.

Avocado Salsa

Makes about 1 cup

The trick to keeping this a coarse-chopped salsa is in the mixing; if you are too vigorous, it may become guacamole. (If it does —don't worry—it will still be delicious.) However, if you can keep your hand light, you will be rewarded with a chunky salsa that glistens on the plate and has a great toothy texture.

Good for Slathering: Tortilla chips; fresh corn tortillas, grilled salmon or other fish, grilled shrimp; grilled vegetables, eggs

> 2 ripe but not mushy avocados, preferably Haas
>
> 1 lime, juiced
>
> 1 roma tomato, seeded and diced
>
> 1 small white onion or shallot, diced
>
> 1 sprig fresh cilantro, leaves only, torn or chopped
>
> 1/4 teaspoon fleur de sel or coarse salt

1. Cut the avocado lengthwise in half around the pit. Carefully lodge a large knife into the pit, twist to pull the pit from the flesh, and then discard the pit.

2. Using a spoon, carefully scoop out the avocado flesh from the peel in one piece (as best as you can). Dice the avocado halves and put in a medium bowl. Drizzle lime juice over the avocado to prevent it from browning. Add a little at a time, since you don't want it swimming in juice.

3. Toss gently with the tomato and onion, keeping the dice intact. Sprinkle with cilantro and fleur de sel and toss again. Serve immediately.

Grilled Mango, Peach, and Poblano Chile Salsa

Makes about 2 cups

This salsa may take a little longer to make than the raw variety, but your patience will be rewarded. It dresses up simple salt-and-pepper chicken thighs with fresh, explosive flavors that complement the richness of the darker, moister chicken meat.

Good for Slathering: Chicken; pork; salmon, tuna; rice and beans; tortilla or pita chips

Grilling Method: Direct/Medium Heat

> 1 green poblano pepper
>
> 1 paper bag or resealable plastic container
>
> 1 large ripe mango
>
> 2 large ripe peaches
>
> About 2 tablespoons peanut or hazelnut oil
>
> Salt
>
> 1/2 cup chopped red onion
>
> 1/4 to 1 habanero or jalapeño chile, seeded and minced
>
> 3 tablespoons chopped fresh mint
>
> 1 teaspoon finely grated lime zest
>
> 1 lime, juiced
>
> 4 tablespoons passion fruit juice or fresh orange juice
>
> Freshly ground pepper

1. To roast the pepper: Build a charcoal fire or preheat a gas grill on high. Place the poblano on the cooking grate. Turn occasionally until the skin blackens and blisters all over. Remove from the grill and immediately put in a paper bag or sealed plastic container until cool to the touch. Skin and seed the pepper (the skin should slip off easily.) Cut into strips and chop roughly. Set aside.

2. Cut the mango lengthwise on either side of the pit. Cut the peaches into quarters, removing the pits. Brush all the fruit on the cut sides with the oil and sprinkle lightly with salt.

3. Place the mango halves and peach quarters cut side down on the cooking grate and grill with the lid down for about 4 minutes or until nicely marked and beginning to warm. Turn and place on cooking grate skin side down. Continue grilling with the lid down until the skin begins to pull away from the flesh, 3 to 4 more minutes. Transfer to a clean platter.

4. When fruit is cool enough to handle, hold one of the mango slices in your hand, flesh side up, and score the flesh lengthwise and then crosswise in a grid pattern, forming 1/2-inch cubes and taking care not to cut through the peel. Press against the center of the peel to force the cubes upward, then slice along the peel, releasing the cubes into a bowl. Repeat with the remaining slice. Remove the skin from the peaches and chop into small cubes, about 1/4-inch pieces.

5. In a medium bowl, combine the roasted poblano, the grilled mango and peaches, onion, chilies, mint, and lime zest and juices, and toss gently to mix. Season to taste with salt and pepper. Let stand at room temperature for 20 minutes before serving.

Chicken Thighs with Grilled Mango, Peach, and Poblano Chile Salsa

Serves 4

Grilling Method: Indirect/Medium Heat

> 4 bone-in chicken thighs and/or breasts, legs etc
> Olive oil
> Salt and freshly ground pepper
> 1 recipe Grilled Mango, Peach, and Poblano Chile Salsa (page 157)

1. Build a charcoal fire or preheat a gas grill. Remove and discard excess fat from the chicken. Pat dry. Brush lightly with oil and season with salt and pepper. Place the chicken, bone side down, in the center of the cooking grate. You do not need to turn the chicken pieces while they cook.

2. Grill-roast until the breast meat near the bone registers 165°F and the thigh meat registers 180°F. If you don't have an instant-read thermometer, cook until no longer pink and the juices run clear, about 30 to 45 minutes, depending on the size of your chicken pieces. Transfer to a platter and let sit for 5 to 10 minutes before serving with the salsa.

Summer's Best Heirloom Tomato Salsa

Makes about 4 cups, depending on the size of the tomatoes

This salsa is easy as can be and is a recipe that I recommend to cooks when they are just starting out. Not only is it delicious, but it also looks pretty—and pretty impressive. You can use the same seasonings with regular ripe tomatoes; it will taste delicious, but it won't look quite as unique as it does with the colorful heirloom tomatoes. Do not make this more than a few hours in advance or you will lose the flavors of the fresh-cut tomatoes.

Good for Slathering: Grilled halibut, scallops, shrimp; chicken; grilled tofu; bread; scrambled eggs

> 4 large heirloom tomatoes (mixed selection), such as green zebra, rainbow, red ruby, black, brandywine, etc.
>
> 2 small shallots, finely chopped
>
> 4 tablespoons chopped fresh herbs (e.g., parsley, mint, lemon thyme, basil), plus sprigs for garnish
>
> 3 large cloves garlic, minced or grated
>
> 1 fresh jalapeño chile, stemmed, seeded, and minced
>
> 1 lime, juiced
>
> Kosher salt

1. Chop the tomatoes into coarse chunks, reserving all the juices. Put the tomatoes and juices into a large glass bowl.

2. Add the shallots, herbs, garlic, and jalapeño; mix gently until all ingredients are well combined. Add the lime juice a little at a time, tasting and adding until you think the balance of the tomato juice with the lime is right—basically it should taste good without too much of a citrus flavor. Season with salt, stir, and let sit covered at room temperature until ready to serve.

Grilled Pineapple Salsa

Makes 2 1/2 to 3 cups

Pineapple is often used to make salsa because its sweet acidity is a perfect match for fiery chilies. The small orange habanero packs a lot of heat in a little body. If you aren't familiar with the chile, start slow—maybe with a quarter of a chile—and build up slowly to a hotter level. Grilling the pineapple concentrates the sugar and lowers the acidity for a sweet and spicy salsa that borrows flavors from the East and the West.

Good for Slathering: Swordfish, shrimp, tuna; chicken; pork; use as a dip for grilled pita bread or tortilla or pita chips

Grilling Method: Direct/Medium Heat

> 1 cup distilled white vinegar
>
> 5 tablespoons sugar
>
> 1/4 teaspoon ground cloves
>
> 1/2 teaspoon Chinese five-spice powder
>
> 1/2 teaspoon sea salt
>
> Two 1/4-inch slices fresh ginger, coarsely chopped
>
> 1/2 to 1 habanero chile, seeded and finely chopped

4 tablespoons untoasted nut oil, plus more for brushing

1/2 teaspoon ground cinnamon

1 very ripe pineapple, peeled, cored, and cut into 1/2-inch-thick slices

1/2 small red onion, finely diced (4 tablespoons)

3 scallions, finely sliced (white and green parts)

2 tablespoons chopped fresh lemon verbena or fresh mint

1. Put the vinegar, 4 tablespoons of the sugar, the cloves, five-spice powder, sea salt, ginger, and habanero chile in a blender. Process until just mixed, then add the oil in a slow stream. Process again until thoroughly blended. Set aside.

2. Build a charcoal fire or preheat a gas grill. Meanwhile, mix the remaining 1 tablespoon sugar with the cinnamon. Brush the pineapple rings on both sides with oil and sprinkle on both sides with the cinnamon sugar.

3. Place the pineapple rings on the cooking grate and grill for about 8 minutes, turning once halfway through the cooking time. Remove from the grill and chop into 1/4-inch pieces. Put the pieces into a medium bowl.

4. Pour 3/4 cup of the reserved dressing over the warm pineapple and toss gently with the onion, scallions, and lemon verbena. Serve warm, cool, or at room temperature. You may have leftover dressing, which will keep, tightly covered, in the refrigerator for up to 2 days.

Fire-Roasted Salsa

Makes about 8 cups

In the summer, I love grilling all kinds of summer vegetables and blending them with red wine vinegar, olive oil, and herbs. The pureed vegetables are good mixed with rosé wine and served as a soup or a great base for grilled shrimp, scallops, or even a full-flavored fish like Chilean sea bass. But most of the time, I serve it with tortilla chips as the world's best grilled salsa!

It takes about 45 minutes to roast and caramelize the garlic. Plan ahead, or do it in advance if you like.

Good for Slathering: Chilean sea bass; grilled chicken or pork; as a dip, salsa, or pasta sauce with grilled shrimp or mussels; tortilla chips; use to make soup, adding sour cream and/or crème fraîche to lighten it up

Grilling Method: Indirect/Medium Heat

6 large, ripe tomatoes, about 3 pounds

1 yellow bell pepper

1 red bell pepper

2 cucumbers

1 large sweet onion, cut in half

2 bunches scallions

Olive oil

1 head garlic

Kosher salt

1/4 to 1/2 cup red wine vinegar, depending on the tartness of the vegetables

2 tablespoons chopped fresh herbs (including basil, mint, parsley, oregano)

2 teaspoons hot smoked Spanish paprika

Freshly ground pepper

1 paper bag or resealable plastic container

2 teaspoons Tabasco sauce

1. Build a charcoal fire or preheat a gas grill.

2. Stem the tomatoes. Clean the peppers but leave them whole for roasting. Peel, halve, and seed the cucumber. Peel the onion and cut the roots off the scallions. Brush with 1/2 to 3/4 cup oil and set aside.

3. Prepare the head of garlic for roasting by cutting about 1/8 inch off the top. Brush the whole head with oil, sprinkle with salt, and place on an 8-inch square of heavy-duty aluminum foil. Close the foil completely around the head of garlic. Place the garlic on the warming rack of the grill or away from any direct heat to roast. Roast for about 45 minutes or until the garlic is soft and golden brown.

4. When ready to grill, place the peppers in the center of the cooking grate over the heat to blacken.

5. When the peppers are blackened, place in a closed container or paper bag until the steam loosens the skin. Remove the skin and seeds and set aside. Check to make sure the garlic is done and remove from grill. Set aside until you are ready to combine.

6. Place the tomatoes, cucumbers, onion, and scallions on the grill and cook until marked, browned, and soft to the touch but not mushy. The vegetables will take different lengths of time to cook—the cucumbers and onions will take the longest, about 20 minutes. The tomatoes will take about 10 minutes, depending on size, and the scallions will only take about 5 minutes. When all the vegetables are done, transfer them to a platter to cool, reserving any juices.

7. Transfer the still-warm grilled vegetables, peppers, and garlic, and the vegetable juices, to a food processor or blender and process at high speed. Slowly add 1/8 to 1/4 cup oil, vinegar, herbs, smoked paprika, salt, pepper, and Tabasco until the salsa is smooth and very thick. Adjust the oil, vinegar, and seasonings to taste. The recipe should be highly seasoned and thick. Transfer to a medium bowl and refrigerate until ready to serve.

Ruben's Super-Hot Salsa

Makes about 3 cups

Ruben Gomez is a retired DEA agent and an active barbecue judge, cook, and caterer living in Rio Rancho, New Mexico. I met Ruben in Murphysboro, Illinois, where we had both traveled for the Apple City Barbecue Contest. He and his wife had spent the day making this salsa for the contest's Friday-night barbecue buffet. The salsa was the hit of the night—it has the kind of heat that sneaks up on you and makes you want to eat just one more bite! If you don't like things quite as hot, reduce the number of jalapeños, or try his dressed-up version with cooling mango, corn, and black beans (see the variation).

Good for Slathering: Grilled fish; chicken; tortilla chips; grilled quesadillas, tacos

- 12 jalapeño chilies, seeded and chopped
- 6 ripe roma tomatoes, chopped
- 2 bunches scallions, chopped
- 4 cloves garlic, minced
- 3 limes, juiced
- 4 sprigs fresh cilantro, chopped
- Sea salt and freshly ground pepper

In a medium bowl, mix the jalapeños, tomatoes, scallions, and garlic together. Add the lime juice and mix. The salsa should be wet but not "swimming" in juice. Add the cilantro and salt and pepper to taste. This is best eaten fresh but can be made up to 1 day in advance.

Ruben's Dressed-Up Salsa Variation

Add 2 chopped mangos, 1 cup of fresh corn kernels, and 1/2 cup cooked and drained black beans to the salsa. Adding these extra ingredients will also dilute the heat.

Note: Use rubber kitchen gloves when handling chilies to avoid burning your skin with the chile oil.

Irene's Hot Pepper Jelly

Makes 5 1/2 cups

Every time I visit my friend, Kirsten Newman-Teissier in Pennsylvania, we plan one day to cook—and always eat—with her mother, Irene. Renie, as she is known to her family, may be food TV's biggest fan. During a recent visit, she had just made a batch of hot pepper jelly that was a little different than all the hot pepper jellies that I had growing up in North Carolina. Her version is made with green bell peppers and both red and green chilies. The jelly was sweet and hot and tangy and had more dimension than most. When I made her version, I added the red chile flakes that have always been present in the Southern jellies and switched up the peppers to red and green bell peppers, since you can always find red bell peppers in the grocery store but you can't always find red hot peppers. I love this jelly so much that I use it for lots of recipes in this book.

Good for Slathering: Cream cheese on a cracker (a classic Southern appetizer); or lamb, pork, or beef as a condiment or glaze

- 1/2 cup chopped green bell pepper
- 3/4 cup chopped red bell pepper
- 1/4 cup chopped jalapeño chilies
- 1 1/2 cups apple cider vinegar
- 6 1/2 cups sugar
- 6 ounces pectin
- 2 teaspoons red chile flakes

1. Put the peppers, chilies, and vinegar in a food processor or blender and puree.

2. Pour the puree into a large pot and add the sugar. Bring to a boil and boil for 3 minutes.

3. Whisk in the pectin and continue boiling for 1 minute. Skim the foam from the top. Remove from the heat and let sit for 5 minutes; skim the foam again. Stir in the red chile flakes.

4. Pour into hot sterilized jelly jars. Seal and store in a cool place.

Note: Store the jelly in sterilized jars. I sterilize my jars in the dishwasher and time it so that the cycle is finished when the jelly is done. If you've never sterilized jars before, before you do, check the procedure online or in books about canning and preserving.

Jezebel Sauce

Makes 4 cups

If you are from the South, you may recognize Jezebel sauce as a sweet-hot condiment that is frequently slathered over cream cheese and eaten with Wheatsworth crackers. No one really knows where Jezebel sauce comes from—some say Tennessee, some say the Carolinas—but regardless, it is perfect with both grilled meats—especially pork—and cream cheese and crackers! When you make the sauce, consider doubling the batch and taking a jar to your favorite griller with a bottle of your favorite Reisling—you'll definitely be their favorite grill friend!

Good for Slathering: Cream cheese; pork chops, tenderloin, ham; toss with grilled chicken salad

One 16- to 18-ounce jar pineapple preserves

One 16- to 18-ounce jar no-sugar-added apricot jam or jelly

1/2 cup prepared horseradish (not cream-style)

3 tablespoons dry mustard, preferably Colman's

2 teaspoons coarsely ground pepper

Combine all the ingredients in a large bowl with a fork or in a food processor. The fork produces a chunkier sauce, the food processor a smoother sauce. The sauce tastes the same; it is just a textural difference. Cover and refrigerate. The sauce will keep, tightly covered in the refrigerator, for up to 1 week.

Note: If you use 12-ounce jars, the yield will be 3 1/2 cups.

Chow-Chow, a.k.a Ultimate Pickle Relish

Makes 6 cups

Chow-chow is a relish with roots in the South and, interestingly, the state of Pennsylvania. It is said that the name derives from the French word for cabbage—*chou*—which makes sense until you consider that this is not a dish that we adopted from any French-speaking region. It is a pickled relish that always includes cabbage and turmeric, which gives it the distinctive yellow color. Other than that, recipes vary greatly from cook to cook. This version includes green tomatoes, which I love. You won't be able to tell where the cabbage starts and the onions end as the flavors blend together perfectly.

Make sure you grate the cabbage to look like a dice, not a slice. You want the vegetables to be close to the same size.

Good for Slathering: Pork; hamburgers; hot dogs, sausages

> 1 medium head fresh green cabbage, grated by hand or with a food processor
>
> 3 cups chopped Vidalia or other sweet onions (about 2 large onions)
>
> 1 1/2 cups chopped green tomatoes or underripe red tomatoes (about 3 tomatoes)
>
> 4 tablespoons kosher salt
>
> 3 cups distilled white vinegar
>
> 2 cups sugar or Sugar in the Raw (turbinado)
>
> 2 teaspoons dry mustard, preferably Colman's
>
> 2 teaspoons ground turmeric
>
> 2 teaspoons pickling spice
>
> 2 teaspoons whole mustard seeds
>
> 1 teaspoon whole cloves
>
> 1 teaspoon whole black peppercorns
>
> 2 teaspoons red chile flakes, optional

1. In a large nonreactive bowl, mix the chopped vegetables and sprinkle with salt. Let stand for 4 to 6 hours in the refrigerator. Drain the vegetables and absorb any excess liquid with paper towels.

2. In a large stockpot, combine the vinegar, sugar, dry mustard, turmeric, pickling spice, mustard seeds, cloves, peppercorns, and chile flakes, if using, and simmer for 10 minutes.

3. Add the vegetables to the simmering vinegar mixture and simmer for another 15 to 25 minutes or until the vegetables are crisp-tender. At this point, bring to a boil for 2 minutes.

4. Pack, boiling hot, into sterilized, heated canning jars, leaving 1/8 inch head space. Place canning lids and rings on the jars and tighten. Turn the hot jars upside down so that all the heat is on the seals. Turn them back upright when the jars are completely cool.

5. After the chow-chow cools, you can start using it immediately. It will keep for up to 6 months in a pantry or 2 weeks in the refrigerator once it has been opened.

Pepper Chow-Chow Variation

Add red or green bell peppers to the mix. I like mine without bell peppers, but feel free to add them; the red color is very pretty in the chow-chow. Sometimes I also add a jalapeño or other chile to add some heat to the mix.

Fresh Cherry–Horseradish Relish

Makes about 3 cups

You cannot believe how good this relish is! I make a similar relish in the fall using cranberries. One summer, I wanted to make the relish to top smoked oysters but it wasn't the season for cranberries. Undaunted, I searched the farmer's market for a cranberry replacement. I picked up a bag of fresh, dark Bing cherries for the relish. Oh, my! What a sweet surprise. Try them both, cranberry for winter with smoked oysters or a smoked turkey and cherry for summer with smoked or grilled oysters or fish—or just eat it with a spoon!

Good for Slathering: Smoked or grilled oysters; shrimp cocktail; trout; grilled pork loin or skirt steak

> 3/4 pound fresh Bing cherries, pitted
>
> Juice and zest of 1 large lemon
>
> Juice and zest of 1 large lime
>
> 1/4 cup Sugar in the Raw (turbinado)
>
> 2 tablespoons vodka
>
> 3 tablespoons prepared horseradish (not cream-style), or more to taste
>
> Tabasco sauce
>
> Kosher salt

1. Chop the cherries into 1/4 inch pieces. In a large nonreactive bowl, mix the cherries, lemon juice and zest, and lime juice and zest. Add the sugar, mix to combine, and let sit for 5 minutes.

2. Mix in the vodka and horseradish and let sit for 5 more minutes. Mix again and season with Tabasco and kosher salt. Let sit for another 5 minutes, taste, and correct the seasonings again. Refrigerate until ready to use. The relish will keep, tightly covered, in the refrigerator for up to 2 days. Mix well before serving.

Smoked Oysters with Fresh Cherry–Horseradish Relish

Serves 4

> Alder or cherry wood chips, soaked in water for 30 minutes
>
> 16 freshly shucked oysters
>
> 16 oyster half-shells (bottom shells)
>
> 4 teaspoons (1/2 stick) unsalted butter
>
> Sea salt
>
> 1 recipe Fresh Cherry–Horseradish Relish (page 165)

1. Build a charcoal fire or preheat a gas grill. In a gas grill, fill the smoker box or aluminum tray with wet wood chips. In a charcoal grill, place two handfuls of wet wood chips directly on the white-gray ash of the briquettes. Alternatively, you can smoke the oysters in the Cameron Stovetop Smoker, but do not soak the Cameron wood dust.

2. Prepare the oysters: Place 1 raw oyster with a little of its juice on each half-shell on a tray. Put a pat of butter—about 1/4 teaspoon—and a pinch of sea salt in the center of each oyster. Refrigerate until ready to cook.

3. When the chips begin to smoke, reduce the heat and place the oysters, shell side down, in the center of the cooking grate and let smoke over low heat for 10 to 15 minutes or until the edges curl and the butter bubbles.

4. Remove from the grill and serve immediately with a dollop of the relish.

Roasted Garlic and Shallot Jam

Makes 3 cups

If you love garlic, you will swoon with delight once you taste this savory jam. Although it takes a little while to make, you'll be glad you have it on hand to top a quick grilled steak or pork chop or to serve with your favorite cheeses. It is also great spread over grilled bread, with or without a little butter. Since you need so many garlic cloves, this is one recipe where it is okay to buy prepeeled garlic cloves.

Good for Slathering: Hanger steak; burgers; pork tenderloin; roasted lamb; sandwiches

 24 shallots, about 2 pounds, peeled
 Olive oil
 1 tablespoon kosher salt, plus more for sprinkling
 30 to 40 large cloves garlic, peeled
 1 cup Sugar in the Raw (turbinado)
 1/4 cup honey
 1 cup spring or bottled water, more as needed
 2 cups red wine vinegar

 2 tablespoons distilled white vinegar
 2 tablespoons Cognac
 2 teaspoons dried thyme, or 4 sprigs fresh thyme

1. Preheat the oven or a grill to 400°F. Coat the shallots in olive oil and sprinkle generously with salt. Lay on a sheet pan fitted with a cooling rack.

2. Place the garlic cloves on a double layer of aluminum foil; drizzle with oil and sprinkle with salt, tossing to make sure each clove is oiled and seasoned—you may need to make 2 foil packets. Place both the shallots and garlic in the oven (or on the grill) and roast for 30 to 45 minutes, checking occasionally. You want them to be pliable and pale golden in color but not completely mushy since you will be cooking them again.

3. Meanwhile, mix the sugar, honey, water, red wine vinegar, white vinegar, Cognac, the 1 tablespoon salt, and the thyme in a large, nonreactive, heavy-bottomed saucepan set over medium heat. Stir to make sure the salt and sugar are dissolved. Add the shallots and garlic and stir gently. Bring to a boil and then reduce the heat. Simmer for 2 hours, stirring occasionally, until the shallots are translucent and soft enough to smash and spread. Taste and adjust the seasoning if necessary with a splash of vinegar.

4. Remove from the heat and cool before serving. The jam will keep, tightly covered in the refrigerator, for about 2 weeks.

Dried Pear and Ginger Chutney

Makes 3 cups

I love dried pears and crystallized ginger. But nothing can compare to what happens when you combine them in this sweet-hot chutney that I created as an accessory for grilled meat. And, as good as it is with grilled pork and game, it is killer spread on toast in the morning or served with cheese in the evening.

Good for Slathering: pork chops, pork loin, fresh ham, game, sausages; chicken, game hen, quail

> 1 pound dried pears, coarsely chopped
> 1/2 pound chunks crystallized ginger
> 1/4 cup golden raisins
> 1/2 cup sugar
> 2/3 cup spring or bottled water
> Juice and zest of 1 lemon
> 1/2 cup champagne vinegar
> 1/2 cup pear eau de vie* or pear juice
> 1 cinnamon stick, broken in half
> 1/4 teaspoon sea salt

1. Mix the pears, ginger, and raisins in a medium, nonreactive, heavy-bottomed saucepan. Cover with the sugar, water, lemon juice and zest, vinegar, eau de vie, cinnamon stick, and salt. Stir to dissolve the sugar and salt.

2. Simmer slowly over medium heat to break down the dried fruit and ginger, stirring occasionally. Bring to a low boil and then reduce the heat. Simmer for

15 to 20 minutes, stirring occasionally, until the mixture resembles a chunky jam. Check the seasonings and adjust if necessary with a squirt of fresh lemon juice and/or a pinch of salt. (It should be plenty sweet, but you don't want it to be too sweet.)

3. Remove from the heat and let cool before serving. Remove the cinnamon stick. The chutney will keep, tightly covered in the refrigerator, for about 1 week.

Eau de vie (translated as "water of life") is the French name for a clear fruit brandy that is prepared with freshly harvested ripe fruit (e.g., pears, peaches, berries) that is crushed whole and fermented prior to distillation. Unlike the brandy from Cognac, eau de vie is not generally aged in wooden casks, which is the reason it remains colorless. The ripe fruit is fermented, distilled, and bottled quickly to preserve the freshness and aroma of the fruit.

Cranberry Chutney with Dried Apricots, Port, and Cherries

Makes about 3 1/2 cups

I created this Thanksgiving chutney the year I discovered dried cherries—many, many years before I knew that I would be writing up recipes for a living. Since that year, this cranberry concoction has been my family's favorite and one of those must-have side dishes. I used to carry it with me on the airplane to Thanksgiving functions, since it can be made up to a week in advance and only gets better. You'll be tempted to eat it with a spoon, but save some for the post-Thanksgiving sandwich. Mixed with a little cream cheese, it makes a "leftovers" sandwich that may rival the original meal.

Good for Slathering: Turkey, turkey sandwiches; venison chops; pork; soft stinky cheese

    Two 12-ounce bags fresh cranberries
    1 cup port
    1 cup spring or bottled water
    1/2 cup fresh orange juice
    Zest of 1 orange
    2 tablespoons balsamic vinegar, divided
    1 cup sugar
    1/2 teaspoon sea salt
    1/4 teaspoon ground nutmeg
    1/4 teaspoon ground cloves
    1/2 teaspoon ground cinnamon
    2/3 cup Turkish apricots, cut into slivers
    2/3 cup dried cherries
    1/2 cup pecan or walnut pieces, lightly toasted, optional

1. Pour the cranberries into a medium, nonreactive, heavy-bottomed saucepan. Cover with the port, water, orange juice and zest, and 1 tablespoon of the vinegar. Stir and add the sugar and salt and stir again. Add the nutmeg, cloves, and cinnamon. Stir and place over medium heat. Stir to make sure the salt and sugar are dissolved in the liquid.

2. Add the apricots and cherries. Simmer slowly to "pop" the cranberries and soften the dried fruit, stirring occasionally. Bring to a low boil and then reduce the heat. Simmer for 45 to 55 minutes, stirring occasionally, until the mixture resembles a chunky jam. Remove from the heat and

add the remaining 1 tablespoon of balsamic vinegar and stir. Check for seasonings and adjust if necessary with a pinch of salt. Add the pecan pieces, if desired.

3. Let cool before serving. The chutney will keep, tightly covered, in the refrigerator for about 2 weeks.

Hell of a Carrot-Jalapeño Relish

Makes 4 cups

If you are in Houston or Austin, you can buy Gail Calder's version of this condiment, called Hell of a Relish. The first time I tasted this, about 10 years ago, I couldn't stop eating it. I used to bring it back on the plane with me every time I visited, but with the current carry-on restrictions, I've been forced to make my own from my recollection of the original. The sweet, hot, crunchy relish is truly addicting. You can make the relish as the recipe reads or double the hot peppers for a "hotter than Hades" relish! Contrary to popular belief, the heat is not in the seeds of the jalapeños but in the white veins or "ribs," but I remove the seeds because I don't like eating them; you can leave them in if you like.

Good for Slathering: Sausages, hot dogs; cream cheese and crackers; out of the jar with a spoon

> 3 pounds carrots, peeled and coarsely grated by hand or with a food processor
>
> 6 shallots, sliced on a mandoline into thin rings (1 cup)
>
> 6 to 10 jalapeño chilies or assorted hot peppers, seeded and sliced into thin rings
>
> 2 tablespoons kosher salt
>
> 3 cups distilled white vinegar
>
> 2 cups sugar or Sugar in the Raw (turbinado)
>
> 2 teaspoons pickling spice
>
> 2 teaspoons red chile flakes, optional
>
> 1 teaspoon whole cloves
>
> 1 teaspoon whole black peppercorns

1. In a large stockpot, mix the carrots, shallots, and jalapeños and set aside.

2. In a medium heavy-bottomed stockpot, combine the salt, vinegar, sugar, pickling spice, chile flakes if desired, cloves, and peppercorns and bring to a boil.

3. When the vinegar mixture is boiling, pour it over the vegetables and stir continually with a long wooden spoon. The boiling water should "cook" the vegetables just enough; they should be brightly colored and crunchy.

4. When the vegetables have cooled to room temperature, transfer the vegetables to sterilized, heated canning jars, leaving 3 inches head space. (I wash and sterilize my jars in the dishwasher, timing it so the cycle is done and the jars are hot when I am ready to pack them.)

5. Bring the remaining liquid to a boil again and pour it into the jars, covering the vegetables but leaving 1/8 inch head space. You want there to be a high liquid-to-relish ratio.

6. Place canning lids and rings on the jars and tighten. Turn the hot jars upside down so that all the heat is on the seals. Turn them back upright when the jars are completely cool.

7. After the relish cools, you can use it immediately. It will keep, tightly covered, in the refrigerator for up to 6 months.

Pomegranate and Mint Salsa

Makes about 1 cup

The red and green color of this salsa instantly brings to mind the holidays, like Christmas or Easter—and it is just the thing for lamb chops. Add a little plain yogurt to the raw salsa and it is a condiment that is at home on grilled meat, fish, or veggies—I really like it on top of grilled eggplant, zucchini, and yellow summer squash. A small note: I generally like to use a Microplane for all my zesting, but in this case, I like the thicker, coarser zest that comes from a traditional zester.

Good for Slathering: Lamb; chicken thighs; swordfish; grilled feta cheese

- 1 tablespoon simple syrup (see page 135)
- 1 tablespoon vodka
- 1 tablespoon pomegranate juice
- Pinch fleur de sel
- 1 whole pomegranate, seeds removed*
- Zest of 1 lemon
- 1/4 cup chopped fresh mint

Mix the simple syrup, vodka, and pomegranate juice together. Add the fleur de sel, stir, and set aside. Gently mix in the pomegranate seeds, lemon zest, and mint. Pour the liquid over the salsa and mix to coat. Serve at room temperature immediately.

*If you can't find fresh pomegranate seeds, substitute the pulp of 3 passion fruits.

Blueberry-Ginger Salsa

Makes 1 3/4 cups

This pretty blueberry salsa has crazy mixed-up origins, borrowing key flavors from lots of different cuisines, but the end result is one of those beautiful fusion dishes that works, elevating the status of anything you add it to. I like to use it on grilled fish as well as skirt steak and grilled fruit. It's a salsa that can go anywhere, anytime. Make this salsa at least 2 hours in advance, allowing the flavors to blend together.

Good for Slathering: Grilled fish; skirt steak; chicken; pork; grilled fruit such as mango or pineapple

- 1 small knob (1/2 inch) fresh ginger, grated
- 1/4 small chile, such as habanero, chopped
- 2 teaspoons extra-virgin olive oil
- Juice of 1 lime
- Zest of 1/2 lemon
- 2 teaspoons honey
- 2 teaspoons Chambord
- 1/4 teaspoon sea salt
- 1 pint fresh blueberries
- Pinch of sweet smoked Spanish paprika
- 4 leafy sprigs fresh basil or mint, leaves removed and cut into chiffonade

1. In a medium nonreactive bowl, mix the ginger, chile (taste a tiny piece of the chile for heat before adding to the mix), olive oil, lime juice, lemon zest, honey, Chambord, and sea salt. Adjust the lime juice, salt, and sugar to taste. There should be a good sweet-tart ratio.

2. Put the blueberries in a medium bowl and pour the "dressing" over the blueberries. Let sit for 5 minutes, tossing to coat all of the berries. Add the smoked paprika and mix again.

3. Refrigerate until ready to use. Just before serving, toss with the basil. Mix again before serving. Use the same day you make it.

Note: My friend Irene Haeckel "preserves" ginger by submerging it in a small, clean jar of vodka. This keeps the peeled ginger fresh and at the ready any time you need to use a little ginger—and can you imagine how yummy that vodka tastes? Add a little club soda and some simple syrup and you have a very adult ginger ale! Brilliant.

Sweet Sauces

Drizzled or spread on foods after cooking to balance savory, tart, or spicy foods or to enhance sweet foods.

Sweet Sauces 101

Sweet sauces are just the thing to turn grilled fruit from good to great! This section of dessert sauces covers some of my favorites, from the Sweetheart Lemon Curd and the passion fruit variation (page 186) to classics like Bittersweet Chocolate Ganache (facing page) and Peach Melba Sauce (page 184). I love to drizzle my favorite sauces on plates before dishing up simple grilled fruit, cobblers, or grilled pound cake, as well as to use them when making full-blown banana splits with chocolate, butterscotch, and strawberry sauce. I also like using the fruit curds as fillings between layers of cake. I love making my mother's fresh grated coconut cake (see *Taming the Flame*) and substituting the passion fruit curd for icing between the layers.

If you don't have time to grill your dessert, make the sauce anyway and serve it on top of ice cream for a sweet ending to a weeknight meal. Most of these sauces can be folded into softened ice cream for a homemade mix-in that will save you a trip to your neighborhood ice cream parlor. A homemade sauce is a great way to dress up and "cheat" a store-bought cake or pie. And—be honest—you might not want all-grilled-all-the-time; there are plenty of times when pancakes, waffles, crêpes, or cheesecake is on the menu. For those times and more, here are a few great sauces that can turn your basics into signatures.

Shelf Life

Most sweet sauces can be made up to 3 days in advance. Sauces that can be made in advance should be stored in a clean glass jar with a tight-fitting lid in the refrigerator. If necessary, warm or bring to room temperature before serving.

Sweet Sauce 101: Bittersweet Chocolate Ganache

Makes almost 1 cup

If there were a "mother sauce for sweets," this would be it. Chocolate ganache is the classic term for the best chocolate sauce you've ever tasted. In its purest form, bittersweet chocolate is thinned out with heavy cream and enhanced with a touch of salt. I add a touch of bourbon to add dimension to the sauce. This ganache is so easy to make that it is plain criminal to buy bottled sauce, which never tastes as good and is always expensive. It can be used any way you like—as a dip for strawberries and other fruit, a glaze for a cake, or a drizzle for a plate or a tart, and it is amazing ladled generously over ice cream and grilled bananas for the ultimate split. Check out the flavor variations below, but imagination and a love of chocolate is all you need to create your own.

Good for Slathering: Grilled bananas, strawberries, poundcake, cheesecake, tarts and pies, ice cream

> 6 ounces bittersweet chocolate (chips or chopped block chocolate), preferably 70 percent cacoa
>
> 1/3 cup heavy whipping cream
>
> 1/8 teaspoon fine-grain sea salt
>
> 1/2 teaspoon vanilla extract
>
> 2 tablespoons liquor or liqueur (e.g., bourbon, dark rum, Frangelico, or your favorite liqueur), optional

Put the chocolate in a medium stainless steel bowl and set aside. Heat the cream in a small heavy-bottomed saucepan to almost boiling, then remove from the heat and add to the chocolate. Whisk vigorously to melt the chocolate, and then place the bowl over a small saucepan of simmering water to finish the melting. Add the salt, vanilla, and liqueur, if using, stirring constantly. Cover with plastic wrap and set aside or refrigerate. The ganache will keep, tightly covered, in the refrigerator for up to 1 week.

Chocolate Ganache Variations

Grand Marnier (Orange) Ganache

Stir in the zest of 1 orange and use Grand Marnier for the liqueur.

Chocolate Peanut Butter Ganache

Increase the heavy cream to 1/2 cup and mix in 1/4 cup smooth peanut butter with the chocolate. Use Skippy Natural for the best results.

Kahlúa Ganache

Add 2 teaspoons instant espresso powder to the heavy cream and use Kahlúa for the liqueur.

Mint Ganache

Use peppermint schnapps for the liqueur. For a festive touch around the holidays, you can also reduce the extract by half and stir in 1/4 cup crushed peppermints or candy canes once the ganache is at room temperature (otherwise it will melt and you'll loose the crunchy texture).

Milk Chocolate and Almond Ganache

Increase the cream to 1/2 cup and substitute 6 ounces milk chocolate for 4 ounces of the bittersweet chocolate. (You will have 2 ounces bittersweet and 6 ounces milk chocolate.) Add 1/4 cup toasted slivered almonds and use amaretto for the liqueur.

Crystalized Ginger Ganache

Stir in 1/4 cup diced crystallized ginger when the ganache is still hot. You can also use Domaine de Canton ginger liqueur, although Grand Marnier or Frangelico combined with crystallized ginger is very nice.

Raspberry Ganache

Stir in 3 tablespoons of no-sugar-added seedless raspberry jam when the ganache is still hot. Use 3 tablespoons Chambord or crème de cassis for the liqueur.

Build-a-Better Banana Split Sundae

Serves 4

Grilling Method: Direct/Low Heat

> 4 firm but ripe unpeeled bananas
> 1 tablespoon Basic Dessert Rub (page 218)
> 8 small scoops best-quality vanilla ice cream
> 1 recipe Bittersweet Chocolate Ganache (page 177) or Butterscotch Sauce (page 182), warmed
> 4 tablespoons coarsely chopped pecans or walnuts, toasted
> Whipped cream, optional
> Maraschino cherries, optional

1. Build a charcoal fire or preheat a gas grill. Slice the bananas in half crosswise and then lengthwise so that each banana yields 4 pieces. Sprinkle the cut sides of the bananas with dessert rub. Let the bananas sit on a baking sheet or platter for 5 minutes.

2. Place the bananas cut side down on the cooking grate over direct low heat. Cook for 2 minutes or until grill marks appear. Using a pair of long-handled tongs, turn over onto the skin sides and let cook for 5 more minutes or until the skin pulls away from the bananas.

3. Let the bananas cool slightly, then remove the skins. Arrange 2 banana halves on each serving plate. Top each serving with 2 scoops of ice cream. Ladle 1/4 cup of warmed chocolate or butterscotch sauce, or a bit of both, over each sundae. Sprinkle each with 1 tablespoon chopped nuts, and if desired, add whipped cream and a cherry on top. Serve immediately.

Dinner Party Crème Anglaise

Makes about 1 cup

Crème anglaise is an English specialty and is simply a pourable custard—or custard sauce. When I was a kid, I could just drink this stuff, although of course I wasn't supposed to! My mother has a thing for floating island and dark chocolate pâte—she would serve both in shallow bowls swimming in the rich, cool crème anglaise. After I said good night to our company, I was always a little nervous that when it came time for her to serve the dessert. One bowl would end up sans crème, as I had been sneaking little tastes all day. Since I was safely tucked in and sleeping by that time, I never knew if that happened, and until now, she may not have known that I was the reason she always had less than she thought!

This is my mother's recipe, which was adapted from Julia Child's *The French Chef Cookbook*. It can be doubled easily and is just as good with fruit. Serve with a bowl full of grilled or fresh berries topped with shavings of dark chocolate.

Good for Slathering: Light, airy cakes like sponge and angel food cake, grilled peaches, berries, all fruit, use as a sauce for floating islands, chocolate pâte, chocolate cake, tiramisu, or ice cream

3 egg yolks

1 1/4 cups whole milk or half-and-half

1 vanilla bean, split in half and scraped, or 2 generous teaspoons vanilla extract

1/3 cup sugar

Pinch fine-grain sea salt

4 1/2 teaspoons Grand Marnier or Cognac

1 tablespoon unsalted butter, softened, optional

1. Whisk the egg yolks in a 3-quart stainless steel or enameled saucepan until thick and sticky, about 1 minute. Meanwhile, in another saucepan, slowly heat the milk, the scrapings from the vanilla bean, and the vanilla bean. When the milk is hot but not boiling, remove the bean and remove the milk from heat.

2. Gradually stir the sugar into the eggs. Beat until light and frothy. Next, add the hot milk bit by bit, stirring gently until it is completely mixed in, tempering the eggs. If you pour the milk in all at once, the eggs will cook and become sweet scrambled eggs!

3. Place the saucepan on the stove over medium-low heat and stir with a wooden spoon or silicone spatula until the sauce thickens enough to coat the spoon. Do not let the sauce come to a boil or the egg yolks will curdle. Remove from the heat and stir in the vanilla, then the liquor and the butter, if desired. Serve warm or refrigerate for at least 3 hours or up to 2 days and serve cold. The sauce will keep, tightly covered, in the refrigerator for 2 days.

Walnut-Honey Sauce

Makes 1 1/2 cups

This super-easy sauce really doesn't need a recipe. Once you start making it, you'll experiment with different nuts and honeys and may even put some up for impromptu guests and gifts (in a decorative jar, it makes a great hostess gift). This is one of my favorite sauces to serve with a cheese course that includes some grilled fruit like apples, pears, and apricots. Try this simple but impressive presentation: Grill pitted and halved apricots over indirect medium heat until warmed through and gently marked, about 5 minutes, Remove from grill and stuff apricots with fresh ricotta cheese and drizzle with this sauce. Serve with a glass of your favorite dessert wine.

Good for Slathering: Ice cream, cake, apple pie, baked apples, grilled strawberries, grilled apricots

1 cup wildwood or your favorite honey
2 teaspoons Chambord, optional
1 cup walnut halves, lightly toasted
(or substitute your favorite nuts)

In a medium bowl, mix the honey with the Chambord, if desired, until it is completely incorporated. Mix the nuts into the honey. Pour the mixture into clean glass jars. The honey and nuts will keep, tightly covered, in a cool place for up to 1 month. If you store it in the refrigerator, you may need to bring it back to room temperature in a warm water bath before using.

Note: To toast nuts for any recipe, place nuts on a dry baking sheet and place in a preheated 300°F oven. Do not toast on a pan on the stove or the nuts will be unevenly toasted, burned in some spots and still "raw" in others.

Hitting the Hard Sauce

Makes about 1 cup

This is my other favorite sweet sauce from childhood. It was originally called hard sauce because it was thinned out with "hard" liquor and spread on fruit cake and fruit compotes. These days, I like it dolloped on a warm apple betty or a fresh fruit crumble. It is typically served cold and "hard" as a contrast to hot desserts like bread pudding, spice cake, and fruit cakes. Once it hits the hot dessert, it melts into a sweet, strong, buttery pool of wonderfulness.

Good for Slathering: Berry crumble, hot gingerbread, bread pudding, grill-baked apples, apple betty, apple pie, homemade fruit cake

1/2 cup (1 stick) unsalted butter, softened

1 1/2 cups sifted confectioners' sugar

Pinch fine-grain sea salt

2 teaspoons vanilla extract

1 to 2 tablespoons brandy or cream sherry

In an electric mixer, cream the butter until soft and fluffy. Gradually, blend in the confectioners' sugar, salt, and vanilla. Add the brandy to taste. The sauce will keep, tightly covered, in the refrigerator for up to 1 week.

Butterscotch Sauce

Makes 1 cup

Butterscotch is the poor man's caramel. Made with brown sugar and butter, and sometimes evaporated milk, butterscotch is completely foolproof and not as intimidating as making caramel. These days I am more apt to make the French caramel or dulce de leche (the recipe-in-a-can version), but I have a soft spot in my heart for butterscotch because my best friend growing up would always order the butterscotch sundaes when the rest of us ordered chocolate! This sauce screams for ice cream, and I prefer its buttery, lighter flavor over traditional caramel when pairing it with acid-rich grilled fruit, especially pineapple.

Good for Slathering: Ice cream, grilled fruit, pineapple, bananas, pound cake

1/2 cup packed light brown sugar

1/4 cup sugar

1/2 cup light corn syrup

1/4 teaspoon fine-grain sea salt

1 cup heavy whipping cream, divided

4 tablespoons (1/2 stick) unsalted butter

1 teaspoon vanilla extract

2 teaspoons dark rum

1. Mix the sugars, corn syrup, salt, and 1/2 cup of the cream together in a medium heavy-duty saucepan. Add the butter and place over medium-low heat.

2. Stir frequently with a wooden spoon or silicone spatula. The mixture will begin to thicken and reach the soft-ball stage (235°F to 240°F) in 10 to 15 minutes. Use a candy thermometer to test for this, or if you don't have a candy thermometer, use this old-fashioned method: Fill a small bowl or even a coffee cup with ice water. Dip a fork into the sauce and let the sauce drip over the ice water. If the sauce forms a soft ball, the texture of taffy, then it is ready. If the sauce dissolves in the water, it needs to cook more.

3. When the sauce is at the soft-ball stage, stir in the remaining 1/2 cup cream, being careful of any "sputters" and splashes of hot sugar. *Note: When adding and stirring in the cream, wear an oven mitt on your stirring hand. The heat of the sugar may create scalding steam when it comes into contact with the cream.*

4. Continue cooking until the sauce is thick and has a smooth, creamy consistency, about 5 more minutes. Remove from the heat and stir in the vanilla and rum. Let cool. The sauce will keep, tightly covered, in the refrigerator for up to 1 week.

Burnt Salted Caramel Sauce

Makes about 1 cup

Salted caramels have become trendy in the past few years, with everyone from Trader Joe's to top confectioners making caramels in the style of the candy makers in Brittany, France. The most inspired of these stateside sweets is a dark chocolate–covered burnt caramel garnished with big chunky crystals of sel gris, gray sea salt. Take a cue from these amazing candies and make this sauce and the Bittersweet Chocolate Ganache (page 177) to top a simple slice of cake or swirl into softened ice cream. And in keeping with the barbecue theme, substitute smoked salt for the regular salt.

Good for Slathering: Warm baked apples, apple pie, ice cream, spice cake, grilled pound cake

  1 cup sugar
  2 tablespoons water
  1 cup heavy whipping cream
  1/4 teaspoon vanilla extract

6 teaspoons fleur de sel, gray sea salt, or smoked sea salt

1. Combine the sugar and water in a medium saucepan—the best pan is a tall 1 1/2-quart pan. Cook over medium heat, but do not stir until the sugar melts and turns dark golden brown, about 7 minutes. (Keep a watchful eye on the sugar, because it will go from being dark brown to being burned in about 1 minute.)

2. Stir to combine and melt any sugar crystals. The mixture will continue to cook and reach the soft-ball stage (235°F to 240°F) in about 5 minutes. Use a candy thermometer to test for this, or if you don't have a candy thermometer, use this old-fashioned method: Fill a small bowl or even a coffee cup with ice water. Dip a fork into the sauce and let the sauce drip over the ice water. If the sauce forms a soft ball, the texture of taffy, then it is ready. If the sauce dissolves in the water, it needs to cook more.

3. Immediately remove the pan from the heat and whisk in the cream and vanilla. Place the saucepan back on the stove and cook over low heat until smooth and thickened, about 12 minutes. Stir vigorously until the mixture is smooth. *Note: When adding and stirring in the cream, wear an oven mitt on your stirring hand. The heat of the sugar may create scalding steam when it comes into contact with the cream.* Remove from the heat and stir in the salt.

4. At this point, the caramel sauce will appear to be thin but will form a ball in ice-water if you use that test. After it cools, it will thicken to the right consistency. The sauce will keep, tightly covered, in the refrigerator for up to 1 week.

One 12-ounce bag frozen raspberries or any other favorite berry

1 to 3 tablespoons superfine sugar, depending on tartness of berries

2 teaspoons fresh lemon juice

1 tablespoon Chambord, optional

Puree the frozen raspberries, sugar, and lemon juice in a blender on high speed. Add the Chambord liqueur, if desired. Strain through a fine-mesh strainer to remove the seeds. Discard the solids. The sauce will keep, tightly covered, in the refrigerator for up to 3 days.

Peach Melba Sauce

Makes about 1 1/2 cups

The classic Melba sauce was created in honor of Dame Nellie Melba, an Australian soprano, and was designed to be served with peaches and vanilla ice cream. The original recipe called for cooking the raspberries with sugar, red currant jelly, and cornstarch. This was the very first sauce that I learned to make, and I loved making it because all I did was blend sugar and raspberries together—it was only recently that I learned there was a cooked version of the sauce. My current version is not cooked and is almost identical to what I made in the fifth grade with my friend Ann Rucker. It is really more of a raspberry coulis—but we thought we were mighty sophisticated making Peach Melba. You can substitute any berries for the raspberries —or use a combination of three or four.

Good for Slathering: Any grilled fruit, chocolate, ice cream, mousse, grilled pound cake

Hungarian Gooseberry Sauce

When I visited Budapest with my Hungarian friend, Marian Temesvary, we ate like kings and queens. And much of the time, we ate home-cooked meals that her sister-in-law Andi and her mother, Maria, made us. Most people have heard of the goulash served in Eastern Europe, but what you don't hear as much about are the fabulous desserts. This gooseberry sauce was served with a simple hazelnut cake and was my favorite of all the sweets. The surprise (for me) was the addition of sour cream to the simple fruit sauce.

Good for Slathering: Grilled fruit; grilled pound cake

1 pound fresh or canned* gooseberries, cleaned

1/4 to 1/2 cup sugar, depending on the tartness of the berries

Juice of 1 lemon
2 tablespoons butter
2 tablespoons flour
Salt
1/2 cup sour cream

1. In a large saucepan, combine the berries with the sugar and lemon juice. Add enough water to cover the berries and cook over a medium heat until soft.

2. Meanwhile, make a light roux (flour thickener) by cooking the butter and flour in a sauté pan until pale brown. You don't want the flour to change color very much but you want to cook out the raw flour taste. Mix the roux with about ½ cup of the cooking liquid and cook until it is thickened. Add the roux mixture to the berries.

3. Simmer the sauce for 2 to 3 minutes and taste. Add a pinch of salt and adjust the sugar if necessary. Stir in the sour cream and let cool to room temperature or refrigerate. Best used the day it is made.

*If you use canned gooseberry skip the "cooking" part.

White Chocolate Mint Sauce

Makes 1 1/3 cups

This is the perfect sauce to make for a special occasion. It is cool and refreshing and adds a touch of elegance to any dessert. The mint flavor comes from the schnapps, so it is easy to vary the flavor of this creamy sauce by choosing another liqueur. I've received rave results when making it with

cinnamon schnapps, green melon–flavored Midori, passion fruit–infused Alizé, and coconut rum such as Malibu—the last three make a perfect match for topping warm grilled tropical fruit.

Good for Slathering: Anything dark chocolate, grilled tropical fruit, dried fruit fondue, ice cream, cake, cheesecake

6 ounces white chocolate (chips or chopped block chocolate)
1/3 cup heavy whipping cream
Pinch fine-grain sea salt
1/8 cup plus 1 tablespoon peppermint schnapps
1/2 teaspoon vanilla extract

1. Put the chocolate in a medium stainless steel bowl and set aside. In a small pot set over medium heat, slowly heat the cream to almost boiling, then remove from the heat and let cool for several minutes.

2. Add the cream to the chocolate and stir vigorously until melted and well combined. If the chocolate is not completely melted, set the bowl over a small saucepan of simmering water. Whisk occasionally until all the chocolate is melted.

3. Remove from the heat and add the salt, liqueur, and vanilla, stirring constantly. The sauce will keep, tightly covered, in the refrigerator for up to 1 week.

Good-for-You Fruit-and-Nut White Chocolate Sauce

Makes 2 cups

When I lived in Paris as a student, I fell in love with a candy bar called Fitness. It was chock full of dried fruits and hazelnuts—albeit held together by a thick coating of rich white chocolate. Well, I was young and gullible and had to agree that anything that tasted good and was full of fruit and nuts had to be good for me. . . right? I've since found out from European friends that they really did think that those types of candy bars were good for them—kind of like the fitness bars of today. Regardless, it's a winning combination for a dessert sauce.

Good for Slathering: Baked apples, grilled pineapple or peaches, ice cream

> 8 ounces white chocolate (chips or chopped block chocolate)
>
> 1/2 cup heavy whipping cream
>
> Pinch fine-grain sea salt
>
> 1/8 cup liqueur (e.g., cherry or apricot kirsch, white rum, etc.)
>
> 1/2 teaspoon vanilla extract
>
> 1 tablespoon dried unsweetened coconut
>
> 1/2 cup assorted diced dried fruit, such as apricots, dried cherries, and currants
>
> 1/4 cup toasted and cracked hazelnuts

1. Put chocolate in a medium stainless steel bowl and set aside. In a small pot set over medium heat, slowly heat the cream to almost boiling, then remove from the heat and let cool for several minutes.

2. Add the cream to the chocolate and stir vigorously until melted and well combined. If the chocolate is not completely melted, set the bowl over a small saucepan of simmering water. Whisk occasionally until all the chocolate is melted.

3. Add the salt, liqueur, and vanilla, stirring constantly. Immediately stir in the coconut, dried fruit, and hazelnuts. Serve warm or at room temperature. The sauce will keep, tightly covered, in the refrigerator for up to 1 week.

Note: Instead of chopping hazelnuts, lay them out on a clean kitchen towel and lay a second towel over the hazelnuts. Use the back of a metal measuring cup or wooden spoon to swiftly tap the nuts. This motion will crack the nuts into pieces.

Sweetheart Lemon Curd and Four Variations

Makes about 1 1/2 cups

We have England and high tea to thank for this cool, sweet, tart, silky treasure that is fruit based and less sweet than custard or cream. If making curd scares you, don't let it. If you have ever made lemon bars, you've basically made a curd. The only difference here is that you are slowly cooking it on the stovetop instead of having it bake on top of a shortbread crust. The flavors listed here include my favorite Meyer lemon, passion fruit, orange, raspberry, and lime curd—all really good with grilled fruit, as a topping for meringues and cheesecake, as a filling for cakes, and folded into ice cream—creamsicle, anyone? For foolproof results, I am passing along a tip that Elinor Klivans gave in an article she wrote for *Fine Cooking* magazine: Cream all the ingredients like you are baking a cake before cooking them so that you don't wind up with curdled bits of egg.

Good for Slathering: Plain grilled fruit, yogurt, grilled brioche; layer shortcake or pound cake with curd and top with grilled fruit such as strawberries, peaches, or plums

 4 tablespoons (1/2 stick) unsalted butter, softened

 3/4 cup sugar

 1/4 teaspoon fine-grain sea salt

 4 egg yolks

 2/3 cup fresh Meyer lemon juice (about 3 lemons)

 1/4 cup spring or bottled water

 Finely grated zest of 2 Meyer lemons (or zest of 1 regular lemon)

1. In an electric mixer, cream the butter, sugar, and salt together until light and fluffy. Add the egg yolks one by one and cream them into the butter-sugar mixture. Add the lemon juice and water and mix until combined.

2. Pour into a heavy-bottomed nonreactive saucepan and cook over medium heat until it coats the back of a spoon, 15 to 20 minutes. The curd will go from transparent to opaque to lemon yellow in color. You will need to stir frequently, and you do not want the mixture to boil or it might curdle.

3. Take the curd off the heat and stir in the zest, mixing well. Turn out into a glass bowl and chill before using. The curd will keep, tightly covered, in the refrigerator for up to 1 week.

Note: If you don't have Meyer lemons, you can substitute 1/3 cup fresh lemon juice (about 1 1/2 lemons) and 1/3 cup orange juice.

Lime Curd Variation

Substitute 1/3 cup fresh lime juice (about 2 limes) and 1/3 cup fresh lemon juice (about 1 1/2 lemons) for the Meyer lemon juice. Stir in the zest of 1 large lime at the end.

Passion Fruit Curd Variation

Substitute 2/3 cup passion fruit puree for the lemon juice and eliminate the water and zest.

Orange Curd Variation

Substitute fresh orange juice for the lemon juice and water and add 2 tablespoons fresh lemon juice. Stir in orange zest instead of lemon zest at the end.

Raspberry/Strawberry Curd Variation

Substitute seedless strained frozen raspberries or strawberries or 1 cup of raspberry or strawberry puree for the lemon juice and water. Stir in the zest of 1 lemon at the end.

Note: To strain frozen berries: Take a 12-ounce bag of frozen raspberries (or strawberries) and let thaw in the bag. You can thaw under running water to speed the process, but do not open the bag and do not cook the berries! Once the berries are thawed, process through the fine blade of a food mill or through a fine-mesh strainer. Use the seedless liquid to make the curd.

Lemon-Orange Sauce

Makes about 2 1/2 cups

This is a versatile sauce that can be drizzled on fresh summer fruit—grilled or raw—or served in the fall over a warm slice of gingerbread, apple crumble, or pancakes. Anytime you want to add a ray of sunshine to a sweet plate, call on this sauce and you won't be disappointed!

Good for Slathering: French toast, pancakes, grilled peaches; ham

> 1 cup sugar
> 1/4 teaspoon fine-grain sea salt
> 1 tablespoon cornstarch
> 1 1/4 cups fresh orange juice
> 3/4 cup fresh lemon juice (about 6 lemons)
> 1 tablespoon cold unsalted butter
> Zest of 1 small lemon

1. Mix the sugar, salt, cornstarch, orange juice, and lemon juice together in a small, heavy-bottomed, nonreactive saucepan. Stir well to make sure there are no lumps.

2. Cook over medium-low heat until the sauce simmers. Let simmer for 2 to 3 minutes or until thick. Reduce the heat and cook for 5 more minutes or until the sauce coats the back of a spoon.

3. Remove from the heat and whisk in the butter. When the butter is fully incorporated, whisk in the lemon zest. Serve the sauce warm or at room temperature. The sauce will keep, tightly covered, in the refrigerator for up to 3 days.

Seasoned

This is the "sprinkle" and "drizzle" section—when "a little dab will do ya"—including:

BBQ Rubs and Spice Blends
Flavored Vinaigrettes • Compound Butters
Pestos and Tapenades • Dipping Sauces

BBQ Rubs and Spice Blends

Mostly dry mixtures of salts, peppers, dried herbs, and spices for flavoring food before cooking. A dry rub can be thought of as a "dry marinade" that adds flavor and promotes a crispy crust on the food. Wet rubs have a thick, wet consistency and are applied much like a traditional marinade.

Rubs 101

RAPID-FIRE CHECKLIST

○ Think of a rub as a dry marinade.

○ Less is more. Do not overseason; you are trying to enhance the flavor of whatever food you are grilling—not cover it up!

○ Unless you are making a wet rub, use dry ingredients in rubs.

○ Never rub hard into the food; sprinkle and pat the spices into the food.

○ Season food 15 to 20 minutes before you plan to cook it.

○ If you want to season food the night before, make sure the rub mixture doesn't have any salt in it, or it will dehydrate the food.

○ If the rub doesn't have salt in it, make sure you season your food with salt before cooking it.

○ Experiment with newly available flavored and dehydrated powders, like dehydrated honey and Worcestershire.

Most people associate rubs with Southern barbecue. However, spice mixtures or blends are used in all parts of the world and can be used to great effect on nearly all food. I even use sweet rubs to season fruit before grilling. My Basic Dessert Rub (page 218) is little more than cinnamon sugar, but it brings out the best in fruit. The bold, in-your-face flavors of grilled food are perfect for dried spice blends and will quickly impart international flavors to your food. For example, instead of laboring over a complicated Mexican mole, you can quickly mix up ground chilies, ground nuts, granulated garlic, dehydrated onion, ground cumin, a pinch of cocoa powder, and a little salt and bring those flavors to a steak, a piece of chicken, fish—even vegetables. Will it have all the nuances of a mole? No way, but it will probably satisfy your craving for Mexican flavors.

A spice or BBQ rub is a mixture of dried spices that is sprinkled or lightly rubbed—thus the derivation of the term—onto food prior to cooking. Think of a rub as a dry marinade. Rubs add flavor and can help form a crispy crust on the food you grill. You don't have to coat your food with the rub as you often do when making Southern barbecue. You can use a light hand to simply season anything that you grill or barbecue. I often use a simple spice rub to reinforce the flavor profile of a dish

A common misconception is that a rub has to have many ingredients in it. Not true. One of my favorite rubs has three ingredients, and it is one of those recipes that everyone loves and makes over and over again. This Original Three-Ingredient Rub (page 206) is made of granulated garlic, cumin seed, and smoked paprika. All three spices are bursting with flavor, and the combination makes a dynamic rub for steak, chicken, and pork—even catfish is better because of it! But I'm not the only one who likes simple combinations. In any reputable kitchen in the world, the chef will have a simple mixture of salt and pepper at the stove for seasoning. This is a rub at its simplest. After you have salt and pepper, anything goes. Salt and pepper are the foundation for all seasoning (see the Grilling Trilogy, page 10). Because I generally like to salt my food just before I put it on the grill, I sometimes make spice blends like the one above that purposefully leave out the salt and pepper. In that case, make sure you season your food with salt and pepper before cooking it.

The Chef Finish

One of the secrets that great chefs have is that they always finish dishes with a drizzle and a sprinkle. It can be as simple as drizzling best-quality extra-virgin olive oil over a piece of grilled fish and finishing it with a sprinkle of fleur de sel (specialty salt from Brittany, France). In this book, I've given you dozens of options for finishing dishes with both seasonings and sauces, from the delicately flavored sea salts like the beautiful magenta Hibiscus Flower Salt (page 217) to the rustic, chunky Reuben's Sauce Vera Cruz (page 97) and the top-secret Steak Love Glaze (page 127) to compound butters and traditional barbecue sauces and glazes. Spice rubs double as a finishing seasoning, they will give even the quickest meal layers of flavor. When you take a bite, you will get both the smoky grilled spicy note as well as the fresher, brasher bite of the uncooked rub. This will bring out the best in your dish; just remember that less is more. You never want to overseason; you are trying to enhance the flavor of whatever food you are grilling—not cover it up!

Rub Your Food the Right Way

The best way to use a rub is to put it on the meat 15 to 20 minutes before you plan to cook it. This gives the spices time to penetrate and season the meat. Some people like to rub (season) ribs and other food the night before it is going to be barbecued—if you do season the night before, make sure the rub mixture doesn't have any salt in it or it will dehydrate the food by drawing the natural juices out of it.

"Rub" Is a Misnomer

In my classes, particularly my Southern-barbecue classes, almost every student will rub their ribs, pork butts, and briskets within an inch of the life of the meat if I don't stop them! Never rub hard into the food; you can damage the meat fibers and texture of the food and run the risk of overseasoning it. What you really want to do is sprinkle the spice mixture evenly over the meat and gently pat it in place.

The Right Way to Use a Rub

Rub your food the right way by holding your hand at least a foot above the food and sprinkling from one side to the other over the food. The height and the back-and-forth motion help the rub get distributed evenly—pretend that you are "raining" over the food. If you drop the pinch of spice rub close to the food, it will all land in the same spot and not be evenly distributed.

Dry vs. Wet Rubs

Dry Rubs

Dry rubs are just that, dry. You don't want to coat the food in wet ingredients if you want that telltale roasty, toasty, crisp, and smoky crust on the exterior of your meat. The food you are cooking, and meat in particular, will develop a great crust only when it is dry. If you are purposefully trying to get the meat to cook in a moist environment, then you *do* want a wet rub.

Wet Rubs

A wet rub is a flavor paste that can be made up of both wet and dry ingredients, but it often contains fresh garlic, raw onions, fresh herbs, and olive oil. My favorite wet rubs are more like pastes and create a crust on their own, like My Favorite Wet Mustard Rub with Bourbon (page 219), which makes a delectable crust for fresh ham. I like using wet pastes on whole fish, chicken thighs, fresh pork roasts, and leg of lamb.

Oil Rubs

This is my term for a dry rub that is mixed with olive oil and patted or poured onto the food before cooking. As long as there isn't a lot of salt in the rub (preferably no salt), this is a great way to prep food up to a day before cooking and let it marinate for an extended time in the refrigerator. The beauty of an oil rub is that you've seasoned the food and coated it in oil, so all you need to do before grilling is season it with a sprinkling of your favorite salt.

Key Rub Ingredients

Pepper

Pepper is best freshly ground from a pepper mill or spice grinder every time you use it. The flavor that you get from pepper is propelled by the oils in the peppercorns. These oils dry up very quickly, which is why already ground pepper has much less taste than freshly ground pepper.

Before putting the peppercorns in your pepper mill, put them in a dry sauté pan, stir or shake occasionally, and heat gently just until a wisp of smoke is present and you can smell the pepper. Remove and let cool before placing in a peppermill. You can grind them in a spice grinder (coffee grinder) while still warm. This is how you roast a spice to bring out its maximum flavor. You can do this with all whole spices before grinding them and they will all taste fresher and deeper in flavor. This is the same basic idea behind coffee roasting, and it's up to you to decide how dark you like your spices—or coffee, for that matter.

Salt

I love salt and all the different kinds of salt that are available to us today. Use kosher or sea salt for the Grilling Trilogy (see page 10) and everyday cooking. My preference is for Morton kosher salt over Diamond Crystal kosher salt because the crystals are harder and don't dissolve so quickly. This matters, because when you season with Diamond Crystal, it dissolves and instantly draws moisture (water) to the surface of the food. The Morton sticks and dissolves just enough to season the food but not make the surface wet. The rest of the crystal adds a nice crunch and texture to the food. This is especially important in grilling, when you do not want the surface of the food to be wet when you put it on the grill. Wet food steams and stews instead of searing and caramelizing.

Obviously, the longer the food sits after it has been seasoned and before it is cooked, the more the Morton or any salt will melt. This is also why I recommend salting the food just before grilling.

Brown Sugar

A note on using brown sugar in rubs: It is important to use fresh, moist brown sugar in a rub. You may use light or dark brown sugar, but given a choice, I always opt for dark because it gives food more depth of flavor. The soft, fresh brown sugar will mix easily with the other spices in the rub. If the sugar is old, it will not mix well and will have the texture of hard pebbles, which will ruin the rub.

THE WORLD OF SALT

Salt tastings are the new wine tastings! There is a world of salts out there, and they are all worth exploring. Try them and see what nuances they bring to your food. I love salt, and I call for lots of different salts and even have recipes for making your own seasoned salts in this chapter. I also like pairing salt from a particular country and region to other flavors from that region. For example, I add a pinch of fleur de sel to my Burnt Salted Caramel Sauce (see page 183). These days the list of salts is far and wide, and every country with a body of water makes a natural sea salt. Here are a few of my favorites:

Splurge and buy *fleur de sel* ("flower of salt"—hand-raked once a year on France's Brittany coast—most notably from Guérande, *fleur de sel de Guérande*) for your table. The natural salinity and shape of the fleur de sel salt crystals adds a mild, distinctive flavor and texture to salads and meat and vegetable dishes. But don't stop there: Try the *pink salt* from Hawaii and the Himalayas; crunchy, delicate *Maldon* crystal salt from England; *black salt* (Kala Namak) from India; *sel gris* or gray salt from Brittany; *Halen Mon* sea salt, smoked over Welsh oak; and *Halen Mon* sea salt with vanilla, as well as any other salt you can find.

MAKE YOUR OWN RUB

This chart will help you make your own dry rub for any food that you wish to season with a blended spice mixture. Follow the columns and mix and match to your heart's content. Be sure to taste along the way, remembering that the seasonings by themselves will be stronger than when distributed over food, but remember too that

Salt Choose 1	Sugar Choose 1–2	Peppers Choose 1–3	Savory Spices* Choose 1–4	Savory Spices* Choose 1–4
Kosher salt	Dark brown sugar	Ancho chile	Celery salt	Celery salt
Fine sea salt	Light brown sugar	Black pepper	Celery seed	Celery seed
Coarse sea salt	Sugar in the Raw (turbinado)	Blended pure chili powder	Coriander	Coriander
	White sugar	Chipotle pepper	Cumin	Cumin
		Cayenne pepper	Dill weed	Dill weed
		Green peppercorns	Dry mustard	Dry mustard
		Hot chile flakes	Fennel	Fennel
		Lemon pepper	Granulated garlic	Granulated garlic
		New Mexico chile powder	Hot smoked Spanish paprika	Hot smoked Spanish paprika
		Pink peppercorns	Sweet Hungarian paprika	Onion powder
		Szechuan peppercorns	Onion powder	Oregano
		White pepper	Oregano	Sage
			Sage	Sweet Hungarian paprika
			Sweet smoked Spanish paprika	Sweet smoked Spanish paprika
			Thyme	Thyme

* All spices are dried and ground unless otherwise noted.
** Per BBQ expert Mike Mills, never use sweet spices when smoking meat for American barbecue.

Soaked, Slathered, and Seasoned

less is almost always more. If you add too many spices you risk having them "fight" with each other, and the result will be a muddy—not a bright—flavor. Be especially careful not to add too much salt, sugar, or hot peppers, and remember this rule of thumb: The stronger the spice, the less you need to use.

Savory Flavored Powders Choose 1	Sweet Spices** Choose 1–4	Sweet Flavored Powders Choose 1	Other Choose 1–5
Horseradish powder	Allspice	Dehydrated honey powder	Dried chives
Lemon juice powder	Anise seed	Maple syrup powder	Dried lavender
Red wine powder	Cardamom	Molasses powder	Dried lemon peel
Soy sauce powder	Cinnamon		Dried parsley
Tomato powder	Chinese five-spice powder		Dried shallots
Vinegar powder	Cloves		Poppy seeds
Worcestershire powder	Mace		Sesame seeds
	Nutmeg		Unsweetened cocoa
	Star anise		Unsweetened lemonade powder

A Note about Flavored Powders

Flavored powders are the future of the barbecue circuit and the backyard barbecue. I was at the annual Murphysboro Barbecue Cook-Off when I noticed that some of the winning ribs had this incredible sheen and a crust that was sweet and savory at the same time. I know that this is difficult to achieve with liquid honey and other sweeteners; they are wet, thus impeding a crust from forming, and they burn very easily. I was perplexed until my BBQ buddy Chris Mills let me in on his secret. You can now purchase dehydrated honey, maple syrup, and molasses, as well as red wine powder, tomato powder, Worcestershire sauce powder, etc., for use in your dry rubs. This is a veritable treasure chest for lovers of dry rubs. You can now balance your herbs and spices with a tangy acid from lemon juice powder, horseradish powder, vinegar powder, soy sauce powder, even cheese powder. These powders have always been available for commercial purchase, but they are a new resource for home cooks and barbecue competitors alike. Check out Suttons Bay Spices at www.suttonsbayspices.com/Flavored_Powders/.

Shelf Life

Dry rubs can be made on the day they are used or up to three months in advance. Rubs made in advance should be stored in clean glass jars with tight-fitting lids in a pantry or away from light.

Rub 101: Salt and Pepper Mix

Makes about 3/4 cup

Every chef has his or her "BAM" mixture of spices to season food. At its simplest, it is usually kosher salt and freshly ground pepper. You can add a mixture of peppercorns or use a fancy salt to make this your own. Make sure you toast your peppercorns before grinding them.

Good for Seasoning: All kinds of meat (pork, beef, veal, lamb); chicken; fish, shellfish; vegetables

> **1/4 cup whole black peppercorns or a combination of different peppercorns**
>
> **1/2 cup kosher salt, preferably Morton**

1. Toast the peppercorns in a dry skillet. Grind the peppercorns while they are still warm in a spice grinder.

2. Empty the ground pepper into a small bowl, making sure that there are no pieces that are cracked (too large) instead of ground. Add the salt and mix. Taste for balance and adjust if desired. The mixture will keep in an airtight container or salt mill fitted with a ceramic blade indefinitely.

Barbecue Circuit Rub

Makes 1/2 cup

This rub is as classic as it gets. It brings out the best in any meat you barbecue. It hits all the right notes of sweet, savory, spicy, and salty, and it even has a little smoke, courtesy of the natural hardwood smoke from the Spanish paprika. The hardwood fire scents the red peppers before they are dried and ground, making this spice the unsung hero of spice rubs.

Good for Seasoning: Pork; ribs; beef; chicken; sausage

- 1/4 cup packed dark brown sugar
- 2 tablespoons hot smoked Spanish paprika
- 1 tablespoon sweet Hungarian paprika
- 1 tablespoon freshly ground pepper
- 1 tablespoon fine-ground white pepper
- 1 tablespoon kosher salt, preferably Morton's
- 2 teaspoons granulated garlic
- 2 teaspoons onion powder
- 1 teaspoon celery salt
- 1/2 teaspoon cayenne pepper

In a medium bowl, combine all the ingredients with a fork or whisk and mix well. The rub will keep, tightly covered, for up to 6 months.

Mike Mills's Magic Dust

Makes about 2 cups

Mike Mills and his daughter, Amy, are award-winning barbecuers and restaurant owners. We wrote books at the same time and share a deep friendship and mutual love of barbecue. As close as we are, though, I can't promise that this is the "real" recipe for the Magic Dust that Mike uses on his award-winning ribs.* When I asked if it was the same Magic Dust that I always bring home from Murphysboro, he just smiled, and as his emerald eyes sparkled, he said, "It's good dust!" That was good enough for me, and now, I offer it to you.

Good for Seasoning: Ribs; pulled pork; beef; poultry; vegetables (asparagus, zucchini, eggplant); even popcorn

- 1/2 cup sweet Hungarian paprika
- 1/4 cup kosher salt, finely ground
- 1/4 cup sugar
- 1 tablespoon dry mustard, preferably Coleman's
- 1/4 cup chili powder
- 1/4 cup ground cumin
- 1 tablespoon freshly ground pepper
- 1/4 cup granulated garlic
- 1 tablespoon cayenne pepper

In a medium bowl, combine all the ingredients and mix well. The rub will keep in an airtight container for up to 6 months.

*Mike says to keep some in a shaker next to the grill or stove. "Keeps indefinitely but won't last long."

John Willingham's W'ham

Makes about 1/4 cup

I was introduced to W'ham on my maiden voyage as a rib maker. A friend and fellow barbecue competitor of John's took me (a real newbie) under his wing. He scored a bag of W'ham—that, a lemon, and a rack of ribs soon became the best ribs that I had ever eaten, at least up to that point—and I made them! I wrote down the simple procedure and named them after the team that taught me, Bubba's Bunch. To this day, I teach these ribs in my monthly Southern-barbecue class at the Institute of Culinary Education and at least half the class still chooses them as their favorite ribs—the secret is in the W'ham! Thank you, John.

Good for Seasoning: Ribs; beer-can chicken; steak; barbecued cabbage

> 2 tablespoons kosher salt, preferably Morton
> 1 teaspoon Worcestershire powder
> 1 teaspoon freshly ground pepper
> 1 teaspoon lemon pepper
> 1 teaspoon cayenne pepper
> 1 teaspoon chili powder
> 1 teaspoon dry mustard, preferably Colman's
> 1 teaspoon dark brown sugar
> 1/2 teaspoon garlic powder

In a small bowl or glass jar with a lid, combine all the ingredients. Stir or shake to mix. The rub will keep in an airtight container for several months.

The Belmontis' House Blend

Makes about 1/4 cup

This is another one of those perfect three-ingredient rubs. Gretchen and Jeff Belmonti are the foundation of my Chicago family and frequent partners in barbecue bliss. When Jeff was in high school, he worked at Poeta's Food Mart in Highwood, Illinois, and this was their secret to the best homemade roast beef in the Midwest—maybe the country! When Jeff and Gretchen got married, moved to the 'burbs, and started cooking in—instead of eating out—this became their house blend. It is good for garlic lovers. They use it on everything and say "The magic is the granulated garlic. It melts into the meat as it cooks and provides a flavor that is simple, yet perfect."

Good for Seasoning: Roast beef, flank steak; lamb chops; pork; chicken

> 2 tablespoons kosher salt, preferably Morton
> 4 teaspoons whole black peppercorns
> 4 teaspoons granulated garlic

Put all the ingredients into a spice grinder. Pulse until combined. The texture can be determined based on whether you like a coarsely or finely ground rub. The rub will keep in an airtight container for up to 6 months.

Bubba's Boogie Butt Rub

Makes about 1/4 cup

Most Southerners are called "Bubba" at least once in their life! On the barbecue circuit, there are many Bubbas of all ages! And I was no exception. My sister Catherine called me "Bubba" when we were tweens and even had a tank top made for me that said "Let's Boogie, Bubba!" The nickname and the tank top are history, but the Bubba stayed in my blood. This barbecue rub is so good that it makes you want to boogie with your favorite Bubba—and after a beer or two; you'll even think you got rhythm!

Good for Seasoning: Pork butt; ribs, chicken; steak; burgers; winter squash

> 2 teaspoons kosher salt, preferably Morton
> 2 teaspoons dry mustard, preferably Colman's
> 2 teaspoons sweet smoked Spanish paprika
> 2 teaspoons granulated onion
> 1 1/2 teaspoons granulated garlic
> 1 1/2 teaspoons coarsely ground pepper
> 1 teaspoon dried thyme
> 1/2 teaspoon cayenne pepper

In a medium bowl, combine all the ingredients and mix well. The rub will keep in an airtight container for up to 6 months.

Rodeo Rub

Makes about 1 cup

If you live in Houston (or anywhere in Texas, for that matter), the barbecue high point is the World Championship Bar-B-Que that takes place right before the Houston Livestock Show and Rodeo. It is the highlight of the Houston social season! This is as real as rodeo gets, with modern-day cowboys and cowgirls competing for big-ticket purses. The wildcatters of Texas may not be striking oil anymore, but they are striking gold with their award-winning barbecue, made with complex rubs like the one below.

Good for Seasoning: Steak, brisket; pork chops; rice; stuffed jalapeños, potatoes, grilled squash, sweet potatoes, pineapple and other tropical fruit

> 1/4 cup sweet Hungarian paprika
> 2 tablespoons sugar
> 2 tablespoons dark brown sugar
> 1 tablespoon ground cumin
> 2 tablespoons chipotle chile powder
> 1 tablespoon coarsely ground pepper
> 1 tablespoon cayenne pepper
> 1 tablespoon onion powder
> 1 tablespoon garlic powder

In a medium bowl, combine all the ingredients and mix well. The rub will keep in an airtight container for up to 6 months.

Pitmaster Pete's Sweet Chile Rub

Makes about 4 cups

Pitmaster Pete Daversa is my favorite kind of cook. As he is smoking the daily fare for Hill Country restaurant—where I work—he is thinking up new recipes and experimenting with smoking everything! One night with lamb chops on his mind, he created this rub with three kinds of sugar and chili powder (among other things). He made them for me and I was blown away! They were so good that I had to figure out a way that I could make them often and anywhere. I created a version of his succulent sweet pink smoked lamb chops using a Cameron Stovetop Smoker (see recipe below) and the results are just as good—no I mean GREAT!

- 4 teaspoons mustard powder
- 4 teaspoons granulated garlic
- 4 teaspoons onion powder
- 4 teaspoons sweet Hungarian paprika
- 4 teaspoons cayenne pepper
- 6 tablespoons chili powder
- 1 1/2 cups packed dark brown sugar
- 1/2 cup Sugar in the Raw (turbinado)
- 1/2 cup kosher salt, preferably Morton
- 1/2 cup white granulated sugar

Mix all ingredients in a bowl and sift through a strainer or flour sifter to make sure that there are no clumps of spice or sugar and ensure that it is well mixed. The rub can be stored in an airtight container for up to 3 months.

Chile-Rubbed Smoked Lamp Chop Lollipops

Serves 4 to 6

Grilling Method: Indirect/Medium-Low Heat

Special Equipment: Cameron Stovetop Smoker; post oak or other favorite wood chips, soaked in water

- 2 racks of lamb, frenched
- Olive oil
- 2 cups Pitmaster Pete's Sweet Chile Rub (left)

1. Using a sharp knife, cut the racks of lamb along the bones into individual chops—you'll have about 14 chops. They should be small and resemble lamb "lollipops." Lightly brush all the surfaces of the lamb with the olive oil.

2. Pour the rub onto a piece of waxed paper. Holding each chop by the bone, dredge each side of the chop through the rub to coat the entire outside of each chop.

3. Once the chips start to smoke, place the chops in the center of the cooking grate and smoke-cook for about 15 minutes for rosy rare like the picture or a little longer for medium (pink) rare. The chops are best cooked to rare, but cook to your preferred level of doneness.

Note: My preferred method is using the Cameron Stovetop Smoker. Set up the smoker per the manufacturers instructions, using the oak wood chips made for the Cameron Smoker. Smoke with the lid closed for 7 to 10 minutes on high heat or until done to your likeness.

Rick Schmidt's Real Texas Market Rub

Makes about 1 1/2 cups

You know, when you are learning a new craft you believe your teachers! Such was the case for me when I took a Texas-barbecue class many years ago. This was before I had taken my first trip to Hill Country or the central Texas barbecue belt. I'm embarrassed to say that I perpetuated what I learned and created a 15-ingredient spice rub for Hill Country brisket. And then I got Texas religion when I learned from a real master. The real story, as told by Rick Schmidt (owner of Kreuz Market in Lockhart, Texas) and all of his compatriots, is that a true Texas rub has but three ingredients: salt, coarsely ground black pepper, and enough cayenne pepper to make the rub take on a pink hue. This is my take on his time-tested rub. (Be forewarned: It is salty, so use sparingly.)

Good for Seasoning: Beef (brisket, beef shoulder); pork; chicken

> 1 1/2 cups kosher salt, preferably Morton
>
> 1/4 cup Tellicherry (black) peppercorns, coarsely ground, or about 1/4 cup plus 1 tablespoon freshly ground black pepper
>
> 1 tablespoon cayenne pepper

In a medium bowl, combine all the ingredients and mix well. The rub will keep in an airtight container for up to 6 months.

THE BITE ON PEPPER

During a recent trip to Kreuz Market, in Texas, I had a pork chop that was studded with great big chunks of coarse black pepper. The smoked pepper took on a leathery consistency and at first I was afraid that it would be too spicy to eat. Rick Schmidt was sitting with me and he anticipated my question. All of the heat and bite in pepper is in the dust. When you coarsely grind the pepper and sift all the dust off the pepper, you are left with relatively mild chunks of pepper. Who knew? I was a little skeptical, but I took a bite of the chop, and it was perfectly seasoned and not hot at all—the pepper-studded crust was just assertive enough to stand up to the rich post oak smoke and juicy pork. When I got home, I tried it for myself and it is true! This is now one of my favorite teaching demos because it is a fun factoid that few already know and everyone is amazed to learn.

Grilling Guru Rub

Makes about 1 1/4 cups

If I were stuck on a desert island and could only have one barbecue rub, this would be it! It has all the classic barbecue notes: salt, spice, sweetness, and smokiness. Even though I have dozens of recipes that I like and a few purchased rubs that I rely on, I find myself making this rub over and over again.

Good for Seasoning: Poultry; pork; ribs; steaks; burgers; new potatoes

- 3 tablespoons sweet smoked Spanish paprika
- 3 tablespoons kosher salt, preferably Morton
- 3 tablespoons Sugar in the Raw (turbinado)
- 2 tablespoons dark brown sugar
- 1 tablespoon ground cumin
- 1 tablespoon chili powder
- 1 tablespoon freshly ground pepper
- 1 tablespoon granulated onion
- 1 tablespoon granulated garlic
- 1 tablespoon Worcestershire powder, optional
- 1 tablespoon celery salt
- 2 teaspoons cayenne pepper
- 2 teaspoons dried oregano, crushed

In a medium bowl, combine all the ingredients and mix well. The rub will keep in an airtight container for up to 6 months.

Note: For a smoother rub, puree the ingredients in a spice grinder until well combined and all the pieces are uniform in size (the rub will be very fine and tan in color).

Hot and Sticky BBQ Rub

Makes about 3/4 cup

Sometimes your food (or your mood) just calls out for something hot and sticky! This rub packs a punch, but the sweetness from the two sugars tempers the heat from the peppers. This is a good example of how the four different peppers contribute as much flavor as they do heat to the rub. Because of the high amount of sugar, which can burn easily, this rub is best used when cooking food by the Indirect Method or when cooking pieces of food that take only a few minutes over direct heat.

Good for Seasoning: Pork tenderloin; ribs; beef; chicken; smashed grilled potatoes; pineapple

- 1/2 cup packed dark brown sugar
- 1 1/2 teaspoons coarsely ground pepper
- 2 tablespoons sugar
- 1 tablespoon molasses powder, optional
- 1 tablespoon kosher salt, preferably Morton
- 1/2 tablespoon hot smoked Spanish paprika

1 teaspoon chipotle chile powder

1/2 teaspoon cayenne pepper

In a medium bowl, combine all the ingredients and mix well. The rub can be stored in an airtight container for up to 6 months.

The Original Three-Ingredient Rub

Makes 1 1/2 tablespoons

This is the original three-ingredient rub, and it packs in a lot of flavor and texture. If I am feeling ambitious, I make a chimichurri sauce to drizzle on top, but the rub itself has so much flavor that all you need is a light coating of olive oil and a sprinkle of salt. The recipe calls for the amount you need for one night's dinner, but because the rub doesn't have any salt or pepper in it, you can increase the amount by simply multiplying. For example, if you are making 10 flank steaks, multiply by 10.

Good for Seasoning: Flank steak; pork; chicken; salmon

2 teaspoons granulated garlic

1 teaspoon smoked Spanish paprika

1 teaspoon whole cumin seeds, toasted in a dry skillet

In a small bowl, combine all the ingredients and mix well. The rub will keep in an airtight container for up to 6 months but you shouldn't have any left over.

Onion Variation

Substitute granulated onion for the granulated onion for a change of pace.

Hot Rod Rub

Makes about 1/2 cup

NASCAR fans are just like barbecue fans —they love to eat, love to drink, and love their sport above all others! The difference is in the design of the rig—NASCAR rigs are quick and ours are real slow. . . Here's a hot rub that is patterned after my BBQ buddy Kenny Hay's championship wing rub—it has a nice kick in the back of the throat. Be forewarned: I've yet to meet anyone who can eat it quick!

Good for Seasoning: Pork; chicken; beef; tomatoes

2 tablespoons hot smoked Spanish paprika

1 tablespoon cayenne pepper

1 tablespoon dry mustard, preferably Colman's

2 teaspoons freshly ground black pepper

2 teaspoons fine-ground white pepper

2 teaspoons garlic powder

2 teaspoons onion powder

2 teaspoons dried oregano

2 teaspoons dried sage

2 teaspoons dried rosemary

In a medium bowl, combine all the ingredients and mix well. The rub will keep in an airtight container for up to 6 months.

Sweet Kansas City Barbecue Rub

Makes about 1 3/4 cups

Kansas City is an adopted "Southern" town of barbecue. The Midwestern geography of the city often causes it to get overlooked when people seek out and talk about "real" Southern barbecue, but no one in K.C. is worried; after all, they support more barbecue restaurants (nearly 100 at last count) than any other place in the world. Kansas City is known for smokin' anything that moves, using lots of sweet, thick, red sauce and it is the home of the American Royal Barbecue contest.

Good for Seasoning: Ribs; pork; brisket; chicken; pineapple, corn

> 1/2 cup packed dark brown sugar
> 1/4 cup kosher salt, preferably Morton
> 1/4 cup sweet Hungarian paprika
> 1/8 cup freshly ground black pepper
> 1 tablespoon ground white pepper
> 1 tablespoon onion powder
> 1 tablespoon dry mustard
> 1 tablespoon honey powder, optional
> 2 teaspoons good-quality chili powder or ancho chile powder
> 2 teaspoons ground cumin
> 1 1/2 teaspoons dried thyme
> 1 teaspoon celery salt
> 1/2 teaspoon cayenne pepper, or to taste

In a medium bowl, combine all the ingredients and mix well. The rub will keep in an airtight container for up to 6 months.

Mexican Spice Rub

Makes about 1/3 cup

Mexican food is one of the most popular cuisines in the United States and one of the easiest to make at home. This basic spice rub will add a south-of-the-border flavor to anything you sprinkle it on. When you are looking for a more sophisticated flavor, eliminate the tangy lime powder and try the cocoa-cinnamon variation.

Good for Seasoning: Meats; fish; chicken; veggies; good for guacamole or salsa or homemade tortilla chips

> 2 teaspoons kosher salt, preferably Morton
> 1 teaspoon freshly ground pepper
> 2 teaspoons ancho chile powder
> 1 teaspoon lime powder or unsweetened limeade drink mix
> 1 teaspoon garlic powder
> 1 teaspoon onion powder
> 2 teaspoons dried Mexican oregano
> 1 teaspoon ground cumin

In a medium bowl, combine all the ingredients; mix well. The rub will keep in an airtight container for up to 6 months.

Cocoa-Cinnamon Variation

In place of the lime powder, add 1 teaspoon each unsweetened cocoa powder and ground cinnamon.

Note: For a smoother rub, puree the ingredients in a spice grinder until well combined and all the pieces are uniform in size (the rub will be very fine and tan in color).

Crazy Mixed-Up Chile-Limon Rub

Makes about 1 cup

The first time I went to Mexico, I was struck by all the snacks and foods flavored with *chile limon*—they even have a canister of chile-limon salt sold in every size, including pocket-sized, so you can take it with you to sprinkle on cut fruit, tacos, beer, etc. I tried it and loved it, and now I use it to spice up food for the grill as well as to make spiced peanuts or rim a Bloody Mary glass.

Good for Seasoning: Chicken; pork; venison; grilled corn, French fries, grilled potatoes, fruit salsa, peanuts, cocktail rimmer

> 1/2 cup sugar
> 1/4 cup kosher salt, preferably Morton
> 2 tablespoons New Mexico or ancho chile powder
> Two .23-ounce packages unsweetened lemon Kool-Aid mix
> 1 tablespoon garlic powder
> 1 tablespoon onion powder
> 1 teaspoon ground cumin
> 1 teaspoon cayenne pepper, or to taste

In a medium bowl, combine all the ingredients and mix well. The rub will keep in an airtight container for up to 6 months.

Hotheads Variation

If you like a hotter chile, use half ancho or New Mexican chile powder and half chipotle chile powder.

Chinese Five-Spice Rub

Makes a generous 1/3 cup

I have long loved Chinese five-spice powder and first started using it in apple pie. The origins of the spice are unclear, but I love the theory that the Chinese created the spice to encompass the five elements of taste—sweet, sour, salty, bitter, and umami (savory). Add this spice to soy sauce, sherry, sesame oil, and honey for a killer marinade for a variety of foods from ribs to duck to carrots. Add a couple of tablespoons of coarse sea salt and it makes an amazing seasoned salt for finishing dishes just before serving.

Good for Seasoning: Duck, chicken; pork chops; carrots, sweet potatoes, butternut squash, apples

> 1 tablespoon ground cinnamon
> 1 tablespoon ground cloves
> 1 tablespoon ground fennel
> 1 tablespoon ground star anise
> 1 tablespoon Szechuan peppercorns, toasted and ground

In a medium bowl, combine the cinnamon, cloves, fennel, star anise, and pepper; mix well. The rub will keep in an airtight container for up to 6 months.

Firecracker Rub Variation

This variation is particularly good on skirt steak, short ribs, and pork chops: Add 2 teaspoons cayenne pepper, 1 tablespoon dehydrated garlic, 1 tablespoon Morton kosher salt, and 1 tablespoon honey powder to the recipe above.

In a medium bowl, combine all the ingredients and mix well. The rub will keep in an airtight container for up to 6 months.

Black Coffee Rub

I was tempted to call this recipe "Mocha Rub" but I thought that might deter folks from using it on steak. It might sound unusual to add cocoa powder and coffee to a pepper rub for steak, but it makes all the difference on the steak. But don't just take my word for it, it is the most popular steak rub that I use in my Steak and Cake class.

    1 tablespoon unsweetened cocoa
    3 tablespoons ground espresso coffee
    2 tablespoons freshly ground black pepper
    2 teaspoons white sugar
    2 teaspoons kosher salt, preferably Morton

In a medium bowl, mix the cocoa, coffee, pepper and white sugar and mix well. The rub will keep in an airtight container for up to 1 month.

American Steakhouse Rub

Makes 1/3 cup

America loves steak. When I survey backyard cooks, the overwhelming favorite food to grill for both men and women is a juicy steak. Turn your backyard into a bona fide steak house by seasoning your steaks with this rub and coarse salt before searing them on red-hot cooking grates. When the steaks are done, top them with Roquefort Butter (page 255) and a sprinkle of chopped parsley—your house will become your family's favorite steak house!

Good for Seasoning: Any steak; burgers; grilled potatoes

    3 teaspoons dry mustard, preferably Colman's
    2 teaspoons granulated garlic
    2 teaspoons coarsely ground pepper
    1 teaspoon sweet smoked Spanish paprika
    1/2 teaspoon dried thyme
    1/2 teaspoon cayenne pepper

Smokin' Four-Chile Rub

Makes about 1/3 cup

This salt-free chile rub is not for the timid. It is one of my favorite rubs but must be used sparingly—this is a real case of sprinkle, don't rub! The subtle nuances of flavor in all the different dried and ground chilies make for a complex rub. The hot smoked chipotle and the sweeter smoked paprika really complement each other. Grill your meat or fish and then serve it up in soft corn tortillas with cooling guacamole—no hot sauce required. The rub is salt free, so remember to season the food with salt as needed just before cooking. And try adding 1 tablespoon of the rub to a stick of butter for slathering on grilled corn on the cob.

Good for Seasoning: Beef; pork; chicken; game; hearty fish such as catfish or snapper; rice, chili

1 tablespoon New Mexican (or any other) chili powder

1 tablespoon ancho chile powder

1 tablespoon chipotle chile powder

1 tablespoon sweet smoked Spanish paprika

1 tablespoons sugar

1 teaspoon fine-ground white pepper

1 teaspoon freshly ground black pepper

In a medium bowl, combine all the ingredients and mix well. The rub will keep in an airtight container for up to 6 months.

Garam Masala Rub

Makes about 3/4 cup

These days the term *masala* has crept into the American vocabulary through music, movies, and the proliferation of really good Indian restaurants and cookbooks. It is a Hindi word that refers to both the physical spice as well as to the ethereal spice (spirit) of life. Chef and cookbook author Suvir Saran embodies this masala, and his restaurant Devi in New York City boasts some of the best Indian food that

I have ever eaten in America, London, or India! This is his recipe for garam masala, a common spice mixture used throughout northern India. (And for those who don't know, curry is the spice mixture used throughout the south of India.)

Good for Seasoning: Chicken; pork; white fish; grilled vegetables; sprinkle on raw whole onions before making the Forgotten Onion (page 43).

2 cinnamon sticks

4 bay leaves

3 tablespoons whole cumin seeds

3 tablespoons whole coriander seeds

1 1/2 tablespoons whole green or black cardamom pods

1 1/2 tablespoons whole black peppercorns

1 tablespoon whole cloves

1 tablespoon ground mace

1. Break the cinnamon sticks into 1/4-inch pieces. Crumble the bay leaves.

2. Heat a heavy frying pan. Add all the spices to the pan. Dry-roast over a medium flame until the color darkens, about 2 minutes, stirring or shaking the pan frequently to prevent any burning. Let cool.

3. Grind the spices in a spice grinder, transfer to a small bowl, then blend in the mace. The rub will keep in an airtight container for up to 6 months.

2. Place the mixture in a salt grinder and grind, or pulverize slightly in a mortar and pestle. The rub will keep in an airtight container for up to 6 months.

Provençal Rub

Makes about 1/2 cup

When you travel to the south of France, the first thing you smell when you walk into a market or a shop is the rich, grassy mixture of dried herbs known as herbes de Provence. This mixture of rosemary, marjoram, basil, thyme, and savory sometimes includes fennel seed, bay leaf, oregano, and the now-popular lavender. It is used throughout the Mediterranean, and I can't think of anything it's not good with! Add 1/2 cup of olive oil to this mixture and it makes a terrific wet-rub marinade.

Good for Seasoning: Beef; lamb; potatoes, root vegetables, tomatoes, eggplant, green beans

> 4 tablespoons herbes de Provence
> 2 tablespoons coarse-grain sea salt
> 1 tablespoon granulated garlic
> 2 teaspoons food-grade lavender buds

1. In a small bowl, combine all the ingredients and stir to mix.

Little Italy Rub

Makes about 3/4 cup

Many major cities have an Italian neighborhood aptly called "Little Italy." The best of these neighborhoods still have Italian bakeries, butchers, and cheese makers who make fresh mozzarella every day. If you live near one of these neighborhoods, you can buy "Italian seasoning" from a butcher who makes it up fresh, or you can do like I do and mix it yourself to have on hand.

Good for Seasoning: Ribs; sausage; roasted meats; sauces, grilled bread; roasted vegetables

> 2 tablespoons dried chives
> 2 tablespoons granulated garlic
> 1 tablespoon dried oregano, crushed
> 2 teaspoons dried basil
> 2 teaspoons dried savory
> 3 teaspoons red chile flakes
> 2 teaspoons dried lemon peel

In a medium bowl, combine all the ingredients and mix well. The rub will keep in an airtight container for up to 6 months.

Chicago Butcher's Rub

Makes about 1/3 cup

Called Hog Butcher to the World for decades, Chicago was the meatpacking center of America. The stockyards, or "yards" as they were known, were built around the railroad tracks for easy access to the West, and they closed in 1971. Today Chicago is still famous for great meat and great butchers, and my favorite steak houses are the old-timers that are still located near the train tracks. This simple butcher's rub is what I envision they used back in the day. It enhances anything that you can buy at a butcher shop—particularly pork chops and big thick steaks.

Good for Seasoning: Steaks; pork chops, pork cutlets; veal chops; chicken pieces

> 2 tablespoons whole Tellicherry black peppercorns, toasted and ground
> 1 tablespoon minced dried garlic
> 1 tablespoon minced dried shallot
> 1 tablespoon kosher salt, preferably Morton, or coarse-grain sea salt
> 1 tablespoon dried parsley
> 1 teaspoon red chile flakes
> 1 teaspoon dried sage

In a medium bowl, combine all the ingredients and mix well. The rub will keep in an airtight container for up to 6 months.

Rosemary and Garlic Rub

Makes about 2/3 cup

This rub just screams out loud for a big ol' prime rib. I almost called this Christmas Rosemary and Garlic Rub because it is what I use every Christmas to season the family prime rib that I grill-roast to pink perfection. This is my favorite meal of the year, but it is too good to only make once a year.

Good for Seasoning: Beef (prime rib or other large roasts, steaks, chops); chicken; potatoes

> 1 tablespoon minced dried garlic
> 2 tablespoons dried rosemary
> 2 tablespoons kosher salt, preferably Morton
> 2 tablespoons sweet Hungarian paprika
> 2 tablespoons hot or sweet smoked Spanish paprika
> 1 tablespoon whole black peppercorns, toasted

In a medium bowl, combine the garlic, rosemary, salt, and both paprikas; stir to mix. Place the peppercorns in a spice grinder and pulverize until they have an evenly coarse grind. Add the rest of the rub and grind again, just to combine. The rub will keep in an airtight container for up to 6 months.

Parsley, Sage, Rosemary, and Thyme Rub

Makes about 1 cup

The Simon & Garfunkel song inspired this rub. Whether or not it makes you whistle the tune, it makes anything you put it on music to your mouth. Add a couple of tablespoons of soft goat cheese or cream cheese for an herb dip, pasta sauce, or topping for your morning bagel.

Good for Seasoning: Grilled steak; chicken; all vegetables, especially asparagus, artichokes, eggplant, mushrooms, tomatoes; grilled bread, dips

- 2 tablespoons dried parsley
- 2 tablespoons dried rosemary
- 2 tablespoons granulated garlic
- 3 tablespoons coarse-grain kosher salt, preferably Morton, or sea salt
- 1 tablespoon dried sage
- 1 tablespoon dried thyme
- 1 tablespoon freshly ground pepper

In a medium bowl, combine all the ingredients and stir to mix. The rub will keep in an airtight container for up to 6 months.

Zydeco Rub

Makes about 1/4 cup

During one of my first visits to southwestern Louisiana, I took a road trip to Lafayette—home to both Cajun and Creole music. I went to a restaurant with live music and felt right at home when the zydeco band took the stage and started playing the frottoir (metal washboard) with a thimble and a spoon. Growing up in North Carolina, I was familiar with "found" instruments like the washboard and the "gut bucket." But what wasn't familiar was the vibrant Creole-spiced food that I ate while I tapped my foot to the beat of the music. This rub will add zydeco zip to all of your foods.

Good for Seasoning: Crayfish, catfish; poultry; vegetables (potatoes, peppers, zucchini, summer squash, baby carrots)

- 2 tablespoons sweet Hungarian paprika
- 1 tablespoon kosher salt, preferably Morton
- 2 teaspoons granulated garlic
- 2 teaspoons dried parsley
- 1 teaspoon freshly ground pepper
- 1 teaspoon granulated onion
- 1 teaspoon dried Greek oregano
- 1 teaspoon dried thyme
- 1/2 teaspoon cayenne pepper

In a medium bowl, combine all the ingredients and mix well. The rub will keep in an airtight container for up to 6 months.

Toasted Sesame Salt

Makes 1 3/4 cups

I use this salt as both a rub and a condiment. I first tried it when I visited my family friend Alan Wagner in India. Alan runs the kitchen at an ashram in Ahmednagar and combines both East and West cooking techniques to come up with dishes that are worth a special trip. I first used this toasted sesame seed salt on soft-boiled eggs, but it perks up grilled vegetables, fish, chicken, pork, and beef as well. A similar Japanese condiment—sold as gomasio—features sesame seeds and salt, sometimes ground with seaweed.

Good for Seasoning: Grilled vegetables, especially asparagus and green beans; chicken; pork; shrimp or beef kabobs

> 1 cup white or black or half and half sesame seeds
>
> 1/2 cup coarse kosher salt, preferably Morton, or sea salt
>
> 1 teaspoon fine-ground white pepper

1. Heat a 10-inch dry skillet over medium heat for 1 minute. Add the sesame seeds and toast, stirring occasionally, until fragrant and golden brown, 5 to 6 minutes. Remove from the heat and let cool.

2. Transfer the sesame seeds to a mortar and pestle and crush lightly. While they are still warm, pour into a bowl and mix with the salt and pepper. The salt will keep in an airtight container for several months.

Note: Be sure to stir just before using, as the salt has a tendency to settle.

Roasted Garlic Variation

If you want to make this salt with even more flavor, add 2 teaspoons of roasted granulated garlic to the sesame seeds while they are toasting.

Szechuan Peppercorn and Black Sesame Variation

Add 2 teaspoons Szechuan peppercorns to the sesame seed mixture and eliminate the white pepper. Grind 1/4 cup of the sesame seeds with the peppercorns and mix with the salt and remaining sesame seeds while still warm.

Lemon-Lime Salt

Makes about 1/4 cup

This is the salt that started me on my love of flavored salt. One night I was tired of the rubs and seasonings I had on hand, so I decided to mix this simple salt and use it like a rub on a skirt steak. The explosion of flavor was intense—even after grilling over high heat! I loved the fresh flavors that came through and started experimenting with all sorts of salts. If you can find Meyer lemons, you will love making the salt with the zest of those sweet beauties. This is great seasoning to use and share at summer gatherings.

Good for Seasoning: Skirt steak, chicken; fish; sprinkle on fresh or grilled fruit (especially citrus and melons); use to rim drink glasses

> Zest of 1 large lemon (about 2 teaspoons)
> Zest of 1 to 2 limes (about 2 teaspoons)
> 2 tablespoons kosher salt, preferably Morton, or coarse-grain sea salt

Mince the zest if necessary; it must be very fine and small. In a small bowl, mix the zest with the salt. Use immediately, or line a baking sheet with a silicone liner or a piece of parchment paper and spread the mixture over the liner. Let sit in a cool, dry place until completely dry, about 4 hours. When dried, the salt will keep in an airtight glass container for up to 6 months.

Meyer Lemon Variation

Use the zest of 2 Meyer lemons instead of the lime.

Lemon-Orange Variation

Use the zest of half an orange, clementine, or tangerine instead of the lime.

Grapefruit Variation

Use the zest of half a grapefruit instead of the lemon.

Green Olive and Lemon Salt

Makes about 1/2 cup

This is an Italian-inspired salt. You can purchase olive salt in Italy, where it is usually made with tiny pieces of black olives. I love mixing small green picholine olives with a little lemon zest for a pretty and tasty salt. I prefer it to the black olive salt that you can buy, as the brininess of the picholine olives and the brightness of the lemon zest round out the salt. For the finest zest, use a Microplane.

Good for Seasoning: Grilled fish, shellfish; chicken; eggplant, tomatoes

> 2 tablespoons minced picholine olives
> 1/2 cup coarse Sicilian sea salt or fleur de sel, preferably Le Saunier de Camargue
> Zest of 1 lemon

1. Place the minced olives at the end of one side of a paper towel and roll the paper towel to wrap the olives. Squeeze the excess moisture out (otherwise, the moisture will melt the salt).

2. In a small bowl, mix the salt, dried minced olives, and lemon zest together. Use immediately, or cover a baking sheet with a silicone liner or a piece of parchment paper and spread the olive mixture over the liner. Let sit in a cool, dry place until completely dry, about 4 hours. When dried, the salt will keep in an airtight glass container for up to 6 months.

Lemon-Pepper Salt

Makes about 1/2 cup

Once upon a time, lemon pepper was the go-to spice. I mostly remember sprinkling it on popcorn with parmesan cheese when I was a teenager. I haven't had a bottle of lemon pepper in my kitchen since then, but the idea is worth reviving. Making it fresh from scratch makes its processed cousin pale in comparison. As my father, Big Lou, is known to say, this salt is "good for anything worth eating."

Good for Seasoning: Fish, shrimp; steak; pork loin; spinach, asparagus; popcorn

> 1/4 cup kosher salt, preferably Morton, or coarse-grain sea salt
>
> 1 tablespoon coarsely ground black pepper
>
> Zest of 1 large lemon (about 2 teaspoons)
>
> 2 teaspoons dried lemon peel
>
> 1 teaspoon fine-ground white pepper
>
> 1/4 teaspoon granulated garlic
>
> 1/8 teaspoon cayenne pepper

In a medium bowl, combine all the ingredients and mix well. The salt will keep in an airtight glass container for up to 6 months.

Rose Pepper and Pink Salt

Makes about 1/3 cup

I created this salt and pepper mixture in honor of my good friend and culinary confidante, baking expert Rose Levy Beranbaum. Rose, as her name may suggest, loves anything with roses on it and rose-colored foods. Each year, Aunt Rose and Aunt EAK (me) take a day to make cookies with my nephews, August, Alexander, and Max, and the reward—besides the cookies—is a very adult feast of 2-inch-thick prime steaks simply seasoned with this mixture.

Good for Seasoning: Steak; chicken; fish, shrimp, oysters; mushrooms, asparagus

> 2 tablespoons pink salt, such as either Hawaiian Alaea or coarse Himalayan
>
> 1 tablespoon pink peppercorns, toasted in a dry skillet
>
> 2 teaspoons sweet smoked Spanish paprika
>
> 1 teaspoon granulated garlic

1. Combine the pink salt and peppercorns in a spice grinder, and pulse until coarsely ground.

2. Pour the mixture into a medium bowl and add the paprika and garlic; mix well. The salt will keep in an airtight container for up to 6 months.

Hibiscus Flower Salt

Makes about 1/3 cup

When I visited Tokyo, I was very lucky to have Stefan Moerth, the executive chef of the famous Park Hyatt, as my food guide to the city. Stefan was schooled in Europe but has worked in Asia for most of his career. Besides the top-notch restaurants at the hotel, Stephan is in charge of the Park Hyatt food shop, creating many of the fresh and pantry items for the store. I flipped out at a bright purply fuschia hibiscus flower salt that I saw in the shop. As if he could read my mind, he served it that night as a condiment with the most exquisite kingfish sashimi that I have ever eaten. Instead of the traditional soy-wasabi condiment combination, the fish was served with a drizzle of olive oil from Tuscany and the hibiscus salt. When I got home, I discovered that many ethnic and gourmet groceries sell the dried flowers, sometimes as tea—think of the bright pink color of Red Zinger! You can also buy them online at www.surfasonline.com, which allows you to make this psychedelic salt in your own kitchen. I promise it will make all your dishes sparkle, and the sweet-tart fruitiness of the hibiscus goes with everything!

Good for Seasoning: Fish, especially seared rare tuna and grilled shellfish; grilled fruit; salads; cheese

> 2 tablespoons dried hibiscus blossoms, ground in a spice grinder
>
> 1/4 cup coarse sea salt or fleur de sel, Maldon sea salt (or crank up the pink quotient by using pink salt)

Combine the ground hibiscus and the salt in a small bowl and mix well. The salt will keep in an airtight glass container for up to 6 months.

Truffle Salt

Makes about 1/4 cup

This aromatic salt will elevate anything it is sprinkled on. Because it is so luxurious, I recommend making it with real fleur de sel (from France). I find the drier type works better than the moist fleur de sel. The salt mixture will keep indefinitely, and a little goes a long way. It can be made with either truffle oil or minced truffle, sometimes sold as truffle pâté. I like it both ways; it mostly depends on your budget and what you have on hand. If you have a hard time finding the salt, try www.isolaimports.com.

Good for Seasoning: Steak; chicken; lamb; grilled asparagus, mushrooms, potatoes; pasta

> 1/4 cup fleur de sel, preferably Le Saunier de Camargue
>
> 2 teaspoons best-quality truffle oil, or 3 teaspoons minced truffles

Mix the fleur de sel with the truffle oil. Spread the mixture out on a piece of parchment paper or a baking sheet. Let sit for 15 minutes. The salt will keep in an airtight glass container for up to 6 months.

Basic Dessert Rub and Five Variations

Makes about 1/2 cup

I coined the term *dessert rub* many years ago when I was a guest on Sara Moulton's TV show *Sarah's Secrets*. I was showing her how to make all kinds of barbecue with rubs, sauces, and mops, but I didn't want to leave out the sweet stuff. (I feel like every meal has to have a little dessert at the end, even if it is just a tiny taste.) At the end of the episode, I made my favorite grilled bananas Foster seasoned simply with cinnamon sugar. In an effort to tie it back to barbecue, I spontaneously said "dessert rub," and I've been using it—and its many variations—even since.

Good for Seasoning: Bananas, peaches, plums, apricots; grilled poundcake

> 3 tablespoons sugar
>
> 2 teaspoons ground cinnamon
>
> Pinch fine-grain sea salt

In a medium bowl, combine all the ingredients and mix well. The rub will keep in an airtight container for up to 6 months.

Mexican Chocolate Variation

Add 1 tablespoon unsweetened cocoa powder to the spice mixture.

Uses: Grilled bananas, apricots, grilled flatbread, ribs with a sauce, and coffee

Five-Spice Powder Variation

Substitute five-spice powder for the cinnamon.

Uses: Eggnog, French toast, apples (tastes like NECCO wafers!)

Orange-Spice Variation

This is the essence of the winter holidays. Add a pinch of cloves and the zest of 1 orange to the basic rub. This will keep for up to 1 week in the refrigerator.

Uses: Apples, pears, duck, pork

Lemon-Sugar Variation

Add the zest of 1 lemon and 1/8 teaspoon ground mace to the mixture. I love the lemon and cinnamon together, but if you don't, eliminate the cinnamon and add the zest of 2 lemons. This will keep for up to 1 week in the refrigerator.

Uses: Strawberries, peaches, nectarines

Vanilla Variation

Split 1 vanilla bean and scoop out the seeds, mix with 1/4 cup of sugar and add a pinch of mace. You can make the vanilla variation with or without the cinnamon.

Uses: Grilled peaches, apples, bananas

My Favorite Wet Mustard Rub with Bourbon

Makes about 3 1/4 cups

This concoction is a cross between a marinade and a paste. It is based loosely on a mustard paste that my Grandmother Odom would make every spring for her fresh ham. Over the years I've doctored it up with some of my favorite things, like bourbon and brown sugar. If I have it, I substitute bacon fat for the olive oil for a pig-on-pig treat.

Good for Seasoning: Pork shoulder roast; fresh ham; chicken pieces

> One 14-ounce jar yellow mustard
>
> One 8-ounce jar whole-grain Dijon mustard
>
> 1/2 cup packed dark brown sugar
>
> 2 tablespoons peanut or olive oil
>
> 2 tablespoons molasses or Steen's cane syrup
>
> 1/2 cup bourbon
>
> 1 teaspoon kosher salt, preferably Morton

In a medium bowl, mix both mustards together until they are combined; add the brown sugar, oil, molasses, bourbon, and salt. Mix well. Coat food and marinate for 2 to 4 hours in the refrigerator, turning occasionally. The rub will keep, tightly covered, in the refrigerator for up to 2 days.

Fig-alicious Wet Rub

Makes about 4 cups

This scrumptious wet rub is unusual but makes a sweet and tenderizing potion. You can also reduce it to make a glaze.

Good for Seasoning: Chicken, duck; venison; pork; lamb chops; cheese; fruit; grilled bread

> 1 cup plus 1 tablespoon balsamic vinegar, divided
>
> 1/2 pound plump black or white figs, cut in half
>
> 1 small shallot, chopped
>
> 1 teaspoon fine-grain sea salt
>
> Pinch pepper
>
> One 10-ounce jar all-fruit, no-sugar-added raspberry or black raspberry jam
>
> 1/2 cup olive oil

1. Place 1 cup of the balsamic vinegar in a small saucepan, and add the figs. Cover and bring to a simmer. Stir and simmer for 1 to 2 minutes. Cover and take off the heat to cool.

2. When cool, place the mixture in a blender and puree, adding the remaining 1 tablespoon vinegar, the shallot, the salt, and the pepper. Puree again.

3. Transfer from the blender to a large bowl; add the jam. Gently blend the puree into the jam. Add the olive oil. Coat food and marinate for 2 to 4 hours in the refrigerator, turning occasionally. The rub will keep, tightly covered, in the refrigerator for up to 2 days.

Pete's Favorite Summer Barbecue Wet Rub

Makes 2 to 3 cups

It wouldn't be a summer barbecue at my friend Pete Savely's house without my Chipotle Chicken Thighs recipe (facing page). Every year he hosts a big bash and grills up about 50 thighs—all marinated in the cool-with-a-kick mayonnaise-chipotle mixture that I learned was the secret to the Oaxacan (Mexican) chicken that is frequently made for *velas* (festivals) and special events.

Good for Seasoning: Chicken pieces, duck breast; pork tenderloin; whole fish, thick fish steaks; doubles as a dip for hot wings or shrimp, and a spread for chicken, burgers, and hot dogs

> One 7-ounce can chipotle chilies in adobo
>
> 1 white onion, chopped
>
> 1 bunch fresh cilantro, chopped
>
> 1 lime, juiced
>
> 1/4 teaspoon kosher salt, preferably Morton
>
> 2 to 3 cups mayonnaise

In a blender, mix the chipotles and adobo sauce, onion, cilantro, and lime juice. Add the salt. Transfer to a large nonreactive bowl. Mix in 2 cups of the mayonnaise. Taste and adjust the seasonings, adding more mayonnaise if it is too hot. Coat food and marinate for 2 to 4 hours in the refrigerator, turning occasionally. The rub will keep, tightly covered, in the refrigerator for up to 2 days.

Chipotle Chicken Thighs

Serves 4

Grilling Method: Indirect/Medium Heat

1 recipe Pete's Favorite Summer Barbecue Wet Rub (facing page)

8 chicken thighs, or 2 chickens cut into pieces

1 lime, quartered

1. Put the rub into a large bowl and add the chicken pieces. Cover and marinate for 2 to 4 hours in the refrigerator, turning occasionally.

2. Build a charcoal fire or preheat a gas grill. Remove the chicken from the refrigerator and place the pieces, bone side down, in the center of the cooking grate. You do not need to turn the chicken pieces while they cook.

3. Grill-roast until the thigh meat registers 180°F and the breast meat near the bone registers 165°F (if you cut up chickens). If you don't have a meat thermometer, cook until it is no longer pink inside and the juices run clear when pierced. Remove and let sit for 10 minutes before serving. Serve with the lime wedges.

Flavored Vinaigrettes

Highly seasoned oil and vinegar blends that are enhanced with olives, jams, and other fresh ingredients. The vinaigrettes are drizzled on cooked or raw food just before serving to add another flavor dimension.

Flavored Vinaigrettes 101

What Is a Vinaigrette?

Learning to make a vinaigrette was a turning point on my culinary path. I majored in French and, like lots of other college students with the same major, I moved to Paris to immerse myself in the culture and the language. The food there was a huge part of my education and my culinary epiphany. However, unlike so many of today's food luminaries, for me it wasn't a complicated dish that transported me. It was the *salade vert*. A simple salad made of tender French lettuce that looked like baby Boston lettuce dressed sparingly with a hand-whisked vinaigrette sharp with real Dijon mustard and tangy with red wine vinegar. It was the salad dressing, or vinaigrette, that made the salad. I tried learning the secret from books and magazines and from making the salad for an entire summer

as an au pair in Perigord, but I never really could get it thick and creamy and perfectly balanced. I finally learned how it was done when I took a class with the late ICE (Institute of Culinary Education) cooking teacher Shirley King. It was she who taught me that whisking was in the wrist and the correct proportions of vinegar to oil.

At its purest, a vinaigrette is a mixture of oil (three parts) to acid (one part), generally vinegar but sometimes lemon or other citrus juice. I sometimes use the three-to-one ratio when I am looking to dial down the acid and increase the creamy mouth feel, with 3/4 cup oil to 1/4 cup vinegar. But most of the time, I choose to make a two-to-one ratio with a 2/3 to 1/3 cup proportion, which will produce a tangier vinaigrette. If you read the marinades chapter on page 32, you will see a similar theme. The big difference is that with a marinade, it is generally the reverse, with more acid and less oil.

Enhancing the Food

If you make your own salad dressing, then you know what a difference it makes to a salad and how it enhances rather than buries whatever you put it on. The same is true with flavored vinaigrettes, which are wonderful on salads but also make amazing quick-and-easy sauces for grilled meat, poultry, fish, and vegetables. You can add whatever you like to flavor a vinaigrette; many top chefs include the drippings from their meat and poultry main courses to tie everything together. Except for the Hot Bacon Vinaigrette (page 238), all of my recipes call for olive, canola, and nut oils. (I love the smoky, rich note that bacon drippings bring to vinaigrettes and dressings, but it can very often become the dominant flavor.) The vinaigrettes in this chapter are flavor-packed, and each of these vinaigrettes would also make a great marinade. Try doubling the recipe and using half for marinating and the other half for drizzling over the cooked food. Since these vinaigrettes are so concentrated, do not marinate food for longer than an hour for large pieces of food, such as butterflied chicken or pork loin, and about 20 minutes for smaller, more delicate foods, such as fish, shrimp, boneless skinless chicken breast, and vegetables.

Oils

Extra-Virgin Olive Oil or Not?

Many of my students ask me if I cook with extra-virgin olive oil. I know that there are some food writers and teachers who say that extra-virgin is too expensive to cook with and that you should only dress and drizzle food with it. However, I use extra-virgin olive oil for everything from scrambling my morning eggs to making a vinaigrette to coating everything that I put on the grill (see the Grilling Trilogy, page 10). I do it because I love the heady, herbaceous flavors of a really nice first-press olive oil, and I want to use the best possible ingredients at all levels of my cooking. I also don't think that home cooks want to buy two or three different kinds of the same oil and keep track of when and where they should use them. (I do, however, reserve my most expensive and most flavorful extra-virgin olive oil for finishing my dishes and making dipping sauces or vinaigrettes.) Unless the higher cost of extra-virgin olive oil is a

concern (and it very well may be), feel comfortable using extra-virgin in all your food prep, from sautéing and grilling to making dressings and sauces—whatever you like. Oftentimes, I will make simple grilled food using the Grilling Trilogy (see page 10) and drizzle a little of my best olive oil on it before serving, to be met with, "What did you do to make this (fill-in-the-blank) taste so good?" I just smile—and now you can too!

If the flavor of extra-virgin olive oil overpowers or is too strong for you, try a different brand. The flavor of olive oil (like wine) varies from country to country, region to region, and producer to producer. By tasting, you can find a more neutral-tasting oil, or you can substitute untoasted walnut or hazelnut oil. You can also buy "light" olive oil. But be forewarned: *Light* refers to the flavor profile, not the calories. Light olive oil has the same calories but has been refined to take out all the flavor. This is the main reason why I don't use this oil. Some people feel that the refining process used to remove all the organic flavors renders the oil "defective." Defective or not, I think there are so many other options out there that light oil is not one that I recommend.

Nut Oils

I often use nut oil when I am grilling fruit or making a flavored vinaigrette. Most of the untoasted nut oils that are widely available on the market are clean oils with very little aroma or flavor. There is one major exception. The beautiful, fresh, cold-pressed nut oils from Jean LeBlanc are so intense that they need to be cut with olive oil or another more neutral oil or they will overpower all the other flavors. These oils and his vinegars are exquisite and worth seeking out. A simple finishing drizzle of one these oils and a sprinkle of fleur de sel will transform any dish—and then you'll also have it on hand for these vinaigrettes. You can buy all his products at www.amazon.com.

Flavored Olive Oils

Just as the type or flavor of vinegar switches up a vinaigrette, so do the fabulous flavored olive oils on the market. Truffle oil is an expensive luxury oil, but there are many others that are equally luscious and not nearly as expensive—and perfect for every-day eating. Don't get me wrong; I think everyone should have truffle oil in the pantry, but it is best used as a flavor ac-cent instead of the main ingredient. My favorite everyday flavored oil is a lemon olive oil (Agrumato lemon oil from www.zingermans.com). A drizzle of this oil alone will transform a grilled dish, but use it in a vinaigrette mixed with fresh juice, zest, and spices and it will magically change a one-dimensional lemon experience into one that's like being in the middle of a lemon grove. Likewise, a robust garlic, chile, basil, sage, or rosemary oil can be your secret weapon to full-flavored, balanced vinaigrettes and great food.

Vinegars

These days there are so many great vinegars on the market that at any one time, I have a collection of a dozen or so bottles on my kitchen counter. In my grandmother's day, she basically had apple cider vinegar and distilled white vinegar to choose from. Because I grew up in a household that used a great deal of apple cider vinegar, I still use it in many of my recipes. But I urge you to break out of the classic ruts and try all the new vinegars out there; you won't believe what a big difference just changing the vinegar will make. For example, one of my favorite vinegars is a white wine vinegar with tarragon. Substitute this in a classic vinaigrette and you have a delicious and speedy sauce for grilled chicken or fish.

If you are really ambitious, vinegar is easy to make. Take a clean dark glass or ceramic crock, and start with an unfiltered vinegar that still has the "mother" in it, like Bragg apple cider vinegar. Add an equal amount of fresh fruit juice or leftover wine. Keep checking it until you like the flavor and acidity level. Put it up in bottles and let it "cure" for about six months—this will allow time for the sharpness mellow out.

You can also make your own flavored vinegars by infusing store-bought vinegars with herbs and dried fruit.

Keep these basics on hand:

- Apple cider vinegar
- Balsamic vinegar
- Unseasoned rice vinegar
- Red wine vinegar
- White wine or champagne vinegar

The Nose Knows

Vinaigrettes rely first and foremost on the freshest, best-quality oils and vinegars to make them what they are, so make sure your ingredients are at their peak. Sometimes oil goes rancid before you can use it all, and it will give everything you put it on an off-taste. Depending on how rancid it is, it can potentially make you sick. Vinegar lasts much longer, but it will begin to grow a culture (the mother) in the bottle if you keep it long enough. You can prevent premature aging of both these ingredients by storing them in the refrigerator. A light settling of debris is normal with vinegar; it is the larger, amoeba-looking blob that is the culture that you need to look out for and toss (the whole bottle) when you see it.

Emulsify

The most difficult thing about making a vinaigrette is getting it to emulsify or become fully blended. The emulsification is what makes the dressing creamy and when done correctly, the oil is suspended in little droplets. There are many tricks to getting the mixture to emulsify. A touch of Dijon mustard, mayonnaise, or cream helps the vinaigrette hold together, and some people even swear by adding a teaspoon of water

to the mixture. After you incorporate these little tricks of the trade, the best advice is to add the oil slowly and fully incorporate each drizzle of oil into the vinegar mixture before adding more oil.

Mustards

The third key ingredient to a perfect vinaigrette is mustard. An authentic, strong Dijon mustard will make a perfect vinaigrette, day in and day out. But just like the vinegar and oil, once you master the basics, there is a world of mustards that can make your vinaigrettes even better. You should have at least the three basics on hand, Dijon mustard, whole-grain Dijon mustard, and yellow mustard, but if you like mustard, branch out and try the flavored mustards sold by Maille (tarragon is a favorite) or the Violet, Cognac, Walnut and Piment D'Esplette Mustards sold by Zingerman's (www.zingermans.com). The violet mustard is not only delicious, but it is also beautiful, with its deep red color adding a nice pink hue to any vinaigrette. The mustard is made from fresh red grape juice and mustard seeds, giving it its distinctive color.

THE MUSTARD PANTRY

- Good, strong Dijon mustard such as Amora, Edmond Fallot, or Maille
- Whole-grain Dijon mustard
- Yellow mustard
- Honeycup mustard
- Creole mustard
- Spicy German or deli mustard

Improvisational Vinaigrettes

Refer to Classic Vinaigrette 101 (facing page) as your basic recipe using red or white wine vinegar. Add a heaping tablespoon of one of your favorite flavors, such as pesto, pureed roasted red or poblano peppers, roasted garlic, tapenade, fruit jam, fresh herbs, etc.—whatever your palate desires. If the vinaigrette seems a little too acidic or too sharp, incorporate a little heavy cream to round it out. And let your imagination guide you to creative combinations, although be careful of trying to blend too many flavored ingredients—such as a flavored vinegar, flavored oil, and flavored mustard. There could be flavor overkill. When you do experiment, try it in small quantities first.

Methods

Ever since I learned how to make homemade vinaigrettes, I've done it with a whisk or even a fork because I get so much satisfaction from making them by hand. But I now know that I am in the minority. Every time I go to a friend's house for lunch or dinner, I am asked to make the vinaigrette, and through this experience

I have discovered that there is a lot of vinaigrette anxiety out there! Blending the dressing is really easy and only takes a little patience. Here are some tips:

By hand: Use a small oval-shaped whisk with a coil for vinaigrettes. I have one that I bought in France many years ago and I use it every day. In fact, it is so easy to get a smooth blend (emulsification) that I take it with me on all my travels and teach all my friends how to make their own "dressings."

- Mix vinegar, dry seasonings, and mustard together.
- Slowly add the oil, little by little, completely incorporating all the oil before adding more.
- Practice; it's all in the wrist, so the right angle and speed will become natural the more you make them.

With a blender: If you own a blender, use it to make vinaigrettes, but don't over-blend or your vinaigrette could come out thick, like a mayonnaise.

Using an immersion blender in a jar: If you own an immersion blender, you can place all the ingredients in a large-mouth glass jar and blend them in the jar—just make sure you have enough liquid to cover the blender part of the stick.

Classic Vinaigrette 101

Makes 1 cup

Use this recipe as a basis for all your vinaigrettes. Switch up the oil, vinegar, and even the mustard to make a whole wardrobe of simple flavored vinaigrettes.

Good for Seasoning: Grilled chicken; fish; green vegetables, salad greens, beets

1/4 cup white or red wine vinegar or balsamic vinegar
1 heaping teaspoon Dijon mustard
Pinch of sea salt and freshly ground pepper
3/4 cup extra-virgin olive oil

In a medium bowl, whisk together the vinegar, mustard, salt, and pepper. Slowly whisk in the olive oil, making sure each addition is completely blended before adding more oil. Adjust the seasoning to taste. Use immediately, or store in the refrigerator in an airtight container for up to 5 days

Shake it: Pour all your ingredients in a Mason jar, screw on the top, and shake.

Shelf Life

Vinaigrettes are fairly stable and will keep, covered, in the refrigerator for about 5 days. However, they are always at their best right after you make them. This is especially true with vinaigrettes made with fresh juices. As soon as they sit, you lose some of the brightness (tartness and clarity of flavor) from the freshly squeezed juices and other highly perishable ingredients. Vinaigrettes made in advance should be stored in a clean glass jar with a tight-fitting lid in the refrigerator. If necessary, warm or bring to room temperature before serving.

Sherry-Shallot Vinaigrette

Makes 1/2 cup

The addition of the violet—red—mustard makes this sherry-shallot vinaigrette a rosy choice for drizzling on grilled chops or a simple salad. To deepen the flavor, sauté the chopped shallots in a little olive oil until they are well caramelized before making the vinaigrette.

Good for Seasoning: Lamb chops; steak; grilled clams, oysters; chicken; green vegetables

1/3 cup sherry vinegar
2 teaspoons violet mustard or 1 teaspoon favorite Dijon mustard
2 tablespoons grated or minced shallot
Pinch sugar
Pinch sea salt and freshly ground pepper
2/3 cup olive or untoasted walnut oil

In a medium bowl, whisk together the vinegar, mustard, shallot, sugar, salt, and pepper. Slowly whisk in the oil, making sure that each addition is completely blended before adding more oil. Adjust the seasoning to taste with salt and pepper. Use immediately, or store in the refrigerator in an airtight container for up to 5 days.

Sweet Poppy Seed Dressing

Makes 1 cup

Every self-respecting Southern girl has a poppy seed dressing in her brunch repertoire. This is not only good on berries and baby lettuce, but it also makes a killer dressing for grilled salmon, among other things!

Good for Seasoning: Grilled strawberries, grilled fruit salad, spinach salad; quinoa salad; salmon, scallops, lobster

- 1 tablespoon sugar
- 2 tablespoons honey
- 1/4 teaspoon sea salt
- 1/4 cup unseasoned rice vinegar
- 1/2 teaspoon dry mustard, preferably Colman's
- 1/2 cup untoasted walnut oil
- 1/4 cup minced shallots
- 1 tablespoon whole poppy seeds

In a medium bowl, whisk together the sugar, honey, salt, vinegar, and dry mustard. Slowly whisk in the oil, making sure that each addition is completely blended before adding more oil. Taste for the acid-

oil balance and adjust if desired. Stir in the shallots and poppy seeds. Use immediately, or store in the refrigerator in an airtight container for up to 5 days.

Southwestern Vinaigrette

Makes 3/4 cup

When I was creating the recipes for Hill Country, a Texas barbecue restaurant in Manhattan, I wanted a salad dressing that would reflect the bright colors and different cultures that come together in the Hill Country. The lime juice, chile pepper flakes, and bright herbs make a peppery green vinaigrette that turns ordinary chicken and greens into a meal that makes cowboys and beauty queens alike feel right at home in New York City.

Good for Seasoning: Grilled fish, scallops; boneless skinless chicken breasts; vegetables, grilled veggie chopped salad

- 3 tablespoons seasoned rice vinegar
- 1 teaspoon Dijon mustard
- Pinch red chile flakes
- Pinch sea salt
- 1 small shallot, grated
- 1 lime, juiced
- 1/2 cup olive oil
- Freshly ground pepper
- 3 tablespoons chopped fresh cilantro or basil
- 2 tablespoons chopped fresh chives
- 1 tablespoon chopped fresh curly parsley

In a medium bowl, whisk together the rice vinegar, mustard, red chile flakes, salt, shallot, and lime juice. When they are well mixed, slowly whisk in the oil, making sure each addition is completely blended before adding more oil. Adjust the seasoning to taste with salt and pepper and add the fresh herbs. Use immediately, or store in the refrigerator in an airtight container for up to 2 days.

French Herb Vinaigrette

Makes 1 1/4 cups

My favorite herb combination is known in France as *fines herbes*, a combination of chervil, chives, parsley, and tarragon. This classic combination is traditionally mixed into the terrific *omelet des fines herbes*, and is what makes Boursin cheese a delicious add-in for almost every savory dish! You can make this fresh herb vinaigrette with the fines herbes or substitute your favorite herb, such as basil or dill, to make it your own.

Good for Seasoning: Salmon, cod; chicken; zucchini, eggplant, asparagus, white beans

1/3 cup champagne vinegar or white wine vinegar

1 teaspoon heavy whipping cream

1 teaspoon whole-grain Dijon mustard

1/8 teaspoon fine-grain sea salt and freshly ground pepper

2/3 cup olive or untoasted walnut oil

1 tablespoon chopped fresh chervil

1 tablespoon chopped fresh parsley

1 tablespoon chopped fresh chives

1 tablespoon chopped fresh tarragon

In a medium bowl, whisk together the vinegar, cream, mustard, salt, and pepper. Slowly whisk in the oil, making sure each addition is completely blended before adding more oil. Add the chervil, parsley, chives, and tarragon and whisk to combine. Adjust the seasoning to taste with salt and pepper. Use immediately, or store in the refrigerator in an airtight container for up to 2 days.

Fresh Basil Variation

Substitute 4 tablespoons of chopped fresh basil for the combination of herbs.

Roasted Red Pepper Vinaigrette

Makes 1 cup

You can roast the red peppers, then cool, peel, and puree them in advance. The puree will keep in an airtight container in the refrigerator for at least a week. If you aren't making the peppers in advance, be sure to allow time to roast them—they'll take 30 to 40 minutes from raw to puree.

Good for Seasoning: Boneless skinless chicken breast; salmon, swordfish; pork tenderloin; Boston lettuce salad, grilled arugula, corn, any grilled vegetable

Grilling Method: Direct/High Heat

> 1 red bell pepper
> 1 paper bag or resealable plastic container
> 1 heaping teaspoon Dijon mustard
> 1/3 cup red wine vinegar or sherry vinegar
> Sea salt and freshly ground pepper
> 2/3 cup extra-virgin olive oil
> 1 tablespoon heavy whipping cream

1. Roast, peel, and seed the pepper as described on page 43. Puree it in a blender or food processor and set aside.

2. Make the vinaigrette: In a medium bowl, whisk together the mustard, vinegar, salt, and pepper. Slowly whisk in the oil, making sure each addition completely blended before adding more oil. Add the pureed red pepper and whisk to combine.

3. Whisk in the cream and adjust the seasoning to taste with salt and pepper. Use immediately, or store in the refrigerator in an airtight container for up to 5 days.

Roasted Poblano and Garlic Vinaigrette

Makes 1 1/3 cups

This dressing is perfect for adding a light Mexican flavor to anything grilled or raw. The roasted poblano pepper adds a bit of smoky heat that is complemented by the rich roasted garlic. This is a great dressing to make while you are leisurely grilling on the weekend; then you can save the vinaigrette for a quick weeknight meal.

Good for Seasoning: Grilled fish tacos, catfish, shrimp; chicken; portobello mushrooms, grilled cactus paddles

Grilling Method: Direct/High Heat

> 1 to 2 poblano peppers, depending on size
> 1 paper bag or resealable plastic container
> 2 heads roasted garlic (see page 262), mashed
> 1/3 cup white wine vinegar
> Pinch sea salt and freshly ground pepper
> 2/3 cup extra-virgin olive oil
> 1 tablespoon heavy whipping cream

1. Build a charcoal fire or preheat a gas grill. Grill the pepper over direct heat, turning until the skin blackens and blisters all over. Remove from the grill and immediately put in a paper bag or sealed plastic container until cool. The steam will loosen the skin from the flesh of the pepper. Skin and seed the pepper (the skin will slip off easily). Puree pepper in a blender or food processor and set aside.

2. Make the vinaigrette: In a medium bowl, whisk together the garlic, vinegar, salt, and pepper. Slowly whisk in the oil, making sure each addition is completely blended before adding more oil. Add the pureed pepper and cream; whisk to combine.

3. Adjust the seasoning to taste with salt and pepper. Use immediately, or store in the refrigerator in an airtight container for up to 5 days.

Black Olive Vinaigrette

Makes 1 cup

This vinaigrette is right out of Restaurant Tricks 101! It dresses up the simplest of foods with pizzazz. Black olive puree or "tapenade" can be found in a jar in the imported-food (French or Italian) section of the grocery store. You can use this same basic recipe and substitute pesto for a fresh,

herby dressing for corn, tomatoes, pasta salad, or fish.

Good for Seasoning: Simple grilled fish (halibut, tuna, swordfish); grilled peppers, eggplant, zucchini; grilled chicken salad

> 2 anchovy fillets, drained and finely minced
>
> 4 cloves garlic, finely minced
>
> 1 tablespoon capers, drained and coarsely chopped
>
> Juice and zest of 1 large lemon
>
> 1 teaspoon strong Dijon mustard
>
> 2 tablespoons white wine vinegar
>
> 2/3 cup extra-virgin olive oil
>
> 2 to 3 tablespoons black olive puree
>
> Salt

Combine the anchovies, garlic, capers, lemon juice and zest, mustard, and vinegar in a blender or a food processor. Slowly add in the oil and olive puree and pulse together until blended. Season to taste with salt (although it probably won't be needed, as several ingredients are naturally salty). Use immediately, or store in the refrigerator in an airtight container for up to 5 days.

Chunky Lemon-Olive Vinaigrette

Makes 1 cup

This version of black olive vinaigrette is chunky, and lighter with the omission of anchovies and the addition of chopped olives and a tablespoon of Meyer lemon marmalade. It is the perfect sauce for any grilled fish.

Good for Seasoning: Halibut, monkfish; chicken paillards; baked goat cheese; frisée

- 3 tablespoons fresh lemon juice
- 1 tablespoon red wine vinegar
- 1 tablespoon lemon marmalade, preferably Meyer lemon
- 1 tablespoon black olive puree
- 1/3 cup extra-virgin olive oil
- 1 tablespoon chopped black olives, such as niçoise
- 2 teaspoons capers in brine, chopped
- 1 shallot, finely chopped
- Pinch fine-ground white pepper

In a small bowl, whisk together the lemon juice, vinegar, marmalade, and olive puree. Slowly whisk in the oil, making sure each addition is completely blended before adding more oil. Add the chopped olives, capers, and shallot. Adjust the seasoning to taste with pepper. Use immediately, or store in the refrigerator in an airtight container for up to 5 days.

Grilled Halibut with Chunky Lemon-Olive Vinaigrette

Serves 4

Grilling Method: Direct/Medium Heat

- 4 fresh halibut steaks, about 3/4-inch thick
- Olive oil
- Kosher salt
- 1 recipe Chunky Lemon–Olive Vinaigrette (left)
- 2 tablespoons chopped fresh chives

1. Build a charcoal fire or preheat gas grill. Brush the fish all over with a thin layer of oil and season lightly with salt. Place the fish on the cooking grate over direct heat. Grill for 10 to 12 minutes, turning once halfway through the cooking time—about 5 minutes per side. Cooking time may be longer depending on the size of the fish.

2. Remove from the grill and place one steak in the center of each plate. Top with 1 to 2 tablespoons of the vinaigrette; you may need to remix the vinaigrette before using to reincorporate all of the ingredients. Sprinkle with the chopped chives and serve.

Note: Halibut steaks with the bone in generally weigh about 1 pound each. Ask your fishmonger to split the steaks along the bone to make individual portions. The remaining meat should be about 6 ounces per portion.

Honey Mustard Vinaigrette and Dip

Makes 3/4 cup

Whenever I think of a basic honey mustard dressing, Houston's restaurant comes to mind. This sweet-tart vinaigrette is made with yellow ballpark mustard and makes a great dipping sauce or glaze in addition to the vinaigrette.

Good for Seasoning: Chicken breasts, kabobs, wings; burgers

> 2 tablespoons apple cider vinegar
> 3 tablespoons honey
> 2 teaspoons sugar
> 3 tablespoons yellow mustard
> 1/4 cup mayonnaise, preferably Hellmann's
> Pinch sea salt and freshly ground pepper
> 1/4 cup canola or untoasted walnut oil

In a medium bowl, whisk together the vinegar, honey, sugar, mustard, mayonnaise, salt, and pepper. Slowly whisk in the oil, making sure each addition is completely blended before adding more oil. Adjust the seasoning to taste with salt and pepper. Use immediately, or store in the refrigerator in an airtight container for up to 5 days.

Fancy Honey Mustard Vinaigrette

Makes 1 1/4 cups

This vinaigrette makes me think of the Honeycup brand mustard that is thick and sticky, sweet and hot. It is tangy and spicy with the addition of hot Dijon mustard. The stronger the Dijon mustard, the better the dressing. The heat is tempered with a light creaminess contributed by a touch of mayo.

Good for Seasoning: Chicken, wings; pork tenderloin; grilled cobb salad

> 1/3 cup apple cider vinegar
> 3 teaspoons honey
> 2 teaspoons dark brown sugar
> 1 teaspoon whole-grain Dijon mustard
> 1 tablespoon smooth, strong Dijon mustard
> 1 tablespoon mayonnaise
> Pinch sea salt and freshly ground pepper
> 2/3 cup olive or untoasted walnut oil

In a medium bowl, whisk together the vinegar, honey, sugar, mustards, mayonnaise, salt, and pepper. Slowly whisk in the olive oil, making sure each addition is completely blended before adding more oil. Adjust the seasoning to taste with salt and pepper. Use immediately, or store in the refrigerator in an airtight container for up to 5 days.

Note: If you can find Honeycup brand mustard in your area, substitute it for the mustards in the dressing above. It makes a killer sweet-hot drizzle or salad dressing.

1 teaspoon favorite dry spice rub
2/3 cup peanut oil
Sea salt, optional

In a medium bowl, whisk together the vinegar, barbecue sauce, molasses, Worcestershire sauce, and spice rub. Slowly whisk in the oil, making sure each addition is completely blended before adding more oil. Adjust the seasoning with salt only if using a salt-free rub. Use immediately, or store in the refrigerator in an airtight container for up to 5 days.

Barbecue Sauce Vinaigrette

Makes 1 cup

This is just the ticket when you want a light barbecue sauce flavor but don't want to slather your food with the sauce. The tanginess of the apple cider vinegar cuts the sweet, thick texture so often associated with barbecue sauce to deliver a lighter and sharper but still sweet sauce with a beautiful consistency. Just perfect! I love the combination of Mike Mill's Magic Dust on page 199 and the Sweet Cherry Cola Barbecue Sauce on page 90—but feel free to mix and match your favorites.

Good for Seasoning: Steak; ribs; pork (chops, loin); burgers; chicken wings; grilled onions

2 tablespoons apple cider vinegar
2 tablespoons your favorite barbecue sauce
2 teaspoons molasses
1 teaspoon Worcestershire sauce

Smoked Paprika Vinaigrette

Makes 1 cup

This is my favorite newfangled savory vinaigrette. It turns fire-roasted vegetables into Spanish tapas and is the perfect complement to any kind of grilled fish or shellfish, especially calamari and shrimp.

Good for Seasoning: Grilled fresh figs; steak (hanger, skirt); butterflied chicken; pork chops; sardines

2 tablespoons quince paste
1/3 cup sherry vinegar
1 scant tablespoon sweet or hot smoked Spanish paprika
Pinch sea salt and freshly ground pepper
2/3 cup olive or untoasted walnut oil

In a medium bowl, mix the quince paste with 1 tablespoon warm water, until almost melted. Whisk in the vinegar, paprika, salt, and pepper. Slowly whisk in the oil, making sure that each addition is completely blended before adding more oil. Adjust the seasoning to taste with salt and pepper. Use immediately, or store in the refrigerator in an airtight container for up to 5 days.

Hot Bacon Vinaigrette

Makes 3/4 cup

We all know that bacon makes everything taste better, but try this on grilled Brussels sprouts and you won't believe the transformation that a little ol' hot bacon dressing can give a much maligned vegetable—it's like magic!

Good for Seasoning: Grilled Brussels sprouts, spinach salad with grilled tomatoes, broccoli, delicata squash, grill-roasted new potatoes

- 6 slices thick-cut bacon
- 3 tablespoons chopped red onion
- 1/3 cup apple cider vinegar
- 2 teaspoons whole-grain Dijon mustard
- 2 teaspoons honey
- 1/8 to 1/4 cup peanut or olive oil, depending on the amount of bacon drippings
- Fine-grain sea salt and freshly ground pepper

1. Fry the bacon in a cast-iron skillet over low heat until crisp. Transfer the bacon to a paper towel–lined plate to drain. Add the onion to the bacon drippings in the skillet and sauté for 5 minutes or until the onion begins to brown and caramelize. Chop the bacon. Transfer the onion to the plate with the bacon.

2. Pour the vinegar into the hot bacon drippings and whisk. Add the mustard and honey and continue whisking.

3. Pour all the pan liquids into a small bowl and slowly drizzle in the oil until the dressing is creamy and completely blended. Add the bacon and onion. Adjust the seasoning to taste with salt and pepper and use immediately.

Note: You can also make a slurry (a mixture of cornstarch and water) and mix it into the hot bacon fat and vinegar to make it creamy and help the dressing blend together.

Blue Cheese and Pecan Vinaigrette

Makes 1 cup

This creamy blue cheese and pecan vinaigrette is a happy alternative to the traditional creamy blue cheese dressing. If you are in the mood for pure blue, double the cheese and eliminate the nuts—and if you are looking for an English twist to this classic, substitute Stilton and walnuts for the Roquefort and pecans.

Good for Seasoning: Beef (tenderloin, kabobs, strip steak, flat-iron steak); grilled romaine, roasted peppers, salads

> 1/4 cup apple cider vinegar or white wine vinegar
>
> 1 heaping teaspoon Dijon mustard
>
> Salt and freshly ground pepper to taste
>
> 1/2 cup olive oil
>
> 1/4 pound Roquefort or other blue cheese, crumbled
>
> 2/3 cup pecan pieces, toasted

1. In a small bowl, whisk together the vinegar, mustard, salt, and pepper. Slowly whisk in the olive oil, making sure each addition is completely blended before adding more oil.

2. Add the blue cheese and set aside until you are about to use. Add the toasted pecans just before serving. Stir to combine, and use immediately.

Meyer Lemon and Mint Vinaigrette

Makes 1 cup

The Meyer lemon comes from China and is thought to be a cross between the more familiar Lisbon lemon and the Mandarin orange. It is sweeter and less tart that the common lemon, with a thinner, darker skin. I think it is the essence of pure lemon and although it is not available in every grocery store, it is very easy to grow in warmer climates and is often grown in large ornamental pots. Grow your own or seek out a specialty store that carries these lemons—they are also known as the "valley lemon" in southern Texas. They will change your lemon life and make you a true lemon-head!

Good for Seasoning: Branzino (sea bass), white fish, shrimp; chicken paillards; veal chops; baby vegetables

> 1/3 cup champagne vinegar
>
> 1 teaspoon mint jelly
>
> 1 teaspoon whole-grain Dijon mustard
>
> Pinch sea salt and freshly ground pepper
>
> 2/3 cup Meyer lemon olive oil
>
> 2 tablespoons chopped fresh mint
>
> Zest of 1 small Meyer lemon

In a medium bowl, whisk together the vinegar, jelly, mustard, salt, and pepper. Slowly whisk in the oil, making sure that each addition is completely blended before adding more oil. Add the mint and zest and stir to combine. Adjust the seasoning to taste with salt and pepper. Use immediately. Or make up to the step where you add the mint and zest, and store in the refrigerator in an airtight container for up to 5 days; add the mint and zest right before serving.

Lemon-Thyme Vinaigrette

Makes 1 cup

Some thyme, any thyme, this vinaigrette works all the thyme!

Good for Seasoning: Chicken; pork; salmon, tilapia, cod; summer squash

    1 heaping teaspoon Dijon mustard
    1/3 cup white wine vinegar
    2 teaspoons minced fresh thyme
    Pinch sea salt and freshly ground pepper
    Zest of 1 lemon
    2/3 cup extra-virgin olive oil

In a small bowl, whisk together the mustard, vinegar, thyme, salt, pepper, and lemon zest. Slowly whisk in the olive oil, making sure each addition is completely blended before adding more oil. Adjust the seasoning to taste with salt and pepper. Use immediately, or store in the refrigerator in an airtight container for up to 5 days.

Lemon Truffle Dressing

Makes 3/4 cup

I first made this vinaigrette to dress up grilled asparagus for a special dinner that I was hosting. The truffle oil transports it to another level and the whipping cream rounds out the sharp lemon note, turning this light vinaigrette into a rich sauce for grilled vegetables and shellfish. If you have a Meyer lemon on hand, substitute it for the regular lemon.

Good for Seasoning: Grilled asparagus, artichokes, new potatoes, arugula, mushrooms; lobster

    1/3 cup fresh lemon juice (about 2 1/2 lemons)
    1 teaspoon heavy whipping cream, at room temperature
    1/3 cup olive or canola oil
    1/4 cup truffle-infused oil
    Sea salt and freshly ground pepper

In a medium bowl, whisk together the lemon juice and cream. Slowly whisk in the oil, making sure each addition is completely blended before adding more oil. Season to taste with salt and pepper Use immediately, or store in the refrigerator in an airtight container for up to 2 days.

Marmalade Vinaigrette

Makes 1 cup

I make this marmalade vinaigrette most often with orange or clementine marmalade, but it is fantastic with any marmalade you can find. The sweet and bitter notes of the candied citrus peel up the ante and turn a simple dish into a superb one. For a real treat, try June Taylor's fabulous handcrafted marmalades and jams in this recipe (www.junetaylorjams.com).

Good for Seasoning: Grilled chicken salad; pork; skirt steak; grilled green vegetables, salad greens

- 2 teaspoons apple cider vinegar
- 1/3 cup fresh orange juice
- 2 teaspoons heavy whipping cream, at room temperature
- 2 tablespoons orange marmalade
- 1/4 cup untoasted hazelnut oil
- 1/3 cup canola oil
- Sea salt and fine-ground white pepper to taste

In a small bowl, whisk together the vinegar, juice, and cream. Add the marmalade and mix again. Slowly add the oil, whisking after each addition until it is completely blended before adding more oil. Adjust the seasoning to taste with salt and

pepper. Use immediately, or store in the refrigerator in an airtight container for up to 2 days.

Fig and Balsamic Vinaigrette with Toasted Walnuts

Makes 1 1/2 cups

Try one of the very good fig balsamic vinegars when making this vinaigrette; it will complement the fig jam and give the dressing a rounder, richer flavor. Add toasted walnuts to this vinaigrette for some crunch.

Good for Seasoning: Turkey, duck; pork; goat cheese; beets

- 1/3 cup balsamic vinegar, preferably fig balsamic
- 1 tablespoon fig jam
- 1 teaspoon whole-grain Dijon mustard
- Fine-grain sea salt and freshly ground pepper
- 2/3 cup olive or untoasted walnut oil
- 2 tablespoons chopped toasted walnuts

In a medium bowl, whisk together the vinegar, figs, mustard, salt, and pepper. Slowly whisk in the oil, making sure each addition is completely blended before adding more oil. Add the walnuts and stir to combine. Adjust the seasoning to taste with salt and pepper. Use immediately. Or make the vinaigrette up to the step where you add the walnuts, then store in the refrigerator in an airtight container for up to 5 days; add the walnuts just before serving.

Garlic-Shallot and Caper Vinaigrette (Raw and Fried)

Makes 1 cup

I make this vinaigrette two ways, and they are equally good. I like mixing all the ingredients together, freshly chopped and uncooked. Or, I heat up 1/4 cup of the oil and flash-fry the capers, garlic, and shallots before mixing them into the vinaigrette. The raw version is more subtle, and the fried version is full of big, bold, in-your-face flavors. The raw dressing is dynamite on drizzled on hot grilled vegetables and the fried version is great drizzled over grilled bread, shellfish, or chicken breasts.

Good for Seasoning: Grilled vegetables; steak, veal; chicken; clams, mussels, oysters; grilled bread

> 2/3 cup olive oil
> 1 tablespoon salt-cured capers, chopped*
> 2 tablespoons chopped shallot
> 1 teaspoon grated garlic
> 1/3 cup red wine vinegar
> 1 teaspoon whole-grain Dijon mustard
> Pinch sea salt and freshly ground pepper

1. If making the fried version, heat 1/4 cup of the oil in a small heavy-duty sauté pan. "Fry" the capers, shallot, and garlic until they are beginning to brown. Let them cool in the oil before making the vinaigrette.

2. In a medium bowl, whisk together the vinegar, capers, shallot, garlic, mustard (and oil you cooked them in if you fried them), salt, and pepper. Slowly whisk in the oil, making sure that each addition is completely blended before adding more oil. Adjust the seasoning to taste with salt and pepper. Use immediately, or store in the refrigerator in an airtight container for up to 5 days.

*When using salt-packed capers, rinse them several times in cold water and squeeze extra moisture out with a paper towel.

Toasted Sesame-Soy Dressing

Makes 1/2 cup

Although this makes a great dressing for chicken, pork, and even beef, my favorite way to use this is to grill long green beans and toss them in this vinaigrette while hot. The green beans, with their heady sesame aroma, will become the main event!

Good for Seasoning: Grilled green vegetables, long beans, asparagus, baby carrots; salmon; chicken, duck breast; pork (chops, tenderloin); beef

> 4 tablespoons unseasoned rice vinegar
> 1 tablespoon low-sodium soy sauce
> 1/2 teaspoon light brown sugar
> 1/4 teaspoon red chile flakes
> 1/4 cup toasted sesame oil
> 1/4 cup olive or canola oil
> Salt and freshly ground pepper
> 1 tablespoon black or white sesame seeds, toasted

1. In a small bowl, whisk together rice vinegar, soy sauce, sugar, and red chile flakes. Slowly whisk in both oils, making sure each addition is completely blended before adding more oil.

2. Adjust the seasoning to taste with extra vinegar and salt, and pepper and add sesame seeds. Use immediately, or store in the refrigerator in an airtight container for up to 5 days.

Ginger-Mirin Variation

Add 3 teaspoons of freshly grated ginger and 1 tablespoon of mirin to the vinegar mixture. This variation is especially good on fish and shellfish.

Roasted Garlic and Honey Vinaigrette

Makes 1 1/4 cups

Roasting garlic mellows out the sharpness and changes the texture from hard to creamy, making it perfect for whisking into a vinaigrette. You can double the garlic punch and add some crunch by adding 3 cloves of thinly sliced and fried garlic to the vinaigrette.

Good for Seasoning: Grilled endive, roasted peppers, veggies; salmon fillet; butterflied chicken

    1/3 cup white balsamic vinegar
    1 head roasted garlic (see page 262)
    1 tablespoon honey
    1 teaspoon whole-grain Dijon mustard
    1 teaspoon smooth Dijon mustard
    Pinch sea salt and freshly ground pepper

    2/3 cup olive oil
    3 cloves sliced and fried garlic, optional

In a medium bowl, whisk together the vinegar, garlic, honey, mustards, salt, and pepper. Slowly whisk in the oil, making sure each addition is completely blended before adding more oil. Add the fried garlic, if using, and stir to combine. Adjust the seasoning to taste with salt and pepper. Use immediately, or store in the refrigerator in an airtight container for up to 5 days.

Thyme-Chile Vinaigrette

Makes 1 cup

The combination of red chilies and thyme leaves is an unexpected flavor revolution. A vinaigrette is the perfect medium to deliver the bold flavors in a way that packs a punch but is not overpowering.

Good for Seasoning: Flank steak, skirt steak, steak salad; chicken thighs; roasted yellow peppers, grilled pattypan squash

    1/3 cup distilled white vinegar
    1 tablespoon hot pepper jelly
    1 teaspoon heavy whipping cream
    Pinch sea salt and freshly ground pepper
    1/3 cup olive or peanut oil
    1/3 cup hot (red) chile oil*
    1 tablespoon chopped fresh thyme

In a medium bowl, whisk together the vinegar, jelly, cream, salt, and pepper. Slowly whisk in the oils, making sure each addition is completely blended before adding more oil. Add the thyme and mix to combine. Adjust the seasoning to taste with salt and pepper. Use immediately, or store in the refrigerator in an airtight container for up to 5 days.

*If you don't have any hot chile oil on hand, mix 1 tablespoon Thai chile-garlic sauce (*sriracha*) with 2/3 cup olive or peanut oil.

Ginger-Chile-Lime Vinaigrette

Makes 3/4 cup

This limy vinaigrette borrows its flavor profile from Southeast Asia. The Thai hot chili sauce—*sriracha*—is mixed with fresh ginger, shallots, and chives for a vinaigrette that could double as a dipping sauce. The sweetness comes from a very American ingredient—hot pepper jelly!

Good for Seasoning: Grilled Napa cabbage, green beans, snow peas, Asian slaw; sausages; pork tenderloin; turkey cutlets; shrimp

- 3 tablespoons seasoned rice vinegar
- 1 teaspoon Thai chili-garlic sauce (*sriracha*)
- 1 tablespoon hot pepper jelly
- Juice and zest of 1 large lime
- 1/8 teaspoon fine-grain sea salt
- 1 small shallot, grated
- 1/2 cup olive or peanut oil
- 2 tablespoons chopped fresh chives
- 1 tablespoon grated fresh ginger

In a medium bowl, whisk together the rice vinegar, chili-garlic sauce, hot pepper jelly, lime juice and zest, salt, and shallot. Slowly whisk in the oil, making sure that each addition is completely blended before adding more oil. Add the chives and ginger. Adjust the seasoning to taste with salt and pepper. Use immediately, or store in the refrigerator in an airtight container for up to 5 days.

Chipotle Adobo Vinaigrette

Makes 3/4 cup

As far as chipotles in adobo sauce are concerned, a little dab will do you, and when they are mixed with smooth tequila, they add a distinctive Mexican flavor to all your grilled fare.

Good for Seasoning: Steaks; grilled chicken; shrimp; pork shoulder; tacos; roasted poblanos, new potatoes

- 1/3 cup distilled white vinegar
- 2 tablespoons agave tequila
- 2 tablespoons seedless raspberry jam, warmed to melt
- 2 teaspoons pureed chipotle chilies in adobo sauce, or more to taste
- Pinch sea salt and freshly ground pepper
- 1/2 cup olive or peanut oil

In a small bowl, whisk together the vinegar, tequila, jam, pureed chipotles, salt, and pepper. Slowly whisk in the oil, making sure each addition is completely blended before adding more oil. Adjust the seasoning to taste with salt and pepper. Use immediately, or store in the refrigerator in an airtight container for up to 5 days.

Note: Puree a can of chipotles with the adobo sauce and keep it in the refrigerator to add a little touch of chipotle to your food anytime. The pureed chipotles will keep for up to a month.

Golden Curry Vinaigrette

Makes 1 cup

Curry seasoning is one of the jewels of India. And although there are as many curries in India as there are cooks, in America, we associate the flavor of curry with the golden yellow curry powder that is spiced with coriander, fenugreek, cumin, black pepper, bay leaves, celery seed, nutmeg, cloves, onion, red pepper, and ginger, and colored with turmeric. I love drizzling this golden vinaigrette on just about everything that I want to spice up with a little Indian flair.

Good for Seasoning: Grilled lamb chops, leg of lamb; chicken kabobs, chicken thighs; fish, shrimp; vegetables, rice

> 1/3 cup white wine vinegar
> 1 tablespoon honey
> 1 teaspoon mayonnaise
> 1 tablespoon curry powder
> Pinch sea salt and freshly ground pepper
> 1/3 cup hot chile oil or olive oil
> 1/3 cup olive oil

In a medium bowl, whisk together the vinegar, honey, mayonnaise, curry powder, salt, and pepper. Slowly whisk in both oils, making sure each addition is completely blended before adding more oil. Adjust the seasoning to taste with salt and pepper. Use immediately, or store in the refrigerator in an airtight container for up to 5 days.

Berry Good Vinaigrette

Makes 1 cup

In the big bad eighties, raspberry vinegar ruled! Since then, so many other vinegars have come to market that it is hard to remember why it defined the gourmet category. The sparkling, fruity, sweet tang and the pleasing pink color pairs with almost every food; fish or fowl—try any number of the great berry vinegars and no-sugar-added jams to make a raspberry, blueberry, strawberry, blackberry, or berry medley vinaigrette and bring back the eighties!

Good for Seasoning: Salads; grilled mushrooms; grilled salmon; chicken salad; duck, quail

> 1/3 cup balsamic or raspberry vinegar
> 1 tablespoon all-fruit no-sugar-added berry jam
> 1 teaspoon whole-grain Dijon mustard
> Pinch sea salt and freshly ground pepper
> 2/3 cup olive or untoasted walnut oil
> 2 tablespoons chopped dried or fresh raspberries or other berries*

In a small bowl, whisk together the vinegar, jam, mustard, salt, and pepper. Slowly whisk in the oil, making sure each addition is completely blended before adding more oil. Stir in the fruit. Adjust the seasoning to taste with salt and pepper. Use immediately, or store in the refrigerator in an airtight container for up to 5 days.

*Add whole berries just before serving for garnish and plate appeal.

Orange and Port Wine Vinaigrette

Makes 1 cup

Make this vinaigrette and drizzle it over grilled bread and cheese or wild game. The sweet citrus notes of the orange zest and the rich port were made to order for red meat, assertive cheeses, and grilled radicchio.

Good for Seasoning: Short ribs; venison; pork loin; grilled bread; cheese; grilled apple and pear salad

- 2 tablespoons sherry vinegar
- 3 tablespoons port
- 1 teaspoon whole-grain Dijon mustard
- Pinch sea salt and freshly ground pepper
- Zest of 1 large navel orange
- 1/3 cup untoasted walnut or olive oil
- 1/3 cup orange-flavored oil (or 1 teaspoon pure orange oil mixed with untoasted walnut oil)

In a medium bowl, whisk together the vinegar, port, mustard, salt, pepper, and orange zest. Slowly whisk in both oils, making sure each addition is completely blended before adding more oil. Adjust the seasoning to taste with salt and pepper. Use immediately, or store in the refrigerator in an airtight container for up to 5 days.

Warm Cassis Vinaigrette

Makes 1 cup

This vinaigrette takes its cue from the Kir Royale, that mixture of champagne and crème de cassis. The olive oil will give the dressing more muscle and the walnut oil will make it more delicate—choose the oil based on what you are serving with this lovely warm vinaigrette.

Good for Seasoning: Grilled duck, grilled duck or chicken salad; steak; artichokes

- 1/3 cup champagne vinegar
- 3 tablespoons crème de cassis
- 1 teaspoon strong Dijon mustard
- 1/8 teaspoon fine-grain sea salt
- Pinch freshly ground pepper
- 2/3 cup olive or untoasted walnut oil

1. In a medium bowl, whisk together the vinegar, crème de cassis, mustard, salt, and pepper.

2. In a small saucepan, slowly warm the oil, taking care not to let it simmer or boil. When it is hot to the touch, remove from the heat and slowly whisk it into the vinegar-cassis mixture, making sure each addition is completely blended before adding more oil. Adjust the seasoning to taste with salt and pepper and use immediately.

Pomegranate-Cherry Vinaigrette

Makes 1 1/4 cups

Pomegranates are the fruit of the twenty-first century. Not only do they taste good, but they are good for you. Here the tart, astringent juice is sweetened by no-sugar-added cherry jam for a ruby-red vinaigrette that dazzles all white meats, fish, and vegetables.

Good for Seasoning: Pork, ribs; smoked chicken; grilled corn; grilled oysters

- 1/4 cup pomegranate juice
- 1 tablespoon balsamic vinegar
- 2 tablespoons no-sugar-added cherry jam
- 1 teaspoon violet mustard
- Generous pinch sea salt and freshly ground pepper
- 2/3 cup olive oil
- 1/3 cup fresh pomegranate seeds, optional

In a medium bowl, whisk together the pomegranate juice, vinegar, jam, mustard, salt, and pepper. Slowly whisk in the olive oil, making sure each addition is completely blended before adding more oil. If adding the pomegranate seeds, add and stir. Adjust the seasoning to taste with salt and pepper. Use immediately, or store in the refrigerator in an airtight container for up to 2 days.

Passion Fruit Vinaigrette

Makes 1 cup

Passion fruit is my all-time favorite fruit flavor. It used to be hard for home cooks to find, but more and more grocery stores carry this fruit. It is great scooped out of its skin and mixed with plain yogurt and light brown sugar or mixed into a classic vinaigrette—seeds and all! Passion fruit is ripe when wrinkled and feels a little hollow.

Good for Seasoning: Grilled mango, roasted peppers; chicken; pork; shrimp, scallops, lobster

- 1/3 cup white balsamic or white wine vinegar
- 1 tablespoon passion fruit (such as Goya) or apricot jam
- 1 teaspoon whole-grain Dijon mustard
- Pinch sea salt and freshly ground pepper
- 2/3 cup olive or untoasted walnut oil
- Pulp from 1 fresh passion fruit or passion fruit puree

In a medium bowl, whisk together the vinegar, jam, mustard, salt, and pepper. Slowly whisk in the oil, making sure each addition is completely blended before adding more oil. Add the passion fruit pulp and stir to combine. Adjust the seasoning to taste with salt and pepper. Use immediately, or store in the refrigerator in an airtight container for up to 2 days.

Compound Butters

Savory and sweet mixtures of high-flavor ingredients—herbs, spices, aromatics (such as garlic), fruit (such as citrus), sweeteners (such as sugar), salt, alcohol, condiments (such as jam)—bound by butter. They are quick, easy, and look beautiful as they melt over hot grilled food.

Compound Butters 101

Compound butters are the secret weapon of steak houses worldwide and of most four-star chefs. The simple addition of a flavored butter transforms a simple piece of grilled meat, fish, vegetable, or fruit from plain Jane to supermodel! What we call compound butters in the United States started as *beuerre maître d'hôtel* in France. Flavored butters were being used as long ago as the early 1900s in France by the famous classic chef Escoffier.

In truth, compound butters can replace most fancy sauces, especially for the grill cook. The innate flavor of grilled food is so delicious and distinctive that all it needs is a brightly flavored compound butter to add that extra level of taste and richness to make it one of your favorite dishes. So often, less is more. When I was creating recipes for *Taming the Flame*, I wanted to re-create my favorite swordfish dish from Nantucket; grilled swordfish with béarnaise and sautéed pecans. I made a brown butter and pecan sauce with three ingredients—butter, sea salt, and pecans—and spooned it over swordfish that was grilled using the Grilling Trilogy of olive oil, salt, and pepper (see page 10). The result was so

compelling that it became my favorite fish recipe in the book and is still one of my all-time favorite recipes (see page 112). And compound butters are even easier to make. The essence of a compound butter is butter and flavorings. These can be sweet or savory and provide an exciting and unexpected burst of flavor to any food you can imagine. It is one of the easiest techniques to execute—even someone who doesn't cook can make a compound butter and add it to a 101 recipe (see pages 14–29) with confidence.

The way compound butters work is that the cold butter has all the great flavors "locked in," and when you put the butter on hot food, it melts and bathes the food with all the seasonings, creating a subtle but very noticeable change in flavor.

Compound butters can be made in advance and stored in either the refrigerator or freezer. I usually make more that I need for a particular grilling recipe so that I have it already made to add to my morning eggs or evening pasta, or to embellish other dishes. Try the Escargot Butter (page 261) on French bread for dynamite grilled garlic bread or the Apricot-Ginger Butter (page 271) between European-style sugar cookies for a quick dessert. Less unusual but equally good, the sweet butters are great on toast, waffles, and pancakes and the savory butters are terrific as a spread for sandwiches—both cold and grilled! Once you add compound butters to your cooking repertoire, you will use them more

and more because they give your food the biggest bang for the least amount of effort. After you try a few of the butters here, try your hand at your own signature butters.

Butter: Salted or Unsalted?

Most food experts, especially those who, like me, are really into salt, prefer to use unsalted butter for everything. Using unsalted butter lets you choose how much and what kind of salt to use. For the most part, I like controlling the saltiness of my food. For example, in Kirsten's Anchovy Butter (page 268), I don't add any salt at all because the anchovies are so salty. Ditto for the Soy-Ginger Wasabi Butter (page 268), the Blue Cheese and Pecan Butter (page 254), and the BBQ Butter (page 265). So many of the flavorings are inherently salty that it is better to season to taste after combining all the ingredients than have a butter that is so salty that the salt overpowers all the other flavors.

Shelf Life

Compound butters can be made on the day they are used or up to a week in advance. Butters made in advance should be stored, tightly wrapped, in the refrigerator or freezer. If you freeze them, they will last for up to a month. Thaw before use, or cut into pieces while still frozen with a vegetable peeler or sharp knife.

MAKING A BUTTER LOG

1. Spread out a sheet of plastic wrap or parchment.

2. Spoon dollops of soft butter in a row about 2 inches from the end.

3. Fold wrap over dollops and roll and tighten.

4. Twist ends to secure butter in the wrap.

5. Twirl ends to tighten and compact butter.

6. Once log is uniform, chill until firm.

Compound Butter Tips

- **Mix It:** If you are making a large quantity of compound butter, a stand mixer works very well. (If restaurant kitchens flavor their house butter, they always make it in an electric mixer.) But do not overwhip or overmix the butter or you will lose the bright bold flavors that you are adding to your butter. If you are making a small quantity for home use, a mixer can actually be more trouble than it's worth.

- **Freeze It:** To make butter for future use, I cut each log into 1/4-inch-thick medallions or mold it using a butter or candy mold. I place these pieces in the freezer to harden and then wrap each individual piece in plastic wrap. When they are all wrapped, I put them in a freezer container or bag so that I can easily remove one or more pieces when I need them.

- **Grate It:** To control how much butter you eat or serve, freeze the whole log of butter and, when it is frozen, use a vegetable peeler to grate or shave the compound butter over the food. You get great butter flavor without overdoing it.

Compound Butter 101

Makes 1 log (1/2 cup)

This is the simplest of compound butters but still adds sophistication to any dish you put it on. It is a simplified version of the classic French compound butter called *beurre maître d'hôtel*. Add a squeeze of lemon juice and a little lemon zest and you have the classic. I also like to add a pinch of granulated garlic to this butter.

Good for Seasoning: Zucchini, yellow squash; steak; scallops

> 1/2 cup (1 stick) unsalted butter, softened
> 4 teaspoons minced fresh curly parsley
> 1/2 teaspoon sea salt or fleur de sel

1. In a medium bowl, mash or stir the butter with a fork until it is smooth and slightly fluffy. Add the parsley and salt. Mix together, mashing with the back of the fork to make sure all the ingredients are completely incorporated. Taste for seasoning. Add more salt if desired.

2. On a piece of plastic wrap or parchment, drop the butter in spoonfuls to form a log. Roll the butter in the plastic wrap and smooth out to form a round log about 1 1/2 inches in diameter. Refrigerate until hard and easy to cut into pieces. The butter will keep, tightly wrapped, in the refrigerator for up to 1 week and in the freezer for up to 1 month.

Nut butters are a cook's ace in the hole. Think how nuts are used by all the best chefs and in your favorite restaurants; think trout amandine, pecan chicken, lamb chops with hazelnuts, macadamia nut–crusted mahi-mahi, etc. You can use virtually any nut that you like to add additional flavor to your favorite foods. Nut butters are also a great way to dress up plain grilled vegetables. Even onions become a house favorite with a little pecan butter melted over the top! Substitute your favorite nut for the pecans in the pecan butter. It is best to lightly toast the nuts on a baking sheet in a low oven to bring out all their flavor. Be sure to let the nuts cool completely before mixing them in the butter. You do not want to melt the butter. If you like the look of parsley on your food, add the chopped curly parsley to the butter. If you are making one of the nut butters for grilled fruit, do not add the parsley; instead, add 1 tablespoon of light brown sugar to the butter.

To make smooth nut butters, add 1/4 cup ground nut butter to softened butter. These are fun to play around with. Use chile-flavored peanut butter for a quick Thai-style peanut sauce. Use a dark chocolate peanut butter for grilled fruit, or use almond or cashew butter with a touch of soy sauce and toasted sesame oil for an Asian flair.

Toasted Pecan Butter

Makes 1 log (1/2 cup)

I chose to use pecans for the basic nut butter because I am from the South, and to Southern cooks pecans go with and in everything, just like salt and pepper. Feel free to substitute the nut of your choice to make your favorite nut butter (see the sidebar, left).

Good for Seasoning: Grilled trout, catfish; boneless skinless chicken breasts; meat; vegetables, fruit

> 1/2 cup (1 stick) unsalted butter, softened
> 1/2 cup toasted pecans, chopped into 1/4-inch pieces
> 1/2 teaspoon sea salt or fleur de sel

1. In a medium bowl, mash or stir the butter with a fork until it is smooth and slightly fluffy. Add the pecans and salt. Mix together, mashing with the back of the fork to make sure all the ingredients are incorporated. Mix well. Taste for seasoning and adjust if desired.

2. On a piece of plastic wrap or parchment, drop the butter in spoonfuls to form a log. Roll the butter in plastic wrap and smooth out to form a round log about 1 1/2 inches in diameter. Refrigerate until hard and easy to cut into pieces. The butter will keep, tightly wrapped, in the refrigerator for up to 1 week and in the freezer for up to 1 month.

Blue Cheese and Pecan Butter

Makes 1 log (1 cup)

Think of the best holiday cheese ball, rich with creamy blue cheese and crunchy pecans. With this butter you can turn a staple dish into a beautiful meal that tastes anything but basic.

Good for Seasoning: Steak; chicken; meaty fish; grilled bread, baked potatoes

> 1/2 cup (1 stick) unsalted butter, softened
>
> 1/3 cup Gorgonzola, Roquefort, or other blue cheese, softened
>
> 3 tablespoons toasted and finely chopped pecans
>
> Sea salt, optional

1. In a medium bowl, mash or stir the butter with a fork until it is smooth and slightly fluffy. Add the cheese and pecans. Mix together, mashing with the back of the fork to make sure all the ingredients are incorporated. Taste for seasoning. The cheese should be salty enough that you don't need to add any additional salt. If you do want to add salt, add it slowly, pinch by pinch, because the butter will taste saltier as it sits and the flavors meld together.

2. On a piece of plastic wrap or parchment, drop the butter in spoonfuls to form a log. Roll the butter in plastic wrap and smooth out to form a round log about 1 1/2 inches in diameter. Refrigerate until hard and easy to cut into pieces. The butter will keep, tightly wrapped, in the refrigerator for up to 1 week and in the freezer for up to 1 month.

Roquefort Butter

Makes 1 log (1 cup)

This is simple and sublime. The salty, pungent flavors of the Roquefort are mellowed out by the sweet butter, and the parsley adds a fresh look and bite to this little black dress of butters. Put a healthy dollop on top of a burger and it will turn the burger into a steak!

Good for Seasoning: Beef; burgers; apples, pears

> 12/ cup (1 stick) unsalted butter, softened
>
> 2/3 cup Roquefort cheese, softened
>
> 2 teaspoons finely minced curly parsley
>
> Sea salt, optional

1. In a medium bowl, mash or stir the butter with a fork until it is smooth and slightly fluffy. Add the cheese and parsley. The cheese should be salty enough that you don't need to add any additional salt. Mix together, mashing with the back of the fork to make sure all the ingredients are incorporated. Mix well and taste for seasoning. If you do want to add salt, add it slowly, pinch by pinch, because the butter will taste saltier as it sits and the flavors bloom and marry.

2. On a piece of plastic wrap or parchment, drop the butter in spoonfuls to form a log. Roll the butter in plastic wrap and smooth out to form a round log about 1 1/2 inches in diameter. Refrigerate until hard and easy to cut into pieces. The butter will keep, tightly wrapped, in the refrigerator for up to 1 week and in the freezer for up to 1 month.

Truffle Butter

Makes 1 log (1/2 cup)

This is a favorite of mine and one that I keep on hand. It is the essence of truffles and so wonderful that I serve it alone or as an accompaniment to cheese and crackers. It's also great on meat, vegetables, and scrambled eggs.

Good for Seasoning: Grilled bread; beef; chicken; fish; veggies; lamb; scrambled eggs, deviled eggs

    1/2 cup (1 stick) unsalted butter, softened
    2 tablespoons minced truffles (sometimes sold as truffle paste), or 1 tablespoon white truffle oil
    3/4 teaspoon fleur de sel or other coarse salt

1. In a medium bowl, mash or stir the butter with a fork until it is smooth and slightly fluffy. Add the truffles and fleur de sel. Mix together, mashing with the back of the fork to make sure all the ingredients

are incorporated. Mix well. Taste for seasoning and adjust if desired.

2. On a piece of plastic wrap or parchment, drop the butter in spoonfuls to form a log. Roll the butter in plastic wrap and smooth out to form a round log about 1 1/2 inches in diameter. Refrigerate until hard and easy to cut into pieces. The butter will keep, tightly wrapped, in the refrigerator for up to 1 week and in the freezer for up to 1 month.

Pernod Butter

Makes 1 log (1/2 cup)

Pernod was created in 1905 to mimic the flavor of the controversial absinthe. The distinctive herbaceous flavor comes from star anise and a unique combination of aromatic herbs and plants. The anise flavor is the perfect complement to the dried tarragon in this butter. Add a chunk of this butter and a drizzle of cream to sautéed spinach to make a quick but delicious "creamed spinach."

Good for Seasoning: Chicken; pork; fish, shrimp, lobster; fennel, pears, sautéed spinach

    1/2 cup (1 stick) unsalted butter, softened
    1 small shallot, minced
    3 sprigs fresh tarragon, leaves only, chopped, or 1/2 teaspoon dried tarragon
    1/2 teaspoon Pernod or Ricard
    1/4 teaspoon fine-grain sea salt
    Fine-ground white pepper

1. In a medium bowl, mash or stir the butter with a fork until it is smooth and slightly fluffy. Add the shallot and tarragon. Mix together, mashing with the back of the fork to make sure all the ingredients are incorporated. Add the Pernod and mix again. When the texture of the mixture is smooth, season to taste with salt and pepper.

2. On a piece of plastic wrap or parchment, drop the butter in spoonfuls to form a log. Roll the butter in plastic wrap and smooth out to form a round log about 1 1/2 inches in diameter. Refrigerate until hard and easy to cut into pieces. The butter will keep, tightly wrapped, in the refrigerator for up to 1 week and in the freezer for up to 1 month.

Tarragon Butter

Makes 1 log (1/2 cup)

So good—it tastes like béarnaise without all the fuss! Substitute any of your favorite herbs for the tarragon to make other herb butters.

Good for Seasoning: Beef; fish; poultry; vegetables

> 1/2 cup (1 stick) unsalted butter, softened
>
> 3 teaspoons dried tarragon, or 5 teaspoons minced fresh tarragon
>
> 2 teaspoons minced fresh curly parsley
>
> 2 teaspoons granulated garlic
>
> 1/2 teaspoon fleur de sel

1. In a medium bowl, mash or stir the butter with a fork until it is smooth and slightly fluffy. Add the tarragon, parsley, granulated garlic, and fleur de sel. Mix together, mashing with the back of the fork to make sure all the ingredients are incorporated. Mix well. Taste for seasoning and adjust if desired.

2. On a piece of plastic wrap or parchment, drop the butter in spoonfuls to form a log. Roll the butter in plastic wrap and smooth out to form a round log about 1 1/2 inches in diameter. Refrigerate until hard and easy to cut into pieces. The butter will keep, tightly wrapped, in the refrigerator for up to 1 week and in the freezer for up to 1 month.

International Herb Butter Variations

For a distinctive Italian flavor, substitute 2 teaspoons of dried Italian seasoning for the tarragon. Oregano and lemon zest will give this butter a Greek flair. Cilantro, lime, and garlic make a nice Mexican butter. Try lemongrass and Thai basil for a Vietnamese butter.

Herbes de Provence Butter

Makes 1 log (1/2 cup)

Make this butter and keep it in your fridge at all times. This is one butter that literally goes with all savory things grilled and is especially good tossed into a goat cheese omelet or tossed with hot pasta and grilled tomatoes.

Good for Seasoning: Grilled lamb chops; shellfish; grilled tomatoes, eggplant; grilled bread, pasta; mixed into goat cheese

> 1/2 cup (1 stick) unsalted butter, softened
>
> 3 teaspoons herbes de Provence
>
> 1 teaspoon granulated garlic
>
> 1/2 teaspoon lavender, if not included in herbes de Provence
>
> 1/2 teaspoon fleur de sel
>
> Pinch lemon zest, optional

1. In a medium bowl, mash or stir the butter with a fork until it is smooth and slightly fluffy. Add the herbes de Provence, granulated garlic, lavender, if using, and fleur de sel. Mix together, mashing with the back of the fork to make sure all the ingredients are incorporated. Mix well. Taste for seasoning and adjust if desired. Add fresh lemon zest if you are looking for a citrus note.

2. On a piece of plastic wrap or parchment, drop the butter in spoonfuls to form a log. Roll the butter in plastic wrap and smooth out to form a round log about 1 1/2 inches in diameter. Refrigerate until hard and easy to cut into pieces. The butter will keep, tightly wrapped, in the refrigerator for up to 1 week and in the freezer for up to 1 month.

Stefan's Steak Butter

Makes 2 logs (1 cup)

Stefan Moerth is the Austrian-born executive chef of the Park Hyatt Tokyo. Classical training has served him well in overseeing all of the first-rate restaurants in the high-profile Park Hyatt. Most Americans know the hotel from the movie *Lost in Translation*. In the famous bar scene, Bill Murray is seated in the bar of the hotel's New York Grill. In Tokyo, the New York Grill is famous for its preparation of the famed Wagyu beef. When you order your steak, you have your choice of this exquisite and complex "hotel butter" created by Moerth or their signature steak sauce (page 115).

Good for Seasoning: Big grilled steaks

> 1 cup (2 sticks) unsalted butter, softened
>
> 2 1/2 teaspoons dry mustard, preferably Colman's
>
> 1 1/2 teaspoons curry powder
>
> 1 teaspoon sweet smoked Spanish paprika
>
> Pinch dried sage
>
> 1 1/2 tablespoons chopped or grated garlic

1 1/2 tablespoons chopped anchovies

3 tablespoons chopped fresh parsley

1 1/2 teaspoons chopped capers

1/2 teaspoon Worcestershire sauce

1 teaspoon fresh lemon juice

2 teaspoons fine-grain sea salt or fleur de sel

1 teaspoon freshly ground pepper

Two dashes Tabasco sauce

1. In a medium bowl, mash or stir the butter with a fork until it is smooth and slightly fluffy. Add the mustard, curry powder, paprika, and sage. Mix well and add the garlic, anchovies, parsley, and capers. Mix until well incorporated and add the Worcestershire sauce, lemon juice, salt, pepper and Tabasco. Mix together, mashing with the back of the fork to make sure all the ingredients are incorporated. Mix well. Taste for seasoning and adjust if desired.

2. On 2 pieces of plastic wrap or parchment, drop the butter in spoonfuls to form 2 logs. Roll the butter in plastic wrap and smooth out to form round logs about 1 1/2 inches in diameter. Refrigerate until hard and easy to cut into pieces. The butter will keep, tightly wrapped, in the refrigerator for up to 1 week and in the freezer for up to 1 month.

Escargot Butter

Makes 1 log (3/4 cup)

If I were a betting woman, I'd be willing to bet that 90 percent of folks who love escargot love it because of the rich, green, garlicky butter. I know that's my fascination

with it! This butter makes the ultimate garlic bread and, is a great way to infuse garlic in any recipe. One of my favorite ways to use it is on top of a grilled flat-iron steak. I call it my Bistro Steak with Escargot Butter.

Good for Seasoning: Flat-iron steak, roast beef; grilled chicken; veal; fish, shellfish; vegetables

1/2 cup (1 stick) unsalted butter, softened

2 tablespoons minced fresh curly parsley

3 cloves garlic, grated

1 small shallot, grated

1/2 teaspoon granulated garlic

2 to 4 teaspoons dry white wine, such as a French Burgundy or French-style Chardonnay

1/2 teaspoon sea salt or fleur de sel

1. In a medium bowl, mash or stir the butter with a fork until it is smooth and slightly fluffy. Add the parsley, garlic, shallot, and granulated garlic. Mix together, mashing with the back of the fork to make sure all the ingredients are incorporated. Add the wine and salt. Mix until smooth and fully incorporated. Taste for seasoning and adjust if desired.

2. On a piece of plastic wrap or parchment, drop the butter in spoonfuls to form a log. Roll the butter in plastic wrap and smooth out to form a round log about 1 1/2 inches in diameter. Refrigerate until firm and easy to cut into pieces. The butter will keep, tightly wrapped, in the refrigerator for up to 1 week and in the freezer for up to 1 month.

Note: Grating garlic with a Grill Friends Super Grater or Microplane provides a garlic paste that is more easily mixed into the butter. Or see page 316 for ways to grate garlic.

Roasted Garlic–Dijon Butter

Makes 1 log (1/2 cup)

The mild caramelized garlic is rich with flavor without the bite of raw garlic. Try this butter on a grilled Cuban sandwich; it's devilishly delicious!

Good for Seasoning: Mashed vegetables; white fish; pork; grilled bread, as a sandwich spread

ROASTED GARLIC

1 head garlic
Olive oil

DIJON BUTTER

1/2 cup (1 stick) unsalted butter, softened
1 tablespoon smooth Dijon mustard
Pinch sea salt or fleur de sel

1. Prepare the roasted garlic: Preheat the oven to 350°F or a grill to high indirect heat. Remove the first layer of papery skin from the garlic. Slice off 1/2 inch from the pointy top. Drizzle with oil. Wrap in foil and roast in the oven or on the hot grill for 60 to 80 minutes or until the cloves are golden brown and soft. Remove from the oven or grill and let cool. Follow the instructions to use it fresh, or squeeze the roasted cloves from their skin and place in an airtight container for up to 3 days, until ready to use.

2. Prepare the butter: In a medium bowl, mash or stir the butter with a fork until it is smooth and slightly fluffy. Remove the garlic from its skin and mix with the mustard until the garlic is completely incorporated and smooth.

3. Add the garlic-mustard mixture and salt to the butter. Mix together, mashing with the back of the fork to make sure all the ingredients are incorporated. Mix well. Taste for seasoning. Add more salt only if needed.

4. On a piece of plastic wrap or parchment, drop the butter in spoonfuls to form a log. Roll the butter in plastic wrap and smooth out to form a round log about 1 1/2 inches in diameter. Refrigerate until hard and easy to cut into pieces. The butter will keep, tightly wrapped, in the refrigerator for up to 1 week and in the freezer for up to 1 month.

Red Wine Butter (*Marchand de Vin* Butter)

Makes 2 logs (1 1/3 cups)

The classic French *marchand de vin* sauce calls for boiling shallots in red wine until the mixture is reduced by half and then adding beef consommé and reducing it again until it is almost dry. If you think it sounds like a lot of work, you are correct! This version is less refined, and the layered flavors come from the addition of Worcestershire sauce and Dijon mustard. Use the rough-textured whole-grain Dijon if you can find it, as it makes a big difference in the flavor and the texture of this butter. It is great with anything that you would normally drink red wine with and reminds me of one of my favorite ways to eat sole, poached in red wine and served with a melted version of this butter.

Good for Seasoning: Steak; lamb; veal; sole or other delicate white fish

- 2 shallots, minced
- 2 tablespoons plus 3 teaspoons red wine, divided
- 1 cup (2 sticks) unsalted butter, softened
- 3 teaspoons minced fresh parsley
- 1/2 teaspoon Worcestershire sauce
- 1/2 teaspoon smooth or whole-grain Dijon mustard
- 1/2 teaspoon sea salt
- Freshly ground pepper

1. Make the butter at least 3 hours in advance. Soak the shallots in 2 tablespoons of the wine for 30 minutes. In a medium bowl, mash or stir the butter with a fork until it is smooth and slightly fluffy. Drain the shallots from the wine and add the

wine-soaked shallots to the butter. Mix well. Add the parsley, Worcestershire, mustard, remaining 3 teaspoons wine, salt, and pepper. Mix together, mashing with the back of a fork to make sure all the ingredients are incorporated. Mix well. Taste for seasoning and adjust if desired.

2. On 2 pieces of plastic wrap or parchment, drop the butter in spoonfuls to form 2 logs. Roll the butter in plastic wrap and smooth out to form round logs about 1 1/2 inches in diameter. Refrigerate until hard and easy to cut into pieces. The butter will keep, tightly wrapped, in the refrigerator for up to 1 week and in the freezer for up to 1 month.

White Wine and Lemon Butter

Makes 2 logs (1 cup)

The first flavor combination that I learned (after peanut butter and banana) was white wine and lemon. This is a fresh and bright butter that will liven up your food.

Good for Seasoning: Any and all seafood (especially shrimp and lobster tail); grilled chicken; pork (paillards, chops); veal paillards; steak; any green vegetable

- 2 shallots, minced
- 2 tablespoons plus 3 teaspoons white wine, divided
- 1 cup (2 sticks) unsalted butter, softened
- 3 teaspoons minced fresh parsley
- Zest of 1/2 small lemon

(continued on page 264)

Whiskey Butter

Makes 2 logs (1 cup)

I created this butter for my take on Steak Diane. Because I am a southerner, I chose Jack Daniel's instead of the traditional French Cognac. The key is soaking the shallots in the whiskey so that the flavor is deeply ingrained in the butter.

Good for Seasoning: Beef (cowboy or any other steak); chicken; pork chops

> 1 cup (2 sticks) unsalted butter, softened
>
> 2 shallots, minced soaked in 2 tablespoons Jack Daniel's or other whiskey for 5 minutes
>
> 3 teaspoons minced curly parsley
>
> 1/2 teaspoon Worcestershire sauce
>
> 1/2 teaspoon Dijon mustard
>
> 2 teaspoons Jack Daniel's or other whiskey
>
> 1/4 teaspoon fine-grain sea salt
>
> Fine-ground white pepper

1. In a medium bowl, mash or stir the butter with a fork until it is smooth and slightly fluffy. Add the shallots soaked in whiskey, parsley, Worcestershire, mustard, Jack Daniel's, salt, and pepper. Mix together, mashing with the back of the fork to make sure all the ingredients are incorporated. Mix well. Taste for seasoning and adjust if desired.

2. Roll the butter in plastic wrap and smooth out to form round logs about 1 1/2 inches in diameter. Refrigerate until hard and easy to cut into pieces.

Steak Jack and Diane

Serves 4

Grilling Method: Direct/Medium-High Heat

> 2 bone-in rib-eye steaks,* about 1 pound each and at least 1 inch thick
>
> Olive oil
>
> Kosher salt or your favorite spice rub
>
> Freshly ground pepper, optional
>
> 1 recipe Whiskey Butter (left)
>
> Fresh parsley, chopped, for garnish

1. Build a charcoal fire or preheat a gas grill. Allow the meat to come to room temperature for 20 to 30 minutes before grilling. Wrap the meat in paper towels to get rid of excess moisture. Just before grilling, remove the towels and brush both sides of the steaks with oil and season lightly with salt and pepper.

2. Place the steaks on the grates over medium-hot heat and grill for about 5 minutes. Turn the steaks and continue cooking for about 5 more minutes for medium-rare. Remove the steaks from the grill. Place a slice of the compound butter on each steak and allow it to rest for at least 5 minutes, but no longer than 10 minutes, before serving.

3. When ready to serve, spread the melted butter around on top of the steaks and place another piece of cold compound butter on each steak. Serve the steaks warm with the butter. Garnish with chopped parsley, if desired.

*Bone-in rib-eyes are also known as cowboy steaks.

1 teaspoon fresh lemon juice
1/2 teaspoon granulated garlic
1 teaspoon fleur de sel
Fine-ground white pepper

1. Make the butter at least 3 hours in advance. Soak the shallots in 2 tablespoons of wine for 30 minutes. In a medium bowl, mash or stir the butter with a fork until it is smooth and slightly fluffy. Drain the shallots from the wine and add the wine-soaked shallots to the butter. Mix well; add the parsley, lemon zest and juice, garlic, remaining 3 teaspoons wine, salt, and pepper. Mix together, mashing with the back of the fork to make sure all the ingredients are incorporated. Mix well. Taste for seasoning and adjust if desired.

2. On 2 pieces of plastic wrap or parchment, drop the butter in spoonfuls to form 2 logs. Roll the butter in plastic wrap and smooth out to form round logs about 1 1/2 inches in diameter. Refrigerate until hard and easy to cut into pieces. The butter will keep, tightly wrapped, in the refrigerator for up to 1 week and in the freezer for up to 1 month.

Hip-Hop (Cognac) Butter

Makes 2 logs (1 1/4 cups)

The Cognac industry claims that hip-hop music saved its export business and that it is now the drink of choice among the young hip-hop generation—making this butter more about Jay-Z than Alistair Cook. It is equally at home on top of steak and lobster as it is on top of a big ole burger.

Good for Seasoning: Grilled beef (steaks, burgers); chicken; pork; lamb; shrimp, scallops, lobster

1 cup (2 sticks) unsalted butter, softened
2 shallots, minced, soaked in 4 tablespoons Cognac for 5 minutes
2 teaspoons minced fresh parsley
3 teaspoons Cognac
1/2 teaspoon granulated roasted garlic
1/2 teaspoon sea salt
Fine-ground white pepper

1. Make the butter at least 3 hours in advance. In a medium bowl, mash or stir the butter with a fork until it is smooth and slightly fluffy. Add the shallots soaked in Cognac and the parsley. Mix together, mashing with the back of the fork to make sure all the ingredients are incorporated. Add the Cognac, garlic, salt, and pepper. Mix well. Taste for seasoning and adjust if desired.

2. On 2 pieces of plastic wrap or parchment, drop the butter in spoonfuls to form 2 logs. Roll the butter in plastic wrap and smooth out to form round logs about 1 1/2 inches in diameter. Refrigerate until hard and easy to cut into pieces. The butter will keep, tightly wrapped, in the refrigerator for up to 1 week and in the freezer for up to 1 month.

are incorporated. Mix well. Taste for seasoning and adjust if desired.

2. On a piece of plastic wrap or parchment, drop the butter in spoonfuls to form a log. Roll the butter in plastic wrap and smooth out to form a round log about 1 1/2 inches in diameter. Refrigerate until hard and easy to cut into pieces. The butter will keep, tightly wrapped, in the refrigerator for up to 1 week and in the freezer for up to 1 month.

BBQ Butter

Makes 1 log (1/2 cup)

Sing hallelujah! Praise the combination of barbecue rub and butter. The only thing better is the addition of a tablespoon of cold rendered bacon fat to the mixture for ultimate piggy pleasure. This butter adds a spicy note to barbecued cabbage (see *Taming the Flame*), beer-can chicken, and pork chops.

Good for Seasoning: Pork; beef; chicken, game hen; squash, root vegetables, potatoes

> 1 tablespoon cool rendered bacon fat, optional
>
> 1/2 cup (1 stick) unsalted butter, softened
>
> 1 to 2 tablespoons your favorite rub, such as Barbecue Circuit Rub (page 199)
>
> 1/2 teaspoon kosher salt, if the rub is salt-free

1. If using the bacon fat, in a medium bowl, mash or stir it into the butter with a fork until it is smooth and slightly fluffy. Add the barbecue rub and, if using, the salt. Mix together, mashing with the back of the fork to make sure all the ingredients

Sun-Dried Tomato Butter

Makes 1 log (3/4 cup)

This butter is best if you use the sun-dried tomatoes that are packed in oil. However, you need to drain and dry them off before using.

Good for Seasoning: Pasta; chicken; tilapia; eggplant, zucchini

> 1/2 cup (1 stick) unsalted butter, softened
>
> 4 large sun-dried tomatoes, drained, dried, and finely chopped
>
> 1 teaspoon tomato powder (available from www.spicehouse.com) or tomato paste
>
> 1/2 teaspoon sea salt or fleur de sel
>
> 1/4 teaspoon freshly ground pepper or grains of paradise (see note on page 321)

1. In a medium bowl, mash or stir the butter with a fork until it is smooth and slightly fluffy. Add the tomatoes, tomato powder, salt, and pepper. Mix together, mashing with the back of the fork to make sure all the ingredients are incorporated.

Mix well. Taste for seasoning and adjust if desired.

2. On a piece of plastic wrap or parchment, drop the butter in spoonfuls to form a log. Roll the butter in plastic wrap and smooth out to form a round log about 1 1/2 inches in diameter. Refrigerate until hard and easy to cut into pieces. The butter will keep, tightly wrapped, in the refrigerator for up to 1 week and in the freezer for up to 1 month.

Sun-Dried Tomato and Goat Cheese Butter

Makes 1 log (1 cup)

Remember how we loved everything goat cheese and sun-dried tomatoes when we first tried it? It may seem a little old fashioned these days, but it is still the ultimate California combination. Try this butter tossed with grill-roasted spaghetti squash for a twist on everyday spaghetti.

Good for Seasoning: Spaghetti squash, apples; grilled French bread, grilled pizza, grilled veggie sandwich; any grilled meat

1/2 cup (1 stick) unsalted butter, softened

4 ounces goat cheese, herb flavored or plain, softened

7 large sun-dried tomatoes, drained, dried, and finely chopped

1/2 teaspoon sea salt or fleur de sel

1/4 teaspoon freshly ground pepper or grains of paradise (see note on page 321)

1. In a medium bowl, mash or stir the butter with a fork until it is smooth and slightly fluffy. Add the goat cheese and stir until it is completely smooth and incorporated. Add the tomatoes, salt, and pepper. Mix together, mashing with the back of the fork to make sure all the ingredients are incorporated. Mix well. Taste for seasoning and adjust if desired.

2. On a piece of plastic wrap or parchment, drop the butter in spoonfuls to form a log. Roll the butter in plastic wrap and smooth out to form a round log about 1 1/2 inches in diameter. Refrigerate until hard and easy to cut into pieces. The butter will keep, tightly wrapped, in the refrigerator for up to 1 week and in the freezer for up to 1 month.

Black Olive Butter

Makes 1 log (3/4 cup)

Think of this butter as the perfect accessory for your food. The butter and fig jam (surprise!) mellow out the pungency of the black olive paste and add a richness that works wonders with shellfish, fish, chicken, or vegetables.

Good for Seasoning: Chicken paillards; fish, shellfish; grilled veggies

> 1/2 cup (1 stick) unsalted butter, softened
> 2 tablespoons black olive puree or tapenade
> 1 1/2 teaspoons fig or orange-fig jam
> 1 teaspoon capers, minced
> 1/4 teaspoon freshly ground pepper or grains of paradise (see note on page 321)
> Sea salt, optional

1. In a medium bowl, mash or stir the butter with a fork until it is smooth and slightly fluffy. Add the olive puree, jam, capers, and pepper. Mix together, mashing with the back of the fork to make sure all the ingredients are incorporated. Mix well. Taste for seasoning. Add salt only if needed, as the olives and capers are inherently salty and should provide all the seasoning you need.

2. On a piece of plastic wrap or parchment, drop the butter in spoonfuls to form a log. Roll the butter in plastic wrap and smooth out to form a round log about 1 1/2 inches in diameter. Refrigerate until hard and easy to cut into pieces. The butter will keep, tightly wrapped, in the refrigerator for up to 1 week and in the freezer for up to 1 month.

Chipotle–Pumpkin Seed Butter

Makes 1 log (1/2 cup)

Hot and spicy, orange and green, with a touch of sweetness from the cinnamon and crunch from the pumpkin seeds. When this butter melts on top of hot-from-the-grill foods, it transports you to Mexico and cries gently for a hand-shaken Margarita —not included but most appropriate!

Good for Seasoning: Shrimp; cornbread; chicken; pork

> 1/2 cup (1 stick) unsalted butter, softened
> 1 small chipotle in adobo, drained and finely chopped finely (about 1 tablespoon)*
> 3 tablespoons lightly toasted green pumpkin seeds (pepitas)
> 1/2 teaspoon ancho chile powder
> Pinch ground cinnamon
> 1/2 teaspoon sea salt or fleur de sel

1. In a medium bowl, mash or stir the butter with a fork until it is smooth and slightly fluffy. Add the chipotle, pumpkin seeds, ancho chile powder, cinnamon, and salt. Mix together, mashing with the back of the fork to make sure all the ingredients are incorporated. Mix well. Taste for seasoning and adjust if desired.

2. On a piece of plastic wrap or parchment, drop the butter in spoonfuls to form a log. Roll the butter in plastic wrap and smooth out to form a round log about 1 1/2 inches in diameter. Refrigerate until hard and easy to cut into pieces. The butter will keep, tightly wrapped, in the refrigerator for up to 1 week and in the freezer for up to 1 month.

*Chipotles vary in strength, so taste yours before adding in order to monitor the heat quotient.

Kirsten's Anchovy Butter

Makes 1 log (1/2 cup)

Kirsten Newman-Teissier is my right hand (and sometimes my left!) and a great cook in her own right. Her father, "Seafood Bob," is a fishmonger, so she grew up with all manner of fresh seafood anytime she wanted. She makes this simple anchovy butter as the foundation for her clams casino.

Good for Seasoning: Clams, shrimp; chicken; steak; lamb; pasta loaded with grilled vegetables

- 1/2 cup (1 stick) unsalted butter, softened
- 1 tablespoon anchovy paste
- 1/2 teaspoon white or regular Worcestershire sauce
- 1/4 teaspoon freshly ground pepper or grains of paradise (see note on page 321)

Pinch cayenne pepper

Sea salt, optional

1. In a medium bowl, mash or stir the butter with a fork until it is smooth and slightly fluffy. Add the anchovy paste, Worcestershire, pepper, and cayenne. Mix together, mashing with the back of the fork to make sure all the ingredients are incorporated. Mix well. Taste for seasoning. Add salt only if needed, as anchovies are inherently salty and should take care of the seasoning.

2. On a piece of plastic wrap or parchment, drop the butter in spoonfuls to form a log. Roll the butter in plastic wrap and smooth out to form a round log about 1 1/2 inches in diameter. Refrigerate until hard and easy to cut into pieces. The butter will keep, tightly wrapped, in the refrigerator for up to 1 week and in the freezer for up to 1 month.

Soy-Ginger Wasabi Butter

Makes 1 log (1 cup)

Here's a modern way to add Asian flavor to your food—mix a little soy, ginger, and wasabi into a stick of butter. The butter rounds out all the sharp flavors.

Good for Seasoning: Grilled white fish, salmon, tuna; chicken; veggies (green beans, asparagus, broccoli)

- 1/2 cup (1 stick) unsalted butter, softened
- 3 teaspoons low-sodium soy sauce
- 3 teaspoons prepared wasabi paste

1 teaspoon minced pickled ginger

1 teaspoon ground ginger

1/2 teaspoon onion powder

1/2 teaspoon sea salt or fleur de sel

1. In a medium bowl, mash or stir the butter with a fork until it is smooth and slightly fluffy. Mix the soy sauce, wasabi, and pickled ginger into the butter. Mix together, mashing with the back of the fork to make sure all the ingredients are incorporated. Add the ginger, onion powder, and salt. Mix well. Taste for seasoning and adjust if desired.

2. On a piece of plastic wrap or parchment, drop the butter in spoonfuls to form a log. Roll the butter in plastic wrap and smooth out to form a round log about 1 1/2 inches in diameter. Refrigerate until hard and easy to cut into pieces. The butter will keep, tightly wrapped, in the refrigerator for up to 1 week and in the freezer for up to 1 month.

Good for Seasoning: Skirt steak; cornbread; grilled pineapple, grilled apples, squash

1 cup (2 sticks) unsalted butter, softened and divided

1 tablespoon fresh orange juice

Zest of 1 orange

1 1/2 teaspoons ancho chile powder

1/2 teaspoon ground cinnamon

1/2 teaspoon ground coriander

1 tablespoon honey

1 teaspoon fleur de sel

Ancho-Honey Butter

Makes 1 log (1 1/3 cups)

I created this butter for Hill Country, a Texas-style barbecue restaurant in New York City. As the executive chef, I had the pleasure of designing the menu and the recipes for the restaurant that the *Wall Street Journal* named one of the top 10 barbecue joints in America. At the restaurant, we serve this butter with our skillet cornbread, but at home I make it to top grilled pineapple and fall squash.

1. In a medium bowl, mash or stir 1/2 cup of the butter with a fork until it is smooth and slightly fluffy. Add the orange juice and zest with half of the butter. Mix together, mashing with the back of the fork to make sure all the ingredients are incorporated. Add the remaining 1/2 cup butter and the cinnamon, coriander, honey, and fleur de sel. Mix well. Taste for seasoning and adjust if desired.

2. On a piece of plastic wrap or parchment, drop the butter in spoonfuls to form a log. Roll the butter in plastic wrap and smooth out to form a round log about 1 1/2 inches in diameter. Refrigerate until hard and easy to cut into pieces. The butter will keep, tightly wrapped, in the refrigerator for up to 1 week and in the freezer for up to 1 month.

Raspberry-Amaretto Butter

Makes 1 log (1 cup)

I first created this butter when I was grilling a summer peach and decided to flavor it by putting butter in the little pocket created where the pit was removed. It slowly melted and caramelized, intensifying the flavors of the fruit. It is my modern-day version of peach Melba. If you like a crunchy texture, add 2 crumbled amaretti cookies to the butter.

Good for Seasoning: Peaches, grilled stone fruit; pancakes, toast

- 1/2 cup (1 stick) unsalted butter, softened
- 2 tablespoons light brown sugar
- 4 tablespoons seedless raspberry jam
- 1/2 teaspoon sea salt
- 2 tablespoons amaretto

1. In a medium bowl, mash or stir the butter with a fork until it is smooth and slightly fluffy. Add the sugar, jam, and salt. Mix together, mashing with the back of a fork to make sure all the ingredients are incorporated. Add the amaretto and mix well. Taste for seasoning and adjust if desired.

2. On a piece of plastic wrap or parchment, drop the butter in spoonfuls to form

a log. Roll the butter in plastic wrap and smooth out to form a round log about 1 1/2 inches in diameter. Refrigerate until hard and easy to cut into pieces. The butter will keep, tightly wrapped, in the refrigerator for up to 1 week and in the freezer for up to 1 month.

Sweet Strawberry Butter

Makes 1 log (1/2 cup)

This is the butter that started it all! When I graduated from college, I moved to Atlanta and was soon invited to have a ladies' lunch at the Swan Coach House Restaurant. It was *the* place for Southern ladies who lunch. As we were seated, we were given iced tea with miniature pitchers of simple syrup, lemon wedges, and mint leaves, and on the table were fresh-from-the-oven biscuits and rolls with strawberry butter. After that lunch, I started mixing jam and butter together for breakfast, brunch and the occasional teatime. I flavor the butter with strawberry here, but feel free to substitute your favorite jam.

Good for Seasoning: Grilled fruit; French bread, muffins, biscuits, cornbread

> 1/2 cup (1 stick) unsalted butter, softened
> 1/4 cup strawberry jam
> Zest of 1/2 small lemon
> 2 teaspoons light brown sugar
> 1/2 teaspoon sea salt

1. In a medium bowl, mash or stir the butter with a fork until it is smooth and slightly fluffy. Add the jam, zest, sugar, and salt. Mix together, mashing with the back of the fork to make sure all the ingredients are incorporated. Taste for seasoning and adjust if desired.

2. On a piece of plastic wrap or parchment, drop the butter in spoonfuls to form a log. Roll the butter in plastic wrap and smooth out to form a round log about 1 1/2 inches in diameter. Refrigerate until hard and easy to cut into pieces. The butter will keep, tightly wrapped, in the refrigerator for up to 1 week and in the freezer for up to 1 month.

Apricot-Ginger Butter

Makes 1 log (3/4 cup)

This is my go-to sweet butter for giving everything that "wow" factor.

Good for Seasoning: Pork; chicken; shrimp; butternut squash, sweet potatoes, fruit (pineapple, apples); spread between sugar cookies

> 1/2 cup (1 stick) unsalted butter, softened
> 1/4 cup apricot jam

> 1 tablespoon crystallized ginger or stem ginger in syrup, finely chopped
> 1 teaspoon fresh lemon juice
> 1/2 teaspoon sea salt

1. In a medium bowl, mash or stir the butter with a fork until it is smooth and slightly fluffy. Add the jam, ginger, lemon juice, and salt. Mix together, mashing with the back of the fork to make sure all the ingredients are incorporated. Taste for seasoning. Add more ginger if desired.

2. On a piece of plastic wrap or parchment, drop the butter in spoonfuls to form a log. Roll the butter in plastic wrap and smooth out to form a round log about 1 1/2 inches in diameter. Refrigerate until hard and easy to cut into pieces. The butter will keep, tightly wrapped, in the refrigerator for up to 1 week and in the freezer for up to 1 month.

Honey Butter

Makes 1 log (1/2 cup)

Honey and butter go together like bees and honey! It is a natural pairing, and the butter brings out the other nuances of flavor in the honey. This simple butter will enhance everything that benefits from a little bit of sweetness.

Add 1 tablespoon cinnamon sugar to this simple butter for a nice variation. You can also add 1/4 cup no-sugar-added preserves to flavor it. I love mixing it with blueberry preserves for a sweet-tart butter.

Good for Seasoning: Grilled fruit (bananas, mango, pineapple); grilled bread; pork; chicken

- 1/2 cup (1 stick) unsalted butter, softened
- 2 tablespoons light brown sugar
- 3 tablespoons orange blossom honey
- 1/2 teaspoon sea salt
- Zest of 1/2 small orange

1. In a medium bowl, mash or stir the butter with a fork until it is smooth and slightly fluffy. Add the sugar, honey, salt, and zest. Mix together, mashing with the back of the fork to make sure all the ingredients are incorporated. Taste for seasoning and adjust if desired.

2. On a piece of plastic wrap or parchment, drop the butter in spoonfuls to form a log. Roll the butter in plastic wrap and smooth out to form a round log about 1 1/2 inches in diameter. Refrigerate until hard and easy to cut into pieces. The butter will keep, tightly wrapped, in the refrigerator for up to 1 week and in the freezer for up to 1 month.

Maple Sugar–Cinnamon Butter

Makes 1 log (1/2 cup)

When I was growing up, I used to love to go to the grocery store with my father. I'd find all kinds of random interesting items that we didn't really need but that he would let me add to the cart. I particularly remember an intriguing round yellow cardboard container of butter with a dark brown drawing of a bee buzzing around it. I had high hopes for that bee inviting me to sample the cinnamon honey butter inside. And it left a great impression. Today I make my own version, substituting sweeter and richer real maple syrup for the honey—if you don't have any maple syrup, substitute honey and make the bees happy!

Good for Seasoning: Cornbread; corn on the cob, butternut squash, grilled fruit

- 1/2 cup (1 stick) unsalted butter, softened
- 1 tablespoon dark brown sugar
- 1 teaspoon ground cinnamon
- 1/2 teaspoon sea salt
- 3 tablespoons pure maple syrup

1. In a medium bowl, mash or stir the butter with a fork until it is smooth and slightly fluffy. Add the brown sugar, cinnamon, salt, and maple syrup. Mix together, mashing with the back of the fork to make sure all the ingredients are incorporated. Taste for seasoning and adjust if desired.

2. On a piece of plastic wrap or parchment, drop the butter in spoonfuls to form a log. Roll the butter in plastic wrap and smooth out to form a round log about 1 1/2 inches in diameter. Refrigerate until hard and easy to cut into pieces. The butter will keep, tightly wrapped, in the refrigerator for up to 1 week and in the freezer for up to 1 month.

Rum Raisin Butter

Makes 1 log (1/2 cup)

This butter instantly conjures up thoughts of grill-roasted sweet vegetables and fruit. Place a pat of the butter on the piping hot fruit and vegetables, toss well to coat all the surfaces, and serve immediately.

Good for Seasoning: Grilled apples, bananas, pineapple, pears, tropical fruits; sweet potatoes, baby carrots, fall squash

- 1/4 cup raisins or currants
- 2 tablespoons dark rum
- 1/2 cup (1 stick) unsalted butter, softened
- 2 tablespoons light brown sugar
- 1/2 teaspoon sea salt
- 1/8 teaspoon vanilla extract

1. Make the butter at least 3 hours in advance. Soak the raisins in the rum for 30 minutes. In a medium bowl, mash or stir the butter with a fork until it is smooth and slightly fluffy. Add the sugar and salt and mix to combine. Add the raisins, the remaining soaking liquid, and the vanilla. Mix together, mashing with the back of the fork to make sure all the ingredients are incorporated. Mix well. Taste for seasoning and adjust if desired.

2. On a piece of plastic wrap or parchment, drop the butter in spoonfuls to form a log. Roll the butter in plastic wrap and smooth out to form a round log about 1 1/2 inches in diameter. Refrigerate until hard and easy to cut into pieces. The butter will keep, tightly wrapped, in the refrigerator for up to 1 week and in the freezer for up to 1 month.

Kirsch (Cherry) Butter

Makes 1 log (1/2 cup)

Kirschwasser, generally referred to as kirsch, is a sharp, clear cherry brandy that originates from the Black Forest region of Germany. It is traditionally used in both sweet and savory cooking and is commonly associated with cheese fondue and the alcohol used to flambé cherries jubilee. It was created for sweets but could be used with any wild game, especially venison— just reduce the amount of sugar by half and add an extra splash of kirsch.

Good for Seasoning: Brie, goat cheese; fruit; grilled pound cake; wild game

- 1/2 cup (1 stick) unsalted butter, softened
- 2 teaspoons light brown sugar
- 1/2 teaspoon sea salt
- 2 tablespoons no-sugar-added cherry or raspberry jam
- 2 tablespoons dried cherries, roughly chopped
- 1 tablespoon kirsch

1. Make the butter at least 3 hours in advance. In a medium bowl, mash or stir the butter with a fork until it is smooth and slightly fluffy. Add the sugar, salt, jam, and cherries. Mix together, mashing with the back of the fork to make sure all the ingredients are incorporated. Add the kirsch and mix well. Taste for seasoning and adjust if desired.

2. On a piece of plastic wrap or parchment, drop the butter in spoonfuls to form a log. Roll the butter in plastic wrap and smooth out to form a round log about 1 1/2 inches in diameter. Refrigerate until hard and easy to cut into pieces. The butter will keep, tightly wrapped, in the refrigerator for up to 1 week and in the freezer for up to 1 month.

2. On a piece of plastic wrap or parchment, drop the butter in spoonfuls to form a log. Roll the butter in plastic wrap and smooth out to form a round log about 1 1/2 inches in diameter. Refrigerate until hard and easy to cut into pieces. The butter will keep, tightly wrapped, in the refrigerator for up to 1 week and in the freezer for up to 1 month.

Brown Sugar Butter

Makes 1 log (3/4 cup)

This butter instantly makes me think of fresh steaming biscuits on a frosty morn. Add a slice of grilled country ham and you have a breakfast to long for. If you like the bitter pairing of molasses or cane syrup (they are not the same thing), substitute your favorite thick black syrup for half the sugar.

Good for Seasoning: Apples, all other fruit; grilled country ham; biscuits

- 1/2 cup (1 stick) unsalted butter, softened
- 3 tablespoons dark brown sugar
- 1/8 teaspoon ground mace
- 1/2 teaspoon sea salt

1. Make butter at least 3 hours in advance. In a medium bowl, mash or stir the butter with a fork until it is smooth and slightly fluffy. Add the sugar, mace, and salt. Mix together, mashing with the back of the fork to make sure all the ingredients are incorporated. Taste for seasoning and adjust if desired.

Sweet Hazelnut Butter

Makes 1 log (1 cup)

Beautifully constructed Mont Blanc pastries have always been a source of fascination for me. When I lived in Paris, I would look longingly at them in the windows of the pastry shops. But I always wound up buying a fruit tart or a quiche. I just couldn't fathom ruining the patisserie's handiwork, and taking a bite of the towering top was a challenge. It looked like a sweet sculpture. True Mont Blancs are made with a vanilla-sweetened chestnut puree, but I always thought hazelnuts would be better. So this compound butter is my ode to Mont Blancs, sweetened with white chocolate and a touch of vanilla bean paste.

Good for Seasoning: Raspberries, pears; chocolate cake, graham crackers, grilled poundcake, apple cobbler

- 1/2 cup (1 stick) unsalted butter, softened
- 1/2 cup ground hazelnuts
- 2 ounces white chocolate, melted and cooled

1/4 cup packed light brown sugar

1 whole vanilla bean, scraped*

1/2 teaspoon sea salt

1. Make butter at least 3 hours in advance. In a medium bowl, mash or stir the butter with a fork until it is smooth and slightly fluffy. Add the hazelnuts, white chocolate, sugar, the seeds from the vanilla bean, and the salt. Mix together, mashing with the back of the fork to make sure all the ingredients are incorporated. Taste for seasoning and adjust if desired.

2. On a piece of plastic wrap or parchment, drop the butter in spoonfuls to form a log. Roll the butter in plastic wrap and smooth out to form a round log about 1 1/2 inches in diameter. Refrigerate until hard and easy to cut into pieces. The butter will keep, tightly wrapped, in the refrigerator for up to 1 week and in the freezer for up to 1 month.

*Although a scraped vanilla bean is best, you can also substitute 1/2 teaspoon Nielsen-Massey vanilla bean paste or 1/4 teaspoon vanilla extract for the scraped vanilla bean.

Lemon Butter

Makes 1 log (3/4 cup)

Think lemon curd, but rougher texture, easier to make, and no eggs to cook. The bright citrus butter is so good that you will be tempted to eat it straight—but restrain yourself! The lemon can be replaced with grapefruit, lime, orange, tangerine, or clementine to change the flavor of the butter—making this the classic sweet citrus compound butter. During the Recipe Testing Boot Camp at the Institute of Culinary Education, one of the students used this butter in an unexpected but absolutely knockout way. She rubbed a flat-iron steak with the Smokin' Four-Chile Rub (page 209), grilled it, and topped it with this butter when it was done. So unexpected, so good!

Good for Seasoning: Grilled fruit; toast, waffles, pancakes; hot gingerbread

1/2 cup (1 stick) unsalted butter, softened

2 tablespoons light brown sugar

Zest of 1 lemon

1/2 lemon, juiced

2 tablespoons confectioners' sugar

1/2 teaspoon sea salt

1. Make butter at least 3 hours in advance. In a medium bowl, mash or stir the butter with a fork until it is smooth and slightly fluffy. Add the sugar and zest and mix until smooth. In a small bowl, mix together the lemon juice, confectioners' sugar, and salt until well mixed. Add the mixture to the butter and mix together, mashing with the back of the fork to make sure all the ingredients are incorporated. Taste for seasoning and adjust if desired. Chill in the refrigerator for 30 minutes or until firm enough to roll into a log.

2. On a piece of plastic wrap or parchment, drop the butter in spoonfuls to form a log. Roll the butter in plastic wrap and smooth out to form a round log about 1 1/2 inches in diameter. Refrigerate until hard and easy to cut into pieces. The butter will keep, tightly wrapped, in the refrigerator for up to 1 week and in the freezer for up to 1 month.

Bittersweet Chocolate Butter

Makes 1 log (1 1/4 cups)

Who ever heard of a refrigerator chocolate sauce that you could slice at will anytime you wanted to add a chocolate kiss? This butter will do just that! Add 1/4 cup unsalted hazelnut butter (you can buy this at a gourmet store or natural food store) to this and you will have your own homemade Nutella.

Good for Seasoning: Grilled fruit; pound cake, graham crakers

> 1/2 cup (1 stick) unsalted butter, softened
>
> 4 ounces bittersweet (70 percent cacao) chocolate, melted and cooled
>
> 2 teaspoons superfine sugar
>
> 1/4 teaspoon vanilla extract
>
> 1/2 teaspoon fleur de sel

1. Make butter at least 3 hours in advance. In a medium bowl, mash or stir the butter with a fork until it is smooth and slightly fluffy. Add the chocolate, sugar, vanilla, and fleur de sel. Mix together, mashing with the back of the fork to make sure all the ingredients are incorporated. Taste for seasoning and adjust if desired. Chill in the refrigerator for 30 minutes or until firm enough to roll into a log.

2. On a piece of plastic wrap or parchment, drop the butter in spoonfuls to form a log. Roll the butter in plastic wrap and smooth out to form a round log about 1 1/2 inches in diameter. Refrigerate until hard and easy to cut into pieces. The butter will keep, tightly wrapped, in the refrigerator for up to 1 week and in the freezer for up to 1 month.

Note: Make no-cook S'mores: Spread one graham cracker with the Hazelnut-Chocolate Butter and spread another with Fluffer. Sandwich the two together and you've got a portable s'more—perfect for picnics and cookouts. Try uping the ante with marmalade, raspberry jam, or any of the chocolate butters in this chapter.

Crystallized Ginger, Orange, and Chocolate Butter

Makes 1 log (1/2 cup)

This classic combination of sweet crystallized ginger, orange, and chocolate can add pizzazz to any dessert. Brush thick slices of pound cake lightly with butter and grill on both sides until warm and golden before topping with this butter.

Good for Seasoning: Pound cake; grilled bananas, pineapple, grilled orange slices, apples

1/2 cup (1 stick) unsalted butter, softened

2 ounces bittersweet (70 percent cacao) chocolate, melted and cooled

1 tablespoon light brown sugar

2 tablespoons crystallized ginger, chopped

Zest of 1 large orange

1/2 teaspoon sea salt

1. Make butter at least 3 hours in advance. In a medium bowl, mash or stir the butter with a fork until it is smooth and slightly fluffy. Add the chocolate, sugar, ginger, zest, and salt. Mix together, mashing with the back of the fork to make sure all the ingredients are incorporated. Taste for seasoning and adjust if desired.

2. On a piece of plastic wrap or parchment, drop the butter in spoonfuls to form a log. Roll the butter in plastic wrap and smooth out to form a round log about 1 1/2 inches in diameter. Refrigerate until hard and easy to cut into pieces. The butter will keep, tightly wrapped, in the refrigerator for up to 1 week and in the freezer for up to 1 month.

Dark Chocolate and Grand Marnier Butter

Makes 1 log (1/2 cup)

This is the ultimate sauce for grilled fruit fondue. Grill the fruit and, when it is still hot, cut it into cubes and toss it with this dark and seductive flavor combination.

Good for Seasoning: Strawberries, peaches, apricots; grilled pound cake

1/2 cup (1 stick) unsalted butter, softened

4 ounces bittersweet (70 percent cacao) chocolate, melted and cooled

1 teaspoon superfine sugar

1/2 teaspoon fleur de sel

2 tablespoons Grand Marnier

1. Make the butter at least 3 hours in advance. In a medium bowl, mash or stir the butter with a fork until it is smooth and slightly fluffy. Add the chocolate, sugar, and fleur de sel. Mix together, mashing with the back of the fork to make sure all the ingredients are incorporated. Add the Grand Marnier and mix well. Taste for seasoning and adjust if desired. Chill in the refrigerator for 30 minutes or until firm enough to roll into a log.

2. On a piece of plastic wrap or parchment, drop the butter in spoonfuls to form a log. Roll the butter in plastic wrap and smooth out to form a round log about 1 1/2 inches in diameter. Refrigerate until hard and easy to cut into pieces. The butter will keep, tightly wrapped, in the refrigerator for up to 1 week and in the freezer for up to 1 month.

Pestos and Tapenades

Concentrated, flavor-packed purees. Pestos are fresh-ground mixtures of herbs bound by oil, and tapenades are mixtures of ground olives and oil accented by dried fruits, vegetables, spices, and liquids.

Pestos and Tapenades 101

RAPID-FIRE CHECKLIST

○ Place all liquid or "wet" ingredients in the blender or food processor and process before adding fresh herbs or other ingredients that might cause a jam in the blender.

○ Have extra herbs or olives on hand in case you need to add them to increase the flavor or adjust the texture.

○ Use the best-quality ingredients—you will taste all of them, and one "off" ingredient will ruin the pesto or tapenade.

○ Store all unused tapenade or pesto in a glass jar with a tight-fitting lid in the refrigerator.

○ Pesto can keep in the refrigerator for 1 week. It can be frozen for up to 6 months and thawed before using.

○ Tapenade can be stored in the refrigerator for up to 1 month.

A few years ago, I came home after a long business trip and I couldn't even think of eating another restaurant meal or more take-out food. So I played a game that I love . . . with nothing in the fridge, let's see what I can create. Kind of my own loaves-and-fishes challenge.

I opened the freezer and found the pristine cryovaced swordfish steaks that Trader Joe's sells and a jar of *pesto alla Genovese* (the original basil pesto) that a friend had brought me from Italy. I thawed the fish and grilled it using the Grilling Trilogy (see page 10) of olive oil, salt, and pepper. When the fish was done, I spooned a generous dollop of the pesto on top of it and waited for the heat of the fish to melt the pesto. It turned out to be the most delightful entrée. That uncapped a whole new way of cooking and eating at home for me. Forget 30-minute meals; at my house it's more like 15-minute meals, and most of that time is simply food cooking on the grill.

Pesto Basics

The term *pesto*, loosely translated, means "pounded or crushed," which makes sense to everyone who has ever made pesto from scratch. And these days, cooks worldwide have embraced and created "pestos" in every form, using every ingredient imaginable. I'm not sure exactly when we, as Americans, first became familiar with the traditional basil-and-garlic pesto from the city of Genoa in the Liguria region of northern Italy. But once we started eating pesto, we couldn't stop! We started with the traditional basil pesto on pasta, and now it is used to great effect on everything from sandwiches and pizzas to meat, fish, and vegetables. And basil is just the beginning of what you can use to create concentrated, flavor-packed purees.

I know that there are some pesto purists who dislike deviating from the classic version, but I embrace being creative. I love having the freedom to make a highly flavored puree out of anything that I can combine and call by the romantic title of pesto. Familiarity breeds comfort, and since everyone knows what pesto is, it's a great way to introduce new flavors or sauces that people aren't familiar with. A great example of using familiar terminology to introduce a new thing is the Argentinean chimichurri sauce. I usually refer to chimichurri as parsley pesto when talking to those who have never heard of it. It is not technically a pesto and is actually closer to the French pistou, since it doesn't have cheese or nuts in the mixture. But calling it parsley pesto sets a frame of reference for people and makes them willing to try something that they have never heard of. I've yet to meet anyone who doesn't love chimichurri on everything! My prediction is that the more familiar we are with chimichurri sauce, the more we will adopt the technique and switch up the ingredients to make as many flavored chimichurri sauces as we have pestos. Stay tuned!

With the exception of pistou, the French provençal version of pesto, pestos generally include nuts and cheese to give the herbs and other ingredients body and layers of flavor. But it is not necessary, and the pistou and chimichurri sauces are great for meat and fish when you don't want the added flavors of nuts and cheese.

To create your own pestos, start with the following list of ingredients, then be creative:

- Herb or main flavor ingredient
- Garlic
- Olive oil or other high-quality nut oil
- Hard cheese
- Nuts
- Other seasonings, optional

Tapenade Basics

Tapenade is another versatile condiment and a favorite of mine—you can add it to a vinaigrette or a compound butter, or use it like a pesto, which is why it is included in this chapter. A tapenade is a puree of olives with different flavoring accents. The name comes from the provençal word for capers, *tapéno*, and so true tapenades must always include capers. After that, anchovies, garlic, and other robust ingredients—even tuna—are added to the olive mixture. I like to add my own twist to a black olive tapenade with figs steeped in Cognac and to a green olive tapenade with preserved lemons or marmalade. If you go to the markets in the south of France, you can choose between lots of different tapenades, but the base is always black or green olive puree.

You can find very high-quality prepared versions of these items at grocery and specialty food stores when you are short on time, but remember, it's always better to make your own fresh.

There are olive purees all over the world, but no place is as famous for them as the south of France. The olive vendors usually have a dozen or so different cured olives and flavored tapenades for sale. Once you start making them at home, you'll find your favorite ways to flavor the tapenades. And, if you look around, you can almost always purchase black olive puree, often sold as *olivada*, from Italy that is ready to be flavored. The good news is that most *olivada* or black olive puree will keep for up to 6 months in the refrigerator if it is stored in a glass jar with a tight-fitting lid.

If you feel like creating your own flavored tapenades, start with the following list of ingredients and then add to it:

- Black or green olive puree
- Capers
- Anchovies, optional
- Dijon mustard

- Lemon juice
- Olive oil

The easiest way to pit olives: If you are making green olive tapenade or prefer to make your black olive paste from scratch, you will need to pit the olives. There are several ways to pit olives, but the easiest way is to crush them with the flat part of a chef's knife (with the blade facing away from you). The olive will crack, and then it will be very easy to pick the pit out of the olive. You want to be very careful to get all the pits when you do this, because a wayward pit could break the blade of your blender or food processor—or someone's tooth if you leave it in the tapenade!

Shelf Life

Most pestos and tapenades actually taste better the day after they are made—perhaps the only exception to this is fresh basil pesto, which is best served the same day it is made because it turns from a brilliant green to a black color very quickly. They are fairly stable and will keep, tightly covered, in the refrigerator for anywhere from 3 days to a month. However, they are always at their best a few days after you make them. Pestos and tapenades made in advance should be stored in a clean class jar with a tight-fitting lid in the refrigerator. Bring to room temperature before serving.

Pesto 101: Basic Basil Pesto

Makes about 2 cups

This is the pesto that started it all! Known in Italy as *pesto alla Genovese*, it is a simple mixture of basil, pine nuts, Parmigiano-Reggiano cheese, and garlic. It is commonly spread on toasted bread or tossed with pasta. When it is brushed onto grilled foods, it takes everything that it touches to a new level. If you can't find pine nuts, you can substitute walnuts.

Good for Seasoning: Swordfish, shrimp; chicken; pasta; potatoes, tomatoes; grilled pizza

> 1 cup pine nuts, lightly toasted
>
> 5 cups fresh basil leaves
>
> 2/3 cup freshly grated Parmigiano-Reggiano cheese
>
> 4 cloves garlic, peeled
>
> 3/4 to 1 cup olive oil
>
> 1/4 teaspoon kosher salt
>
> 1/4 teaspoon freshly ground pepper

Put all the ingredients in a food processor or blender and process until smooth and well combined. Taste and adjust the oil, salt, and pepper, if desired. The pesto will keep, tightly covered, in the refrigerator up to 3 days or in the freezer for up to 6 months.

Tapenade 101: Basic Black or Green Olive Tapenade

Makes 2 cups

A simple puree of olives seasoned with anchovies and capers is a dynamic way to flavor many foods. When smeared on bread and crackers, it is a great appetizer!

Good for Seasoning: Fish; chicken or other poultry; pork; lamb; grilled portobello mushrooms; use as a spread

> 2 anchovy fillets, rinsed
> 1 tablespoon capers, rinsed
> 1 clove garlic, peeled
> 2 teaspoons Dijon mustard
> 1 tablespoon fresh lemon juice
> 1 pound pitted black or green olives (about 3 cups), or 1 1/2 cups olive puree
> 1/2 to 2/3 cup extra-virgin olive oil
> Freshly ground black or white pepper

1. Put the anchovies, capers, garlic, mustard, and lemon juice in a food processor and process until everything is pureed and well combined. Add the olives and process until smooth and paste-like. Slowly add the oil through the feed tube and process until the tapenade is gleaming with oil. Season to taste with pepper.

2. Transfer to a glass jar with a tight-fitting lid. The tapenade can be served immediately but gets better as it sits in the refrigerator, where it will keep for 1 month. Let come to room temperature before serving.

Sun-Dried Tomato Pesto

Makes about 2 cups

This is my favorite way to eat those sweet-tart and slightly chewy sun-dried tomatoes. Pureeing them in a pesto that is rich with olive oil and walnuts complements the tomatoes and brings out their sun-dried goodness.

Good for Seasoning: Grilled flatbread; flank steak; tuna; chicken, duck breast; veal chops; pork chops

> 1/4 cup chopped walnuts, lightly toasted
> 1/2 cup fresh basil leaves
> 1/3 cup freshly grated Parmigiano-Reggiano cheese
> 1 clove garlic, peeled
> 1 cup oil-packed sun-dried tomatoes (one 8.5-ounce jar) or rehydrated dried tomatoes, plus 1/3 cup of the oil (top off with olive oil if necessary to make 1/3 cup)
> 2/3 cup olive oil
> 1/8 teaspoon freshly ground pepper

Put all the ingredients in a food processor or blender and process until smooth. The pesto should be perfectly seasoned without adding any salt, as many of the ingredients are inherently salty. Taste and adjust the pepper if desired. The pesto will keep, tightly covered, in the refrigerator for up to 2 weeks.

Sicilian-Style Pesto

Makes 3 1/2 cups

The first time I saw this tomato-rich pesto, I was shopping at a specialty store and saw a bag of "Made in Italy" pasta dressed with "Sicilian pesto." The picture on the bag was red and so I naturally thought it was red-pepper pesto. I read further and saw it was tomato pesto. Then I went home and did some research and tried it myself. This tomato-based pesto recipe is true to its Sicilian roots, as it is made with tomato and much less basil. I'm not sure about the rest of the ingredients, but what I am sure of is that is delicious!

Good for Seasoning: Eggplant, grilled mushrooms; chicken; pasta; grilled pizza

> 2 pounds plum tomatoes
>
> 1 cup blanched almonds, lightly toasted
>
> 4 large cloves garlic, peeled
>
> 1 cup fresh basil leaves
>
> 2/3 cup freshly grated Pecorino Romano cheese
>
> 3/4 cup olive oil
>
> 1/2 teaspoon kosher salt
>
> 1/4 teaspoon freshly ground pepper

1. Place a large saucepan over high heat and bring to a boil. Once the water boils, add the tomatoes for 5 to 10 seconds. Transfer to a bowl of ice water to stop the cooking. It might be easier to do this a few tomatoes at a time with a slotted spoon. When you've blanched all the tomatoes, peel the skin—it should slip right off. Cut the blanched and peeled tomatoes in half and squeeze out the seeds. Place on paper towels for 10 minutes to drain.

2. Meanwhile, put the almonds in the bowl of a food processor and process until ground. Add the garlic and basil and process until finely chopped. Add the tomatoes and pulse to chop and mix with the other ingredients. Add the cheese and pulse just to combine. Slowly add the oil while processing until the pesto is thinned out and you like the texture. Add the salt and pepper and pulse again. Taste and adjust the salt and pepper, if desired.

3. The pesto will keep, tightly covered, in the refrigerator up to 3 days or in the freezer for up to 6 months.

Simple "Pistou" Pesto

Makes about 1 cup

This version of "pesto" comes from Provence, where it is known as pistou. It is generally made with olive oil, basil, and garlic only. Cheese may be added if you like but nuts are not used. This basil-rich paste is most commonly used to season *soupe au pistou*, a fresh vegetable soup bursting with summer basil.

Good for Seasoning: Grilled vegetable soup, grilled vegetables; white fish; beef; lamb

> 3 to 4 cloves garlic, peeled
>
> 1/2 teaspoon fine-grain sea salt
>
> 3 cups fresh basil leaves
>
> 1/2 cup extra-virgin olive oil

You can make pistou one of two ways:

To make this recipe traditionally, you need a large mortar and pestle. Crush and pound the garlic and salt together until you have achieved a creamy garlic paste. Add the basil a few leaves at a time until they are crushed and you have a paste-like consistency. Slowly add the olive oil to thin out the paste and give it a looser texture.

Alternatively, put all the ingredients in a food processor or blender and puree until smooth but still a bit chunky. Taste and adjust the salt if desired. The pistou is best a few hours after you make it, but it will keep, tightly covered, in the refrigerator for up to 3 days or in the freezer for up to 6 months.

Classic Chimichurri

Makes about 1 1/2 cups

In Argentina, chimichurri sauce is as common as ketchup is in the USA—and for good reason, because the bright green sauce is rich with flavor but not heavy at all. Chopped parsley, garlic, and shallots are combined to create a refreshing sauce that sparkles with sherry vinegar and fresh lemon juice. Red wine vinegar can be substituted, but it is worth seeking out the sherry vinegar for this recipe.

Good for Seasoning: Grilled beef (steak, flank steak); lamb; chicken; fish; pasta, baked potatoes

> 3 to 5 cloves garlic, peeled
> 2 tablespoons roughly chopped shallot or onion
> 3/4 cup vegetable or olive oil
> 3 tablespoons sherry vinegar or red wine vinegar
> 3 tablespoons fresh lemon juice
> 1 teaspoon salt
> 1/2 teaspoon freshly ground pepper
> 1/2 teaspoon red chile flakes
> 4 to 6 cups lightly packed chopped fresh curly parsley*

Put the garlic, onion, oil, vinegar, lemon juice, salt, pepper, and red chile flakes in a blender or food processor and process until pureed. Add the parsley a little at a time and blend until it is incorporated. You may need to scrape down the sides of the container with a spoon or spatula to aid in the pureeing. The sauce should be very green and thick—the texture of pesto. The chimichurri will keep, tightly covered, in the refrigerator for up to 3 days.

*I call for 4 to 6 cups of parsley because it is hard to measure parsley exactly. I tend to use more parsley because I like a parsley-rich chimichurri.

Three-Herb Chimichurri

Makes about 2 1/2 cups

I was inspired by the classic chimichurri sauce and added cilantro and fresh mint to the parsley for a sauce with more dimension. I especially love the addition of mint, which cools off the fiery chile rub in Beef Tenderloin with Chimichurri (right).

Good for Seasoning: Beef tenderloin, steaks, roast beef sandwiches; chicken; leg of lamb

- 3 cloves garlic, peeled
- 2 shallots, peeled and cut into quarters
- 3/4 cup olive oil, or more to taste
- 3 tablespoons sherry vinegar or red wine vinegar
- 3 tablespoons fresh lemon juice
- 1 teaspoon fine-grain sea salt
- 1/2 teaspoon freshly ground pepper
- 1/2 teaspoon red chile flakes
- 3 cups tightly packed chopped fresh curly parsley
- 2 cups tightly packed fresh cilantro
- 1 cup tightly packed fresh mint

Put the garlic, shallots, oil, vinegar, lemon juice, salt, pepper, and red chile flakes in a blender or food processor and process until pureed. Add the parsley, cilantro, and mint a little at a time and blend until they are incorporated. You may need to scrape down the sides of the container with a spoon to aid the pureeing. The sauce should be very green and thick—the texture of pesto. The chimichurri will keep, tightly covered, in the refrigerator for up to 3 days.

Beef Tenderloin with Chimichurri

Serves 8 to 10

Grilling Method: Combo/Medium-High Heat

- 1 1/2 teaspoons to 1 tablespoon chipotle chile powder, to your taste (if not available, substitute ancho chile powder)
- 1 tablespoon sweet smoked Spanish paprika
- 1 teaspoon coarsely ground pepper
- 3 tablespoons dark brown sugar
- 1 tablespoon kosher salt, preferably Morton, or coarse-grain sea salt
- 1 whole beef tenderloin, about 5 pounds, at room termperature
- 2 tablespoons olive oil
- 1 recipe Three-Herb Chimichurri (left)

1. Preheat the grill. In a small bowl, whisk together the rub ingredients.

2. Roll tenderloin in paper towels to remove excess moisture. Sprinkle half the rub mixture evenly over the tenderloin. If you like it spicy, continue sprinkling until you've used all the mixture. Pat the spices into the meat gently to adhere.

3. Place the tenderloin on the cooking grate and sear for 2 minutes on each side over direct high heat. After all the sides are seared, move to medium-high indirect heat and finish cooking, about 40 more minutes for medium-rare or until a meat thermometer inserted in the thickest spot reads 130°F. (If the tenderloin is larger, it will take longer to cook.)

4. Transfer meat to a platter and let rest 15 minutes. Slice thinly and serve with sauce.

Roasted Red Pepper Pesto

Makes about 2 cups

The chile oil changes the character of this pesto from mild to magnificent. If you don't have any hot chile oil, use all olive oil and add a generous tablespoon of Thai chili-garlic sauce (*sriracha*). Besides turning basic grilled steaks and fish into great gourmet meals, it is addictive as a dip for chips and raw veggies.

Good for Seasoning: Fish, shellfish; steaks; grilled veggie pasta; use as a dip for grilled and raw vegetables

- 1/4 cup chopped walnuts, lightly toasted
- 1/2 cup fresh curly parsley
- 2/3 cup freshly grated Pecorino Romano cheese
- 2 large cloves garlic, peeled
- 3 roasted red peppers (see page 45)
- 1/3 cup hot chile oil
- 2/3 cup olive oil
- 1/4 teaspoon kosher salt
- 1/4 teaspoon freshly ground pepper

Put all the ingredients in a food processor or blender and process until smooth. Taste and adjust the salt and pepper if desired. The pesto will keep, tightly covered, in the refrigerator for up to 3 days.

Mushroom Pesto

Makes 2 cups

I love mushrooms any and all ways. This versatile pesto is terrific as a spread for a steak sandwich or a relish for an Italian sausage, stuffed into mushroom caps before grilling for a double whammy, or as a pizza sauce. The addition of Cognac adds a sophisticated note to this herbaceous mushroom paste. Substitute your favorite wild mushrooms when you want to up the flavor ante.

Good for Seasoning: Steak sandwiches or steaks; chicken; Italian sausages; grilled mushrooms; pizza, grilled bread

- 1 pound baby portobello or wild mushrooms
- 3/4 cup olive oil, divided
- 1 1/2 cups fresh basil leaves
- 1 sprig fresh rosemary, leaves only
- 1/2 cup fresh curly parsley
- 2/3 cup freshly grated Pecorino Romano cheese
- 1/2 cup walnuts, lightly toasted
- 4 cloves garlic, peeled
- 1 tablespoon Cognac, optional

1/4 teaspoon kosher salt

1/4 teaspoon freshly ground pepper

1. Slice or chop the mushrooms very fine (minced). Add about 2 tablespoons of the olive oil to a heavy-duty sauté pan and cook the mushrooms over medium-high heat until they are beginning to caramelize on the edges and darken. Let cool. Chop into small pieces and set aside.

2. Meanwhile, put the basil, rosemary, parsley, cheese, walnuts, and garlic in a blender or food processor. Process with the remaining oil until pureed and paste-like—you may not need all the oil. Add the Cognac, if desired, and the salt and pepper.

3. Add the mushrooms to basil paste and mix well by hand.

4. Taste and adjust the salt and pepper, if desired. The pesto will keep, tightly covered, in the refrigerator for up to 3 days.

Ancho Chile and Cashew Pesto

Makes 2 cups

This powerful pesto packs a punch. I love the combination of rehydrated ancho chilies and roasted cashews. It is very unconventional but delicious. The cashews mellow the heat of the anchos and make this pesto a seasoning agent that can also double as a wet rub. I particularly like rubbing it on fish and wrapping it in a banana or lettuce leaf before grilling—that way the rich flavors of this pesto bake into the food as it

grills. If you want to use this recipe as a wet rub to flavor food before grilling, reduce the olive oil by half, or until you have a consistency like a nut butter.

Good for Seasoning: Chicken; whole fish, shrimp; grilled vegetables; rice or pasta dishes

6 to 8 dried ancho chilies, stemmed and seeded

1 cup roasted cashews, preferably unsalted

1/2 cup fresh flat-leaf parsley

1/2 cup fresh Thai basil leaves

1 cup fresh cilantro leaves

Juice and zest of 1 to 2 limes (about 1/8 cup juice and 2 tablespoons zest)

1 large shallot, peeled

6 cloves garlic, peeled

Pinch red chile flakes

1 teaspoon kosher salt

1/4 teaspoon freshly ground pepper

1/2 cup olive oil

1. Place the ancho chilies in a single layer in a shallow heatproof dish. Boil 2 cups of water and pour over the chilies. Let cool in the water for about 15 minutes to soften and rehydrate. Drain the water and set the chilies aside.

2. Put the chilies in a blender or food processor and process until chopped and they resemble a rough paste. Add the cashews and pulse until ground. Add the parsley, basil, cilantro, lime juice and zest, shallot, garlic, red chile flakes, salt, and pepper. Pulse until the pesto is pureed.

3. Slowly add the oil and pulse until the consistency is creamy but still a little thick (for dolloping on food, or paste-like for seasoning food).

4. Taste and adjust the salt and pepper, if desired. The pesto will keep, tightly covered, in the refrigerator for up to 3 days.

Arugula-Lemon Pesto

Makes 2 cups

This is the perfect pesto to make in the winter when you are in need of some sunshine on your plate and palate. One bite of this happy pesto and you'll forget the grayness of any day. The tart lemon and peppery arugula are balanced by the richness of pecans and real parmesan cheese. It's like your favorite salad in a sauce. If you can find Meyer lemons, which taste like a cross between a lemon and a Mandarin orange, in your market, substitute them for the conventional lemons and you'll be rewarded with an extra sweetness.

Good for Seasoning: White fish, scallops, clams, shrimp; pork tenderloin; boneless skinless chicken breasts; grilled bread

1 cup pecans, lightly toasted

4 cups fresh arugula leaves

1 cup fresh lemon verbena, lemon basil, or basil

1/3 cup freshly grated Parmigiano Reggiano cheese

4 cloves garlic, peeled

Zest of 2 lemons

1 lemon, juiced

3/4 cup extra-virgin olive oil

1/2 teaspoon kosher salt

1/4 teaspoon freshly ground pepper

Put all the ingredients in a food processor or blender and process until smooth. Taste and adjust the salt and pepper, if desired. The pesto will keep, tightly covered, in the refrigerator up to 3 days or in the freezer for up to 6 months.

Sweet Mint Pesto with Grappa

Makes 1 1/2 cups

Alone, grappa might be an acquired taste, but add it to other ingredients in cooking and grappa adds depth and flavor. This sweet pesto is a welcome change from cloying dessert sauces. Look for grappa di Moscato, which is crystal clear with a peachy, honeysuckle-y, Muscat lusciousness. If you can't find the grappa, substitute an apricot eau de vie from France or an apricot palinka from Hungary.

Good for Seasoning: Grilled fruit (white peaches, plums, strawberries); melon and proscuitto; grilled pound cake; use as a light spread on shortbread or sugar cookies

1 cup hazelnuts, lightly toasted

1/3 cup sugar

2.5 ounces (5 tablespoons) grappa di Moscato or apricot eau de vie

1 tablespoon chopped crystallized ginger

4 cups fresh mint leaves

1/2 cup untoasted hazelnut or walnut oil

1/4 teaspoon fine-grain sea salt

1. Put the hazelnuts, sugar, grappa, and ginger in a food processor or blender and process until smooth. Add the mint and pulse until the mint is chopped and the pesto is well blended. Slowly add the oil until the consistency is a little thinner than a paste.

2. Add the salt, then taste and adjust the salt and/or sugar if desired. The pesto will keep, tightly covered, in the refrigerator up to 3 days or in the freezer for up to 6 months.

Red-Hot Chile Pepper Tapenade

Makes about 3 1/2 cups

Walk up to any olive stand in the south of France and you will see the red and black mosaic of oil-cured olives and bits of red chile peppers. Although you lose the visual in this tapenade as the black olive obliterates the red pepper's color, what you get in return is a perfect mélange of flavor in every bite.

Good for Seasoning: Grilled chicken; pork; grilled vegetables; scallops, grilled bread

1 to 2 dried ancho chilies, stemmed and seeded

3 anchovy fillets, rinsed

2 tablespoons capers, rinsed

5 cloves garlic, peeled

1 tablespoon fresh lemon juice

1 tablespoon strong Dijon mustard

1/2 teaspoon red chile flakes

1 roasted red pepper (see page 43)

1/2 pound pitted black olives (about 2 cups), or 1 cup olive puree

1 cup extra-virgin olive oil

Freshly ground black or white pepper

1. Put the ancho chile in a bowl and pour 2 cups of boiling water over to rehydrate. Allow to cool to room temperature, about 30 minutes. Drain and set aside.

2. Put the chile, anchovies, capers, garlic, and lemon juice in the bowl of a food processor. Pulse until everything is pureed and well combined.

3. Add the mustard, chile flakes, roasted red pepper, and olives. Process until they are smooth and have a paste-like consistency.

4. Slowly add the oil and process until the tapenade is gleaming with oil. Stop occasionally to scrape down the sides of the bowl, making sure that all the ingredients are incorporated. Adjust the pepper, if necessary.

5. Transfer to a glass jar with a tight-fitting lid. The tapenade can be served immediately but gets better as it sits in the refrigerator, where it will keep for 1 month. Let come to room temperature before serving.

Green Olive and Lemon Marmalade Tapenade

Makes about 1 cup

If you've never noticed lemon marmalade in your store, look again. Although it is not as widely produced or as popular as orange marmalade, it is often on the grocery shelf. It makes a lovely glaze by itself and is a great ingredient in everything from this tapenade to almost anything that is made better by a bit of sweet lemon. This sweet and tangy green tapenade makes everything it touches sparkle with good taste and flavor—everyone will wonder "where you learned to cook like that!"

Good for Seasoning: Swordfish; grilled bread; cheese; grilled vegetables

> 2 anchovy fillets, rinsed
>
> 1 tablespoon capers, rinsed
>
> 1 tablespoon fresh lemon juice
>
> 2 to 3 tablespoons lemon marmalade, to your taste

> 1/2 pound pitted green olives (about 2 cups), preferably picholine
>
> 1/3 cup very green extra-virgin olive oil or lemon olive oil
>
> Freshly ground black or white pepper

1. Put the anchovies, capers, and lemon juice in the bowl of a food processor. Pulse until everything is pureed and well combined. Add the lemon marmalade and olives and process until they are smooth and have a paste-like consistency.

2. Slowly add the oil and process until the tapenade is gleaming with oil. Stop occasionally to scrape down the sides of the bowl, making sure that all the ingredients are incorporated. Season to taste with pepper.

3. Transfer to a glass jar with a tight-fitting lid. The tapenade can be served immediately but gets better as it sits in the refrigerator, where it will keep for 1 month. Let come to room temperature before serving.

Green Olive, Apricot, and Pastis Tapenade

Makes 2 1/4 cups

Come along now, let's have a pastis! In fact, I am sipping on a pastis as I write this recipe. It is the much-loved and often-drunk anise-flavored aperitif from the south of France. It was created after absinthe was banned and contains many of the same aromatics, minus the reputed craze-inducing wormwood. The herbs and spices used in making the drink are very food friendly. Often, pastis is served with seasoned olives, making this tapenade a natural flavor combination. I've added the sweet, fruity apricots to balance the bitter and briny green olives. Pernod is a cousin to pastis and very easy to find and therefore often substituted, but it is not technically considered a pastis—look for Ricard first and use Pernod second.

Good for Seasoning: Chicken; lamb; grilled fish; grilled flatbread

> 1 cup dried Turkish apricots, cut into strips
>
> 1/2 cup Ricard or Pernod
>
> 2 anchovy fillets, rinsed
>
> 2 tablespoons capers, rinsed
>
> 1 tablespoon strong Dijon mustard
>
> 2 tablespoons chopped fresh tarragon
>
> 1 tablespoon fresh orange or clementine juice
>
> Zest 1/2 orange or clementine
>
> 1 pound pitted green olives (about 2 cups)
>
> 1 cup extra-virgin olive oil
>
> Fine-ground white pepper

1. Put the apricots and Ricard in a small saucepan. Cover, bring to a boil, and simmer for 2 to 3 minutes. Turn off the heat and let the apricots sit until they have absorbed most of the pastis. Let cool to room temperature or slightly warm.

2. Put the apricots and any remaining liquid in the bowl of a food processor. Pulse to puree. Add the anchovies, capers, mustard, tarragon, orange juice, and zest, and pulse until everything is pureed and well mixed, but still chunky.

3. Add the olives and process until they are smooth and have a paste-like consistency. Slowly add the oil and process until the tapenade is gleaming with oil. Season with pepper. Stop occasionally to scrape down the sides of the bowl, making sure that all the ingredients are incorporated.

4. Transfer to a glass jar with a tight-fitting lid. The tapenade can be served immediately but gets better as it sits in the refrigerator, where it will keep for 1 month. Let come to room temperature before serving.

Finger-Lickin'-Good Brandy-Steeped-Fig Tapenade

Makes about 2 cups

My friend and fellow Francophile Sarah Leah Chase spent many summers peddling through Provence, leading food and bike tours. On these trips, she was inspired by all the glorious tapenades in the markets. When she came back to the United States, she made her own, adding brandy-steeped figs to her tapenade to temper the strong flavors of anchovies and capers. It more than tempers the tapenade—it turns it from a condiment that you use sparingly into something you can't stop eating on everything! If you are not a fig lover, substitute dried plums (prunes) and Armagnac for an equally great fruit-brandy tapenade. Here, I've adapted Sarah's recipe but kept her spirit.

Good for Seasoning: Grilled duck; pork loin; beef tenderloin; grilled bread; cheese

> 1 cup dried black Mission figs, stemmed and cut in half
>
> 1/2 cup your favorite best-quality brandy or Cognac
>
> 4 anchovy fillets, rinsed
>
> 2 tablespoon capers, rinsed
>
> 1 tablespoon strong Dijon mustard
>
> 1 tablespoon fresh lemon juice
>
> Zest of 1/2 lemon
>
> 1 pound pitted black olives (about 3 cups), or 1 1/2 cups olive puree
>
> 1/2 cup extra-virgin olive oil
>
> Freshly ground black or white pepper

1. Put the figs and brandy in a small saucepan. Cover, bring to a boil, and simmer for about 3 minutes. Turn off the heat and let the figs sit for about 30 minutes or until they have absorbed most of the brandy. Let cool to room temperature or slightly warm.

2. Put the figs and any remaining liquid in the bowl of a food processor. Pulse to puree. Add the anchovies, capers, mustard, lemon juice, and zest, and pulse until everything is pureed and well mixed.

3. Add the olives and process until they are smooth and have a paste-like consistency.

4. Slowly add the oil and process until the tapenade is gleaming with oil. Stop occasionally to scrape down the sides of the bowl, making sure that all the ingredients are incorporated. Adjust the pepper, if necessary.

5. Transfer to a glass jar with a tight-fitting lid. The tapenade can be served immediately but gets better as it sits in the refrigerator, where it will keep for 1 month. Let come to room temperature before serving.

Note: If using Calimyrna (white) figs, add 2 tablespoons fig jam for sweetness.

Dipping Sauces

Sweet or savory mixtures that you dip your food into after it is cooked. Almost any sauce can be used as a dipping sauce.

Dipping Sauces 101

When some people think of dipping sauces, they instantly think of the bowls of big, bold flavor from the many Southeast Asian cuisines that we have adopted into our own favorite foods repertoire. But the idea of dipping and dunking food in liquid for added flavor and moisture is an old and international one—from dunking Japanese sushi and dumplings in soy sauce to the very American tradition of dipping cookies in milk.

You don't have to stay in the Asian realm of Vietnam, Thailand, Cambodia, China, Japan, or other eastern countries to use a dipping sauce. Aioli is a dipping sauce in Provence, where the Friday lunch tradition of the "grand aioli" is an excuse to eat the garlic-rich homemade mayonnaise. The plain steamed codfish and vegetables of the grand aioli are not just made palatable by the addictive aioli but are turned into a sought-after specialty by the garlicky sauce. I love all kinds of aioli and use them often as a dipping sauce—especially with grilled shellfish and grilled vegetables of all kinds. Another favorite is pesto thinned out with some extra-virgin olive oil. It makes a fresh, clean, and bright dipping sauce for any fish, shellfish, vegetable, white meat, or grilled bread. Ketchup is the original American dipping sauce, and homemade ketchup is lick-your-fingers good on most anything from grilled burgers, dogs, and sausages to chicken breasts. When it comes to dipping sauce, everyone gets their own bowl, so double dipping is not only permitted, it is encouraged.

If a dipping sauce can come from anywhere, how do you define it? I define it as anything that you can put into a small bowl and dip cooked food into. This turns barbecue sauce that you serve on the side into a dipping sauce. Melted butter served with grilled lobster or shrimp is a dipping sauce, as are the more complicated sauces such as Romesco Dipping Sauce (page 323) and Blue Cheese Dip (page 310) for hot wings. Because almost everything can be turned into a dipping sauce, I've included an eclectic group of sauces in this chapter, but I encourage you to use any of the sauces and condiments in this book to dip into.

Since dipping is personal, why not create your own dipping sauces based on your favorite condiments or flavors? When I was a kid, I loved to dip knockwurst into a mixture of ketchup and mayonnaise.

When I am feeling in need of childhood comfort foods, I make a homemade Thousand Island Dressing (page 325) and dip my grilled sausages and dogs in that. Try it, you might like it, or try your own blends.

Classic Asian Dipping Sauces

In America, the most familiar Asian dipping sauce (besides soy sauce) is the peanut sauce served with Thai satays, or grilled chicken or beef on a stick. But there are so many other Asian dipping sauces to choose from, and most of them are lighter, saltier, and have a healthy dose of chilies in them. There are many dipping sauces that we are used to using in restaurants, but since we don't know the names of them, we don't make them at home. For example, the thin red chile-soy sauce that is flavored with the distinctive and ubiquitous fish sauce and served with spring rolls, egg rolls, and dumplings is an equally great dipping sauce for grilled shellfish, as well as for grilled mushrooms, and it's easy to make (see page 332).

How to Dip

Dipping allows you to apply as little or as much sauce to your food as you like. In the Asian dipping tradition, you dip a corner or so of the food in the sauce before taking a bite. Dips are concentrated and not intended for slathering. But if you subscribe to the "more is more" style, feel free to dip deeply!

Shelf Life

Many dipping sauces taste best used the day they are made. And some, like the Blue Cheese Dip on page 310, taste better the next day. The rule of thumb is the more fresh citrus juice and fresh herbs the dip has in it, the better it is to make just before serving. As soon as these sauces sit, you lose some of the brightness (tartness and clarity of flavor) from the freshly squeezed juices and other highly perishable ingredients. Dipping sauces made in advance should be stored in a clean glass jar with a tight-fitting lid in the refrigerator. If necessary, warm or bring to room temperature before serving.

Dipping Sauce 101

Makes 1 1/2 cups

This is the simplest of all mustard sauces and makes a great dip for grilled chicken, sausage, steak—and raw veggies. If you make this dip once, you'll end up making it all the time because it is a real crowd-pleaser—just don't let them know how easy it is!

Good for Seasoning: Chicken; smoked salmon; grilled vegetables, raw veggies; sausages; savory pigs in a blanket

> 1 cup mayonnaise, preferably Hellmann's
> 1/2 cup smooth Dijon mustard
> 1 tablespoon whole-grain Dijon mustard
> 1/2 teaspoon granulated garlic
> Freshly ground pepper

In a medium bowl, mix the mayonnaise with the mustards until creamy and well combined. Add the garlic. Add pepper to taste. Serve immediately, or store, tightly covered, in the refrigerator for up to 5 days.

Creole Mustard Sauce

Makes 1/2 cup

I fell in love with Creole mustard when I lived in New Orleans. The spicy but not too hot mustard is as common as yellow mustard in Louisiana and Mississippi, but there have been many times where I couldn't find it, so I created my own quickie version of this smooth and grainy mustard using a bit of mayonnaise to bind the two mustards. It may not be the same as the classic Creole favorite Zatarain's, but it is good in a pinch or if you can't get the original.

Good for Seasoning: Grilled potatoes; chicken; sausages; salmon

> 1/4 cup whole-grain Dijon mustard
> 2 tablespoons strong Dijon mustard
> 2 to 3 tablespoons mayonnaise, preferably Hellmann's, plus more if needed

In a small bowl, mix the mustards and mayonnaise together until smooth. Taste for seasoning. If the mustard is too strong, add another tablespoon of mayonnaise. Use as a dipping sauce or use as directed in a recipe. Serve immediately, or store, tightly covered, in the refrigerator for up to 5 days.

Rémoulade Sauce

Makes 2 cups

This dipping sauce is the heart and soul of New Orleans. It is served on just about everything but most often associated with shrimp. If you can't find Creole mustard in your grocery store, use the preceding recipe to make Creole mustard, and then make the Rémoulade Sauce.

Good for Seasoning: Green tomatoes, roasted potatoes; shrimp, crayfish; turkey; pork chops

- 1 cup mayonnaise, preferably Hellmann's
- 2 tablespoons Creole or other grainy mustard
- 2 tablespoons ketchup
- 3 tablespoons scallions, finely chopped
- 2 tablespoons fresh curly parsley, finely chopped
- 1 stalk celery, finely chopped
- 2 cloves garlic, grated
- 1 teaspoon sweet smoked Spanish paprika
- 1 teaspoon Louisiana-style hot sauce
- Kosher salt
- Freshly ground pepper

In a medium bowl, combine the mayonnaise with the mustard and ketchup. Add the scallions, parsley, celery, garlic, paprika, and hot sauce. Mix thoroughly. Season to taste with salt and pepper. Serve immediately, or store, tightly covered, in the refrigerator for up to 3 days.

Rough-and-Ready Mustard

Makes about 1/3 cup

When I visit my associate and good friend Kirsten Newman-Teissier and her French-born husband, Nat, at their home in Pennsylvania, we always eat in. Sometimes making elaborate meals, sometimes testing recipes, and sometimes having an easy evening of our favorite cheeses, sausages, and bread. On one of these "easy" evenings, I made a couple of quick sauces to serve with grilled and dry sausages and cheese. The winner of the night was the Rough-and-Ready Mustard. It is almost as simple as mixing mustards and jam together, and the variations are endless. I've always called this mixture Rough-and-Ready Mustard—I am not sure why, but I love the sound of it.

Good for Seasoning: Grilled pork; chicken; cheese; grilled sausages, dried salami

- 1/4 cup apricot jam
- 1 tablespoon whole-grain Dijon mustard
- 2 teaspoons smooth Dijon mustard
- Pinch of dry mustard, preferably Colman's
- Pinch dried parsley or other dried herb

In a small bowl, mix the jam and Dijon mustards together until combined but still chunky. Add the dry mustard and parsley and mix until combined. Serve immediately, or store, tightly covered, in the refrigerator for up to 3 days.

Rough-and-Ready Mustard Variation Ideas

Raspberry jam and mint

Fig jam and dehydrated shallots

Red currant jelly and red chile flakes

Blackberry jam and tarragon

Classic Aioli

Makes 1 1/2 cups

Praise aioli! The homemade garlic-rich mayonnaise is so good that you'll want to slather it on everything from fish, chicken, and roast beef to grill-roasted veggies and grilled fries. As good as the original aioli is, try all the variations for a family of dipping sauces that will make you want to dip daily!

Good for Seasoning: Grilled bread; fish, shrimp; chicken; lamb kabobs; raw veggies

- Juice and zest from 1 to 2 large lemons
- 6 large cloves garlic, roughly chopped
- 1 heaping tablespoon Dijon mustard
- 1 large egg
- 1 large egg yolk
- 1 1/2 cups vegetable oil, plus more if needed
- 1 cup best-quality extra-virgin olive oil
- 1/2 teaspoon kosher salt

1. In a food processor, combine the lemon juice and garlic and pulse until the garlic is pureed (about 15 seconds). Add the mustard and pulse again until combined. Add the egg, egg yolk, and lemon zest and process for 10 seconds (if you are concerned about the raw eggs, use pasteurized eggs).

2. Very slowly, add the oils in a trickle through the feed tube of the food processor until the sauce is thick and well combined. As the aioli becomes thicker, the noise will sound more like a purr than a whirr, and you'll know it is done. If you like a firmer texture, add a little more oil. Add the salt and process until well combined. Serve immediately, or store, tightly covered, in the refrigerator for up to 1 week.

Note: The older the garlic, the stronger it tastes. If your garlic is a little past its prime but hasn't started sprouting yet, you can still use it; just reduce the quantity by half if you don't like a strong garlic flavor. Likewise, if you love the taste of garlic and your garlic is extremely fresh and firm, increase the amount of garlic for a more pronounced flavor.

Lemon Aioli or Mayo

Makes 1 1/2 cups

To turn this lemon aioli into lemon mayonnaise, simply eliminate the garlic from the recipe. Add fresh basil to this recipe for a summertime aioli that will make any tomato sandwich or BLT explode with flavor!

Good for Seasoning: Asparagus and other spring vegetables; grilled salmon; BLT or tomato sandwich

> Juice and zest from 2 large lemons
>
> 4 large cloves garlic, roughly chopped, optional
>
> 1 heaping tablespoon Dijon mustard
>
> 1 large egg
>
> 1 large egg yolk
>
> 1 1/2 cups vegetable oil, plus more if needed
>
> 1 cup best-quality extra-virgin olive oil
>
> 1/2 teaspoon kosher salt

1. In a food processor, combine the lemon juice and garlic, if desired, and pulse until the garlic is pureed (about 15 seconds). Add the mustard and pulse again until combined. Add the egg, egg yolks, and lemon zest and process for 10 seconds (if you are concerned about the raw eggs, use pasteurized eggs).

2. Very slowly, add the oils in a trickle through the feed tube of the food processor until the sauce is thick and well combined. As the aioli becomes thicker, the noise will sound more like a purr than a whirr, and you'll know it is done. If you like a firmer texture, add a little more oil. Serve immediately, or store, tightly covered, in the refrigerator for up to 1 week.

Herbed Aioli

Makes 1 1/4 cups

Rich with garlic and fines herbes, this is the dipping sauce equivalent to Boursin cheese—but better because it is homemade. If you prefer the straight herb flavor, omit the garlic and increase the herbs. This beautiful green aioli is best made with fresh herbs and eaten within 2 days.

Good for Seasoning: Grilled and raw vegetables, especially peppers and asparagus; chicken; salmon, shrimp, trout

1 large egg, at room temperature

1 large egg yolk, at room temperature

2 1/2 tablespoons fresh lemon juice

Zest of 1/2 lemon

6 cloves garlic, peeled

1 tablespoon chopped fresh chives

1 tablespoon chopped fresh chervil

1 tablespoon chopped fresh parsley

1 tablespoon chopped fresh tarragon

1 tablespoon strong Dijon mustard

Fine-grain sea salt

Freshly ground pepper

1 cup olive oil

1/2 cup neutral olive oil, canola oil, or untoasted walnut oil

1. In a food processor, combine the egg, egg yolk, and 1 tablespoon of the lemon juice. Pulse to mix. Add the garlic, herbs, mustard, and a pinch of salt and pepper and process until fairly smooth. With the motor running, slowly add the oils through the feed tube of the food processor. The aioli will begin to thicken; watch closely and add the oils until it is the right consistency. Taste and adjust the seasoning, adding more lemon juice (the mayonnaise should be tart), herbs, salt, and pepper to suit your taste.

2. Cover and refrigerate for at least 2 hours to develop the flavors before using. For best results, the mayonnaise should be used within 2 days. It will keep, tightly covered, in the refrigerator for up to 1 week.

Saffron Aioli

Makes 1 1/2 cups

This golden yellow aioli looks as rich as it tastes and pairs with any Middle Eastern–spiced food or simple grilled lamb chops, shrimp, and green vegetables like asparagus and zucchini. Save any leftovers for sandwiches and raw vegetables.

Good for Seasoning: Lamb chops; asparagus and other spring vegetables, pattypan squash; shrimp, lobster, mussels, cod; French fries

Juice and zest from 1 large lemon

1/4 teaspoon saffron stems, crumbled and dissolved in a little lemon juice

6 large cloves garlic, roughly chopped

1 heaping tablespoon Dijon mustard

1 large egg

1 large egg yolk

1 1/2 cups vegetable oil, plus more if needed

1 cup best-quality extra-virgin olive oil

1/2 teaspoon kosher salt

1. In a food processor, combine the lemon juice, saffron, and garlic and pulse until the garlic is pureed and the saffron is dissolved (about 15 seconds). Add the mustard and pulse again until combined. Add the egg, egg yolks, and lemon zest and process for 10 seconds (if you are concerned about the raw eggs, use pasteurized eggs).

2. Very slowly, add the oils in a trickle through the feed tube of the food processor until the sauce is thick and thoroughly combined. As the aioli becomes thicker, the noise will sound more like a purr than a whirr, and you'll know it is done. If you like a firmer texture, add a little more oil. Add the salt and process until well combined. Serve immediately, or store, tightly covered, in the refrigerator for up to 1 week

"Dijonnaisse"

Makes 1 1/2 cups

Who doesn't love the mustardy-tangy mayonnaise? It's so much better made at home that I included it in this collection of dipping sauces. Add a little honey and it becomes Honey Dijonnaisse.

Good for Seasoning: Grilled chicken; salmon; sandwiches; raw and grilled vegetables

- 2 tablespoons distilled white vinegar
- 2 heaping tablespoons Dijon mustard
- 1 teaspoon dry mustard, preferably Colman's
- 2 tablespoons honey, optional
- 1 large egg
- 1 large egg yolk
- 1 cup peanut or other vegetable oil, plus more if needed
- 1/2 cup best-quality extra-virgin olive oil
- 1/2 teaspoon kosher salt

1. In a food processor, combine the vinegar, Dijon mustard, and dry mustard; pulse until pureed (about 15 seconds). Add the honey, if desired. Add the egg and egg yolks and process for 10 seconds (if you are concerned about the raw eggs, use pasteurized eggs).

2. Very slowly, add the oils in a trickle through the feed tube of the food processor until the sauce is thick and well combined. As the mixture becomes thicker, the noise will sound more like a purr than a whirr, and you'll know it is done. If you like a firmer texture, add a little more oil. Add the salt and process until well combined. Serve immediately, or store, tightly covered, in the refrigerator for up to 1 week.

Spicy or Not Horseradish Cocktail Sauce

Makes 2 cups

To me, the essential ingredient in classic cocktail sauce is the fresh horseradish. I love it in almost equal proportions to the ketchup. But I realize that many people prefer it sweeter and less spicy. This is a cocktail sauce made to order for everyone, since the horseradish is served on the side and quickly whisked in by each diner. If everyone in your party likes it spicy, mix 1/4 cup fresh horseradish into the base recipe.

Good for Seasoning: Shrimp, calamari, grilled oysters

- 1 cup ketchup
- 1 cup Heinz Chili Sauce
- Juice and zest of 2 lemons
- 8 shakes Tabasco sauce
- 1/2 teaspoon sea salt
- Freshly ground pepper, optional
- 2 to 4 heaping tablespoons prepared white horseradish (not cream-style)

1. In a medium nonreactive bowl, mix the ketchup, chili sauce, lemon juice, zest, Tabasco, and salt until well combined. Add the pepper, if desired. Serve immediately, or store, tightly covered, in the refrigerator for up to 1 week.

2. Just before serving, divide the horseradish between 4 small saucers and divide the sauce into 4 bowls. Serve a bowl of sauce with the horseradish on the side for diners to customize as they desire.

Green Tabasco and Tomatillo Cocktail Sauce

Makes 1 3/4 cups

I love this cool green cocktail sauce with grilled shellfish and fruit cocktails. The tart, spicy sauce is full of big, bold flavors —it is in-your-face in a good way—if you like it a little smoother, add a 1/4 cup of sour cream to the sauce.

Good for Seasoning: Grilled tacos; shrimp, scallops, lobster; shellfish cocktails made with mango, passion fruit, grilled pineapple, or grilled peaches

> 1 large shallot, chopped
> 4 cloves garlic, minced
> 1 lime, juiced
> 3 to 6 large tomatillos, about 1 pound, brown husks removed and cut into quarters
> 1 cup chopped fresh cilantro
> 1/2 cup baby spinach leaves
> 1/8 teaspoon sea salt

> 1/4 cup Tabasco Green Pepper sauce
> Sour cream, optional

In a food processor, process the shallot, garlic, lime juice, tomatillos, cilantro, spinach, and salt until smooth. Mix in the Tabasco and season to taste with salt and extra lime juice if desired. If using sour cream, stir in a few tablespoons just before serving. Serve immediately. If you leave out the sour cream, you may store, tightly covered, in the refrigerator for up to 2 days; add the sour cream, if desired, just before serving.

Basil-Lemon Dipping Sauce

Makes about 3/4 cup

Basil and lemon go together like sunshine and summer. This olive oil–based dipping sauce is light and lets the natural flavors of the citrus and basil shine through—try it with orange juice and zest for a nice change of pace.

Good for Seasoning: Pasta with grilled clams; grilled shrimp, salmon; grilled bread; grilled asparagus

> Juice and zest of 1 large lemon
> 2 large cloves garlic, grated
> 1/2 cup best-quality extra-virgin olive oil
> 8 to 10 large fresh basil leaves, cut into chiffonade

In a small bowl, combine the lemon juice, zest, garlic, oil, and basil. Mix well. Use immediately.

1-2-3 Pesto Dipping Sauce

Makes 1 cup

This easy 1-2-3-Dipping Sauce turns thick pesto into a thinner dipping sauce. It is one of my favorite sauces and goes with just about everything. You mix best-quality pesto with really good olive oil and a pinch of coarse sea salt. This is a great way to use all that extra pesto that you make at the end of the summer, when basil grows like weeds.

Good for Seasoning: Grilled bread; chicken; shrimp, fish; grilled vegetable pasta

> 1/2 cup best-quality pesto, store-bought or homemade (see Pesto 101, page 282)
> 1/2 cup best-quality extra-virgin olive oil
> Pinch coarse-grain sea salt or fleur de sel

Put the pesto in a medium bowl. Add the oil and stir until fully combined and "runny." Season with salt. Serve immediately, or store, tightly covered, in the refrigerator for up to 1 week.

Parmesan and Black Pepper Dipping Sauce

Makes 3/4 cup

The first thing that my good friend Michael Krusch does when he sees a bowl of olive oil is to add parmesan cheese to it before dipping his food in. And why not? Olive oil is good, but olive oil and parmesan is great. I add a hefty dose of coarsely ground black pepper to the mix, making it a tasty dip for bread, veggies and grilled meat.

Good for Seasoning: steak (turns it into steak au poivre); grilled chicken; grilled bread; grilled antipasto salad

> 1/4 cup vinegar of your choice, such as red, white, or balsamic, etc.
> 1 teaspoon warm water
> 1/2 cup extra-virgin olive oil
> 2 teaspoons freshly ground pepper
> 1/2 cup freshly grated Parmigiano-Reggiano cheese
> Pinch sea salt

In a small bowl, mix the vinegar and water. Slowly whisk in the oil until it is completely blended. Add the pepper and cheese and stir to combine. Season with salt. Serve immediately, or store, tightly covered, in the refrigerator for up to 2 days.

Greek Islands Dipping Sauce

Makes about 3/4 cup

The combination of freshly squeezed lemon juice, pungent garlic, and herbaceous oregano makes me want to take a trip to Greece—or at least to a great Greek restaurant. Try this dipping sauce at home with Salt-Crusted Shrimp (right), grilled calamari, or any other seaside fare. It was designed to be served with salty dishes and thus has no salt in the sauce. If you are serving it with milder foods, add a pinch of salt at the end.

Good for Seasoning: Any salt-crusted grilled foods; shrimp; vegetables; chicken; lamb kabobs

- 1/2 cup best-quality extra-virgin olive oil
- 2 lemons, juiced
- Zest from 1/2 lemon
- 2 cloves garlic, grated
- 4 sprigs fresh oregano, leaves only
- Freshly ground pepper

In a small bowl, whisk together the oil, lemon juice, and zest. Stir in the garlic. Add the oregano leaves. Let sit for at least 20 to 30 minutes to marry the flavors—or make up to 12 hours in advance. Add a grind of pepper, just before serving. Use the sauce within 24 hours.

Salt-Crusted Shrimp with Greek Islands Dipping Sauce

Serves 4

Grilling Method: Direct/Medium Heat

- 16 jumbo or colossal shrimp in the shell
- 3 tablespoons olive oil
- 1/4 cup kosher salt or other coarse salt
- 1 recipe Greek Islands Dipping Sauce (left)

1. Build a charcoal fire or preheat a gas grill. Put the shrimp in a large bowl and toss with the oil to coat lightly all over. Just before putting on the grill, sprinkle the salt evenly over the shrimp and toss well to make sure each shrimp is thoroughly coated in a crust of salt. Do not use fine-grain kosher salt, as it melts too quickly.

2. Place the shrimp in the center of the cooking grate, and grill for 3 to 4 minutes per side or until the shrimp is pink and the flesh is opaque. Serve immediately with the dipping sauce.

This is my favorite party ice-breaker appetizer. I place the oil-tossed shrimp in a bowl on a tray with a small bowl of kosher salt, tongs, lots of napkins, a platter, and the prepared dipping sauce. Once everyone is armed with a cocktail, we hit the deck where the whole party feels like they're in on the backyard action. While we are talking, I toss the shrimp in the salt and grill them (see photos).

When the shrimp are cooked, pile them on newspaper or a platter and the fun begins! Everyone takes a shrimp, peels it, and dips it in the sauce for a fun, casual, and interactive appetizer! The salt on the shells stays on your fingers as you peel the shrimp, seasoning the shrimp as you dip into the potent lemon-garlic sauce. By the time the shrimp and our cocktails are gone, we are either fast friends or better friends! Alternatively, you can arrange 4 shrimp on each serving plate and accompany with a small ramekin of the dipping sauce, but I think serving them hot off the grill is much more fun.

Tex-Mex Queso Dip

Makes about 3 cups

This is really more of a dip in the classic sense instead of a dipping sauce, but it makes a dynamite appetizer for any gathering and is terrific served with smoky grilled tortillas. The key ingredient is a can of Ro-Tel tomatoes. If you can't find them in your area, substitute diced fire-roasted tomatoes and green chilies.

Good for Seasoning: Boneless skinless chicken breasts; boneless pork chop sandwiches; tortilla chips; grilled bread

> One 10-ounce can Ro-Tel* tomatoes
> 16 ounces Velveeta, cut into cubes
> 1/2 cup shredded Monterey Jack or jalapeño Jack cheese
> 1/2 cup cooked and crumbled Mexican chorizo, optional

Place the tomatoes and Velveeta in a medium heavy-bottomed saucepan over low heat. Stir frequently as the cheese melts.

When the mixture is smooth and warm, add the Jack cheese and stir as it melts. If desired, add the chorizo on top just before serving. Serve immediately, or store, tightly covered in glass jars, in the refrigerator for up to 3 days. Before serving, warm the glass jars in a water bath in the oven. Stir and serve.

*If you can't find Ro-Tel tomatoes, substitute 10 ounces (about 4) diced plum tomatoes and their liquid and 1 seeded and stemmed minced jalapeño chile.

Blue Cheese Dip

Makes 2 cups

This blue cheese lover's dip can be used as a dressing as well as a dip, but it is the quintessential dip for Buffalo wing lovers. Make this dip the day before you want to use it and let it sit overnight to let the garlic, shallots, and blue cheese mellow and marry.

Good for Seasoning: Any grilled meat; chicken wings; grilled romaine lettuce, potatoes, crudités

1 cup mayonnaise, preferably Hellmann's
1/2 cup sour cream
4 ounces blue cheese, crumbled
1 to 1 1/2 tablespoons grated shallot
1 tablespoon fresh lemon juice
2 cloves garlic, grated
Fine-grain sea salt, optional
Freshly ground pepper

In a large bowl, combine all the ingredients except the salt and pepper, and refrigerate for at least 3 hours to let the flavors develop. Taste and add the salt and pepper as desired. You probably won't need any salt, as all of the ingredients are naturally salty. Refrigerate for at least 3 hours and serve chilled. It will keep tightly covered, in the refrigerator for up to 1 week.

Horseradish Cream

Makes 4 cups

This is hands-down the best sauce to eat with grilled prime rib, and it is my family's tradition every Christmas. It is so simple that it hardly needs a recipe; once you make it a few times, you'll have it committed to memory. The only thing you have to decide is whether you like it plain or with a squirt of fresh lemon juice. I usually make it without, but my sister, Mary Pat (and many others) thinks the lemon is the key ingredient, so if she is making it, we have it with lemon—try them both and decide which one you like better. They are both divine.

Good for Seasoning: Prime rib; grilled meat sandwiches; lobster

1 pint heavy whipping cream

1 to 2 tablespoons prepared horseradish (not cream-style)

Sea salt

1/2 lemon, juiced, optional

1. Pour the cream into a large stainless steel bowl. Using an electric beater, whip on high until the cream forms soft peaks. Add the horseradish.

2. Taste and adjust, adding more horseradish if you like it stronger. Season with salt and a generous squirt of lemon juice, if desired. Serve immediately.

Forgotten Onion Dip

Makes 2 1/2 cups

Serve a little of this Forgotten Onion Dip with grilled vegetables and boneless skinless chicken breasts and it will become everyone's favorite weeknight meal—easy on the cook and tasty for the diners! This can be done with any onion, including shallots.

Good for Seasoning: Grilled veggies, crudités; grilled bread; grilled chicken

Grilling Method: Indirect/Medium Heat

4 medium onions, preferably Vidalia

Olive oil

One 5.2-ounce container Boursin cheese

1/2 cup sour cream

1/8 teaspoon Tabasco sauce

1 1/2 teaspoons kosher salt

1/8 teaspoon freshly ground pepper

1. Roast the 4 onions following the recipe on page 43. Let the onions cool.

2. Put the onions in a food processor and pulse till they're chunky but not pureed. Add the Boursin and pulse until well mixed. Remove and mix in the sour cream by hand. Season with the Tabasco, salt, and pepper.

3. Put in the refrigerator for a minimum of 3 hours to chill and let all the flavors mellow. Taste and adjust the seasonings as desired. Serve immediately, or store, tightly covered, in the refrigerator for up to 3 days.

Garry Roark's Come Back Sauce

Makes 3 1/2 cups

The first time that I met Garry Roark was at Memphis in May, but we didn't really bond until he drove from Yazoo City, Mississippi, to New York City for the Big Apple Barbecue Block Party. Accustomed to taking a little snort (drink) while tending his hawg, he came to New York prepared. But unsure of the laws, he packed his Jack Daniel's in a medicine flask. Naturally, I said yes when he offered me a drink—but when he started pouring it out of the Pepto-Bismol bottle (I know the shape by heart), I started laughing so hard that I couldn't stop. Since laughter is contagious, Garry joined in, and it was quite some time before we were calmed down enough to share that snort—but after that, he became one of my all-stars. This sauce is just as fun; it's a dipping sauce that is called "Come Back" because, as Garry said, "It's so good, folks come back for more!"

Good for Slathering: Pork ribs, pulled pork; chicken, wings; sausage, fried pickles or as a salad dressing for a redneck Caesar

    1 cup mayonaise
    1/2 cup ketchup
    1/4 cup packed dark brown sugar
    1/4 cup cider vinegar
    2 tablespoons favorite hot sauce
    2 tablespoons Worcestershire sauce
    1 small onion, minced
    Kosher salt
    Freshly ground black pepper
    Red pepper flakes or lemon pepper to taste.

1. In a medium bowl, mix the mayonnaise, ketchup, brown sugar, vinegar, hot sauce, Worcestershire, and onion together. Season with salt and pepper to taste. Add a pinch of red pepper flakes or lemon pepper to taste.

Note: This recipe was created by Garry's daughter, Leslie—the real muscle behind their restaurant (Ubon's) and award-winning barbecue. You can also make this sauce with their rub and sauce by ordering it from Ubon's at www.ubons.net.

Ubon's Come Hither Sauce (for those who don't like mayo!)

    1/2 cup yellow mustard
    1/4 cup honey
    1/4 cup packed light brown sugar
    1/2 cup ketchup
    2 tablespoons favorite hot sauce
    2 tablespoons Worcestershire sauce
    Kosher or sea salt
    Freshly ground black pepper

In a medium bowl, mix the mustard, honey, brown sugar, ketchup, hot sauce and Worcestershire together. Season with salt and pepper to taste.

Honey Mustard Dipping Sauce

Makes 1 cup

Who knows where this came from? The classic honey mustard dipping sauce has but three ingredients: mustard, honey, and mayo. I've added a splash of raspberry vinegar as the secret ingredient in my version of one of America's favorite condiments. Once you make it at home, you'll never buy it again. It is so simple and tastes so much fresher than the bottled variety.

Good for Seasoning: Pork tenderloin; fresh ham; chicken wings, grilled chicken tenders; vegetable crudités

    3/4 cup mayonnaise, preferably Hellmann's
    3 tablespoons yellow mustard
    1 tablespoon raspberry vinegar
    3 tablespoons honey
    Kosher salt
    Fine-ground white pepper

In a medium bowl, whisk the mayonnaise and mustard together. Mix the vinegar and honey together and add to mayo-mustard mixture. Mix well and season with salt and pepper. Refrigerate for at least 3 hours before serving. Serve immediately, or store, tightly covered, in the refrigerator for up to 1 week.

Chinese Mustard Dipping Sauce

Makes 1 cup

When I was growing up in North Carolina, there was one take-out Chinese restaurant, complete with a mural of a big green dragon in the parking lot. I loved nights when we'd eat Chinese food, and to me, the best thing about it was dipping the egg rolls in the hot, sinus-clearing mustard sauce. It is so easy to make at home, and the flavors are so much brighter than the packaged variety. Serve it with all your grilled food—it makes a dynamite dipping sauce and glaze for beef or pork tenderloin, steaks, and chops!

Good for Seasoning: Grilled chicken; grilled pork; grilled mushrooms; dumplings; egg rolls, use as a seasoning for soup; doubles as a glaze

> 1/2 cup boiling water
> 1/2 cup dry mustard, preferably Colman's
> 2 tablespoons low-sodium soy sauce
> 1 tablespoon apple cider vinegar
> 1 teaspoon dark brown sugar
> 3 tablespoons peanut or canola oil

In a medium bowl, whisk together the boiling water and mustard until smooth. Add the soy sauce, vinegar, and sugar and mix well. Slowly add the oil and whisk together until completely combined. Serve immediately, or store, tightly covered, in the refrigerator for up to 1 week.

Note: Substitute 1 tablespoon of the oil with toasted sesame oil or hot chile oil to change the flavor of the mustard sauce. I always make it with 2 tablespoons peanut oil and 1 tablespoon toasted sesame oil.

Sweet-and-Sour Dipping Sauce

Makes 1/4 cups

Sweet-and-sour sauce is said to come from the Hunan region of China. Western recipes typically call for using rice wine vinegar, but I find the flavor of dry sherry more complex and appealing. Feel free to substitute all rice vinegar if you prefer. Like many Chinese sauces, the glossy thickness of the sauce comes from making a cornstarch slurry and heating the ingredients.

Good for Seasoning: Duck breast, chicken; grilled pork egg rolls; grilled Asian vegetables

> 1/4 cup dry sherry
> 2 tablespoons seasoned rice vinegar
> 2 tablespoons light brown sugar
> 1 tablespoon sugar
> 1 tablespoon red currant jelly
> 2 tablespoons chili sauce, preferably, or ketchup
> 2 teaspoons low-sodium soy sauce
> 2 teaspoons cornstarch mixed with 4 teaspoons water

1. In a small saucepan over low heat, stir together the sherry, vinegar, sugars, jelly, chili sauce, and soy sauce and bring to a simmer.

2. Add the cornstarch mixture to the other ingredients and stir. Bring the mixture to a boil for 1 minute. Lower the heat and continue cooking for 2 to 3 minutes to thicken.

3. Serve the sauce warm. It can be made up to 2 days in advance and refrigerated, tightly covered; reheat before serving.

Pineapple-Scallion Variation

When the sauce has thickened and cooled a bit, add a 3-ounce can of crushed pineapple and 3 to 4 finely chopped scallions.

Irene's Garlic-Ginger-Chile Dipping Sauce

Makes 1 cup

My friend Kirsten's mother, Irene, is a fantastic cook, and Asian food is her passion. If you are leery of making an Asian sauce, think of Irene's late husband, Udo. Udo was a German-born meat-and-potatoes man and wanted nothing to do with Asian cuisine, so one day Irene slipped this sauce on the table without telling him what it was. Not surprisingly, he loved it.

Good for Seasoning: Shrimp, grilled oysters or clams; chicken; grilled bok choy, scallions, mushrooms

> 3 medium cloves garlic, grated (see page 316)
> 1 small knob (2 inches) fresh ginger, grated
> 1 dried red bird chile, seeded and minced
> 1/2 serrano chile, seeded and minced
> 1/2 teaspoon Thai chili-garlic sauce (*sriracha*)
> 2 tablespoons Asian fish sauce
> 3 tablespoons fresh lime juice

> 5 tablespoons fresh orange juice
> 2 tablespoons water
> 1 1/2 teaspoons honey

In a small bowl, mix the garlic, ginger, and chilies with the chili-garlic sauce to form a paste. Stir in the fish sauce, lime juice, orange juice, honey, and water. Serve immediately, or store, tightly covered, in the refrigerator for up to 1 week.

Italian Red Dipping Gravy

Makes 4 3/4 cups

Dip or drizzle this sauce over Italian sausages, grilled eggplant, or chicken.

Good for Seasoning: Grilled chicken; meatballs; shrimp; noodles; crostini

> 4 pounds plum tomatoes, cored
> 2 sprigs fresh sage or basil
> 2 teaspoons kosher salt
> Pinch sugar
> 4 cloves garlic, roughly chopped
> Best-quality extra-virgin olive oil

1. Place a heavy-bottomed 5-quart saucepan on the stove. Break each tomato open by squeezing it with your fist over the saucepan. Once each tomato is cracked, place it in the saucepan. Add the sage leaves, salt, sugar, and garlic. Cover.

2. Cook on medium heat for 45 to 60 minutes, stirring occasionally. When the tomatoes are thick and saucy, remove from the heat. Let cool to room temperature. Process through a food mill. Taste and

1. Ceramic grater

2. Spice mill or coffee grinder
3. Microplane

adjust the seasonings; whisk in a little olive oil. Serve immediately or store, tightly covered, in the refrigerator for up to 1 week.

Pineapple and Cucumber Raita

Makes 1 3/4 cups

The traditional cucumber is mixed with sweet fresh pineapple and mint in a raita that is made quickly—and without toasting the spices. The cooling, smoky flavor is a welcome dip for spicy grilled foods. I suggest you buy the very good Greek

yogurt that is already drained and very thick (such as FAGE Total). If you use regular yogurt instead, you will need to drain it for an hour.

Good for Seasoning: Spice-rubbed grilled chicken; shrimp, salmon; sweet potatoes, peppers; grilled bread

2 cups predrained whole-milk yogurt, such as FAGE Total

1/4 teaspoon fine-grain sea salt

1/4 teaspoon ground cumin

1/2 teaspoon hot smoked Spanish paprika

Pinch of Sugar in the Raw (turbinado)

3 tablespoons chopped fresh mint leaves

1 small English cucumber, peeled and finely

chopped (about 3/4 cup)

1/2 cup chopped fresh pineapple

Pinch cayenne pepper, optional

1. Put the drained yogurt in a medium bowl. Add the salt, cumin, paprika, and sugar and mix to combine. Add the mint leaves and mix well. Add the cucumber and pineapple and stir to combine. Season with cayenne, if desired.

2. Cover and refrigerate for at least 1 hour to cool and blend. Stir well and serve immediately, or store, tightly covered, in the refrigerator for up to 2 days.

Banana and Cilantro Raita

Makes 1 1/4 cup

Raitas are yogurt-based Indian condiments that contain spices and vegetables such as onions and cucumbers. I love the addition of fruit, such as the banana in this raita.

Good for Seasoning: Snapper, mahi-mahi, tuna; chicken; pork kabobs

2 teaspoons olive oil

1/2 teaspoon whole coriander seeds

1/4 teaspoon ground cinnamon

1/4 teaspoon ground cumin

1/4 teaspoon ground ginger

1/4 teaspoon ancho chile powder

1 large slightly green banana, cut into 1/2-inch pieces

1 generous cup predrained whole-milk yogurt, such as FAGE Total

Pinch salt

2 cloves garlic, grated

2 teaspoons fresh lime juice

Zest of 1/2 lime

2 tablespoons chopped fresh cilantro leaves

1. Heat the oil in a small frying pan over medium heat. Add the coriander seeds and "fry" until they start popping. Add the ground cumin, cinnamon, ginger, and ancho chile powder and mix well. Add the banana to the pan. Let cook until warmed through, about 2 minutes, stirring constantly. Remove from the heat and mash with the warm spices. Let cool.

2. Mix the yogurt with the cooled spice-banana mixture. Add salt, garlic, lime juice, zest, and cilantro. Mix thoroughly. Cover and refrigerate for at least 1 hour to cool and blend. Stir well and serve immediately, or store, tightly covered, in the refrigerator for up to 2 days.

Pomegranate and Mint Raita

Makes 1 1/3 cups

Most people think of cucumber and mint in this cool, green-flecked yogurt condiment that is standard Indian fare. I love the addition of the tart red pomegranate seeds in this variation on the traditional. If you want to use cucumber instead of the pomegranate seeds, substitute 1 cup chopped English cucumber.

Good for Seasoning: Chicken; lamb; a pita with grilled shrimp

2 teaspoons olive oil

1/2 teaspoon whole mustard seeds

1/2 teaspoon whole cumin seeds

1/4 teaspoon ground cumin

1/4 teaspoon ancho chile powder

1 generous cup predrained whole-milk yogurt, such as FAGE Total

Pinch salt

1 tablespoon fresh lemon juice

Zest of 1/2 lemon

1/2 cup pomegranate seeds (about 1 small pomegranate)

3 tablespoons chopped fresh mint leaves

1. Heat the oil in a small frying pan over medium heat. Add the mustard and ancho chile powder seeds and "fry" until they start popping. Add the ground cumin and cayenne and mix well. Remove from the heat and let cool.

2. Mix the yogurt with the cooled spice mixture. Add salt, lemon juice, zest, pomegranate seeds, and mint. Mix thoroughly. Cover and refrigerate for at least 1 hour to cool and blend. Stir well and serve immediately, or store, tightly covered, in the refrigerator for up to 2 days.

Passion Fruit Variation

Substitute the pulp of 3 passion fruits for the pomegranates.

Tzatziki Dipping Sauce

Makes 1 1/2 cups

This Greek cucumber-yogurt dip can be used as a dressing for meat, fish, chicken, or vegetables.

Good for Seasoning: Chicken; lamb; kabobs; grilled zucchini

2 cups nonfat or full-fat yogurt, drained for 1 hour

1/2 medium seedless cucumber, peeled and diced

3 cloves garlic, finely grated

1 tablespoon olive oil

1/2 teaspoon fresh lemon juice

Kosher salt

Fine-ground white pepper

Put the yogurt in a large bowl. Add the cucumber, garlic, olive oil, and lemon juice. Season with salt and pepper. Mix well and refrigerate to chill before serving. Serve immediately, or store, tightly covered, in the refrigerator for up to 3 days.

Note: Make the Tzatziki up to three days in advance. The flavors intensify and actually taste better once they've had a chance to meld.

Melted Butter Dipping Sauces

Makes 1 cup

Melted butter and a touch of salt is a simple way to enhance grilled shellfish. And, although it is old-fashioned, some vegetables, including artichokes and roasted root vegetables, still cry out for a touch of melted butter. All good cooks have a way that they melt butter. A lot of restaurant cooks place a saucepan with butter on the "back burner" and let the pilot light slowly melt the butter. Modern-day home cooks swear by the microwave. Whatever method you choose, make sure to melt the butter at a low temperature or you run the risk of burning it. If time is of the essence, cut the butter into smaller pieces before melting and it will melt faster. When you are looking for a change of flavor from the simple salted butter sauce, try the variations that I have here—and try your own. In fact, most of the compound butters in this book can be slowly melted to become a dipping sauce.

Good for Seasoning: Shrimp, lobster, any mild fish; vegetables

- 1 cup (2 sticks) unsalted butter
- 1/4 teaspoon sea salt or fleur de sel

Place the butter in a medium heavy-bottomed saucepan over low heat. You can cut the sticks into chunks or leave them whole, depending on your time schedule. Stir the butter occasionally and remove from the heat when it is all melted and warm. Add salt to taste and serve immediately.

Drawn Butter Variation

Drawn butter is a fancy term for clarified butter, and it sounds so much more luxurious! Probably because lobster with drawn butter is one of the iconic American fancy foods. *Drawn* or *clarified* simply refers to skimming the milk solids from melted butter, leaving the pure butter fat as a dip-

ping sauce. The easiest way to do this is to melt the butter the day before you need it and refrigerate it overnight. Once cooled, the milk solids rise to the top and the clarified butter is left below.

- 1 cup (2 sticks) unsalted butter
- 1/4 teaspoon sea salt or fleur de sel

Place the butter in a medium heavy-bottomed saucepan over low heat. You can cut the sticks into chunks or leave them whole, depending on your time schedule. Stir the butter occasionally and remove from the heat when it is all melted and warm. Pour into a glass container, cover with plastic wrap, and refrigerate overnight. When the butter is cooled, remove and discard the disk of milk solids that have risen to the top. (If you don't have all night to wait, you can place the butter in an ice bath to rapidly cool it down and skim the solids from the top.) Just before using, slowly reheat the clarified butter and add salt to taste. Serve immediately.

Garlic Butter Variation

This simple mixture is the key to making homemade garlic bread and a sauce for dipping grilled shellfish and vegetables.

- 1 cup (2 sticks) unsalted butter
- 6 to 8 cloves garlic, smashed
- 1/4 teaspoons sea salt or fleur de sel

Place the butter in a medium heavy-bottomed saucepan over low heat. You can cut the sticks into chunks or leave them whole, depending on your time schedule. Add the garlic. Stir the butter occasionally and remove from the heat when it is all melted and begins to bubble. Remove from the heat and let sit for 15 minutes. Strain the butter through a fine-mesh strainer to remove the garlic. Add salt to taste and serve immediately.

Old Bay Butter Variation

This is the classic shrimp boil combined into one dynamite dipping sauce.

- 1 cup (2 sticks) unsalted butter
- 3 teaspoons Old Bay Seasoning

Place the butter in a medium heavy-bottomed saucepan over low heat. You can cut the sticks into chunks or leave them whole, depending on your time schedule. Stir the butter occasionally and remove from the heat when it is all melted and warm. Add the Old Bay and serve immediately.

Smoky Paprika Butter Variation

This is my favorite melted butter variation. The smoked paprika is enhanced by the melted butter, making it a silky sauce exploding with flavor. Make this sauce and I guarantee all your guests will think you are a master saucier! No one ever believes that this sauce only has three ingredients.

1 cup (2 sticks) unsalted butter

1 scant tablespoon sweet smoked Spanish paprika

1/4 teaspoon sea salt or fleur de sel

Place the butter in a medium heavy-bottomed saucepan over low heat. You can cut the sticks into chunks or leave them whole, depending on your time schedule. Stir the butter occasionally and remove from the heat when it is all melted and warm. Add the paprika and salt to taste and serve immediately.

Herb and Garlic Variation

This dipping sauce takes melted butter one step further for any shellfish, fish, and especially grilled potatoes!

Good for Seasoning: Grilled white fish; chicken; veal paillards; potatoes, tomatoes; breadsticks

1 cup (2 sticks) unsalted butter

6 to 8 cloves garlic, smashed or grated

2 tablespoons minced fresh herbs, such as chives, parsley, tarragon, and/or oregano

Pinch sea salt or fleur de sel

Place the butter in a medium heavy-bottomed saucepan over low heat. You can cut the sticks into chunks or leave them whole, depending on your time schedule. Add the garlic. Stir the butter occasionally and remove from the heat when it is all melted and begins to bubble. Remove from the heat and let sit for 15 minutes. Strain the butter through a fine-mesh strainer to remove the garlic. Add the herbs and salt to taste. Serve immediately.

Warm Anchovy Butter Dipping Sauce

Makes about 3/4 cup

I like to think of this as the Italian version of a garlic-butter sauce. If you want to reach for the stars, substitute the soft and sublime white anchovies for the tin of regular anchovies. Serve this butter with lobster or a double-cut veal chop and you'll be in heaven.

Good for Seasoning: White fish, shrimp, lobster; grilled portobello mushrooms, grilled asparagus; grilled bread; steak; veal chops

1/2 cup (1 stick) unsalted butter

2 tablespoons olive oil

2 cloves garlic, finely minced

1 can (2 ounces) anchovies, drained and finely minced (about 16 fillets)

1/4 teaspoon freshly ground grains of paradise,* optional

1 lemon, cut into wedges

1. Heat the butter and oil in a small skillet over medium heat.

2. When the butter is melted, add the garlic and sauté until fragrant, about 1 minute. Add the anchovies and sauté for 1 minute more. Season with the grains of paradise, if using.

3. Keep warm over very low heat. Serve warm, with the lemon wedges for diners to add a squirt of fresh lemon juice.

*Grains of paradise is a seasoning from West Africa whose taste resembles a mix of black pepper, coriander, and cardamom. If you don't have grains of paradise, make a substitution by grinding green cardamom pods and black peppercorns. Mix 1/4 teaspoon pods with 1/2 teaspoon peppercorns. Grind and mix to approximate the flavor of grains of paradise. Use the ground mixture sparingly to season your recipe.

Maple Ginger Butter Dipping Sauce

Makes 1 cup

This unexpected sweet and spicy dipping sauce is perfect for grilled peaches in the summer and grilled squash and apples in the fall. The crystallized ginger adds a nice balance to the sweet maple syrup in this versatile sauce.

Good for Seasoning: Grilled acorn or spaghetti squash, grilled peaches, baked apples, strawberries; pound cake; crêpes; applesauce

> 1 cup (2 sticks) unsalted butter
> 2 tablespoons pure maple syrup
> 2 tablespoons chopped crystallized ginger
> 1/8 teaspoon ground ginger
> 1/8 teaspoon sea salt or fleur de sel

Put the butter in a medium heavy-bottomed saucepan over low heat. You can cut the sticks into chunks or leave them whole, depending on your time schedule. Stir the butter occasionally and remove from the heat when it is all melted and begins to bubble. Add the maple syrup, crystallized ginger, ground ginger, and salt to taste. Serve immediately.

Apricot-Ginger Dipping Sauce

Makes 1 cup

My friend Bob Blumer elevates every kid's favorite, chicken fingers, to chicken lollipops. Instead of the ubiquitous honey mustard sauce, he serves them with a variation of this delicious apricot-ginger sauce that is equally at home with grilled quail and salmon as it is with chicken fingers.

Good for Seasoning: Salmon, shrimp; chicken tenders; chicken kabobs, spring rolls; grilled yellow and orange bell peppers

> 3/4 cup no-sugar-added apricot jam
>
> 1 jalapeño chile, seeded and minced
>
> 2 tablespoons seasoned rice vinegar or fresh lime juice
>
> 1 tablespoon finely grated fresh ginger
>
> 1 tablespoon Dijon mustard

In a medium nonreactive bowl, mix all the ingredients together until well blended. Serve immediately, or store, tightly covered, in the refrigerator for up to 3 days.

Bourbon, Brown Sugar, and Butter

Makes 1 1/4 cups

What could be better than the three Bs? Even though this butter sauce is sweet, it works well with vegetables or grilled pork. Try it with sweet potatoes, Brussels sprouts, squash, and a whole host of grilled fruit.

Good for Seasoning: Fruit kabobs, bananas, grilled apples, peaches, carrots, sweet potatoes; use as a glaze for grilled salmon, ribs, short ribs, pork

> 1 cup (2 sticks) unsalted butter
>
> 1/4 cup packed dark brown sugar
>
> 2 tablespoons bourbon, preferably Maker's Mark
>
> Pinch sea salt or fleur de sel

1. Put the butter in a medium heavy-bottomed saucepan over low heat. You can cut the sticks into chunks or leave them whole, depending on your time schedule. Stir the butter occasionally and add the sugar.

2. Remove from the heat when it is all melted and begins to bubble. Add the bourbon and salt to taste. Serve immediately.

Mignonette Sauce

Makes 1 cup

This simple French dipping sauce is most often associated with raw oysters and is the preferred sauce for oyster purists. Traditionally, it is made with cracked white peppercorns, minced shallots, and red wine vinegar. I prefer using sherry vinegar and a combination of peppercorns that lend a bit more complexity and color to this classic sauce. Interestingly enough, I think of this as the French version of the Asian dipping sauces, and you can switch up the vinegar and the flavorings to make a sauce suited to just about everything.

Good for Seasoning: Grilled and raw oysters, clams; grilled vegetables, barbecued cabbage

> 1 tablespoon assorted whole peppercorns, such as green, white, black, and pink
>
> 1 cup sherry wine vinegar
>
> 2 shallots, finely minced

Coarsely grind the peppercorns in a spice grinder or coffee grinder. Mix the vinegar and shallots in a small bowl. Add the peppercorns. Divide into small dipping bowls and serve immediately.

Mexican Mignonette with Tomatoes and Chilies

Makes 1 1/2 cups

The smaller you cut the shallots, tomatoes, and jalapeño, the better this sauce is. This chunky sauce is pretty on the plate and adds a Mexican flair to many dishes. Surprisingly, it is the perfect accompaniment to rich and rare steak.

Good for Seasoning: Skirt steak; poultry; oysters, scallops, whole grilled snapper, grouper

> 1 tablespoon assorted whole green and white peppercorns*
>
> 1 cup champagne vinegar
>
> 2 shallots, finely minced
>
> 1 plum tomato, peeled, seeded, and minced
>
> 1/2 small jalapeño chile, seeded and minced

Coarsely grind the peppercorns in a small spice grinder or coffee grinder. Pour the vinegar into a medium bowl. Add the peppercorns. Stir in the shallots, tomato, and jalapeño. Divide into small dipping bowls and serve immediately.

*If you can't find dried green peppercorns, substitute brined green peppercorns and chop them instead of grinding them in the spice grinder.

Romesco Dipping Sauce

Makes 3 cups

This grilled tomato sauce from the Catalan region of Spain is served in bars and restaurants with everything from grilled meats to vegetables and bread—it is even stirred into soups to add body and seasoning. It takes a little while to make, but it is worth it in the end. Make a double batch and you'll wind up using it on everything from simple sandwiches and pasta to steaks and chops. If time is tight, substitute canned fire-roasted tomatoes for the fresh-grilled tomatoes.

Good for Seasoning: Flank steak; grilled bread; spaghetti squash, grill-roasted potatoes

Grilling Method: Indirect/Medium-High Heat

> 2 pounds ripe plum tomatoes, or two 14.5-ounce cans fire-roasted tomatoes
>
> 1/2 cup extra-virgin olive oil, preferably Spanish, plus more for drizzling
>
> 1 to 2 teaspoons kosher salt or sea salt, plus more for sprinkling
>
> 1/4 teaspoon freshly ground pepper, plus more for sprinkling
>
> 1 roasted red pepper (see 43)
>
> 1 head garlic, roasted (see page 262)

3 tablespoons red wine vinegar

1/2 cup blanched almonds

1 tablespoon ancho chile powder

1 tablespoon sweet smoked Spanish paprika

1. Build a charcoal fire or preheat a gas grill. Core the tomatoes and drizzle the center of each tomato with olive oil and season with salt and pepper. Place in a disposable aluminum tray and place in the center of the cooking grate. Grill-roast for 30 to 45 minutes or until the tomatoes are caramelized and soft. (If you haven't already done so, this is also a good time to roast the pepper and the garlic. The pepper will take about 15 minutes, and the garlic will take about 45 minutes.) Remove from the grill and let cool in the pan, making sure to keep any of the juices that escape.

2. Peel and seed the peppers and remove the skins from the garlic. Set aside.

3. Using a food processor or blender, puree the tomatoes, their juices, the roasted pepper, and roasted garlic. Add the vinegar and almonds and puree until smooth and uniformly chunky. Add the ancho chile powder and smoked paprika and pulse to combine. Slowly add the remaining oil until you like the consistency of the sauce. Add salt and pepper to taste and pulse to combine. Taste and adjust the seasoning if desired with salt and pepper. Serve immediately, or store, tightly covered, in the refrigerator for up to 1 week.

Tartar Sauce

Makes 1 cup

Tartar sauce has a special place in my heart. When I was a kid, I wasn't sure that I liked fish, but when I went to the beach with the Rucker family, we ate at the Sanitary Fish Market every night. I had no choice but to eat the fish, and it was the pickle-laden tartar sauce that eased me into my love affair with anything that swims! This homemade sauce is a fresh alternative to jarred sauce.

Good for Seasoning: Grilled catfish, fried white fish; potatoes; hamburgers and all fried seafood

1 cup mayonnaise, preferably Hellmann's

2 teaspoons fresh lemon juice or pickle juice

1/4 cup finely chopped dill pickles

1 shallot, finely chopped

Sea salt and freshly ground pepper

In a small bowl, mix the mayonnaise and lemon juice until smooth and no lumps are left. Add the pickles and shallot and mix well. Season to taste with salt and pepper. Serve immediately, or store, tightly covered, in the refrigerator for up to 1 week.

Note: Some people use sweet pickles, but I prefer dill pickles—if you prefer it sweet, substitute sweet pickle relish for the dill pickles.

Thousand Island Dipping Sauce

Makes 1 1/4 cups

There are many stories about the origin of this dressing, which is used by just about every genre of restaurant from continental to fast food to Jewish deli. My favorite story about its name is that the specks of pickle look like a thousand islands! I've added capers and lemon zest to the dressing, giving it a lighter, fresher flavor—this is not your bottled dressing. If you are a purist, stick with the three basics: mayo, ketchup, and sweet pickles.

Good for Seasoning: Cocktail sauce for grilled shrimp, shellfish, us as a dipping sauce for fish; grilled vegetables, especially tomatoes and romaine; chicken; hamburgers; hot dogs, sausages

- 1 cup mayonnaise, preferably Hellmann's
- 1/4 cup ketchup
- 1/8 teaspoon dry mustard, preferably Colman's
- Zest of 1 lemon
- 3 teaspoons capers or green olives, minced
- 2 tablespoons sweet pickle relish
- Sea salt and fine-ground white pepper

In a small bowl, whisk the mayonnaise and ketchup together until smooth and no lumps are left. Add the mustard, lemon zest, capers, and relish. Mix well. Season to taste with salt and pepper. Serve immediately, or store, tightly covered, in the refrigerator for up to 1 week.

Buttermilk "Ranch" Dipping Sauce

Makes 1 cup

This is probably the first dressing that a lot of Americans remember making, adding buttermilk and mayo to a seasoning packet and shaking everything in a jar. This homemade version is still made by shaking, but you mix your own combination of herbs and spices.

Good for Seasoning: Chicken wings; salmon; burgers; salads, grilled veggies, potatoes

- 2 teaspoons granulated garlic
- 2 teaspoons dried basil
- 1 teaspoon dried thyme
- 1 1/2 teaspoons dried parsley
- 1 teaspoon sugar
- 1 teaspoon dried dill
- 1/2 teaspoon freshly ground pepper
- 1/2 teaspoon fine-grain sea salt
- 1/3 cup buttermilk
- 2/3 cup mayonnaise, preferably Hellmann's
- Apple cider vinegar, optional

In a small bowl, mix all the herbs and spices together. Pour the buttermilk and mayonnaise into a bowl or a glass jar with a tight-fitting lid and whisk or shake well, making sure there are no lumps. Add the herb-spice mixture. Whisk or shake well until smooth. Let sit for 15 minutes, and then shake again. Taste for seasoning, adding vinegar if you want more tang. If it is too thick, add a little more buttermilk to thin it out. Pour into a jar if it is not already in one. Shake well before each use. Store, tightly covered, in the refrigerator for up to 3 days

Green Goddess Dipping Sauce

Makes about 1 1/4 cups

Bright green, creamy, and herby. This dipping sauce will make anything you dip into it taste heavenly! Try it with grilled scallops when you are feeling flush or grilled chicken fingers when you are serving the under-five set—they will love the bright green color!

Good for Seasoning: Lamb; pork; chicken; crudités, grilled vegetables, chopped grilled salad

- 2 anchovy fillets, optional
- 2 scallions, green parts only, sliced
- 2 tablespoons chopped fresh chives
- 2 tablespoons chopped fresh parsley
- 1 tablespoon chopped fresh tarragon
- 1 tablespoon chopped fresh basil
- 2 tablespoons tarragon or white wine vinegar

- 1 1/2 tablespoons fresh lime juice
- 1/8 teaspoon freshly ground pepper
- 1/4 teaspoon fine-grain sea salt, if not using anchovies
- 3/4 cup mayonnaise, preferably Hellmann's
- 1/4 cup sour cream

1. Combine the anchovies, if desired, the scallions, chives, parsley, tarragon, basil, vinegar, lime juice, pepper, and optional salt in a small food processor. Process to a rough puree. Or mince the herbs and the anchovies by hand.

2. Transfer the puree to a medium bowl and whisk in the mayonnaise and sour cream. Taste and adjust the seasonings if desired. Cover and refrigerate for at least 1 hour to let the flavors meld. Taste and reseason if necessary. Shake well before each use. Store, tightly covered, in the refrigerator for up to 3 days.

Classic Ketchup

Makes 1 quart

So what if salsa sales surpassed those of ketchup! This is still the number-one dipping sauce in America. Make it from scratch for a gourmet burger party and send your guests home with their own bottle as a party favor that no one will forget.

- 3 tablespoons olive oil
- 3 small red onions, diced
- 5 cloves garlic, grated
- 4 pounds ripe plum tomatoes, cut into quarters
- 1/3 cup apple cider vinegar
- 1/2 cup molasses

2 tablespoons sugar

1 tablespoon Worcestershire sauce

1 teaspoon ground allspice

1 teaspoon whole mustard seeds

1/2 teaspoon ground celery seed

1/4 teaspoon ground cloves

1/4 teaspoon ground cinnamon

1 tablespoon salt

2 teaspoons freshly ground pepper

1. In a large, heavy saucepan, heat the olive oil over medium heat and cook the onion until it begins to caramelize, stirring occasionally, about 8 minutes. Add the garlic and cook for another minute. Add the tomato quarters. Cover and bring the mixture to a boil, then reduce the heat and simmer until the tomatoes have completely broken down, about 30 minutes.

2. Uncover and add the vinegar, molasses, sugar, Worcestershire, allspice, mustard seeds, celery seed, cloves, cinnamon, salt, and pepper. Stir well and continue to simmer for 15 more minutes, uncovered. Take off the heat and let cool in the saucepan. When cool, process the mixture through a food mill into a bowl. Return to the pot.

3. Bring the mixture back to a simmer and cook until it has reduced and is very thick, stirring occasionally, about 30 minutes. Allow the ketchup to cool. Serve immediately, or store, tightly covered, in the refrigerator for up to 1 month. If you seal it in sterilized jars, it can be kept indefinitely.

Quick Fire-Roasted Ketchup

Makes 1 quart

This simple ketchup uses canned fire-roasted tomatoes, which makes it a snap to make, but if you have the time, substitute 2 pounds of tomatoes that you grill yourself (see the directions below). This sweet and spicy tomato-based dipping sauce gets its depth of flavor from the star anise, making it a very distant cousin to the grocery store variety.

Good for Seasoning: Hamburgers; grilled chicken; bratwurst; steak; grilled scallops

2 tablespoons olive oil

1 large yellow onion, diced

2 cloves garlic, grated

1/2 cup red wine vinegar

1 cup packed dark brown sugar

1/2 teaspoon salt

2 teaspoons ground allspice

1/2 teaspoon dry mustard, preferably Colman's

1/2 teaspoon ground cloves

3 star anise, ground in a coffee grinder

One 28-ounce can whole fire-roasted plum tomatoes

1. In a sauté pan over medium-high heat, add the oil, onion, and garlic and sauté for about 4 minutes, until translucent. Add the vinegar and sugar. Increase the heat and reduce the liquid by half.

2. Add the salt, spices, and tomatoes (including liquid). Simmer for about 20 minutes, until the mixture begins to thicken. Let cool, then puree. Serve immediately, or store, tightly covered, in the refrigerator for up to 1 month. If you seal it in sterilized jars, it can be kept indefinitely.

Fire-Roasted Tomatoes

Core the tomatoes and drizzle the center of each tomato with olive oil and season with salt and pepper. Place in a disposable aluminum tray and place in the center of the cooking grate. Grill-roast for 30 to 45 minutes, or until the tomatoes are caramelized and soft.

Blueberry Ketchup

Makes 1 quart

Berries put the fun into ketchup and have a perfect affinity for the rich and spicy tomato condiment. I love using blueberries, but raspberries and cranberries are also good substitutes in this berry, berry good ketchup. If you use cranberries, make sure you balance the sugar, since they are much tarter than blueberries or raspberries.

Good for Seasoning: Venison; game; steak; sausages

3 tablespoons olive oil

2 small red onions, diced

2 cloves garlic, grated

3 pounds ripe plum tomatoes, cut into quarters

1 pound fresh or frozen blueberries or raspberries

1/3 cup blueberry or raspberry vinegar

1/2 cup no-sugar-added blueberry or raspberry jam or preserves

2 tablespoons light brown sugar

1 tablespoon molasses

1 1/2 teaspoons ground allspice

1/2 teaspoon ground cloves

1/2 teaspoon ground ginger

1/2 teaspoon dry mustard, preferably Colman's

1/2 teaspoon ground cinnamon

1 tablespoon salt

2 teaspoons freshly ground pepper

1. In a large heavy saucepan, heat the olive oil over medium heat and cook the onions until they begin to caramelize, stirring occasionally, about 8 minutes. Add the garlic and cook for another minute. Add the tomato quarters and blueberries. Cover and bring the mixture to a boil, then reduce the heat and simmer until the tomatoes have completely broken down, about 30 minutes.

2. Uncover and add the vinegar, jam, sugar, molasses, allspice, cloves, ginger, mustard, cinnamon, salt, and pepper. Stir well and continue to simmer for 10 more minutes, uncovered. Take off the heat and let cool in the saucepan. When cool, process the mixture through a food mill into a bowl. Return to the pot.

3. Bring the mixture back to a simmer and cook until it has reduced and is very thick, stirring occasionally, about 30 minutes. Allow the ketchup to cool. Serve immediately, or store, tightly covered, in the refrigerator for up to 1 month. If you seal it in sterilized jars, it can be kept indefinitely.

Peanut Sauce I

Makes 2 cups

If you've eaten Asian satays, then you instantly think of peanut sauce when you think of their "food on a stick." This sauce is inspired by Southeast Asian cuisine but is great with whatever you put it on. I also like to mix it with rice that I serve as a side dish for virtually everything. If you make this sauce for "peanut rice," toss the rice with the reserved chopped peanuts and 2 scallions that have been sliced into thin rings just before serving.

Good for Seasoning: Grilled chicken and beef kabobs; spicy shrimp; noodles; broccoli rabe

> One 13-ounce can unsweetened coconut milk
>
> 4 tablespoons natural peanut butter, preferably crunchy
>
> 1/2 cup roasted unsalted peanuts, chopped, divided
>
> 4 1/2 teaspoons Thai chili-garlic sauce (*sriracha*)
>
> 2 teaspoons Asian fish sauce
>
> 2 teaspoons unseasoned rice vinegar or malt vinegar
>
> 1/2 lemon, juiced

1. Put the coconut milk, peanut butter, half of the peanuts, the chili-garlic sauce, fish sauce, and vinegar in a blender. Process to combine. Remove from the blender and place in a small saucepan. Simmer for 10 minutes, and then taste. Add the lemon juice and adjust the seasonings if desired. Set aside to cool. If the ingredients separate, put the mixture back into blender or use a immersion blender to reblend.

2. Transfer the sauce to a bowl and sprinkle the remaining peanuts on top of the dipping sauce. Serve immediately, or store, tightly covered, in the refrigerator for up to 3 days.

"The Heat Is On" Peanut Sauce II

Makes 1 1/2 cups

There are so many ways to make peanut sauce, and I love making this quick satay sauce with Peanut Butter & Co.'s hot chile peanut butter called The Heat Is On. It's almost ready to go by itself but even better mixed with some traditional and untraditional ingredients. I like adding the very untraditional toasted coconut for extra texture and sweetness.

Good for Seasoning: Chicken; shrimp; skirt steak

> 1/2 cup unsweetened coconut milk
>
> 3/4 cup peanut butter mixed with 4 teaspoons Thai chili-garlic sauce (*sriracha*), or 3/4 cup chile-flavored peanut butter
>
> 2 tablespoons toasted sesame oil

3 tablespoons toasted sweetened dried coconut

1 tablespoon fresh lime juice

1 teaspoon soy sauce or Asian fish sauce

1/4 cup roasted peanuts, chopped

Pour the coconut milk and peanut butter into a small heavy-duty saucepan set over low heat. Cook until warm and the peanut butter is melted. Whisk together and remove from the heat. Slowly whisk in the sesame oil until it is well mixed—it might not be completely smooth, but it will be once you add the rest of the ingredients. Add the coconut, lime juice, and fish sauce and mix well. Mix in the chopped peanuts. Serve immediately, or store, tightly covered, in the refrigerator for up to 3 days.

Note: One day during the Recipe Testing Boot Camp, friend and tester Ken Hartmann made us all sandwiches with this sauce and the the homemade hot pepper jelly on page 163. A star was born. Not only did it stick to our ribs, Ken couldn't stop thinking about it and plans to make the Spicy PB&J his signature item in his new bar and grill.

Lime and Salt Japanese Dipping Sauce

Makes 1/8 cup (4 servings)

By coincidence, I landed in Tokyo at the same time that my cookbook editor, Linda, was in Japan's largest city. We had dinner at Kyoto's Kikunoi, a famous kaiseki restaurant where the presentation is as important as the way the food tastes. My favorite course was the rare matsutake mushroom that was served on a tabletop grill with a simple dipping sauce made of fresh sudachi* (similar to a lime) and salt. We grilled the fat pieces of mushroom using chopsticks to turn them and mixed our own dipping sauce by squeezing the wedge of sudachi and mixing it with salt. To make this simple dipping sauce in the U.S., substitute your favorite lime or even a Meyer lemon—or try the other variations. Use this for any grilled vegetable or fish and mix it at the table.

Good for Seasoning: Grilled mushrooms, veggies; fatty fish, shellfish

2 limes, cut into wedges

4 teaspoons sea salt or fleur de sel

Divide the lime wedges between 4 bowls. Divide the salt into 4 saucers, or pass the salt for everyone to add to suit their own taste. Squeeze the lime wedges and stir the salt into the juice with a chopstick. Use immediately.

*Sudachi is a small, round, green citrus fruit that resembles a lime and is relatively unknown outside Japan. It is considered to be a delicacy and to have a "zestier" flavor and aroma than lemons or limes. A wedge of sudachi is often served with traditional Japanese dishes of fish, soba, udon, and even some alcoholic beverages.

Variations

1 cup Japanese rice vinegar and 4 teaspoons sea salt, divided into four dipping bowls

1/2 cup soy sauce, 1/2 cup rice wine vinegar, and 2 teaspoons light brown sugar, divided into four dipping bowls

Note: There is no difference between rice wine vinegar and rice vinegar. Rice vinegar, which is available seasoned (meaning sweetened) or unseasoned, is lower in acid than many vinegars and is an essential part of Asian cuisine and has been widely adopted by American cooks. Rice wine vinegar is made from rice that has been fermented and made into rice wine, and then fermented a second time to create the vinegar.

Orange-Ginger-Soy-Wasabi Sauce

Makes about 3/4 cup

The name is almost the recipe. This "juiced" up soy sauce follows the format of the many simple soy sauce–based dipping sauces in Japan. Be sure to use the low-sodium soy sauce, as the regular type makes this sauce too salty.

Good for Seasoning: Tuna steaks, shrimp; zucchini, grilled peppers; flank steak

> 1 tablespoon wasabi powder
> 1/2 cup low-sodium soy sauce
> 1 tablespoon grated fresh ginger
> Juice and zest of 1 orange

1. Put the wasabi powder in a small bowl and add enough water to form a paste. You don't want it too watery, so start with 1 teaspoon and add a little at a time as needed.

2. Mix the wasabi paste with the soy sauce, ginger, orange juice, and orange zest. Taste and adjust the wasabi if you like it a little hotter. Serve immediately.

Helen Chen's Sweet and Sour Dip

Makes about 1 1/2 cups

Helen Chen is the daughter of Joyce Chen—the woman who brought Chinese cookery to the United States. This sweet and sour dipping sauce is her favorite of all the many Chinese sauces. Helen says that it can be used in place of duck sauce as a dip or condiment with finger foods of any sort. It should be served hot, warm, or at room temperature. If it has been refrigerated, reheat over low heat, stirring constantly, until warm.

Good for Seasoning: Pork chops, pork tenderloins; chicken; grilled shrimp; grilled red peppers

> 1 tablespoon canola, corn, or peanut oil
> 1 clove garlic, crushed
> 2/3 cup sugar
> 1/4 cup ketchup
> 1/2 cup apple cider vinegar
> 2 tablespoons low-sodium soy sauce
> 1/3 cup water
> 2 tablespoons cornstarch dissolved in 1/3 cup water

1. Heat the oil in a medium saucepan over medium heat. Brown the garlic, then discard it (leaving only a hint of flavor in the pan).

2. In a medium bowl, combine the sugar, ketchup, vinegar, soy sauce, and water. Pour into the pan with the oil and stir constantly with a spoon or whisk until the mixture is smooth and comes to a boil.

3. Add the cornstarch mixture and bring to a boil for 1 minute. Lower the heat and stir until the sauce thickens and takes on a sheen. Keep warm over very low heat, stirring occasionally to prevent scorching, until ready to serve. Or serve at room temperature.

Vietnamese Soy Sauce

Makes 1/2 cup

When I visited Ho Chi Minh City (Saigon), in Vietnam, I stayed at the Park Hyatt hotel, where the food was so good that I would fly back any day of the week just to eat there. The first morning, executive sous chef Hein Nguyen Ngoc took me to the bustling market, where we looked and shopped before going back to the hotel kitchen to cook. We made many things that morning, but there are two sauces that I make over and over again as dippers for many different foods: the Fish Sauce Dip and the Vietnamese Soy Sauce Dip. They both have a perfect balance of salty and sweet and take just a few minutes to whisk together.

The Vietnamese Soy Sauce Dip has it all! Sweet, salty, spicy, and sour notes; the soy sauce even supplies umami—the Japanese-named "fifth taste" that gives food, and in this case soy sauce, that round, rich, almost meaty complex flavor.

Good for Seasoning: grilled kabobs; chicken, beef, pork, shrimp or beef; grilled asparagus and mushrooms

> 1/4 cup low-sodium soy sauce
> 1 clove garlic, minced
> 1 teaspoon Sugar in the Raw (turbinado)
> 1 teaspoon fine-ground white pepper
> 1 dried or fresh red bird chile, seeded and minced
> 3 tablespoons fresh lime juice
> 1 tablespoon crushed roasted unsalted peanuts, optional

In a small bowl, combine all the ingredients and mix well. Serve immediately.

Saigon Sauce

Makes 1/2 cup

Coconut water is the milky liquid that is drained from a fresh coconut. Vietnam and other Asian countries use the coconut so often that they always have some of this "juice" in the kitchen. It's worth cracking a coconut just for this sauce (and then use the coconut in your favorite recipes). For me, it's a good excuse to make my mother's fresh coconut cake. If you like, you can also buy prepared coconut water.

Good for Seasoning: Vegetables, grilled scallions; grilled white fish, shrimp, oysters, clams

> 1/4 cup water or fresh coconut water (not cream of coconut)
> 2 teaspoons unseasoned rice vinegar

JAPANESE SOY SAUCE–BASED DIPPING SAUCES

I have long loved the salty-spicy Japanese flavor combination of wasabi and soy sauce in which we dip sushi and sashimi. I have often used the idea and mixed the two to glaze a simple piece of fish. But it wasn't until I went to Japan that I realized that there were so many soy sauce–based dipping sauces. Usually, the proportions of ingredients are mixed to taste. For example, I usually add more wasabi than most people at the table, and I always use low-sodium soy sauce—not for the lower sodium but because I think it has a richer flavor.

Good for Seasoning: Grilled fish; chicken; beef kabobs; sushi

Here are the most commonly used dipping-sauce combinations. In Japan, the amounts of each ingredient are mixed according to personal taste; however, I am providing basic measurements to get you started. Feel free to increase or decrease according to your personal taste.

- 1 to 2 teaspoons wasabi (preferably freshly grated) plus 1/4 cup soy sauce (*washbi jo-yu*)—used for most kinds of raw fish.

- 1 teaspoon grated fresh ginger plus 1/4 cup soy sauce (*sho-gajo-yu*)—used for "blue" or oily raw fish, such as mackerel and bonito.

- 1 teaspoon grated garlic plus 1/4 cup soy sauce (*ninniku jo-yu*)—used sometimes for meat and fish.

- 2 teaspoons dry mustard (preferably Colman's) plus 1/4 cup soy sauce—for meat and vegetables.

- 1/4 teaspoon chile oil plus 1/4 teaspoon toasted sesame oil (*ra-yu*) and 1/4 cup soy sauce—the most popular dipping sauce for steamed gyoza dumplings.

- 1 tablespoon rice vinegar plus 1/4 cup soy sauce (*su-jo-yu*)—used for fish, vegetables, and meat.

- 2 teaspoons fresh lemon juice (*yuzu* in Japan) plus 1/4 cup soy sauce—used for everything (bottled as ponzu sauce).

- 1/2 cup mirin plus 1 tablespoon light brown sugar and 1 cup soy sauce (*tsuyu*), heated until bubbly and the sugar is melted. This is the only one of these soy sauce–based sauces that is cooked. It is the standard Japanese dipping sauce for noodles, tempura, and some dumplings. In Japan, you can buy bottled sauce often called *mentsuyu*, which roughly translated means "noodle sauce."

3 teaspoons Sugar in the Raw (turbinado) or agave syrup

1 dried or fresh red bird chile, seeded and minced

2 cloves garlic, finely grated

2 tablespoons fresh lime juice

4 tablespoons Asian fish sauce

1. Bring the water, vinegar, and sugar to a boil in a small saucepan. Remove and set aside to cool.

2. In a small bowl, combine the cooled mixture with the chile, garlic, and lime juice. Mix well, then stir in the fish sauce. Serve immediately.

Carrot Variation

Add about 2 tablespoons grated carrot to the dip.

Ginger-Tahini Dipping Sauce

Makes 3/4 cup

I like to think of tahini as Middle Eastern peanut butter. Tahini is made of ground sesame seeds. It is available in most grocery stores, natural food stores, and Middle Eastern markets, but if you can't find it, you can make your own by blending lightly toasted sesame seeds and a little olive oil—at a ratio of 5 to 1.

Good for Seasoning: Grilled chicken; shellfish; scallion pancakes; noodles; veggies; Asian-inspired coleslaw of napa cabbage, bok choy, and carrot

1/4 cup tahini

2 tablespoons hot chile oil

1 tablespoon toasted sesame oil

2 tablespoons low-sodium soy sauce

1 tablespoon rice vinegar

2 tablespoons light or dark brown sugar

3 cloves garlic, minced

1 small knob (2 inches) fresh ginger, minced

Put all the ingredients in a blender or food processor and blend until smooth. Serve immediately, or store, tightly covered, in the refrigerator for up to 3 days.

Acknowledgments

Every book has a set of characters who need to be thanked. In my case, the home team needs to be thanked once again. Great big bear hugs to Kirsten Newman Teissier and Rose White who keep my boat in ship-shape, despite my very challenging travel schedule—I quite literally couldn't keep it together without them. As always, thanks to Alfred Geller at Geller Media Management for his unconditional support.

I must thank Rick Smilow, the owner of the Institute of Culinary Education (ICE) and his staff for not only embracing the Recipe Testing Boot Camp, but for also getting behind it and taking on the gargantuan task of organizing the students. I especially want to thank Andy Gold and Jessie Craig, Kristen James, Mary Bartolini, and the entire Stewarding Department. My friend and assistant, Andrew Lavenski is affectionately referred to as "Squirrel" because of his unrivaled organizational skills. I would not have been able to maximize the 14 hours a day for two weeks if I hadn't had him to help me. Every recipe in this book was touched in some way by Andrew. Two students in particular came every chance they had—working with me all day and then going to night jobs after 6 p.m. when we wrapped for the day. Heart-

felt thanks go to Kathleen Lucier and Ken Hartmann for being so cheerful, so exacting, and so willing to test anything, all day long. Kathleen graduated around the time of the Boot Camp and she was/is my culinary godsend, pitching in to help me with my classes at ICE, television appearances, events at Hill Country, and in finishing this book. She carefully proofread the book—not once, but twice—shopped and styled the photographs, and literally did anything else that needed to be done. Christina Ferranti baked her first cake during the boot camp and has gone on to be a valuable assistant, helping me with classes and events. Special thanks to all of the other students who participated in the Recipe Testing Boot Camp for their hard and conscientious work—they know who they are— 42 in all!

I need to thank everyone in the different areas of my life for letting me put everything but this book on the back burner for a couple months when I was in lockdown, writing the book.

I again thank my immediate and extended family for saying and doing all the right things as I was trying to write the book and celebrate the holidays at the same time— not doing either very well! Especially my parents and my always understanding sister and BFF, Mary Pat; my brother-in-law, Karl; and all their "shorties"—August, Alexander, and Max—my loving and handsome nephews who are going to need another nickname as they quickly grow taller than Mary Pat and me. I love how much they love food and barbecue!

When you work on your own, you have lots of colleagues and a few confidants. I am thankful for my friendship and collaborations with John Lineweaver, Bob Blumer, Rose Levy Beranbaum, Marian Temesvary, Amy Mills Tunnecliffe, and my sister, Mary Pat, the resident shrink—*merci* to them all for being members of my kitchen cabinet.

Other friends and members of my sounding board include my culinary resource, Lynn Karmel, CFO and boss of bubbly Pete Savely; BBQ partners Gretchen and Jeff Belmonti; my French connection, Nat Teissier; equipment expert Sharon Franke; food and wine mavens extraordinaire Sarah Powers and Mary Burnham; Bon vivants Bill Barrick and Tony Kemp; "UP" Roger Sawhill; foodie Irene Haeckel; sage David Lineweaver; and mastermind Howie Rumberg. A big round of appreciative applause goes to all of the editors, writers, reporters, and producers who continue to support and promote me, my books, products, Hill Country, and anything else I do by asking me to write for their magazines, appear on their television and radio shows, and interview me all year 'round. I owe a lot of my success to you all.

On the Grill Friends front, thanks go to my friend and housewares mentor Robert Laub and everyone at Harold Import Co., for being so helpful and supportive at all times and for distributing all of my cookbooks. Special thanks to Nicole, Millie, John D., Pamela, Dave, Danielle, Alicia, Allyn, Dan, and Jason for all your hard work on behalf of Grill Friends. And, to all the retailers who carry my books and products, thank you for making my dream come true. More thanks go to my NYC barbecue family, Marc Glosserman, John Shaw, Pete Daversa, Sarah Abell and the crew at Hill Country. Thanks to all the members of my Girls at the Grill Web site and my Institute of Culinary Education recreational students (past and future) who help me to keep my finger on the pulse of what home cooks want. Thank you for keeping it real.

This book wouldn't have been possible without my wonderful and thoughtful editor Linda Ingroia who worked graciously with my hectic schedule to get this book edited and produced. Thanks to publisher Natalie Chapman for being such a big supporter of my books. Also to others on the Wiley team: the lovely and calm Alda Trabucchi, senior production editor; Jeff Faust, the cover designer; Tai Blanche, the art director and interior designer; and Jennifer Greenstein, freelance production editor; for pulling the complex components of this book together beautifully.

It is always a pleasure to work with the marketing and publicity team at Wiley, kindred spirits all: Todd Fries, Michael Friedberg, Gypsy Lovett, David Greenberg and Jana Nordstrand—here's to the celebration of food and wine, and to more lunches like the one we shared at Galatoire's.

The beautiful photography in this cookbook is compliments of Jamie Tiampo. We grilled and then shot all the photography on his rooftop in Manhattan. Without grills, there would be no grilled food. A big thank you to Jeanine Thompson and all my friends at Weber for providing the gas and charcoal grills. Our team was tight—Jamie, Kathleen, Linda, and myself —and it was so much fun that it felt more like summer camp than work. Thanks to Jamie for making this long process an enjoyable partnership and for picking out fabulous food from around the world for our lunches. I love all of the photographs and am so pleased with the rustic and organic look and feel of them—they make this book accessible to everyone!

Our lean, mean photo shoot team flourished with the support and generosity of Saukok Chu Tiampo who cheerfully let us move in for six weeks; Jim Peterson who generously lent us lights, lenses and his grandmother's heirloom silver; and thanks to Mark Kelly and Bob Kellerman from Lodge Manufacturing, makers of the best cast-iron products in the world.

Many thanks to Dominique Dobson and Shun Knives for my new favorite knives including the rocking U2—my everything knife! More thanks to Lisa Callahan and Nick Jendrejeski and All-Clad for their generous, photogenic, and useful collection of pots and pans; and Rachel Litner and Mary Rogers from Cuisinart and Waring for all the electrics and my favorite workhorse of a (Waring) blender. Thanks to Julia Stambules for coming through with products from her clients, Microplane,

Wusthoff, and the delicious Terra Medi olive oil and vinegar from Greece.

Our beautiful backgrounds are compliments of Marcie Parmet and Chilewich—I am a huge fan of these colorful and modern placemats. Thanks to Bruce Flack and Amin Mysorewaia of K&A for the color-coordinated linens. The key to my favorite smoked catfish recipe is the Cameron Stovetop Smoker; thanks to Ann and Chris Malone for their support of all my projects and classes.

I toast Julie D'Ancona for tracking down the awesome Bulleit bourbon glasses and the bourbon to go in them. Heroic thanks to Robert Schueller of Melissa's for sending us out-of-season pomegranates and lots of other exotic produce including the stunning pink variegated lemons seen on page 303. More thanks go to Laura Baddish of The Baddish Group for her Funkin fruit purees, especially the passion fruit for my fruit curds and the delicious Pama pomegranate liqueur, which inspired me to make the best sweet tea/cocktail known to mankind. More thanks go to Mandy Sheehan from John Boos & Co. for helping us secure the perfect work surface. And finally, my heartfelt thanks to everyone who buys my books and products —you are all my Grill Friends.

Index